THE ASTROLOGY OF
Great Sex

THE ASTROLOGY OF
Great Sex
What Your Lover Wants

MYRNA LAMB

HAMPTON ROADS
PUBLISHING COMPANY, INC.

for the evolving human spirit

Cover design by Jane Hagaman
Cover art by Robert Lamb

Hampton Roads Publishing Company, Inc.
1125 Stoney Ridge Road
Charlottesville, VA 22902

434-296-2772
fax: 434-296-5096
e-mail: hrpc@hrpub.com
www.hrpub.com

If you are unable to order this book from your local
bookseller, you may order directly from the publisher.
Call 1-800-766-8009, toll-free.

Lamb, Myrna, 1942-
   The astrology of great sex : what your lover wants / Myrna Lamb.
       p. cm.
   Summary: "Offering a twist on traditional sexual astrology, Lamb surveyed more than
1,200 men and women about their turn-ons and turn-offs, fantasies and dreams. Lamb not
only offers guidance on compatibility—which signs meld well with others-—but, by including the respondents' real-life sexual confessions, she provides insight into your lover's—and
your own--deepest desires"—Provided by publisher.
   ISBN 1-57174-509-2 (7 x 10 tp : alk. paper)
   1.   Astrology and sex.   I. Title.
   BF1729.S4L36 2006
   133.5'864677--dc22

                            2006017940

                  ISBN 1-57174-509-2
                  10 9 8 7 6 5 4 3 2 1
           Printed on acid-free paper in Canada

Dedication

This book is dedicated to three men.

TOM SEERS
In Memoriam
Gifted astrologer, friend, and mentor, without
whom this book would never have been started

RON NELSON
Quintessential Virgo, a man who embodies
the meaning of friendship—steadfast, patient,
ever-present—and without whom this book would
never have been finished

ROBERT LAMB
Extraordinary artist, husband, and soul mate,
without whose love and encouragement this book
would be missing its heart

Contents

Aries
March 21–April 19
THE RAM
PAGE 1

Taurus
April 20–May 20
THE BULL
PAGE 19

Gemini
May 21–June 20
THE TWINS
PAGE 37

Cancer
June 21–July 22
THE CRAB
PAGE 55

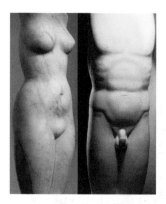

Sagittarius
November 22–December 21
THE ARCHER

Capricorn
December 22– January 19
THE GOAT

Aquarius
January 20–February 18
THE WATER BEARER

Pisces
February 19–March 20
THE FISH

Acknowledgments

I wish to extend my appreciation to:

My literary agent, Bill Gladstone at Waterside Productions, and Ming Russell, with appreciation for their commitment to this project and for their excellent representation;

Jack Jennings, Robert Friedman, Sara Sgarlat, Jane Hagaman, Tania Seymour, Matt Genson, and the rest of the fine staff at Hampton Roads Publishing Company for daring to publish this very different astrology book;

Faye Mandell for introducing me to Bill Gladstone;

Jason Marzini of Exposure #1 for the fine photography he did of Robert Lamb's paintings and sculptures;

Judy Ammerman, Claire Bracaglia, Patricia Cohen, Susan Epstein, Jan Grant, Ariela McCaffrey, Helene Scheff, and Linda Sheally for reading and providing feedback on the material;

Jeff Gellman of MIKO Exoticwear for getting me started in the distribution of the Sex Survey, and to Options of Rhode Island for promoting that questionnaire; and

Jakob for occupying himself and letting Gram work.

A special debt of gratitude is due to the hundreds of men and women who gave of their time to complete the sex questionnaires that form the basis for this book.

Introduction

WHAT'S INSIDE THIS BOOK?

Sex and lots of it.

More than 1,200 men and women completed a sex survey that provided the information presented in this book. Quotes from hundreds of these people have been included. Their explicit comments and generous contributions made it possible to write this very different kind of astrology book. Firsthand, learn what your lover likes, dislikes, wants, and fantasizes about in the world of sex.

Throughout the book, I have listed the questions asked on the sex survey and my summary answers that explain the astrological connection. Beneath my comments, in most cases, are quotations taken directly from the questionnaires.

Here's an example from the Aries chapter:

The Aries Woman in Her Own Words

WHAT ATTRACTS YOU TO SOMEONE?

Aries always responds to a man's energy. Vitality goes a long way to compensate if a man isn't really her type physically.

"I am attracted by energy, personality, humor. Physical attributes aren't extremely important. Personality and a pleasant disposition and behavior outweigh looks."

"A man's smile, energy, behavior, plus the ability to dance. Height matters as I want a man who's a bit taller than I am, and I don't want him to be fat. Penis size never really counts. I want to know if he can snuggle and whether he likes himself."

How to Use This Book

Go to the table of contents to find your birthday* and Sun Sign, and those of your lover or anyone else you might want to check out. When you turn to that chapter, feel free to open to any page and read whatever parts interest you. The way this book is laid out, in question-and-answer format, there is no need to read any chapter from beginning to end. Most pages have short vignettes, set off with a sun or moon symbol. These are the sexual fantasies and memories that hundreds of men and women wrote on their questionnaires.

The questions come from the sex questionnaire and all the answers have been taken directly from the completed surveys. Frequently you will find repetition among the answers. Repetition shows the consistency with which people of a given Sun Sign responded to a question.

SEXUAL COMPATIBILITY THROUGH THE ZODIAC

The second part of this book describes the way each Sign relates to every other. It begins with Aries partnered with Aries, and then with Taurus, and then with Gemini. It continues all the way through Pisces with Pisces. The compatibility overviews are broken down into men versus women within each Sign (the Aries Woman with a Taurus Man and then the Aries Man with a Taurus Woman).

On a few occasions there are sections that seem somewhat contradictory. This is because some Signs bring out certain traits in an individual, but put that same person with another Sun Sign, and the result is apt to be quite different. For example, Libra and Sagittarius relate beautifully, whereas Libra and Pisces have little common ground.

PREMISE OF THIS BOOK

The Astrology of Great Sex: What Your Lover Wants began with a simple premise. The Sun Sign is the most basic and deepest level of the astrology of personality. Sex is among the most basic of human urges. It follows that the characteristics of one's Sun Sign should relate to that individual's sexual behaviors and preferences.

To test that relationship I devised a sex questionnaire and asked people to fill it out anonymously. The consistency of the answers received from people of the same Sign, down to the use of exactly the same words, was remarkable. For instance, the Sign of Aries rules the head, and so it is that the head is a focal point in sex for Aries. Without exception every Aries, in responding to the question, "What do you like most sexually?" mentioned kissing. "Kissing, oral sex, having my breasts fondled and sucked . . ." Another example is with Gemini, the Sign of Communication. When asked, "What do you like to do on a date?" Gemini always mentioned talking. "Talking, getting together with friends, having good conversations over dinner."

*If you were born on the first day or the last day of a Sign, you may not be sure which chapter to read. There are many websites online that will let you know which one of the two is your actual Sun Sign. You may also write to me and I'll check it for you. Go to www.MyrnaLamb.com and send me an email request.

THE QUESTIONNAIRE

The questionnaire consists of seven sections regarding an individual's attitudes toward sex and relationships, sexual behaviors, fantasies, memories of significant encounters, and interest in sexual fetishes. A copy of the survey is included at the end of this book. Fill out the survey with your lover and compare your answers to enrich and broaden your sex life.

The questionnaire was distributed to thousands of men and women who learned of it through my website, advertisements, and announcements in newspapers and on radio programs. I also handed it out at fetish fairs and gave it to my astrology clients.

WHO THIS BOOK IS FOR

This book is for people of all ages, whether in new or long-standing relationships, who want to know more about how to make their sex lives more fulfilling. What better way to learn than to read your lover's own words?

USING WHAT YOU'VE LEARNED

Some people, even those in committed relationships, are reticent about telling their lovers how to please them. In the pages of this book, you'll find out. For instance, when a Capricorn man is asked, "How do you demonstrate affection for your partner?" he mentions being attentive and leaving her notes. "I'll take her out to a candlelit dinner, send cards and small gifts." In this way he's indicating how he would appreciate being treated.

In some cases one partner wants to explore that sexual territory existing beyond the bounds of mainstream sex, also called "vanilla" sex. *The Astrology of Great Sex: What Your Lover Wants* will help you determine what behaviors your lover might accept and what areas are apt to be taboo.

Learning about your lover's fantasies can add considerably to your sex life. Fantasies are safe, an opportunity to think anything without breaking laws or taboos, and many people don't want to act out their fantasies. But introducing some element of a fantasy, even talking about images from it during a sexual encounter, will spice things up for your lover. For example, a Leo man wants to tie a woman to a bed and have sex with her so much and so often that she passes out from exhaustion. So, if your lover is a Leo, you might offer to be his sex slave for a session. A Capricorn woman imagines getting a well-deserved spanking followed by intercourse. You might take your Capricorn lover across your knee and give her a gentle paddle or two.

THE ELEMENTS: Fire, Earth, Air, and Water

The Signs of the zodiac fall into four categories. They are Fire, Earth, Air, and Water. Within each element are three Signs and they have some common qualities, so it might be of interest to scan all three for added insights. For example, if your lover is an Aries, check out Leo and Sagittarius and so on through each of the elements. When it comes to compatibility, though there are some surprises, as a general rule the Fire Signs and Air Signs are harmonious and the Water Signs and Earth Signs suit each other well.

Fire: Aries, Leo, and Sagittarius

The Fire Signs are perhaps the most active sexually. Their passion is intense, but sex may be quick. For Aries, sex can be about showing off how good she/he is. Leo is never to be outdone at anything and Sagittarius—well, even the symbol of Sagittarius, half man/half horse—speaks of their desire to prove their animal magnetism. With all three, praise is a vital stimulus.

Earth: Taurus, Virgo, and Capricorn

The Earth Signs are the "earthiest" Signs as to the range of their sexuality. They love to touch, taste, and smell. While Taurus may like sex that lasts longer, Virgo may be more open to experimentation, and Capricorn is perhaps most open to extreme sex, all three Earth Signs are very physical. Food turns them on and material goods are important to them.

Air: Gemini, Libra, and Aquarius

The Air Signs are turned on by ideas, conversations, and stimulus to the brain. Where the heart of the matter for most men might be squarely between his legs, the Air Sign man needs to be turned on first verbally. While the Air Sign woman may be drop-dead gorgeous and turn every head in the room, it's the person who has plenty to say who will score with her.

Water: Cancer, Scorpio, and Pisces

The Water Signs are likely to be the most passionate in terms of the expression of emotion in sex. Cancer's sexuality grows out of a need to nurture, Scorpio's out of the need to be desired, and Pisces' comes from idealized romantic passion. All three Water Signs are extremely sexual and sensitive to their partner's mood. Getting turned on results from a sense of emotional closeness.

ARIES

March 21–April 19

THE RAM

Fire Sign Aries is impulsive, assertive, and in some ways a perpetual child. Ruler of the head and the features of the face, the Ram loves oral sex. To satisfy Aries in lovemaking, that which is indispensable above all else is passionate kissing.

She says: "I enjoy deep kissing on the mouth, and all over my lover's body. Everyone praises my tongue and how I bring them to orgasm."

He says: "When it comes to sex I am a man for all seasons, but if I had to choose between intercourse and cunnilingus, I would choose cunnilingus."

"I'll never grow up, never grow up, never grow up . . . not me."
—Carolyn Leigh

The Aries Woman in Her Own Words

A Memory

"Out on a boat, drifting in the sun. Lying naked on the deck. Rubbing oils on each other. The rocking motion. Occasional splash of a fish. The cry of seagulls. Smell of sweat and suntan oil. His cigar smoke. Me tasting of Zima and him of beer, all mixing when we kiss. Sitting on his lap, moving up and down with the motion of the boat, and him inside me. Moving faster and faster. Him thrusting harder and harder until I explode in an incredible orgasm."

Attraction and Dating an Aries

WHAT ATTRACTS YOU TO SOMEONE?

The Aries woman always responds to a man's energy. Vitality goes a long way to compensate if a man isn't really her type physically.

"I am attracted by energy, personality, humor. Physical attributes aren't extremely important. Personality and a pleasant disposition and behavior outweigh looks."

"A man's smile, energy, behavior, plus the ability to dance . . . Height matters as I want a man who's a bit taller than I am and I don't want him to be fat. Penis size never really counts. I want to know if he can snuggle and whether he likes himself."

"Confidence is the biggest turn-on though not to the point of arrogance . . . intelligence, sense of humor, sensitivity, karma, chemistry."

A Memory

"He was a very attractive, romantic man. His body was lean and clean. He brought flowers and wine and we lingered over a delicious seafood dinner. Then we began making out, taking our time. He talked dirty, adding to the excitement. I remember us lying there with the sun streaming in through the windows, warm on our bodies."

WHAT MIGHT TURN YOU OFF?

As Aries is the Sign that rules the head and loves to kiss, poor dental hygiene is her number one turnoff. A lack of a sense of humor comes next.

"A man who is ultra-reserved, has poor manners, or is too quiet. I want to have a good time."

"I am definitely turned off by a man who talks about other lovers, has low self-confidence, and is insensitive."

"Poor style, bad teeth, inconsiderate behavior."

WHAT DO YOU ENJOY DOING ON A DATE?

Aries women, in addition to listing the traditional things to do on an evening out, include sex as a dating activity. Regardless of her willingness, however, she'll be completely turned off if she feels she's being hurried into bed. A smart man will watch for Aries to signal her availability before suggesting sex too soon after supper.

"Dining out at a great restaurant, casual stuff, movie, antique hunting, dog shows, passionate kissing, holding hands, touching, sex of course, first date, always."

"Dancing, talking about anything, holding hands, touching, passionate kissing."

A Fantasy

"*Making love outdoors, on a warm sunny afternoon, in a country setting. It starts with my lover and me slowly undressing and then massaging each other. It ends with us lying spent and naked on a blanket with warm sun on our bodies and the scent of plants and wildflowers in the air.*"

ARE YOU FLIRTATIOUS?

Flirtatiousness is not an innate Aries trait. She has an ingenuous quality and an open, frank way of interacting with people which can be disarming. It's the rare Aries who is truly a flirt.

"Maybe in a lighthearted way: trading jokes or banter."

"Somewhat, but I'd be more so if I had more confidence in myself."

"Perhaps, subtly flirtatious with strangers, moderately with men I know better."

ARE YOU JEALOUS?

Yes she is. How much so may vary, but Aries being the first Sign of the zodiac, the Sign whose key words are "I am," certainly expects to be the center of attention with her lover.

"If I am with someone who is talking about other lovers, I get jealous."

"Not in casual relationships, but when I really like someone I can be possessive."

"I can be, because I am a loyal friend and want others to be the same."

A Memory

"*It was a warm and breezy February day and no one else was around. We were hiking at Race Point in Provincetown and had walked for about an hour, talking about philosophy. We came upon a little offshoot of a path. The afternoon sun made the trees a sort of golden color. It was magical looking and we thought somehow that it was all meant only for us. I truly felt that I was with my soul mate. We held each other for quite a while and let nature take its course. I remember looking at him*

[and] thinking that his eyes were the same color as the sky."

HOW DO YOU FEEL ABOUT PUBLIC DISPLAYS OF AFFECTION?

Aries wants displays of affection kept to a minimum. Showing regard by holding hands pleases her, but anything that seems to be sexual should be done in private.

"I enjoy letting the world know that I'm in love subtly. I'm not into intercourse in public."

"Lots of hand holding, even an occasional provocative kiss—that's fine in front of others."

"Nothing sexual: discreet holding hands, that's okay. Deep kissing is not."

"Fine as long as they aren't mauling each other . . . I love seeing happy couples. It certainly beats looking at people fighting or walking around with long faces."

Sexual Attitudes and Behaviors

HOW OFTEN DO YOU THINK ABOUT SEX AND HOW OFTEN PER WEEK DO YOU WANT TO HAVE SEX?

Aries is a highly sexual woman. She thinks about sex at least once a day and Aries wants sex at least three times a week.

A Memory

"*I was falling asleep. My lover [lay] down, spooned me, and began gently kissing and sucking on my neck while stroking my breasts. His touch and lips felt warm, soft, and loving. When I was writhing with desire he pulled me on top of him. We had intercourse while kissing deeply and holding hands. [We] reached orgasm together. The low moans he made just before he reached orgasm were intensely exciting to me. We fell asleep, spooned.*"

HOW LONG DO YOU LIKE TO SPEND HAVING SEX AND HOW MUCH OF THAT TIME IS FOREPLAY? DO YOU ENJOY QUICKIES?

She prefers spending about an hour having sex with twenty to thirty minutes of foreplay, but she won't reject quick encounters. If she's had a stressful day or if she's distracted, some passionate kissing and a quickie will prove very satisfying. A night of great sex might begin with a short, passionate encounter and climax, followed by cuddling, kissing, and a slower second round.

"Time depends on my mood, the complexities of the day. Sometimes I like it to last, with foreplay about an hour. At other times I prefer no foreplay at all and a quickie is perfect."

"I like to forget time when having sex. I wouldn't say no to a quickie, but I prefer an open expanse of time."

"Quickies are okay once in a while, but I prefer taking my time."

"I prefer extended lovemaking, [but] an occasional quickie can be very exciting."

"I like a lot of foreplay. Teasing and pleasing someone enhances the actual act."

"On foreplay, as much as needed to build us both up to the point where we have to have [sex]."

WHAT TIME OF DAY DO YOU PREFER TO HAVE SEX?

Sex at any time of day is fine with her though she has some preference for early morning and late night.

"I prefer sex in the dark, whether at night or before dawn breaks."

"My favorite times are mornings, just before getting out of bed, and at night in the dark."

"I like all different times, especially night and first thing in the morning as long as there's enough time."

Memories

"*Being awakened by my partner, who is really horny early in the morning.*"

"*Sex on the hood of my car in a private parking lot, with people watching.*"

"*The moon was out, very dark sky; you could smell the dew on the ground. There was a chill in the air. It was very aggressive.*"

"*In my bed . . . he caressed me all over until I was so turned on, so wet with desire, that his penis slid right in and I felt transported to another world.*"

"*I got into a sexy bra, garter belt, and stockings and we had sex on the kitchen table.*"

HOW OFTEN DO YOU MASTURBATE?

She masturbates two to four times weekly, depending on whether she is unattached or seeing someone.

"I masturbate more, maybe four times weekly, if I am not in a relationship in which I regularly have sex."

HOW LONG DO YOU WANT TO KNOW SOMEONE BEFORE GETTING SEXUAL?

She has no set time or number of dates, days, or weeks before becoming sexual, but it's not likely to be a long time. Having sex on a first date isn't unheard of as long as she hasn't felt pressured by her partner.

"I don't like rules. Time isn't important, chemistry is. If you feel like sleeping with someone right away, go for it. Trust your instincts."

"One day plus . . . it depends on the person."

"Maybe two dates, although sometimes it's been a shorter period."

WHAT'S YOUR ATTITUDE TOWARD CASUAL SEX?

Aries is generally pretty good at distinguishing lust from love, making her quite comfortable with casual sex as long as it's practiced safely.

"When I'm not in a relationship, I don't see anything wrong with casual sex."

"It is fine if precautions are taken."

"It's okay as long as both people are on the same page and don't confuse it with a committed or lasting relationship."

Fantasies

"I am a hopeless romantic. My fantasy is being made love to in the shower, ocean, hot tub, in the snow, in front of the fireplace."

"I think of my husband's hard body."

"Start with neck, go on to breast, [and] then go down."

"For me to have the ultimate perfect body and to be desired and to have intercourse and multiple orgasms with the sexiest man who happen[s] to be my soul mate."

DO YOU BELIEVE IN MONOGAMY?

For her monogamy is not about sex; it's about commitment and bonding. In essence, she believes in serial monogamy, one lover at a time for as long as it works.

"I hope for monogamy, but I know some people aren't suited to it. I've never been faithful. Sometimes the moment overtakes you."

"I'm faithful when in a relationship for as long as it lasts. I don't believe we mate for life, but that each relationship is a learning and growing experience. Some short, some long . . . no pun intended."

"I do believe in it, but I haven't been faithful yet."

"I don't think monogamy works for many people. There is too much pressure on each to satisfy all of the other's desires."

DOES SEX HAVE A SPIRITUAL SIGNIFICANCE FOR YOU?

While she may feel comfortable having sex outside an otherwise bonded relationship, sex isn't merely physical. She is quite private about her concept of spirituality and an element of that is the high that sex brings.

"Sex allows me to feel that I can mingle my spirit with another's—that we can exchange breath—especially if I feel I am with a soul mate whose pleasure/passion is every bit as strong as my own."

"Yes, in the sense that love is spiritual and sex is a wonderful expression of love."

"There is nothing like it. Sex takes me to another plane of experience."

"Sex is the physical manifestation of love, God's gift."

ARE YOU COMFORTABLE INITIATING SEXUAL ACTIVITIES?

Aries has a take-charge nature. She is usually the one to initiate sex.

"Definitely . . . I like being the one in control."

A Memory

"My most wonderful encounter was made extraordinary by the circumstances. I was in love with one of my best friends, and it was unrequited for years. But we became emotionally intimate over time and crossed some boundaries—sleeping in the same bed, touching, caressing, partial nudity—but had never kissed or made love. One very hot night we were sleeping in his single bed. It was raining, thunder and lightning. The window was open. We were in our underwear, caressing each other and he was lying on top of me. The room was dark except for the lightning. I asked him to kiss me; he said no. But then in another moment he did and I felt like the room exploded. A huge bolt of lightning came down at that moment and I couldn't stop shaking. I think about that moment a lot. He's the only actual man I fantasize about and it is always in that bed."

HOW DO YOU COMMUNICATE TO YOUR PARTNER YOUR SEXUAL WANTS AND NEEDS?

Aries is a Fire Sign, the Sign of action. When it comes to communicating about sex, especially in bed, she prefers body language to words, but she welcomes having her partner tell her what he does and doesn't like.

"I guide him and respond to what he does that pleases me."

"I use both [body language and words], but mostly through gestures until I am very comfortable with a partner."

DO YOU THINK OF YOURSELF AS BEING IN THE MAINSTREAM SEXUALLY, MORE EXPERIMENTAL, OR OPEN TO ANYTHING?

Her range of sexuality goes from the mainstream to experimental, from intercourse and oral sex to using food, ice cubes, and hot wax. She might accept an occasional spanking, use a leather or latex accessory, or wear a blindfold or high-heeled boots to add excitement. She might also put on a costume, use a vibrator, and try light bondage. Forget the chains, paddles, and electricity. She'll be turned off by the unusual behaviors these items suggest.

"I'd say I am experimental though not extreme. I am into spanking but not genital torture, piercing, et cetera."

"I consider myself mainstream, though with the right person I could become quite experimental."

Her fantasies extend beyond the mainstream.

A Fantasy

"*I like to imagine my man sitting with me standing in front of him, telling me which articles of clothing to take off and how slowly. Then he tells me what positions he wants me in. Sometimes he ties me up, blindfold[s] me, and uses whipped cream, ice cubes, hot wax, and [then] finally has intercourse with me.*"

HOW DO YOU DEMONSTRATE AFFECTION FOR YOUR PARTNER?

Aries loves to feel that she's helping her partner, and she strives to be considerate. It is important to her to be noticed and to be told that her efforts are appreciated.

"Cooking, listening, understanding a different point of view, I like taking care of my part-

ner . . . making sure that he is remembered on special occasions."

"I help him accomplish personal goals, and send him chocolate kisses, special notes and cards."

"I strive to be thoughtful, make his breakfast in the morning, [run] his bath after work, give him a rubdown and kiss him all over."

Fantasies

"*My partner is kissing me, beginning at my forehead and working his way down to my inner thighs, staying there, teasing me, without touching my vagina until I can't take it any more. Finally he thrusts inside me and brings me to orgasm.*"

"*Having my legs massaged and admired, kissed; oral sex performed on me and the intercourse lasting for a long time—until I am satisfied.*"

"*I have fantasies in which I am forced to have sex in unusual positions and with more than one male partner.*"

The Five Senses

HOW IMPORTANT TO YOU IS THE SEXUAL ENVIRONMENT?

As Aries rules the head, aromas are a stimulant for her. Cleanliness matters. The smell of clean sheets is probably the most important element in the environment for sex.

"Cleanliness is extremely important. The rest doesn't matter at all."

"[Personal] cleanliness is most important. I don't care whether the place is messy."

"A modicum of privacy and cleanliness is important."

WHERE DO YOU LIKE TO HAVE SEX?

Privacy matters. Smells of grass, trees, flowers, the lapping of waves on the beach might be turn-ons, but not if anyone else is remotely nearby. Her favorite place for sex is the bedroom.

"Outdoors, but in a deserted area or situation . . ."

"The car or the beach is fine, never really in a public place."

"Outside is fun—in a pool, Jacuzzi, even on the roof."

A Fantasy

"He picks me up in a limo and brings me red roses. We have dinner at a lovely restaurant and go dancing. Then we go to his hotel room and he does a striptease for me. The sex is hot and he climaxes inside me, and he tells me he loves me."

WHAT PUTS YOU IN THE MOOD FOR SEX?

Two different kinds of behaviors, romantic and highly physical, put Aries in the mood. On the one hand, lavish some attention on her, bring her a flower (it needn't be a bouquet). A token that shows her lover cares about her is very sexy to Aries. On the more active side, working out, roughhousing, and playing at forcing her to have sex get her very excited.

"Music, candles, eating in bed, French kissing, a small gesture like holding hands, can be very arousing to me. Erotic touching, kissing from toes up or eyes down."

"Thunderstorms!! Lying in the sun, talking about sex, reading erotica, romantic movies . . . all put me in the mood."

WHAT'S YOUR ATTITUDE TOWARD PORNOGRAPHY?

Pornography is either of no interest to her or a turnoff. After all, Aries wants her lover to think she is the best there is. Watching some woman with enhanced breasts performing multiple acts of sex on a video is likely to trigger competitive feelings and undermine her own sex drive.

"Porn doesn't have enough emotions and feelings in it. Perhaps if it included a good love story I'd like it a whole lot more."

"Mainstream heterosexual porn does noth-

ing for me. Gay male porn is much more interesting. I think heterosexual porn could be satisfying, but it's just not done well."

"I think porn tends to separate sex from love and even affection and makes it just another spectator sport like football or wrestling. I suppose it enhances sex for some people but that doesn't redeem it for me."

HOW MUCH CUDDLING DO YOU ENJOY, ASIDE FROM SEX?

She likes to cuddle but isn't one to hang on to her lover. She needs her space and respects his. A little hug in public is a pleasure. Cuddling while watching a video at home usually leads to sex.

"I like sitting close and holding hands, walking arm in arm, hips together in rhythm."

"If I like someone a lot, I want a lot of affection."

A Fantasy

"I imagine that he has been away for a while and we are about to meet at a friend's house. We don't have a chance to be alone there, but we talk with each other and hold hands. On the drive home we kiss at red lights, like kids, and I stroke his hand or place my hand on his thigh; not too high up, just a suggestion. Without saying anything, he pulls the car over and we begin to kiss, softly at first and then more passionately. He unbuttons my blouse, I help him out of his clothes, and we make love in the front seat."

HOW TACTILE AND HOW ORAL ARE YOU?

Touching is certainly important to her, but Aries is the Sign that rules the head. So it is that kissing and oral sex are of great significance to her for the most satisfying sex.

"I love touching and being touched, sometimes feather light [and] sometimes rough handling with force."

"I enjoy deep kissing on the mouth, all over my lover's body and penis."

WHAT SEX ACTS DO YOU LIKE MOST AND LEAST?

She loves to kiss and be kissed. Nothing tops the pleasure and excitement that kissing stimulates. She loves to give and receive oral sex, and she enjoys intercourse. Anal sex is her least favorite sex act.

"Favorites: kissing, receiving oral sex, intercourse, anal stimulation, though not anal penetration."

"Kissing, mutual masturbation, fondling breasts, intercourse, oral sex . . . Never anal . . ."

"Kissing, oral sex, having my breasts fondled and sucked, intercourse . . ."

AS A LOVER, WHAT'S YOUR BEST SKILL?

She wants to please her man as well as prove her skill in bed. Aries is especially proud of her abilities at oral sex.

"Everyone praises my tongue and how I bring them to orgasm."

"How I move my body; that I am not easily shamed in bed."

"How I like to initiate and be in control, also being a flirt."

A Memory

"My partner is verbal about appreciating my body and our compatibility. He makes it a priority to bring me to orgasm; in fact, [he] becomes more aroused by my orgasm. He says sentimental or tender things such as, 'Do you realize that we met three months ago today?' He respects and trusts me and is willing to experiment with me and laughs at the word 'dirty.'"

WHAT SMELLS AND TASTES ON YOUR PARTNER DO YOU ENJOY?

Many Aries women love their partners' colognes. The tastes she finds appealing are natural: skin, mouth, lips, and her lover's fresh sweat. She enjoys flavored oils and if she likes to mix food with sex, strawberries are her favorite.

"Smells: cologne on his neck, his skin, hair, scalp, and the smell of his scrotum."

"His cologne just melts me. I like the taste of his cum, his body, his everything."

"I like the smell of his skin and his breath and the taste of his tongue and the salty taste of his penis just before he cums."

"Skin, genitals, colognes, his hair . . ."

A Memory

"Music, great wine, dancing, snuggling, taking off each other's clothes piece by piece, petting, cuddling, laughing, rolling around, massaging each other's feet, kissing all over. Holding each other in the afterglow until we both fell asleep breathing together as one unit."

FOR SOME PEOPLE THE TASTE OF THEIR PARTNER'S CUM OR SECRETIONS IS UNPLEASANT. IF THAT'S TRUE FOR YOU, WHAT DO YOU DO ABOUT THE TASTE?

Some Aries women enjoy their partner's cum and find tasting it an exciting part of the sexual experience. The Aries who isn't enthusiastic about the taste will strive to overlook it.

"I love to swallow, lick, rub cum on my stomach and breasts; this excites me."

"I keep a glass of water handy and take sips of it to dilute the taste."

DO YOU ENJOY WATCHING YOUR PARTNER DURING SEX AND ORGASM? DO YOU ENJOY BEING WATCHED?

She "most definitely" loves watching her partner during sex and orgasm. She is equally comfortable being watched "when I'm with someone I know very well."

A Memory

"We showered together. He surprised me, coming into the bathroom while I was bathing. We washed each other, performed oral sex on each *other. The hot water pouring over us and the smell of soap was intoxicating. Continuing out of the shower into the bedroom with intercourse; reaching climax together, still wet from the shower, and sweet talking afterward."*

The Big "O"

HOW DO YOU REACH ORGASM AND HOW OFTEN?

She can generally reach orgasm with various sex acts, especially those involving oral sex and from any position. Aries is likely to climax every time.

"I reach orgasm through oral sex, masturbation, and intercourse—but usually only with grinding or direct clitoral stimulation."

"I orgasm all the time . . . with [my] latest partner, multiple times . . ."

"I cum through oral sex, being fondled, or masturbation . . ."

WHAT'S YOUR FAVORITE POSITION?

Her favorite position for intercourse may be woman on top, man on top, or doggie style, dependent upon her partner's size. Depth of penetration is what matters to Aries.

"My favorite positions are being on top [and] spooning with clitoral stimulation."

SOME PEOPLE ARE CONCERNED ABOUT BRINGING THEIR PARTNER TO CLIMAX BEFORE HAVING AN ORGASM THEMSELVES. OTHERS STRIVE TO REACH ORGASM TOGETHER. WHICH IS TRUE FOR YOU?

Aries has the reputation of doing almost everything quickly, and this includes reaching orgasm. But generally, she is not concerned about whether she achieves orgasm before, after, or along with her partner.

"It doesn't matter as long as we're both satisfied. My boyfriend doesn't cum every time, but he's content."

"I'd like to cum together, but my partner is always later and I don't worry about it."

 Fantasies

"The kinkiest things I fantasize about are gay sex or a threesome with me and two men."

"Five guys and me . . ."

"Being stroked by a very strong man wearing leather gloves. He takes total control but with respect. I give all of me with wild passion."

"Sex on an airplane . . . a red-eye and everyone's asleep. It turns me on to think of this because it's public but discreet at the same time."

ARE YOU VOCAL DURING SEX?

She is vocal during sex, but not necessarily verbal. The Aries woman does express her feelings, sometimes subtly and at others more overtly.

"I purr like a kitten."

"I am a screamer."

AFTER SEX WHAT DO YOU LIKE TO DO?

After sex she is content to spend a little quiet time with her lover. It isn't important to her whether this time is spent at home or out doing something relatively simple.

"Fall blissfully asleep, or if it's in the morning, cuddle quietly before facing the day."

"Walk by the ocean, hold hands, cuddle, stay in bed, laugh together, sleep."

"Play some more, shower, and sleep."

The Aries Man in His Own Words

A Memory

"We wrestled. She's a pianist and has great strength in her arms and shoulders. Naked, we knelt on the bed. She flailed around in a mock fistfight. I grabbed her arms, pinned her down but couldn't hold her. She had me hanging half off the bed. I demanded, 'Let me up.' She did, then straddled me and held my arms down. I made a quick move, startling her. She was quicker and pinned me again. I conceded the contest. Our rule was the loser must rim the winner. She got up on her elbows and knees to best present her ass to me. I rimmed her affectionately and thoroughly, including penetration. Then she signaled readiness for intercourse. I got on top of her and it was great."

Attraction and Dating an Aries

WHAT ATTRACTS YOU TO SOMEONE?

Aries is playful, so a sense of humor is paramount in attracting his attention. Though looks first turn his head, good conversation, broadmindedness, and personality further involve him.

"Breast size isn't important. Good grooming is nice. I enjoy a nice ass and shapely pair of legs, but those won't motivate me in the absence of intelligence."

"I am first attracted by one's sense of humor. Regarding physical attributes, the only one that really matters is weight in the sense of height/weight in proportion."

"Turn-ons include pleasant voice, nice smile and teeth, warm natural body fragrances, not covered over with perfumes or other artificial scents, and a self-assertive personality."

"A pretty face, nice eyes, and a smile attract me much more than a great body. What matters more is a woman who is honest, mature, and doesn't play childish head games."

WHAT MIGHT TURN YOU OFF?

Even if he is attracted to a woman because she has a lot of personality, he will be put off by any kind of excess. Too much makeup, too much

jewelry, too much perfume, being too heavy, or talking too loudly will push him away.

"I don't find women who are extreme, eat or drink too much, laugh too loudly, and are argumentative at all attractive."

"Too much makeup, putting others down, being selfish."

"Turnoffs include arrogance, self-righteousness, narrow-mindedness, being overbearing."

"Bad teeth have often been a turnoff. I notice them like radar notices a 747. Behavior is a definite factor, from immoral (in my eyes) to annoying or questionable."

"Eats, drinks, or smokes too much; wears too much perfume; looks around too much at others while conversing with me; argumentative; negative."

A Memory

"I was walking through the woods with my partner and we had walked for quite a while. I was taking pictures of her. On the way back she pulled me aside and said 'I am so horny right now.' It all started with her giving me oral sex. It was late afternoon and the area was deserted. Then we had intercourse in the woods and came to orgasm simultaneously."

WHAT DO YOU ENJOY DOING ON A DATE?

He is a traditional and romantic lover. Dinner, long walks, and time to talk are his favorite activities. He may not mention having sex as a part of the evening, but it's certainly one of his hopes.

"A nice romantic dinner and sex after . . ."

"Walking by the ocean, dancing, hiking and camping, doing things we both enjoy."

"Going to a movie, play, parade, theme park, museum, community event, concert, dinner and dance . . ."

"Talking, dancing, flirting, sexual suggestions with food or actions . . ."

"Take a coffee break in a crowded place, get to know her likes and dislikes, match hers to mine and go from there."

ARE YOU FLIRTATIOUS?

He's flirtatious and doesn't realize his manner may be misinterpreted. His motive is innocent. The truth is he's a tad insecure, needs reassurances that he's wonderful, and revels in admiration.

"I am flirtatious, perhaps because I enjoy sincere friendships with many women."

"Yes, I am, up to the point of exchanging phone numbers when I have a girlfriend that I am one-to-one with. If I'm single, I will get as far as I can."

"In a rather obtuse way . . . I try to get a woman to make the first move most times, but if she doesn't, I just go for it."

ARE YOU JEALOUS?

While he's reputedly jealous, the Aries man doesn't view himself that way—at least not much.

"Life is too short to be dwelling on bad, useless emotions."

"I am to a certain extent. I've had my trust broken and it leaves me feeling guarded."

"I'm not usually. One time I got terribly jealous of one of my girlfriends. She said she needed time to think about us and I figured something was up, but later I was proved wrong. That taught me a lesson."

HOW DO YOU FEEL ABOUT PUBLIC DISPLAYS OF AFFECTION?

Aries may be something of a show-off, but when it comes to sex, he's no exhibitionist. Holding hands and some provocative kissing are fine in front of others; after all, Aries does want attention. More than that, and Aries thinks you ought to get a room.

"Slight displays are fine, major displays aren't. My 'affection' is no one else's business."

"I'm proud to show my love for my partner, but not to the point of making her or anyone else uncomfortable."

"What is wrong with it? If the kids are around, watch the breast and buttock touching, but kissing and holding hands, not being afraid to show your love for one another is a beautiful thing."

A Memory

"I was working as a lifeguard at a country club. I started to go out with the receptionist. On our first date we went to a party. It got to be pretty late and we knew the club would be closed, but she had a key so we went to the clubhouse. We had sex on the pool table, then in the steam room, and then in the pool. This was over the course of a long and wonderful night. It was a wonderful beginning of an all-too-short summer romance."

Sexual Attitudes and Behaviors

HOW OFTEN DO YOU THINK ABOUT SEX AND HOW OFTEN PER WEEK DO YOU WANT TO HAVE SEX?

Aries has sex on the brain: thinks about it daily and perhaps is preoccupied with it. He enjoys having sex four times a week.

HOW LONG DO YOU LIKE TO SPEND HAVING SEX AND HOW MUCH OF THAT TIME IS FOREPLAY? DO YOU ENJOY QUICKIES?

Aries prefers sex to last at least an hour, but he tends to be the wham-bam lover of the zodiac, so quickies can serve an important function. Having a quick orgasm sets him up to last a lot longer for a second round.

"I enjoy quickies under the right circumstances, not as a steady diet. I prefer about a half hour for foreplay, about an hour from start to finish. Sometimes a quickie can be a prelude to starting all over again later."

"One good thing about a quickie is that I won't have to worry about cumming too fast when I'm trying to please my lover."

"I like to spend as long as it takes, with foreplay about an hour, but quickies are enjoyable too."

WHAT TIME OF DAY DO YOU PREFER TO HAVE SEX?

He enjoys sex at any time of day, with a little preference for nighttime sex.

"Time on the clock is not important."

"I prefer to do everything at night. Expressions of affection are no different."

"Nighttime, before we fall asleep, holding each other, lying together still as one."

"Evening is great, a rainy afternoon is better."

"I like foreplay to last long enough to get her wet and just about ready to explode, then I go down and get her off first and then . . ."

HOW OFTEN DO YOU MASTURBATE?

If he's in a relationship and having sex frequently, he doesn't masturbate often. Otherwise, Aries masturbates three to five times weekly.

 A Memory

"In a bathroom in a restaurant. About six years ago. I walked in to check on this girl to make sure that she was okay. She stood up and rubbed her butt on my penis. Then I grabbed her breasts. She moved my hands to her belt buckle, which I undid and dropped her pants and then her underwear. She bent over and grabbed the wall and I slid right into her and it was exciting. We got caught by some guy who walked in on us, but it was fun."

HOW LONG DO YOU WANT TO KNOW SOMEONE BEFORE GETTING SEXUAL?

He says, "I'm not in a hurry. I'm willing to wait twenty-four hours." Not every Aries expects sex on the first date, but most of them do.

"Sex is likely within three weeks. Delaying sex is a good thing because sex tends to foreshorten the interesting dating and getting-to-know-you phase."

"I can do casual sex on a first meeting, but people who become regular play partners require some devotion of time and effort."

"Five minutes to fourteen days."

"Right after dinner . . ."

"Two to three dates or less . . . I believe in love at first sight and I am willing to take a leap."

In bed, if no passion is ignited, he realizes he isn't really interested. He'll try a couple of times more and then back off, but not out. He'll want to remain friends.

WHAT'S YOUR ATTITUDE TOWARD CASUAL SEX?

He is of two minds on this question, saying that he loves it and at the same time that it's unsafe. Overall, Aries is not interested, or only occasionally, and sees casual sex as immoral.

"I enjoy it for an amusement, but it is no replacement for sex in a committed relationship."

"I am not against it, but personally I prefer to have some emotional commitment."

DO YOU BELIEVE IN MONOGAMY?

Aries truly desires a total commitment to one woman. For him, the richest relationship is one of constancy.

"I believe that you share most things with the world. Your body is the one thing that you can give and share with one special person, and that commitment brings you both closer to each other."

"When I find the right woman I will be totally devoted to her in every way and wouldn't risk hurting her"

"I am a one-woman man."

DOES SEX HAVE A SPIRITUAL SIGNIFICANCE FOR YOU?

Aries is very positive about the spiritual aspect of sexuality. Within a loving relationship, sex touches his soul.

"Sex, at its best, is the closest to heaven I'll ever get. I think it's the ultimate form of communication."

"How better to define spirituality? There is giving, submission, concern for the other's pleasure and ecstasy."

"I believe sex is the purest union of two people, a way to show their mutual love, the 'of one flesh' thing."

ARE YOU COMFORTABLE INITIATING SEXUAL ACTIVITIES?

Aries is comfortable initiating sex when he's confident his advances are welcome. He doesn't want to offend a woman any more than he wants to deal with rejection. He also welcomes having his partner start things off.

HOW DO YOU COMMUNICATE TO YOUR PARTNER YOUR SEXUAL WANTS AND NEEDS?

Aries is a Fire Sign, a Sign of action. When it comes to expressing his wishes to his partner, especially in bed, he prefers to use body language.

"The body tells more than words . . . listen."

"It's my hope that I turn her on so much direction isn't needed."

"I feel spontaneity is better than a menu. A woman who doesn't do something has a reason for that, and I respect her choice, so I let things go the way they go. Generally I feel if a woman really experiences good sex she will accommodate me. What happens, happens and most of the time it is fulfilling."

DO YOU THINK OF YOURSELF AS BEING IN THE MAINSTREAM SEXUALLY, MORE EXPERIMENTAL, OR OPEN TO ANYTHING?

He's a mainstream lover, sticking primarily to oral sex and intercourse. When he's naughty, a good spanking is just the thing. Having his partner wear a costume complete with high heels turns him on. The more experimental Aries lover is open to some mild bondage, wearing a blindfold, using food, and playing with sex toys like vibrators, dildos, and cock rings.

The most open Aries, few in number, enjoy dominance and submission, ménage à trois, cross-dressing, and more extensive bondage. For them, sex toys might include ticklers, paddles, and handcuffs.

"I am open to damn near anything . . . sado-masochism, body clips, water sports, orgies, fisting, and sex toys such as chains, piercing needles, riding crops, and electrical devices."

"I am pretty open, into dominance and submission. I love to spank my partner to the point [of] orgasm."

Aries' sexual fantasies are quite straightforward. Even those Aries on the most experimental range of this Sign have limits within their fantasies.

Fantasies

"When I masturbate I think about something I've done that was hot and worth reliving."

"I fantasize about sex with a celebrity or my ex."

"My fantasies involve a natural setting, a waterfall near by, a slight rain, very passionate."

"I just imagine having sex after a great day of friendship."

HOW DO YOU DEMONSTRATE AFFECTION FOR YOUR PARTNER?

When Aries is attracted to a woman, he looks at her with an expression so loving, so attentive, that the feeling is almost physical. She expects that he is hanging on her every word. Well, he strives to be considerate and is willing to help his partner, but more often than not he will need gentle reminders.

"I think of ways to make her life easier . . . I try to assess her mood and show her sensitivity doing a household or yard chore. I take her seriously and listen to her problems."

"I bring her tokens of love such as a little doll or cook a special meal. I might create an intimate atmosphere and dance to soft music, or perhaps share a romantic bath."

"Bringing her potted or cut flowers, doing a household or yard chore that is creative and makes a difference, writing poems to her."

"Being sensitive to her mood in whatever helpful ways possible, bringing practical and cute gifts."

The Five Senses

HOW IMPORTANT TO YOU IS THE SEXUAL ENVIRONMENT?

Aries doesn't need a romantic setting to be turned on. He'd like the environment to be somewhat clean, but beyond that it isn't of great significance to him. In fact, throwing in a new sex toy or putting on a costume will prove much more stimulating than candles or incense.

"All that matters is the girl and me."

"It sets the mood. A wide variety is okay as far as décor is concerned. The room should be clean, but not necessarily orderly. Light should be subdued."

"Cleanliness matters. Dim light is nice, but if we're feeling passionate, especially at the beginning of relationship, anywhere is just fine."

"A clean house is a clean body."

WHERE DO YOU LIKE TO HAVE SEX?

He isn't fussy about where to have sex, but if it's outdoors, in the woods or in a car, seclusion matters. Having sex on a deserted beach is a turn-on. Trying to find a private spot among the dunes of an otherwise populated beach where there's a good chance of being seen is a turnoff.

"Anywhere is a good place."

"My preference is in a bed where it is comfortable."

"I prefer the bedroom mostly because that leads to longer and, for me, more enjoyable sex. But I also like public places, when relatively obscure. I did it in an elevator once."

A Memory

"It was a dominance and submission scene where I spanked my partner almost to the point of orgasm, but [I] would not let her touch herself though she really wanted to. I used a hairbrush and a leather belt, and had her strapped down. I kept this up for a long time until finally I let her masturbate to orgasm while I continued talking to her and spanking her."

WHAT PUTS YOU IN THE MOOD FOR SEX?

Considering that this man has sex on the brain most of the time, it doesn't take anything special to put Aries in the mood. Mostly it is the sight of his lover, the sound of her voice, and the smell of her perfume that excite him.

"The right partner puts me in the mood. Set and setting are much less important."

"Spending time getting to know partner . . . this could take minutes or weeks."

"I am an Aries. I am always in the mood. But perfume and slow music and dim lights add to the stimulus."

"Showering together, porn, wine, looking at her when she puts on the leather or latex with the choker and heels . . . sometimes just the plain black vest that she puts on when we are going to dinner . . ."

"From her body language to her clothes, to her smell . . . I can smell a woman, not her perfume, but her. I can't explain it but I know it and it works always."

WHAT'S YOUR ATTITUDE TOWARD PORNOGRAPHY?

It's while masturbating that pornography has its rather limited use for Aries. Just watching the sex act is sufficient to turn him on. Some Aries men completely disapprove of pornography.

"It's sexually arousing, but I still think there's something wrong with it . . . the participants degrade themselves with immoral behavior."

"I am not fond of pornography, but I have nothing against looking at erotica."

"Most porn is like bad acting . . . Ba-ba-boom. Ba-ba-boom, et cetera . . . Boring after a while."

"As a tool for interest or to excite, perhaps when I'm alone, it's okay on occasion. I'm not particularly interested in it."

HOW MUCH CUDDLING DO YOU ENJOY, ASIDE FROM SEX?

With Aries, a sexual session will include considerable cuddling and kissing. Even aside from sex, he loves physical closeness.

"I like sitting close and holding hands, walking arm in arm and with hips together in rhythm."

"I love to cuddle when I am in a serious relationship, feeling her next to me, smelling her hair, kissing her on the head, rubbing her body, without words letting her know how much I appreciate and love her."

"A lot, even more than most women want to give, from my experience anyway."

HOW TACTILE AND HOW ORAL ARE YOU?

As Aries is the Sign that rules the head and the mouth, this is a man who is an expert at kissing and oral sex. In addition to that, he loves to touch, to feel his lover respond to his fingers.

"I love all things oral. I believe that I bring great pleasure and it is also a pleasure for me."

"I am mainly oral and get so much pleasure from it, maybe even more than genital sex if that is possible."

"I use my mouth for everything that makes her excited."

"I am extremely oral; in fact, I have not failed to bring a woman to orgasm this way. I kiss everywhere and miss nothing."

"Where sex is concerned I would rather lose any other sense than touch."

"Touch is teasing, and I love this in foreplay. I love to see my partner crave for more."

 Fantasies
"My girlfriend in a leather outfit, with a choker and black studded heels. She is in the role of a dominatrix and makes me do things to her. Then I stop and become the dominant one and take her however I want her."

"I would like to have a session where I would tie up my partner to a bed, give her oral sex, and have her try to escape. I would also like to spank my partner."

"No whips, no hard pain, but I usually fantasize about being humiliated and violated by a dominant woman."

WHAT SEX ACTS DO YOU LIKE MOST AND LEAST?

He lists the big three: kissing, intercourse, and oral sex. Performing anal sex is the least favorite sex act for Aries men.

"When it comes to sex I am a man for all seasons, but if I had to choose between intercourse and cunnilingus I would choose cunnilingus."

"I love performing oral sex, then fondling her breasts and intercourse. I like to receive oral sex but not all women are good at it. I like anal sex occasionally."

"I dislike any anal penetration, no fingers or probing."

"Stay away from the rectum."

AS A LOVER, WHAT'S YOUR BEST SKILL?

His skills may be many and varied, but high on the list is his ability to please a lover with his mouth.

"My imagination . . ."

"The use of my hands and being able to stay at an erection for a long period of time; enabling my partner to achieve multiple orgasms . . ."

"Inventiveness first of all, then my oral skills . . ."

WHAT SMELLS AND TASTES ON YOUR PARTNER DO YOU ENJOY?

On the subject of aromas, he's more turned on by Dove soap than Poison perfume. The tastes that Aries enjoys on his partner are natural: her skin, mouth, and lips. Very few Aries men are interested in using food with sex.

"I like the scent of skin, freshly showered or bathed, with a scent of cold cream or soap."

"I love all her smells, skin, vagina, panties . . . everything except perfume."

"It is a package; all is good. You can't like someone in slices."

"Good question. I like the natural smell of her clean pussy. But I don't like perfume. I want to experience her real smell. Women smell different from each other. Real turn-on for me."

"I love kissing [a woman after she] has eaten something cold and tasty."

FOR SOME PEOPLE THE TASTE OF THEIR PARTNER'S CUM OR SECRETIONS IS UNPLEASANT. IF THAT'S TRUE FOR YOU, WHAT DO YOU DO ABOUT THE TASTE?

Aries rarely has complaints on this subject. He is a very oral lover and enjoys virtually everything connected to oral sex.

"I love eating pussy. The secretions are pleasant . . . I like the taste."

DO YOU ENJOY WATCHING YOUR PARTNER DURING SEX AND ORGASM? DO YOU ENJOY BEING WATCHED?

He loves being the center of attention and that includes having his partner watch him during sex and orgasm. Watching her is an integral part of the experience for Aries.

"Nothing is as beautiful as a woman when she cums."

"I love watching her. I wouldn't miss it."

The Big "O"

HOW DO YOU REACH ORGASM AND HOW OFTEN?

Most of his sexual encounters end in orgasm, usually achieved through a combination of foreplay, oral sex, and intercourse.

WHAT'S YOUR FAVORITE POSITION?

Aries is satisfied with a range of positions, from lying on his back and being masturbated to doggie style when he's performing anal sex. If he has a favorite position for intercourse and orgasm, it's with the woman on top.

"As long as my dick is covered by flesh (mouth, hand, pussy, ass, tits) I can cum."

SOME PEOPLE ARE CONCERNED ABOUT BRINGING THEIR PARTNER TO CLIMAX BEFORE HAVING AN ORGASM THEMSELVES. OTHERS STRIVE TO REACH ORGASM TOGETHER. WHICH IS TRUE FOR YOU?

Aries is a Sign of action and he does most things fast. As a lover, he sees himself as caring and prefers to bring his partner to climax before cumming himself. At the same time he frequently cums quickly.

"I want my partner to cum first: ego, pride reasons."

"I'd love to cum with my partner but that's difficult to pull off. I would rather make sure my partner has cum than risk her orgasm as I tried to finesse the timing."

"I like both. My partner generally enjoys orgasm through oral stimulation of the clitoris, and then we enjoy mutual orgasm after. It works most times."

ARE YOU VOCAL DURING SEX?

As Aries communicates primarily with gestures, he isn't very vocal during sex.

"There is some crooning and expression of pleasure, but very little talking. That would be a distraction."

AFTER SEX WHAT DO YOU LIKE TO DO?

For Aries sex is the end of the evening, not a prelude to other activities.

"After sex, I pass out."

"I like to kiss and relax with her in my arms."

"If we don't fall asleep I might enjoy having something to eat or watching TV."

"It's usually nighttime so I like to follow sex with a little talking, cuddling, then sleep."

TAURUS

April 20–May 20

THE BULL

Earth Sign Taurus—loyal, dependable, passionate, and highly physical—wants to move slowly and luxuriate in a back or full-body massage. The Sign of Taurus rules the throat and the neck, the tongue, and the sense of touch. Taurus lovers have exceptionally sensitive hands.

She says: "My best sexual skill is how I use my hands to stroke his penis and my tongue to lick all over his body."

He says: "I love to cuddle. I'd like to be a blanket around my date."

"Let's get physical, physical . . . let me hear your body talk."
—Olivia Newton-John

The Taurus Woman in Her Own Words

A Memory

"My wedding night. Best sex of my life. The emotions of the day made me very vulnerable. It was late. We had showered and were lying in bed. He took his time. Lots of foreplay. Lots of oral sex on me, and then I had an amazing orgasm through intercourse. Quiet room and two people who really loved each other expressing that love."

Attraction and Dating a Taurus

WHAT ATTRACTS YOU TO SOMEONE?

Taurus is an exceptionally physical sign. She says that energy, sense of humor, and self-confidence matter. But, in fact, appearance and being in good shape are indispensable.

"He has to be in shape. That shows he cares about himself and it spills over into the rest of his personal life. Penis size does matter."

"It is all one big package: physical appearance, as well as sense of humor, and being emotionally available."

"Physique and eyes, confidence, sense of humor, [being] physically fit but not preoccupied with himself . . ."

WHAT MIGHT TURN YOU OFF?

Talking about his other lovers, being out of shape, and being cheap all turn Taurus off. A man need not be rich to involve a Taurus, but he must have financial security. Stability and security are crucial to her.

"I don't like aggressiveness, like some people say 'come suck this.' Taking the romance or sensuality out of sex is a big turnoff."

"No sense of humor, dirty fingernails, being cheap, putting others down."

WHAT DO YOU ENJOY DOING ON A DATE?

The Taurus woman has an inner quality rather like Cinderella. She wants her man to ride in on a white steed, make that a stretch limo, and take her off for a magical night. But no, he doesn't have to do that every time. She enjoys quiet evenings and an occasional concert. One constant on any date is sharing food, whether at home or at a restaurant.

"I like having fun, to go out and do something. A weekend at Daytona Bike Week is the best date I ever had. Fun, adventure, and more fun, but I also enjoy cooking dinner together and hanging out at home."

"Dinner, walk in the park, art show, something outside. Not going to a movie, being stuck inside. I love nature."

"I enjoy time with just him and me, and time with crowds, walking on the beach in the late day, riding bikes, going to concerts, hanging out at the local pub with friends."

ARE YOU FLIRTATIOUS?

Taurus is flirtatious. Her innate warmth is attractive to men and, although she is loyal by nature, her partner had best let her know she is appreciated or she'll find a way to compensate.

"Often my general friendliness is mistaken for flirtation. Well, I guess I just enjoy flirting on many levels."

"Yes, with anyone I find attractive to see if they are attracted to me."

"Yes, very much so especially because my husband, a Capricorn, is too work oriented and doesn't give me the kind of attention I crave. I got that from my gorgeous former lover. Wow! He was something."

Her fantasies reveal how important it is for her partner to be attentive.

Fantasies

"*Having sex with my former boss in a secluded area somewhere. Him paying total, one hundred percent, attention to me.*"

"*My ultimate fantasy is romantic and sensual. The more my partner wants to seduce and satisfy me, the more arousing it is. The more he reacts when I tease or seduce him, the greater the arousal for me.*"

ARE YOU JEALOUS?

For Taurus the key words are "I have." She holds on to things that are important to her and definitely has a possessive streak.

"I can be, but only in my insecurities. When I feel confident and secure with myself and a partner I am not jealous."

"Yes, I feel jealous, but on the other hand, if another woman can take my man, then I never had him to start with."

"I like to be secure in my relationships or it won't work."

HOW DO YOU FEEL ABOUT PUBLIC DISPLAYS OF AFFECTION?

Taurus considers public displays of affection pretty natural, within limits, of course. It pleases her to have her lover show the world his affection by holding her arm and hugging her in public.

"Great within reason, hand holding, caressing, kissing. Groping is out. If you look and act like you need a room, get one."

"I'm not overly showy, but some can be

exciting, like sneaking a handful in a crowded place or slipping off to somewhere more intimate, but in general I like mild affection in public, hand holding, a few kisses or strokes."

"If it's not too bold I like it, but grabbing at the crotch or breast, no."

A Memory

"*I was not quite nineteen and a virgin. He was my first lover, a lifeguard, tanned and fit. He invited me to a party, after which we went back to his place, a dive of a beach house. We had extremely physical sex that night and several more times in the following weeks. I was an avid runner/cyclist at the time, very muscular and strong. The first night we rolled about his bed and I threw him off and we rolled all around the floor.*

"*When he began intercourse, I pushed him off me with my legs—it hurt, especially because I was pretending it wasn't my first time. Then I let him crawl back on top of me and repenetrate me. We slept. Later, I woke up and he spread some lubricant between my breasts and proceeded to rub his penis between them until he came. We fell asleep again—we must have had sex six or seven times. The smell was sweaty and full of release, of salty air and cum. I loved it. Sex with this guy was like [with] two wild animals. It was quite fantastic, the loss of my virginity in a mixture of passion, pain, aggressiveness, summer, ocean, pride, and strength.*"

Sexual Attitudes and Behaviors

HOW OFTEN DO YOU THINK ABOUT SEX AND HOW OFTEN PER WEEK DO YOU WANT TO HAVE SEX?

Taurus thinks about sex almost every day and would like to have sex that often. If time doesn't permit, she will be content with four encounters weekly.

"I'd like sex every day, some days more than once."

"I don't have a partner right now, but this questionnaire is making me want to go out and find a man right away."

"How often depends on how happy I am with my partner. If he's good to me, every day . . ."

"I'd say four or five times a week at least would be a good average."

HOW LONG DO YOU LIKE TO SPEND HAVING SEX AND HOW MUCH OF THAT TIME IS FOREPLAY? DO YOU ENJOY QUICKIES?

Taurus, being a highly physical Earth Sign, likes to take her time having sex. Foreplay should never be less than 15 to 30 minutes. She wants to make sure that every one of her erogenous zones is attended to. Quickies can be fun, though not as a steady diet.

"I love foreplay, in-between play, after play, foreplay to round 2, 3, 4, 5, et cetera. All sensual touch is wonderful."

"I want more than an hour, quickies, not really. I would rather have long, slow sex."

"Lots, though sometimes we get impatient . . . When we are most relaxed, it is the best and we enjoy it for a long time."

A Fantasy
"Passionate kissing, staying at a bed and breakfast, romantic settings, the roar of the ocean, the smells of flowers, fresh sheets, soap, the ocean."

WHAT TIME OF DAY DO YOU PREFER TO HAVE SEX?

She relaxes when the sun goes down, and so Taurus prefers to have sex in the early evening or at night.

"Anytime, but twilight is a very sexy time."

"All times . . . I am primarily comfortable after my daughter goes to sleep or when she isn't home. I could spend all day in bed, but nighttime is more often my chosen time."

HOW OFTEN DO YOU MASTURBATE?

She seldom masturbates, primarily because this very earthy woman wants to share sex with a partner. It just isn't very gratifying by herself.

HOW LONG DO YOU WANT TO KNOW SOMEONE BEFORE GETTING SEXUAL?

Taurus is not a Sign that likes to feel rushed. That's manipulation in her book and it will make her wary. If she feels comfortable, she'll become sexual in short order. Generally, Taurus wants to know a man for a few weeks before going further than some hugs and kisses.

"It depends on the chemistry. I can feel very sexual and close with someone in a short time. I want to know there's mutual affection and respect along with the sexual attraction, and that takes a bit of time."

"It's not so much the time as it is the quality of time spent. Most often, more than a few weeks . . ."

WHAT'S YOUR ATTITUDE TOWARD CASUAL SEX?

On no level does casual sex fit Ms. Taurus' personality. The physical is too important to her and her feelings are easily hurt.

"It can be unsafe, and why would I want to give my body casually anyway?"

"It usually screws me up; I always think it will be less trouble than it is. I used to wish that I was better able to handle casual sex. I'm better off without it."

"I did it for physical reasons, but suffered emotionally."

Fantasies
"Being with a woman, performing oral sex on another woman, or being with two men."
"I often think about being with a woman and her performing oral sex on me with my boyfriend or another guy helping himself."

DO YOU BELIEVE IN MONOGAMY?

Considering that Taurus is somewhat jealous and is the Sign of stability and security, in her relationships she is loyal and expects monogamy in return.

"Monogamy helps build trust to experiment and to enjoy lovemaking, not just sex."

"Yes, I don't like sharing sexual partners or the chance of getting a disease."

DOES SEX HAVE A SPIRITUAL SIGNIFICANCE FOR YOU?

Taurus may be considered the most physical Sign of the zodiac. It is the Sign that fully appreciates the value of all things tangible, and all things that she touches. This idea extends to relationships, especially sexual ones. As a result Taurus views sex as spiritual.

"Yes. It is almost like meditation, you are not thinking, just feeling. You feel a connection to the person, to the universe, and to God."

"When the mind and the body and the soul and the heart touch each other during sex, then it is very great sex and it is spiritual. I don't always have sex like this, but I have felt it happen this way."

"Yes, it is the melding of two spirits."

"Intimacy, good sex, can leave you spiritually fulfilled. It is healing as well as gratifying."

ARE YOU COMFORTABLE INITIATING SEXUAL ACTIVITIES?

With her appetite for sex, once the relationship has become sexual, Taurus is not shy about initiating.

"Yes. If I've already been intimate with a man, then watch out!"

HOW DO YOU COMMUNICATE TO YOUR PARTNER YOUR SEXUAL WANTS AND NEEDS?

She starts with gestures and progresses to words, as time passes and the relationship deepens.

"If he doesn't get my more subtle gestures, I feel it's only right to tell him what I want."

"I do so verbally, but only after knowing him better."

"Mostly by gestures, but if need be I will come out and say what I want."

DO YOU THINK OF YOURSELF AS BEING IN THE MAINSTREAM SEXUALLY, MORE EXPERIMENTAL, OR OPEN TO ANYTHING?

She is primarily a mainstream lover and far prefers sensuality, touching and kissing, to the use of toys or role-playing activities. Of all activities beyond straightforward sex, the one that Taurus most likely enjoys is incorporating food into sex play.

"I think those toys are a turnoff, frankly, and get in the way of the sensuous experience of making love, clean and natural."

The Tauran who is more experimental might be open to anal sex, spanking, bondage, having sex in public places, role playing in underwear, and would like to have attention paid to her feet.

"I want to explore and experiment. I've always been a little off mainstream, and I'm opening to more and more."

"I am very open, but I don't usually initiate kinky activities because I don't think my lover is interested in it."

In her fantasies she is usually forced to have sex and often with two partners.

 A Fantasy
"*Being captured and forced to be a sex slave to a powerful man or woman. Having to worship and service a man or group of men. Being part of a group of women who are sexual servants to one man. Being trained to obey, worship, and sexually satisfy a particular powerful man for a long period. Being penetrated in all orifices at the same time. Being fed through fellatio and not having any other source of nourishment. Having a man feed me with his penis*

as a baby uses a bottle. Having intercourse with one man while performing fellatio on another man, usually in a ritualistic setting/context. Living only to please one man sexually while spending my 'off time' in bed pleasuring myself with a woman friend. This man has complete control over both of us."

HOW DO YOU DEMONSTRATE AFFECTION FOR YOUR PARTNER?

Taurus is a remarkably caring and loyal lover. She has a knack for buying just the right gift for her partner and generally shows affection for him through her attentiveness.

"I buy him little gifts, things I know he likes, and stock his favorite kind of ice cream in the freezer. I might initiate a new little sexual experience, adding something in that he has dreamed of."

"Do things for him, pick up his clothes, call when I am going to be late, buy him things, touch him."

"I love doing things for my partner. I love to touch and kiss when he is not expecting it. I just love to show him how much I care."

"Having things ready for him, anticipating what he will need. Love notes, initiating sex, taking some of his workload off him."

The Five Senses

HOW IMPORTANT TO YOU IS THE SEXUAL ENVIRONMENT?

Taurus cares about being warm. Beyond that, the environment for sex is not overly important, though cleanliness and soft lighting are a plus.

"Cleanliness is a big issue. The others just fall into place."

"The only thing that matters to me is lighting—no harsh lights. I do like candlelight, clean sheets are important: I hate crumbs or gritty sheets."

"I prefer candlelight and a space that is somewhat neat, but I am not overly picky, especially if I'm with a man I've known quite a while."

"Not as important as our feeling for each other at that moment, but it can set the mood."

 Memories
"*Making love on a balcony in Barbados, overlooking the ocean. The sound of the ocean, the soft trade winds, the bright moon.*"

"*The first time my husband and I did it on his mother's couch, when she was upstairs sleeping. It was risky, fast, and aggressive.*"

WHERE DO YOU LIKE TO HAVE SEX?

Anywhere that can be comfortable and warm will suit a Taurus—most of the time that's the bedroom. Of course, if that bedroom is in a cozy bed and breakfast or in a motel by the sea, her pleasure will be enhanced.

"I used to like having it wherever I wanted it: library, floor, car, beach. Now I wait 'til we get home to enjoy the comfort of a warm bed. Maybe at twenty-eight I'm just getting old."

"Bedroom . . . I'd love to do it outdoors or in a public place, but my husband will have no part of it."

"Primarily where I am comfortable, in the bedroom, but I like a bit of adventure too."

WHAT PUTS YOU IN THE MOOD FOR SEX?

Taurus is a very sensual woman. Stimulating her senses, sights, sounds, smells, and tastes are her turn-ons. Passionate kissing and a massage will almost always work, and food definitely will. From preparing a meal together to dining out to even shopping at the supermarket, food will get all her senses juicy.

"Exercising, Indian food, when he cooks me a great meal."

"Sunsets by the ocean, seeing my lover in a jock strap or nude, the roar of the ocean, jazz music, my lover whispering . . ."

"Music, hot salsa Latin beats, being near the ocean, walks in the park, getting undivided attention from my mate, dinner with just the two of us."

"Eating strawberries with whipped cream . . ."

"Sexy music, love scenes in a movie (not porn), showering together, talking about sex with my husband, snuggling . . ."

A Memory

"My partner came over to pick me up for the evening. He walked in, told me I looked beautiful, and locked the door behind him. He ravished me right there. He was assertive, but not aggressive, dressed nicely, and smelled like he had just stepped out of the shower. When we went for dinner afterward, all I could think about was how wonderful it was and how I couldn't wait to get home and do it all over again."

WHAT'S YOUR ATTITUDE TOWARD PORNOGRAPHY?

Above all, Taurus is the Sign of touch. It is the physicality of being with her partner, the feeling of intimacy, and passionate kissing that excite her. Pornography is a poor substitute for caring embraces.

"Pornography is just so unemotional. It is mechanical. I don't care for it."

"It can be okay as a casual thing, but porn shouldn't be necessary to get turned on. If it is, then something else is wrong."

"I love erotic stories more than movies."

HOW MUCH CUDDLING DO YOU ENJOY, ASIDE FROM SEX?

Taurus loves physical closeness. Watching TV, she wants to be right beside her partner. Out walking, she wants to hold hands. She enjoys falling asleep in her lover's arms.

"A ton, [I] love the sensual feeling of skin to skin."

"I love affection. Holding hands, feet or head in the other's lap while watching a movie, a stroke or a hug as you walk past, falling asleep in each other's arms, all that and more."

"I enjoy cuddling all the time with my honey."

"Cuddling is okay, but I would rather have sex."

HOW TACTILE AND HOW ORAL ARE YOU?

This extremely sensual woman is equally tactile and oral. She loves running her hands all over her partner, deep kissing, and both performing and receiving oral sex.

"I want to know every spot on his body."

"I think touching and exploring is a definite turn-on."

"I enjoy deep kissing very much: his mouth, his body, giving fellatio, and receiving cunnilingus."

"I am really oral. I like kissing all over his body . . . all over. He likes when I do that."

WHAT SEX ACTS DO YOU LIKE MOST AND LEAST?

Her favorite sex acts include intercourse, kissing, and oral sex. Her least favorite sex acts are mutual masturbation and anal intercourse, though some amount of anal play is okay.

"Oral sex is great. Fondling/touching all over is great. I love kissing. I like having intercourse with his finger penetrating my ass."

Fantasies

"To rub my partner with yogurt and lick it all off. To slide my tongue up and down his body until we are both wild with passion."

"I have sex with a special guy in my bed and use strawberries and cream. I spray the cream on his penis and I lick it off with my tongue while romantic music is playing."

AS A LOVER, WHAT'S YOUR BEST SKILL?

She is especially skillful at exciting her partner with the use of her hands. Whether giving him a very sexual massage or masturbating him, her touch is remarkable.

"I give great massages. I also love to kiss and lick."

"How I use my hands to stroke his penis, and the way I use my tongue to lick all over his body."

WHAT SMELLS AND TASTES ON YOUR PARTNER DO YOU ENJOY?

She loves the smell of his clean skin right after a shower and finds it fun to use food on occasion. Non-sticky foods like whipped cream work better than honey. If her lover wants to put food on her body, all she asks is that it be nice and warm.

"I love that clean smell, like right after a shower, but something about just plain and simple man smell is great. Many colognes smell fabulous, too."

"I love the salty taste of skin, but I like to add love oils and food play. I really like that, too."

"The taste of their skin, the saltiness of their sweat . . ."

FOR SOME PEOPLE THE TASTE OF THEIR PARTNER'S CUM OR SECRETIONS IS UNPLEASANT. IF THAT'S TRUE FOR YOU, WHAT DO YOU DO ABOUT THE TASTE?

She seldom has a problem with this and when she is in a committed relationship Taurus is usually comfortable swallowing. The Tauran who objects to the taste tries to avoid getting cum in her mouth, but she still likes performing oral sex.

"It's not a problem. I usually swallow. Sometimes I rub it on him or myself."

"I swallow, but use the deep throat method. That way it doesn't really pass over my tongue."

"There's no taste to it, except sweetness. Sometimes I swallow, occasionally spit it out."

"I like the taste of my partner's cum. I swallow it mostly or rub it on me."

"The taste is nasty, but I like giving head. I don't swallow."

A Fantasy

"Being led by a man who I know is my soul mate into a luxurious suite in a posh hotel, great fabrics and scents around. We lounge on overstuffed couches, drink wine, fill the Jacuzzi with bubbles and very hot water, sit in it together and take lots of time to explore each other's bodies, [and] then make love over and over. Later, doing the same on the huge high bed, on the couches, and the deck. It is intimate, emotional, and yet also extremely physical."

DO YOU ENJOY WATCHING YOUR PARTNER DURING SEX AND ORGASM? DO YOU ENJOY BEING WATCHED?

Taurus enjoys watching her partner during sex and climax but isn't so sure about being watched. She is, by nature, a bit self-conscious.

"I normally close my eyes, but [I] do like to see his eyes light up and [I] watch him sometimes."

"Recently I have come to enjoy being watched. It is new to me, but quite pleasurable if I am comfortable with a man."

"It is okay for him to watch me if it turns him on."

The Big "O"

HOW DO YOU REACH ORGASM AND HOW OFTEN?

Taurus doesn't achieve orgasm every time she has sex. To ensure that she does requires oral or digital stimulation of her clitoris. Intercourse by itself won't bring her to climax on any regular basis.

"I will reach orgasm every time there is oral sex performed on me. It doesn't happen through intercourse. I wish it could because I love intercourse."

"I don't climax as often as I would like with my partner. He usually only makes it happen when he gives me oral sex."

"I have an orgasm pretty regularly, thank God!"

"Unfortunately, masturbation is the only way that I have been able to achieve."

WHAT'S YOUR FAVORITE POSITION?

She enjoys a range of sexual positions, though to achieve orgasm, woman on top and spooning are most successful. Being on top allows Taurus to grind her clitoris against her partner. Spooning is a good position for combining masturbation with intercourse.

"Being on top, spooning, and sixty-nine are the positions by which I'm most likely to achieve orgasm."

"Woman on top is great, and doggie style is great, and all the rest is great too."

SOME PEOPLE ARE CONCERNED ABOUT BRINGING A PARTNER TO CLIMAX BEFORE HAVING AN ORGASM THEMSELVES. OTHERS STRIVE TO REACH ORGASM TOGETHER. WHICH IS TRUE FOR YOU?

While it's exciting to achieve orgasm simultaneously with her partner, this is a rare experience for Taurus. When she does have an orgasm, it is usually before her partner.

"I like getting to orgasm at separate times so that each of us can focus on the other."

"I try to climax before my partner. Reaching orgasm together is the ultimate, but [it's] not always possible."

She understands that it's difficult for her partner to bring her to climax through masturbation.

"I usually have to masturbate after sex to satisfy myself. My husband has tried, but it goes on and on and I just end up sore."

ARE YOU VOCAL DURING SEX?

From moderately to quite a lot, Taurus vocalizes her pleasure. Sometimes talking dirty really adds to her sexual pleasure.

"Yes. I moan and make comments and talk dirty."

"I am very vocal. Yahoo!"

AFTER SEX WHAT DO YOU LIKE TO DO?

Most of all Taurus wants her lover to spend some time interacting with her: talking, cuddling, and even watching TV. She doesn't want her lover to roll over immediately and go to sleep.

"Walk by the ocean, hold hands, laugh together, talk . . ."

"Be massaged, kiss, hold hands, listen to music, cuddle, stay in bed, laugh together."

"Anything as long as we are doing it together . . . It makes me feel that I am not there just for the sex."

"Afterward, talk, cuddle. Beyond that depends on the time of day."

"Shower and do it again and again."

The Taurus Man in His Own Words

A Memory

"I ordered my partner to strip and [I] put a collar and lead on her. I led her to the bedroom on her hands and knees. The room was lit with candles. I put restraints on her wrists and ankles. I tied her in various positions and used different toys on her: a vibrator, butt plug, nipple clamps, a flogger and riding crop, and [I] spanked her as well. I caressed her body, ate her out, made her blow me. She had multiple orgasms and the sex lasted a long time that night."

Attraction and Dating a Taurus

WHAT ATTRACTS YOU TO SOMEONE?

Looks first. Taurus is primarily a physical Sign and so it is that physical characteristics are of paramount importance to him.

"Smile, openness, friendliness, and weight are important. She has to take care of herself. Little or no makeup is a big plus with me."

"Health, beauty, intelligence, physical and psychological compatibility . . ."

"Petite, long hair, sweet smile and eyes, graceful, intelligent, warmhearted, submissive."

"Eyes, skin, teeth, nice breasts, energy, confidence . . ."

"Hair, breasts, a sense of spirit, weight, energy, intellect . . ."

"Very long hair, very long fingernails, big firm breasts, and intelligence . . ."

WHAT MIGHT TURN YOU OFF?

While physical fitness is important to him and a woman who is out of shape will turn him off, there are certain negative behaviors that are equally off-putting. He is a devoted man and wants a partner who focuses her attention on him when they are out in public. Without that sense of connection, this good-hearted man will lose interest.

"Negative behavior, a 'who cares' attitude, poor teeth for sure—and bad breath."

"Insensitivity, someone who doesn't listen . . ."

"Rude behavior, poor dental hygiene, excessive facial or body hair, bad language . . ."

"Not taking care of their teeth, neediness, insecurity, infidelity."

WHAT DO YOU ENJOY DOING ON A DATE?

Taurus may not be overly talkative, but he loves to listen to his partner, so any evening out must include plenty of time for conversation. He also enjoys having a meal together, whether at home or at a restaurant. Overall he prefers romantic, quiet evenings to such things as hiking, biking, or other more active pursuits.

"Driving around, talking, listening to music, going to a club, being in a romantic location."

"Talking, getting to know the person."

"Sharing a home-cooked meal, cuddling."

"Talk, watch the stars, walk along the coast and in the woods."

"Talking, feeling out the person's energy, exploring things I may not have previously experienced."

"Maybe a film, a walk to look at the stars, then sex in front of the fire all set up in advance."

Taurus is a romantic.

Memories

"One truly memorable sexual encounter happened when I was 18. I made love to my girlfriend on a covered pontoon boat, in the middle of a lake, during a rainstorm on a warm summer evening."

"My lover told me she would marry me. The sex that followed was indescribable."

ARE YOU FLIRTATIOUS?

Not often. Taurus has a way of giving a woman his total attention while engaged in conversation with her. It's an honest, straightforward behavior and, in fact, well mannered. On occasion this can be misinterpreted as a come-on.

"I don't think I'm flirtatious, but friends say I flirt a lot."

"I'd say I am, but only occasionally."

"Just a shade to keep the interest always fresh . . ."

ARE YOU JEALOUS?

Taurus is a tenacious Sign. It is against his nature to let go of things, and people fit into that category, so it is that he can be possessive and perhaps more jealous than he realizes.

"I'm not jealous, more heartbroken."

"I am a recovering jealous freak."

"Yes. I suffer silently, internalize, and accept the lady's choice."

"I would say a little. It is a beast I have fought with before. I know it is there but I have worked around it."

HOW DO YOU FEEL ABOUT PUBLIC DISPLAYS OF AFFECTION?

He is very into touching, so hugging and holding hands will please him. However, Taurus also has a slightly shy quality and displays of affection must be within limits.

"Hugs and kisses and holding hands are fine, but I don't enjoy people hanging on me all the time."

"They are okay in moderation but must be politically correct in public."

"How I respond to public displays of affection depends upon how sloppy they get. Holding hands and little kisses are fine."

Sexual Attitudes and Behavior

HOW OFTEN DO YOU THINK ABOUT SEX AND HOW OFTEN PER WEEK DO YOU WANT TO HAVE SEX?

Being with his woman, the scent of her perfume, even just the thought of her during the course of the day will turn his mind to sex. If he is single, any pretty woman passing by, especially one with full lips and an elegant neck, will do the same. If he could have sex as often as he wanted, that would be daily. He will settle for five times a week.

"I'd say I'm borderline preoccupied with sex and I want to have sex every day."

"Sex is on my mind more than five times a day and I'd like sex five times per week."

"When I have a partner, I enjoy having sex about five days weekly."

A Fantasy

"I have been thinking about slavery, as a male to be in the service of a group of women. Sometimes I am a master, watching sex by the slaves at a party. In some of the images I spank a woman, tie her up, place weights on her, put her through humbling behaviors, then tickle her with feathers and give her a massage."

HOW LONG DO YOU LIKE TO SPEND HAVING SEX AND HOW MUCH OF THAT TIME IS FOREPLAY? DO YOU ENJOY QUICKIES?

Taurus likes to take his time when he is doing virtually everything. He certainly doesn't want to rush through the pleasures in life, whether eating or having sex. For sex, he usually prefers at least an hour, and quickies are okay but not particularly satisfying.

"I like spending hours, only once in a while a quickie. I want all the taste."

"As much time as humanly possible, say two hours a day with 30 to 40 minutes for foreplay . . . and, yes to quickies on occasion . . ."

"I like having sex go for three hours plus, with roughly about 75 percent of the whole session for foreplay. I hate quickies."

"I like long sessions and quickies. I love foreplay. I like to tease myself as long as I can."

WHAT TIME OF DAY DO YOU PREFER TO HAVE SEX?
Time of day is irrelevant to Taurus. Whatever pleases his lover will work for him.

"All times have their special appeal."

"Doesn't matter, anytime is fine."

HOW OFTEN PER WEEK DO YOU MASTURBATE?
He may have a week when he masturbates only two or three times, but most often he masturbates daily.

HOW LONG DO YOU WANT TO KNOW SOMEONE BEFORE GETTING SEXUAL?
Taurus has no set time frame. A few dates or a couple of weeks is quite common, but it is not likely that a Taurus will wait several months. As a general rule Taurus relates to people on a physical level and for that reason he will want a relationship to become sexual in short order.

"It's not merely a matter of time. It's more a matter of comfort and trust."

"I have no standard. It is based on feelings of her spirit and openness."

"If there is a strong physical attraction, the first date . . ."

"It depends on the individual. Usually the first date."

 Fantasies

"I love fantasies about bondage and teasing, both as the dominant and as the submissive."

"I would love to have sex with body oils and candlelight, with my partner whispering my name to me very, very slowly."

"Having my partner meet me dressed in stockings and heels and a long coat. We drive off to a quiet location and have sex outdoors on a picnic table."

"I fantasize about having an orgy, couples having intercourse including anal, fisting, oral, et cetera."

WHAT'S YOUR ATTITUDE TOWARD CASUAL SEX?
When not in a relationship, the Taurus male enjoys having sex with many partners. Casual sex is fine as long as safety precautions are taken.

"It is okay, but [it] can be unsafe."

"I don't mind it as long as I know the person. I can't have sex with a total stranger."

"It's fine but in moderation."

"Casual sex is okay if you take precautions."

"It's okay, but I prefer to have an emotional bond with my lovers."

 Fantasies

"Sex with two partners. It's a fantasy, I am not sure I would really like it in reality."

"I'd like to be uninhibited enough to yell when cumming, to really release in every sense."

"They usually involve BDSM in some fashion. I also often fantasize about impregnation."

"I imagine dominating my partner with a collar and lead, caging her, using restraints, and hot wax. Sometimes I am the one being dominated."

DO YOU BELIEVE IN MONOGAMY?

Taurus is a very loyal partner and expects loyalty in return. He may find monogamy difficult to sustain, but he values it within a committed relationship.

"Yes, a noble and wise aspiration."

"It is practically impossible for me because I get bored very easily."

"Yes, for social and moral reasons. Monogamy is important when there are children."

"No STDs please . . ."

"Yes, when I am in a serious relationship I am monogamous."

"I believe in it, but it is not always achievable."

DOES SEX HAVE A SPIRITUAL SIGNIFICANCE FOR YOU?

Even though sex is primarily a physical release for Taurus, he is a loyal, devoted, and romantic man and sex always has a deeply emotional aspect for him. When he truly loves his partner, sex is spiritual.

"Sex is a union of energies and the connective feeling it gives is spiritual."

"Sex is a blessing. It raises the total being since you are somehow one with nature."

"Yes, it is the most intimate expression of love and union."

"I view sex as a physical representation of love. For me, sex without love is a bit bland."

"Yes, because it helps you to understand your partner better and [it] gives you a time when you are as one."

ARE YOU COMFORTABLE INITIATING SEXUAL ACTIVITIES?

Taurus seems so quietly confident, no one would ever suspect that he has any insecurities. At the core, though, he is somewhat shy. He is also likely to move slowly. Nevertheless, when he is at ease with a woman he will initiate sexual activities.

HOW DO YOU COMMUNICATE TO YOUR PARTNER YOUR SEXUAL WANTS AND NEEDS?

Taurus, so into touch, is much more likely to make his wants known with body movement and hand gestures than with words. He does make sounds, however, that clearly indicate his pleasure.

"I am just getting comfortable with this. I used to be silent, but now I am getting comfortable with guidance."

"I ask, sometimes, by touch."

 A Memory

"We had an extraordinary Indian meal and went back to her place, listened to Baroque music, and drank wine. We lit candles and undressed each other. I bound her to the point that she was helpless and teased her with strokes of leather, fur, licks, kisses, and [then] masturbated her to orgasm. Then I freed her and we made love in several positions, had wondrous orgasms followed by gentle loving, stroking, and caressing after play. Then we snuggled and fell asleep together."

DO YOU THINK OF YOURSELF AS BEING IN THE MAINSTREAM SEXUALLY, MORE EXPERIMENTAL, OR OPEN TO ANYTHING?

He is a somewhat experimental lover who may be interested in trying bondage, dominance and submission, wearing costumes, and using food to enhance his sexual pleasure. The most experimental Taurus is open to exhibitionism, sex in public places, and spanking his partner. Taurus is not particularly interested in using toys for sexual play.

His fantasies range from the romantic to scenes of bondage, dominance and submission, and multiple sexual partners.

 A Fantasy

"I'm into romantic settings as seen in the old '60s movies, where the pirate or knight takes the damsel to bed in a candlelit room, which has a huge four-poster bed *in the middle. We share a few moments on the balcony, under the moonlight, preferably drinking wine. Then I, in the role of the pirate, sweep the lady off her feet, carry her to bed, lay her down, and spread her hair on the pillow . . ."*

HOW DO YOU DEMONSTRATE AFFECTION FOR YOUR PARTNER?

He is an affectionate lover who compliments his partner frequently. He also buys her gifts and sends loving cards. He likes the role of gallant knight, opening doors and pulling out her chair in a restaurant.

"I go out of my way to do things for her."

"I show her consideration, loyalty, and honesty."

"I hide love notes where she will find them later, buy her small gifts. Once I sent her an evening dress as a present, with a note saying 'don't cook tonight.'"

"I buy her flowers; take care of things for her."

"By striving to keep her happy, helping out with things, recognizing that the relationship is not all one-sided."

 A Fantasy

"I fantasize about a neighbor lady, that one day we are alone in her house, when her husband is away. She sees the expression in my eyes, friendly and inviting. I reach for her hand and say, 'I want to whisper something in your ear.' Embracing her I tell her, 'You really turn me on. What would you say if I kissed you?' She blushes and says, 'I don't know.' My lips kiss her softly on one cheek and brush across her skin to meet her lips. The fire between us is mounting. We kiss and caress until we are burning with desire for the ultimate expression of love and I quickly undress in her bedroom. She is as starved for love as I am. I feel the wetness between her legs. We wrestle and kiss for only a few minutes before I slide my cock into her. It is so easy and natural. She says, 'Fuck me, honey. It feels so good.'"

The Five Senses

HOW IMPORTANT TO YOU IS THE SEXUAL ENVIRONMENT?

The environment for sex and lovemaking is important to Taurus. He wants the room to be clean, and dim lighting will add to the romance. Attention to the décor and creating an ambience that is warm, inviting, and cozy will heighten his sexual pleasure.

"The setting is very important; the nicer it is the more I enjoy lovemaking. I like candlelight a lot."

"I like it to be clean. Lighting can be super romantic."

"Being clean is important. Dim lights or candles and music make it even better."

"It should be clean and a nice smell is very important."

WHERE DO YOU LIKE TO HAVE SEX?

Taurus is a traditional Sign and one that loves creature comforts. When it comes to having sex, he likes a warm, comfortable place, preferably the bedroom. Being in public places is a turn-on as long as the likelihood of being seen is very slim.

"The bedroom is best, but anywhere free of onlookers is okay. I hate giving public shows."

"Sex is healthy and fun anywhere. As to the risk of being caught, I kind of let go of that back in high school. It is not a turn-on anymore."

"Bedroom, shower, couch, or on the kitchen counter. Outdoors in the car, in a movie theater or pool, Jacuzzi, [or the] beach are all okay so long as we are alone."

"The beach, in the car, a parking garage top floor, on a balcony . . ."

"The bedroom is best for comfort, but the car works or a blanket outdoors, or the floor or the couch."

A Memory

"*We were returning from a fetish fair with our new toys. We were playing with them in the car on the way back to our hotel. We were both excited but could not do anything about it. The sexual tension was immense. When we finally got to the room, wow! What a time we had.*"

WHAT PUTS YOU IN THE MOOD FOR SEX?

A full range of romantic settings and activities, the "jug of wine, a loaf of bread, and thou" will put Taurus in the mood for sex. In fact, food in any fashion turns him on. This means that dining out, cooking at home, going on a picnic, and even grocery shopping can get him started.

"Feeling emotionally close, cuddling, romantic settings, my lover whispering . . ."

"Good food and wine, romantic dinners, good perfumes, shared bath, sexy clothes, cuddling, affectionate gestures, music."

"Listening to slow R&B music, perfumes, the environment, and that special look in my lover's eyes . . ."

"Touching my hand in a sexual manner, kissing, aromas, a romantic atmosphere."

WHAT'S YOUR ATTITUDE TOWARD PORNOGRAPHY?

Taurus is somewhat conventional by nature and therefore ambivalent about pornography. When he is alone, he may find it exciting, but at the same time a bit unsettling. Even if he loves pornography he is apt to be uncomfortable watching it with another person.

"I love it. It is like an off-color joke."

"I enjoy it as long as it is healthy."

"I'm somewhat ambivalent about it, though I find it stimulating and overall harmless."

"I separate erotic from porn. I love the former and find the latter crude."

HOW MUCH CUDDLING DO YOU ENJOY, ASIDE FROM SEX?

Taurus is very touchy-feely and loves lots of cuddling. He loves to feel his partner's hand on his knee when he is driving, to sit close to her when watching TV, and to walk arm in arm.

"I'd like to be a blanket around my date. On the warmer days, I like walking with my arm around her waist and hers around mine."

"I like it a lot, but in truth, it usually leads to sex."

A Memory

"*It was at the end of a Take Back the Night rally. I was walking to the bus. A woman ran after me, attacking me for being male. Somehow she knew my name. I had no idea who she was. The discussion got heated and then she invited me to her house. I stripped her on the floor, then carried her to her bed. The sex was intense.*"

HOW TACTILE AND HOW ORAL ARE YOU?

Taurus is a very physical and tactile Earth Sign. He is capable of bringing his partner to ecstasy just with the use of his hands, but he also loves giving and receiving oral sex.

"I like doing everything: deep French kissing, kissing her entire body, performing cunnilingus."

"I love to touch. I need to feel everything, almost like I'll never see my partner again. I'm not nearly as oral, although I like having oral sex performed on me."

"I like to explore in all ways, with my hands and with my tongue."

"I am very tactile, slow and gentle, and enjoy oral aspects as well. I see sex as the only way to the unity of the spirits."

"I like it all: deep kissing, kissing her body, oral sex, and sixty-nine."

WHAT SEX ACTS DO YOU LIKE MOST AND LEAST?

He loves being given a blow job, performing intercourse, and using some light bondage. In fact, there's little he doesn't like in the mainstream of behaviors. He doesn't necessarily dislike anal sex, but he puts it at the end of the list of pleasurable acts.

"I love fondling my lover's body, and intercourse."

"Mutual masturbation is a lot of fun. It allows my partner and me to break through [the] boundaries of vulnerability."

"I don't think I have a least favorite sex act."

AS A LOVER, WHAT'S YOUR BEST SKILL?

Taurus is quite attentive, not in a hurry, and considerate of his partner's needs. He is especially skillful with his hands.

"The use of my hands, physical endurance, and mental control . . ."

"Perhaps it's the way that I listen to what she wants."

"My hands, massaging her body with my own . . ."

"Using my fingers up inside her to make her climax and keeping them there for multiple orgasms."

A Memory

"Oh man. I like to get her really wet. When our chakras are aligned everything clicks and we completely open up. I have just started to explore having anal sex with her and that is very sensual, much to my surprise."

WHAT SMELLS AND TASTES ON YOUR PARTNER DO YOU ENJOY?

For Taurus the sense of taste is highly erotic. Eating is a decided turn-on and he may enjoy mixing food with sex. In addition, the aromas he finds exciting are more likely to be vanilla and cinnamon than costly perfumes.

"I love the smell of her skin, especially after she has been outdoors, and also her panties."

"I enjoy anything that is naturally her scent, her hair, sweat. No perfumes or hairsprays."

"I prefer cleanliness and only some light perfumes or fragrances."

"I enjoy her clean smells, and sometimes her vaginal fluid tastes like chocolate. I love it!"

FOR SOME PEOPLE THE TASTE OF THEIR PARTNER'S CUM OR SECRETIONS IS UNPLEASANT. IF THAT'S TRUE FOR YOU, WHAT DO YOU DO ABOUT THE TASTE?

His partner's secretions are more likely to excite him than to turn him off.

"No problem for me . . . depends on my level of ecstasy. Generally I swallow every drop."

"If it bothers me, I breathe through my mouth so I won't smell or taste anything."

DO YOU ENJOY WATCHING YOUR PARTNER DURING SEX AND ORGASM? DO YOU ENJOY BEING WATCHED?

Watching his lover is a major turn-on for Taurus. Her climax increases his level of excitement. And, while the thought of being watched by his partner may make him uncomfortable when a relationship is new, over time he enjoys that too.

A Memory

"She met me at a hotel. I took her to our room; it was very dark. I blindfolded her and stripped her down to her stockings and heels, then tied her hands behind her and made her lie face down on the bed. I lubed her thoroughly and made her take it anally from me as she tried to resist."

The Big "O"

HOW DO YOU REACH ORGASM AND HOW OFTEN?

Taurus has no trouble climaxing and he achieves orgasm virtually every time he has sex. Though generally through intercourse, the Taurus male will sometimes climax with intercourse in combination with oral sex.

"I have an orgasm every time, often multiple orgasms, most often through intercourse."

"I cum all the time, in all ways: from intercourse to mutual masturbation, oral or anal sex . . ."

WHAT'S YOUR FAVORITE POSITION?

In the course of a sexual encounter he enjoys being in several different positions, but to achieve orgasm he prefers the missionary style, being on top of his partner.

"They all work: missionary, spooning, doggie style, woman on top, and side by side."

 A Memory

"We had a wonderful evening: a movie followed by coffee. On the way home, we parked the car in a secluded place and cuddled and kissed. Soon we had stripped off our clothes and were in the back seat. She had an orgasm first and I had one in the doggie position. I was sweating profusely even though it was the middle of winter. What an exciting night."

SOME PEOPLE ARE CONCERNED ABOUT BRINGING A PARTNER TO CLIMAX BEFORE HAVING AN ORGASM THEMSELVES. OTHERS STRIVE TO REACH ORGASM TOGETHER. WHICH IS TRUE FOR YOU?

When it comes to orgasm, Taurus is concerned about pleasing his partner. He finds that works best if they cum together or very close.

"I strive to make sure my partner enjoys herself, however she defines it, whatever she wants: just a warm feeling, one orgasm, or multiples."

"I try to get us as close together as possible, so as to relax together, and not have one of us still waiting."

"I like to allow her to cum first, just because sometimes I can be quick."

"I want her to enjoy the time, so I try to have us cum at the same time."

ARE YOU VOCAL DURING SEX?

He may be fairly vocal during sex and orgasm, but quietly so: whispering, not yelling.

AFTER SEX WHAT DO YOU LIKE TO DO?

After sex Taurus prefers to stay at home and relax or cuddle rather than going out or doing anything particularly active.

"Shower together, cuddle, watch a movie, sleep."

"The best is lying beside one another and then doing it again."

"I like to just lie there and fall asleep."

GEMINI
May 21–June 20
THE TWINS

Air Sign Gemini is into experimentation in all things, from types of food to sexual behaviors. Ruler of the shoulders, arms, hands, and the sense of hearing, Gemini is turned on by all things auditory: the sounds of nature, music, and sexy talk.

She says: "I show my affection with love notes, email, sweet cards, computer cards . . . long intimate talks, praise, and compliments."

He says: "I like the sex environment to be dark with some candlelight and sexy music playing, sometimes using erotic videos."

"Love is the wind, the tide, the waves, the sunshine."
—Henry David Thoreau

The Gemini Woman in Her Own Words

A Memory

"We met on the Internet, got close through email and extensive telephone conversations. When we met, that first touch was electric. We sat on the couch kissing. I placed my hand inside his shirt. The feel of the hair on his chest against my palm nearly drove me over the edge. The lighting was low. I could smell his cologne, Escape for Men. There was a blue moon shining through the blinds, adding a touch of the ethereal to the atmosphere. A fantastic night."

Attraction and Dating a Gemini

WHAT ATTRACTS YOU TO SOMEONE?

Looks and physical fitness matter to her. Beyond that, the Gemini woman is attracted by a man's intellect. To keep her involved, a man must be intense about his work and curious about the world around him.

"A man's energy and ability to communicate, a fit physique, a man with a full head of hair, appealing features, little body hair, and a person who is good at dirty, sexy talk."

"Laughter, sincerity, witty conversation with innuendo, fun loving, provocative and with a mischievous smile, good imagination, trim, fit, and vigorous . . ."

WHAT MIGHT PUT YOU OFF?

She is turned off by a man who is cocky, boring, unkempt, immature, or self-absorbed. She is prone to health problems involving the lungs, so smoking is a deterrent to a relationship with her.

"I'm turned off by men talking about other lovers, blowing in my ear, biting my ear."

"Slow thinking, ignorant behaviors."

WHAT DO YOU ENJOY DOING ON A DATE?

Beyond wining and dining, she loves doing things that stimulate her mind such as attending lectures, poetry readings, and going to the theater. She is curious about a broad spectrum of activities and, above all else, she wants time to talk.

"Laughing—lots of it—music, dancing, touching, and socializing . . ."

"Seeing a play, going to the aquarium, zoo, playing board games . . ."

"Quiet dinner in a restaurant, then finding a place outdoors to sit and talk and get to know each other . . ."

A Fantasy

"I imagine that I'm a dancer in a strip club. I get approached by two very sexy guys who lead me into a dark, secluded room. They force me to have rough, hard sex with both of them at the same time. When one guy finishes, a new guy takes his place from the bar. As I am blindfolded, I have no idea who the other guys are."

ARE YOU FLIRTATIOUS?

Absolutely! Gemini has a positive knack for paying attention to a man, making him feel as though he is the most important person in the world to her. And she does this with everyone, old and young. In fact, she does this with women as well. It is her way of courting the attention of people.

"I love to be flirtatious, a little more than friendly occasionally."

"With that select someone whose mind attracts me as much as the rest of him."

"Wicked . . ."

ARE YOU JEALOUS?

Dual Gemini is of two minds on the question of jealousy. One Gemini will say, "No." The next one will say, "Unfortunately, yes. Very." Be assured, a man who comes on to another woman in Gemini's presence will regret his behavior later. She may not terminate a relationship because of this transgression, but she will use her considerable creativity to make him sorry he was so ill mannered.

 A Memory

"I was getting ready to go out. My boyfriend was watching me brush my teeth. Next thing I knew he was behind me, hugging me. He started kissing my neck and rubbing his hardening penis against my body. I could taste the toothpaste and smell his cologne. I remember reaching behind me and touching his hard cock. My skirt went up; his pants went down as I was still watching in the mirror. He began making love to me in the bathroom. We tried to go to the bedroom, but we never made it. We finished in the living room and it was wonderful."

HOW DO YOU FEEL ABOUT PUBLIC DISPLAYS OF AFFECTION?

Public displays are fine. She is accepting of them from others, and participates in them herself. However, Gemini doesn't want her lover hanging on to her too closely because she is such a flirt.

"I'm crazy about them. I think couples should be open about how they feel about each other. There isn't enough hand holding and kissing."

"I don't think about who's watching. I just enjoy the way that I'm feeling."

"I think it's wonderful to see couples in love, holding hands, looking into each other's eyes, small kisses. But making out in public is not classy."

Sexual Attitudes and Behaviors

HOW OFTEN DO YOU THINK ABOUT SEX AND HOW OFTEN PER WEEK DO YOU WANT TO HAVE SEX?

Gemini thinks about sex daily. On average, she enjoys sex three or four times per week.

 A Memory

"A quickie in the attic at his work. Hot and humid. Sweat dripping and running. The only furniture was a single metal folding chair that we used every way: him sitting, me straddling, me standing with one foot on the chair or bent over it. We were trying not to make too much noise, and that only made our lust hotter and more fervent. I had a squirt bottle full of ice-cold water that we sprayed on our overheated bodies. We used my sundress as a towel and off I went."

HOW LONG DO YOU LIKE TO SPEND HAVING SEX AND HOW MUCH OF THAT TIME IS FOREPLAY?

She prefers long sex sessions, at least 45 minutes, including a lot of foreplay. Because Gemini loves variety she wants to include several different sexual behaviors, including oral stimulation and intercourse, in a variety of positions.

"Quickies are great sometimes—they take care of business—but I prefer hours of multiple orgasms."

"Sex might go from ten minutes to whatever, with one minute to hours of foreplay. And yes, I like quickies as well."

WHAT TIME OF DAY DO YOU PREFER TO HAVE SEX?

As the Sign of experimentation, Gemini will welcome sexual activity at any time of day or night, but she does have some preference for late night.

HOW OFTEN DO YOU MASTURBATE?

Gemini doesn't masturbate frequently, doing it virtually not at all or at most a couple of times weekly.

A Memory

"*There were candles all over the room, sweet flowerlike smells, perfume, cologne, and slow romantic music playing. We read love letters to each other, gave full body massages with oils and cream, [fed] each other fruit and chocolate, [licked] and [sucked] flavored oils off each other. We kissed for a long period, foreplay, sixty-nine position, oral sex, different sex positions, several orgasms, [and] ending with going to sleep in each other's arms.*"

HOW LONG DO YOU WANT TO KNOW SOMEONE BEFORE GETTING SEXUAL?

Communication is of major importance to Gemini. Before becoming sexually involved she wants to know something about what's important to a man, what they have in common. It won't take her long to figure this out and she has no set rule before allowing a relationship to become physical.

"Varies with the nature of the relationship, but not on the first date . . ."

"If I have gone out with a man three times that means I think he's a keeper, and if those feelings are reciprocated, then we are likely to become sexual."

A Memory

"*I was working as a manager for a convenience store and I had to close the store by myself this particular night. There was a younger male who frequented the store and I found him very sexy and hot. I openly flirted with him every time he came in. As I was closing the store, I saw that he was parked outside, leaning against his truck. My heart skipped a beat. I walked over to him and we talked for a while. Then he started kissing me. He opened his truck door, [laid] me across the front seat, reached under my dress, and took off my panties. He proceeded to drive me wild with his tongue and hands, and then gave it to me rough and hard. All the way home, alone in my car, I could smell his cologne all over me. I have to admit part of the thrill was realizing that we might get caught being in the parking lot.*"

WHAT'S YOUR ATTITUDE TOWARD CASUAL SEX?

This experimental woman is likely to have gone through a period of having casual sex, but this behavior isn't likely to satisfy her for more than a very short period.

"I think it is unsafe, though I admit it's exciting and honest."

"All in all, it's not for me. It works for others and that is fine."

"I've done it. I'm over it. It's okay for a while."

"It's fine as long as protection is used and both parties involved are not in serious, committed relationships."

DO YOU BELIEVE IN MONOGAMY?

Following her experiences with casual sex, she comes to value the qualities of commitment and monogamy. In fact, she won't tolerate betrayal from a partner and, if he strays, she will retaliate in kind.

"Yes. I think there is the greatest potential for openness, experimentation, growth, and fulfilling sexual relationships in a monogamous relationship."

"Yes; however, if a relationship does not give you everything needed, I could see how someone could wander."

DOES SEX HAVE A SPIRITUAL SIGNIFICANCE FOR YOU?

When Gemini is committed to a lover she finds sex to be greater than just physical pleasure. It has a significance that is decidedly spiritual. It lifts Gemini above the mundane plane.

"It's a pure giving of oneself to another."

"Sex is the meeting of two souls, bodies, minds, and passions."

"It's the most beautiful way of expressing emotion. It is a magical bonding experience."

"When you have a true connection with someone it changes sex to a spiritual act."

 Memories

"My husband and I went to a resort in the Berkshires. While he was out horseback riding with friends I had my first massage. When he returned to our cabin I was all oiled up and totally ready for action. He just died!"

"One night I came home after a long class. My lover was in bed and half-asleep. I was really turned on and initiated lovemaking, which took him by surprise. He gave in to me and let me direct the entire act. I found his complete submission so erotic."

ARE YOU COMFORTABLE INITIATING SEXUAL ACTIVITIES?

Add up the fact that she is flirtatious with the fact that she is a gifted conversationalist, and you get a woman who has no difficulty broaching the subject of sex.

"Yes, very much so . . ."

"Definitely . . ."

HOW DO YOU COMMUNICATE TO YOUR PARTNER YOUR SEXUAL WANTS AND NEEDS?

Gemini is the sign of communication. She is at ease discussing virtually anything, and this includes her sexual preferences.

"I use both. If gentle gestures do not get the point across, then I use words."

"I have no trouble expressing desires, verbally and physically."

 A Memory

"A romantic evening with the man I love. He came to the door with a single rose. We had dinner at home, candles lit around the house. Music playing, very gentle and sensual. It was magical. I felt that we truly connected and our souls fell in love as we were making love. I guess I am an old-fashioned sort of girl at heart."

DO YOU THINK OF YOURSELF AS BEING IN THE MAINSTREAM SEXUALLY, MORE EXPERIMENTAL, OR OPEN TO ANYTHING?

Gemini loves to experience many of life's pleasures, in food, in travels, and in her lovemaking style. In terms of sexual expression, beyond the traditional mainstream range, she will try a broad spectrum of behaviors. These might include anal sex, dominance and submission, sex in public places, spanking, using food, and sampling a variety of sex toys such as cock rings, vibrators, dildos, strap-ons, anal beads, sex shop lotions, body paint, sex games, edible undies, French ticklers, and flavored condoms. Most of the time, however, she prefers to remain within the mainstream of sexuality: kissing, fondling, oral sex, and intercourse.

"I think of myself as kind of mainstream, but open to fun with toys and other things."

"I am very open. Life is good and kinky."

Of her fantasies she says, "They venture into avenues that I could never see myself acting out. I love prison and rape fantasies. I have zero control of the situation. Bound and held with no sign of relief. Also, I enjoy orgasm denial and control."

 A Fantasy

"Seeing someone I know that I always wanted, or even someone I don't know, [and] feeling raw amazing attraction. Without saying anything we look at each other, start to touch, kiss, squeeze, *suck, undress each other, then move on to foreplay, intercourse, and multiple orgasms."*

HOW DO YOU DEMONSTRATE AFFECTION FOR YOUR PARTNER?

Gemini, as an Air Sign, a Sign of communication, demonstrates her feelings for her partner verbally. She is apt to leave him love notes in his briefcase or tucked in a pant pocket or to send cards and emails. She is also an excellent listener.

"Love notes, email notes, sweet cards, computer cards, gifts for occasions, and randomly long intimate talks, praise, and compliments."

"Lots of hugs and snuggling and making sure to say, 'I love you.'"

"Buying special gifts, sending cards, making special meals, and leaving notes around the house."

Fantasies

"I fantasize about a particular guy, going to his apartment and putting him against the wall, disrobing him, running my mouth all over him, and sucking on him until his breathing is fast and he can't stand not to be inside me. I imagine the look on his face, the taste of his skin, the touch of his hands, the closeness."

"I fantasize having sex with two men, vaginal and anal sex simultaneously."

The Five Senses

HOW IMPORTANT TO YOU IS THE SEXUAL ENVIRONMENT?

Gemini appreciates being in a place that enhances sex, a clean place with soft lights, candles, and fragrant air. Given her nervous disposition, messiness and noise could be distracting.

"I feel depressed if my surroundings are not in order."

"Cleanliness, lighting, and decor are all important to me."

"Must be clean and if outside, secluded."

A Memory

"My mate and I had just purchased a minivan. As we pulled into our driveway, we were listening to seductive music and began fondling each other. We became very aroused, started shedding our clothes, and moved to the back of the van, where we made passionate love for hours in every imaginable position with no thought of anyone but each other."

WHERE DO YOU LIKE TO HAVE SEX?

For sex on a regular basis, Gemini wants to be comfortable in her bed, but this is the Sign of variety as well as the Sign that rules automobiles. Add those traits and making love in a car—as well as in other out of the ordinary locations, especially on the spur of the moment—taking advantage of a dark and secluded area is a turn-on.

"The more different the place is, the better the sex."

"Outdoors in a secluded place . . ."

"Anywhere, but [in] bed is my favorite, simply because it is more comfortable."

WHAT PUTS YOU IN THE MOOD FOR SEX?

Gemini is the sign that rules hearing; therefore, sound is a turn-on for her. Natural sounds, like the lapping of ocean waves and rain, as well as listening to music and the sounds of other people making love, all excite her.

"I am turned on by erotic romance novels, by poetry, seeing my lover's nude body, the smell of his skin, romantic settings, and by the sound of my lover whispering."

"Hip-hop and slow music, candles, warmth, love showers, erotic/porn movies, massaging, dirty talk."

"Sensual music, good food/wine, acts of kindness, herbal candles, massage, passionate kissing . . ."

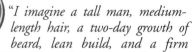

A Fantasy

"I imagine a tall man, medium-length hair, a two-day growth of beard, lean build, and a firm round ass. He's dressed like one of the Three Musketeers: velvet jacket, fitted pants that lace together, and knee-high leather boots. I have been hot for him for some time, but he is forbidden. It is nearing dusk. He's standing in the shadows of a doorway and as I walk past, he grabs my wrist, covers my mouth, and pulls me forcefully into the barn. He drags me over to a stall full of grain and wrestles me down onto it. He restrains my hands with a bit of rope, saying he knows I want it. Then he takes me roughly and with little fanfare."

WHAT'S YOUR ATTITUDE TOWARD PORNOGRAPHY?

Gemini is an intellectual Sign and so both the auditory and visual stimulus of pornography excite her on several levels. Whether or not she wants to try them out, since her range of sexuality is usually mainstream, watching a variety of sexual behaviors triggers her fantasies and turns her on.

"I find mild porn enticing. It can be fun to watch if it's tastefully done. You're always safe with erotica."

"I like it—helps build arousal and excitement, gives the imagination a boost."

"I think it can enhance a sex life."

HOW MUCH CUDDLING DO YOU ENJOY, ASIDE FROM SEX?

Cuddling is fine at the right time and place but she doesn't want to feel confined. Out in public she wants to be free to flirt with anyone, anytime—but harmlessly, just being friendly. A partner who stays too close, who appears possessive, will annoy her.

"I am a very affectionate person, and like the same in return. I love giving and receiving massages."

"I love hugging and being close, but resent it when a partner always turns it into sex."

HOW TACTILE AND HOW ORAL ARE YOU?

The Sign of Gemini rules the shoulders, arms, and hands. Gemini is also the Sign of experimentation. As a result, lovemaking that satisfies her includes equal amounts of kissing, touching, fondling, oral sex, and intercourse.

"The only way to get to know every inch of my lover is by touching."

"I enjoy deep kissing. Oral sex is one of my favorite acts as long as my partner is clean."

"I love kissing. That first kiss is always a turn-on. Oral sex, I love giving, but I am not so good at sitting still for receiving."

A Memory

"A massage, some laughing and talking, kissing, and cuddling. Then oral sex, his fingers inside me to feel the orgasm, intercourse, and then feeling like I am cherished. Talking long into the night, forgetting sleep, and going out for breakfast. Coming home, sleeping into the afternoon, sharing a newspaper and some coffee, listening to music, and enjoying us."

WHAT SEX ACTS DO YOU LIKE MOST AND LEAST?

She likes most everything, especially if there is variety in her lover's approach. She may not be interested in S&M, but bondage can be a lot of fun. She'll try anal sex, but in most cases it doesn't interest Gemini.

"Hmmm . . . can't think of one I don't like."

"The only sex act not on my list is anal sex. I tried it and didn't like it."

AS A LOVER, WHAT'S YOUR BEST SKILL?

As a lover, Gemini is proud of all her abilities to please her lover, from the use of her tongue to the way she handles his penis, from being seductive to the variety she brings to the sexual experience.

"My oral abilities, I have no gag reflex."

"Hands, tongue, body—I'm flexible—tight, noises, moaning."

"Vocalizing my needs and pleasure, providing encouragement . . ."

"The intensity that I put into pleasing my partner; I am told I am fantastic at giving blow jobs, too."

A Memory

"In a luxurious hotel, king-size bed, whirlpool tub, aroma therapy (sandalwood, jasmine) candles, scented rubbing oils. An entire evening of enjoying my lover's body and him enjoying mine with no distractions: just the two of us pleasing each other to the fullest."

WHAT SMELLS AND TASTES ON YOUR PARTNER DO YOU ENJOY?

Gemini is the Sign of experimentation. When it comes to the senses of smell and taste she likes it all; colognes and sweat, clean or a bit salty. Food isn't a big part of her repertoire, but sliding around on a plastic sheet slathered with baby oil can be fun.

"My partner's skin and cologne and even his sweat as long as he's clean."

"His fresh sweat, skin, and cum . . ."

"Strawberry lotion on his body . . ."

FOR SOME PEOPLE THE TASTE OF THEIR PARTNER'S CUM OR SECRETIONS IS UNPLEASANT. IF THAT'S TRUE FOR YOU, WHAT DO YOU DO ABOUT THE TASTE?

The taste of cum isn't a problem for Gemini and she loves oral sex. Nevertheless, most of the time she prefers her lover to climax on her body or during intercourse rather than in her mouth.

"The taste isn't that bad, but I rarely swallow cum. Sometimes I rub it on my breasts."

"I keep a glass of soda beside the bed [so I can] take a drink afterward to get rid of the taste."

"I swallow and rub, lick. It doesn't matter."

"I like him to cum on me."

DO YOU ENJOY WATCHING YOUR PARTNER DURING SEX AND ORGASM? DO YOU ENJOY BEING WATCHED?

Gemini is curious about everything, so she always enjoys watching her partner during sex and orgasm. But, maybe because she has a nervous disposition, she has mixed feelings about being watched.

"Sometimes I love having him watch me, sometimes I hate it. It depends on how I am feeling about myself."

A Fantasy

"We are sitting on the couch, begin deep kissing and rubbing each other through our clothes. We are getting very hot and start pulling at each other's shirts but take it painfully slowly. I sit on my partner's lap, facing him, and start to fondle him under his shirt. He does the same to me. We head for the bedroom, on our way groping each other. On the bed I start kissing him all over and playfully take out two scarves. I tease him with the silky fabric. He ties my hands to the bedposts and tells me not to move. Kissing my body all over, he is making me wild and wet. He spreads my legs apart and begins to move his tongue toward the direction of my clitoris, teasing me all the while until I can't take it any longer. He thrusts his tongue inside me and I have a violent orgasm. After getting my breath back I start to caress my lover's back, butt, and legs and then, ever so slowly, his penis. Then he slides his rock-hard penis inside me and we both orgasm together."

The Big "O"

HOW DO YOU REACH AN ORGASM AND HOW OFTEN?

Gemini has no trouble reaching orgasm and usually cums every time she has sex. A combination of oral sex, finger manipulation of her clitoris, and intercourse will bring her to orgasm.

"I achieve orgasm by masturbation and oral sex every time. By intercourse, hardly ever . . ."

"I climax every time with masturbation; sometimes with intercourse."

WHAT'S YOUR FAVORITE POSITION?

She enjoys many positions for intercourse but when it comes to climaxing, doggie style is Gemini's favorite because it allows for finger manipulation of her clitoris.

Fantasies

"Mine are very simple: being met at the door, slowly undressed, tied up, teased, and finished off with intercourse."

"My fantasy is to have sex in a tub of chocolate, extra sticky."

SOME PEOPLE ARE CONCERNED ABOUT BRINGING THEIR PARTNER TO CLIMAX BEFORE HAVING AN ORGASM THEMSELVES. OTHERS STRIVE TO REACH ORGASM TOGETHER. WHICH IS TRUE FOR YOU?

The Gemini woman loves to climax with her partner. If not, it's preferable for her to cum first—especially because she loves making love in the doggie position. It's the easiest position for her to achieve orgasm.

"Do me first and I will do you."

"I usually reach orgasm first, then my partner, since most men do not last too long after they have an orgasm."

A Memory

"I went over to my lover's house. Without even shutting the door, he grabbed me and deep-kissed me. Vanilla-scented candles were burning and the lights were dim. For the next hour he did everything to pleasure me both orally and touching me gently all over my body. We then took turns orally exciting each other and trying various positions for intercourse. After we reached orgasm he lay next to me and caressed me softly."

ARE YOU VOCAL DURING SEX?

Gemini is a verbal sign and is highly vocal during sex. In fact, some talking during the sex act heightens her pleasure.

"I am very loud."

"I am very vocal, loud. I make a lot of noises."

"Sometimes a little, sometimes a lot; depends on my mood."

A Memory

"I have many wonderful memories. Surprisingly, several of them involve observing sex rather than participating in it. I have been invited to watch men masturbate and to observe other couples having intercourse. To me, voyeurism is much hotter than watching porn videos."

AFTER SEX WHAT DO YOU LIKE TO DO?

She wants to get up, have some dinner, or perhaps listen to some music. Sex tends to invigorate her rather than prepare her for sleep.

"Afterward I like to kiss passionately, be massaged, share food, have dinner cooked for me, laugh together."

"Talk, listen to music, snuggle, then sleep together."

The Gemini Man in His Own Words

A Memory

"We were in the parking lot at the beach making out in the back of my Ford Explorer. We were [doing] sixty-nine, and then ended up going at it doggie style. I had the front window slightly open and the wind's cool breeze and the smell of food barbecuing on the beach mixed in with the wonderful aroma of my girlfriend's perfume and her hair. It was so stimulating. There were a good many people walking to and from the beach. Just the thought that they could see and/or hear what we were doing made it the best experience I ever had."

Attraction and Dating a Gemini

WHAT ATTRACTS YOU TO SOMEONE?

As a little boy he took everything apart to see how it worked. As a man he still likes to examine. He likes looking up . . . including up dresses. Bend over and he has a hard time appearing discreet as he tries to look up her dress or down her cleavage. The physical attributes that turn his head are many and varied. Gemini is a multifaceted sign, after all. But make no mistake; beauty alone won't cut it with Gemini. A positive, upbeat attitude counts for more in the long run than pretty features.

"I think the first thing I notice about a woman is the sound of her voice."

"I respond to a woman with positive energy; someone I can communicate with easily, who has some intellect and a sense of self."

"A beautiful face, I will have to wake up to that every day, so I appreciate good facial features, smaller breasts and ass, pretty legs—and stockings are a turn-on—plus moderate height, hair that's not too short, and a woman who has a sense of style."

"I'm attracted to a woman who is intelligent, witty, beautiful; with nice hips and butt first of all and nice breasts secondly."

"I am attracted by her general appearance and brains. I have never really cared whether a woman has large breasts. All that matters is that she be in fairly good shape."

WHAT MIGHT TURN YOU OFF?

There are not many physical characteristics that he finds objectionable other than that he prefers a woman who is not too heavy. Gemini is the Sign that rules the lungs, so he may object if she smokes. Not being able to hold up her end of a conversation and taking herself too seriously will turn him off because Gemini wants to keep things light. In addition, he has a nervous disposition, so a woman who is overly anxious, jumpy, or fidgety is likely to make him very uneasy.

"I am put off by a woman who says too little, has limited interests, or talks about other lovers."

"Being able to enjoy a good discussion is important to me, so a dull conversationalist will not be in my life for long."

"I am turned off by a woman who is uptight sexually or who will not at least talk about it and try to move past her inhibitions."

"I do not like women who have to be pampered or have negative attitudes toward others."

"What turns me off is a woman who is insensitive and has no sense of humor. Life is tough enough. We have to be able to laugh."

A Memory

"My wife and I were watching TV late at night in bed. She reached over and began to stroke my penis and continued giving me quite a hand job. I tried to reciprocate but she pushed my hand aside, making it clear I was just to lie there and let her take the initiative. She went on stroking and rubbing my prick as I became more and more excited. After some time, her hand still firmly clasping my penis, I heard her snoring gently. If I had not needed to get up and use the bathroom, she would probably have held on all night. It was great."

WHAT DO YOU ENJOY DOING ON A DATE?

Gemini frequently answers this question with one word: talking. A perfect night out may include a variety of other activities, but always time for talking. This is the Sign of the brain, of learning and of experience; a Sign that wants to touch on a wide range of life's offerings, and so he is curious about many subjects, from politics to community affairs, to business and cultural events. He wants a woman who has a similar broad spectrum of interests. He also enjoys quiet evenings at home, and dinner with a couple of friends.

"Dinner, conversation, long walks in the rain, movies, and outdoor stuff like hiking, going skiing, [and] activities such as bowling,"

"At first listening, getting to know her, going some place where both of us are comfortable to talk and relax together."

"Talking, getting together with friends, having good conversations over dinner."

ARE YOU FLIRTATIOUS?

While he never really means to lead anyone on, never really means to drive his partner mad with jealousy, the Gemini man continues to flirt. He loves to. He is charming, charismatic, and has a ready wit. He finds it easy to communicate with almost anyone at any time.

"I really enjoy flirting, even with women who I would not sleep with."

"Yes I am. Sometimes too much . . ."

ARE YOU JEALOUS?

He is, by nature, trusting and not likely to suffer from jealousy—unless given reason. He also believes that his lover is exceptionally attractive to all other men and he is intrigued by the thought that others may envy what he has.

"No, never, though I will get angry if someone is teasing me or playing games in order to make me jealous."

"I have suffered from it, but not overly so."

Memories

"I pulled a fully clothed girl into the shower with me. I had never had relations with her before. It was hot, steamy, aggressive, and intense. Her hair was hanging over me wet. It was wonderful."

"We were fucking and I was going at it with great force and speed. We fell off the bed into the clothes hamper and did not care. We just kept on going until we both came."

HOW DO YOU FEEL ABOUT PUBLIC DISPLAYS OF AFFECTION?

He is very comfortable with moderate displays in public. Gemini is affectionate and enjoys holding hands, some hugging, and some kissing in front of other people. But he also needs his space, and too much closeness doesn't suit him well publicly.

"It is good but one should not overdo it."

"My mood changes . . . kissing is always okay, and when I am really involved with a girl I am more adventurous."

Sexual Attitudes and Behaviors

HOW OFTEN DO YOU THINK ABOUT SEX AND HOW OFTEN PER WEEK DO YOU WANT TO HAVE SEX?

Gemini seems to have the ability to do many things and think many thoughts simultaneously. He can move from one activity to another, having dozens of projects going on at once. And in the course of his day, he will most definitely think of sex at least once. He would be quite happy to act on those thoughts daily as well.

 ### A Memory

"It was our wedding night. We were very much in love and we wanted to have a child right away. Though we had lived together for several months and the sex was satisfying, that first night my new wife fucked like she had never done before. She seemed transformed, more responsive and more giving than ever. It was wonderful."

HOW LONG DO YOU LIKE TO SPEND HAVING SEX AND HOW MUCH OF THAT TIME IS FOREPLAY? DO YOU ENJOY QUICKIES?

The Gemini man is satisfied to spend an hour making love, with about 30 minutes of foreplay. He'll never turn down a quickie, especially in an out-of-the-way place, an elevator, in the car, or on a rooftop.

WHAT TIME OF DAY DO YOU PREFER TO HAVE SEX?

Gemini is not fussy about any set part of the day for sex. If his lover is a morning person he will accommodate her; and, if she does not get turned on until the sun sets, he will be just as pleased to kiss her in the moonlight—or in the middle of the night for that matter.

"Morning feels good, like fresh, perfect heaven. Night is nice as well."

 ### A Memory

"My wife worked second shift during the first couple of years of our marriage. Quite often I would be asleep when she came home. I loved it when she was so horny that she would wake me up for sex. There were times when I was having a sexy dream and then I'd wake up to find my wife masturbating me. Sometimes I did not even wake up until I was inside her. Hot!"

HOW OFTEN DO YOU MASTURBATE?

How often Gemini masturbates varies from week to week: sometimes once and sometimes seven times.

HOW LONG DO YOU WANT TO KNOW SOMEONE BEFORE GETTING SEXUAL?

It is the Gemini man's nature to get sexual quite quickly, in part because the sex must be pretty good for him to want to continue the relationship.

"Thirty seconds . . . a few hours . . . one day . . . a few dates."

"I would prefer to not know a woman very long before getting sexual."

WHAT'S YOUR ATTITUDE TOWARD CASUAL SEX?

He considers casual sex to be a natural part of his dating life: drinks, dinner, perhaps a walk or drive in the car, and sex—not always in this order.

"It should be a regular part of your daily life."

"It is okay. I would say it is normal."

"With caution . . . I am certainly aware that there is such a thing as disease, but I enjoy sex with strangers, and certainly in my fantasies."

Fantasies

"Having two girls on the beach . . . an orgy."

"There are many images that get me hot and I don't need them to be elaborate. I imagine watching someone have sex, sex with two partners, interracial, or intergenerational."

"My sexual fantasy is to be ravaged by numerous women (a minimum of five) who basically do whatever they want with me."

"In my fantasies, I am a voyeur. Sometimes I am looking at the action through the lens of a camera. Other times, I see myself sitting in a chair masturbating while watching."

DO YOU BELIEVE IN MONOGAMY?

Gemini is a nervous sign. Having several partners would be more stress than pleasure for him. But faithfulness depends on his sex life remaining vital and somewhat varied. Adding new elements into the lovemaking will strengthen his resolve to be true to his partner.

"It is a safe haven in the insanity of life."

"Yes, but I also believe that a little excitement is needed in life."

"Only in serious relationships . . ."

"Not if I am bored."

DOES SEX HAVE A SPIRITUAL SIGNIFICANCE FOR YOU?

Gemini is an Air Sign, a Sign that has a core of spirituality. As sex brings him closer to his partner and enables him to feel one with her, he finds a spiritual quality in the act of lovemaking.

"Yes, I believe a person feels better about the world and themselves when they are having great sex."

"Indeed, it's transcendental. It takes you out of yourself and into a spiritual realm."

ARE YOU COMFORTABLE INITIATING SEXUAL ACTIVITIES?

Gemini has a nervous disposition and is not an aggressive man. Nevertheless, there is no doubt that he almost always wants a relationship to become sexual quickly and he may lead the conversation along that path. As soon as he recognizes that a woman is willing, he will initiate sexual activities.

"Yes, if I sense that she is willing. Being shot down ruins my confidence for such things."

HOW DO YOU COMMUNICATE TO YOUR PARTNER YOUR SEXUAL WANTS AND NEEDS?

This Sign is known for its ease in communicating. As a result, Gemini lets his partner know what pleases him in bed verbally, though he won't do this right away.

"I only tell my lover how to please me after I know her better."

"I always ask for what I want, and gestures help a great deal."

"I make gestures and say things like 'That feels good' very passionately."

DO YOU THINK OF YOURSELF AS BEING IN THE MAINSTREAM SEXUALLY, MORE EXPERIMENTAL, OR OPEN TO ANYTHING?

His range of sexual activities is experimental. Gemini is open to bondage, blindfolds, being ordered about by a mock dominatrix, and having sex in a variety of locations. He also enjoys shaving his partner or being shaved. He likes trying sex toys including vibrators, dildos, paddles, floggers, handcuffs, crops, and electric stimulation.

His sex fantasies range from straightforward and romantic, to being with two women, interracial sex, and being dominated. The common element in all his fantasies is time: enough of it to luxuriate in the experience.

A Fantasy

"I am a sex slave to a group of three women who demand that I service them with my enormous penis. Their cheeks are flush[ed]. They are excited and almost fearful of my huge organ. I make them deep throat my weapon. Then they tie me up and take a sound and drop it all the way into me and tie electrodes to it and start electric shock. I am halfway between torture and ecstasy."

HOW DO YOU DEMONSTRATE AFFECTION FOR YOUR PARTNER?

When Gemini is attentive he is truly attentive, but when he is preoccupied with other things he may seem a very distant lover and a partner needs to signal him. "Earth to Gemini, come in Gemini!" His attention wanders and he is apt to overlook birthdays and other special dates. A woman who cares about these things would be wise to slip some mention of said date into the conversation a few days in advance.

"I buy random gifts, flowers . . . [give] midday calls for no reason."

"Just listening seems to help, doing spontaneous things . . . making her laugh."

"Doing favors without being asked, giving gifts, being considerate."

A Fantasy

"A long, secluded getaway with a hot tub and a fireplace and satin sheets on the bed. Erotic massages with oils and being alone with that one special person with no other worries."

The Five Senses

HOW IMPORTANT TO YOU IS THE SEXUAL ENVIRONMENT?

He may not consider the environment to be of great consequence all the time, but attention to the setting will heighten his pleasure. Because Gemini is an Air Sign, sound is of importance in the setting. Music or a video playing quietly in the background does have a positive effect.

"I like the environment to be dark, with some candlelight and sexy music playing; sometimes using erotic videos."

"Being clean and comfortable is important, and low lighting is fine."

A Memory

"We were at my grandmother's house and she was not home. We had some candles going, and made love on the couch. We had dated for months before this came about. It was so extraordinary because I never had to wait to have sex with a woman before. The buildup, excitement, and anticipation made the experience incredible. It was romantic and sensual and passionate all at once. "

WHERE DO YOU LIKE TO HAVE SEX?

Gemini is the sign of transportation. He is attracted to a woman who drives a sexy automobile and many men of this Sign truly love having sex in a car.

"Sex is great everywhere: bed is nice, shower is sensual, car is exciting."

"Sex is fun anywhere, and also with the risk of being caught by someone."

"With a willing partner, anywhere, even public places, but hidden."

WHAT PUTS YOU IN THE MOOD FOR SEX?

Gemini, the Sign of experimentation, the Sign that rules hearing is turned on by all types of sounds. He is also stimulated by taste. Put on some soft, sensuous music and he starts feeling itchy. Serve him something he has never eaten before and he will get in the mood. Serve the meal by candlelight and he will be ready. Wear revealing clothes and sex cannot start soon enough. In other words, Gemini's desire for sex is easily triggered.

"Aromas put me in the mood: the smells of

chocolate and vanilla, also love songs, my lover whispering, and hearing other people make love, the sound of rain, or the roar of the ocean."

"I don't need anything special to be in the mood for sex, just a person willing to comply."

"I'm turned on by cuddling, erotic wrestling, seeing my lover's nude body or her sexy lingerie, and by sex videos."

"Talking about sex, passionate kissing."

"Wine, cheese, low music, all leading up to sex throughout the night . . ."

 A Memory

"I had been seeing this woman for some months and the sex was good. Then one night she invited me to dinner at a formal restaurant that had long white cloths on the tables. She insisted on sitting to my right side. When dinner was served she slipped her hand under the table and unzipped my fly and proceeded to masturbate me throughout the meal. I never enjoyed dinner more."

WHAT'S YOUR ATTITUDE TOWARD PORNOGRAPHY?

Gemini likes pornography today and doesn't like it tomorrow. He likes films by one director, but not by another. In other words he has an on-again, off-again relationship with pornography. If he does find an X-rated video that he really likes, he will watch it repeatedly for months.

"It's okay, but only when I am single."

"I love it. When properly done, it depicts art and creativity."

HOW MUCH CUDDLING DO YOU ENJOY, ASIDE FROM SEX?

Gemini appreciates closeness and affection, especially when he is alone with his partner. When they are out in public he does not want her to hang on him.

"Cuddling is better than sex."

"I enjoy it all the time, lots of holding and touching. I like affectionate women."

 Fantasies

"A long secluded getaway, with a hot tub and a fireplace and satin sheets on the bed. Erotic massages with oils, and being alone with that person with no other worries."

"Everything related to a hot girl turns me on. Short and mid-length skirts are my favorites, so are slips. Always wanted to do it in an elevator. Fantasize about co-workers or classmates."

HOW TACTILE AND HOW ORAL ARE YOU?

Gemini loves all aspects of sex, and it is really difficult for him to choose between oral and tactile pleasure. He thoroughly enjoys giving and receiving oral sex, and he is gifted with his hands. In fact, the pleasure he derives from touching may slightly exceed his love of kissing.

"I love to give massages, to explore the feel of her skin. Touch is a very important part of love-making for me."

"I love kissing and extremely enjoy offering oral sex. I love sucking on a firm clit."

"I enjoy deep kissing a lot, all over the body; licking and giving oral sex."

WHAT SEX ACTS DO YOU LIKE MOST AND LEAST?

He loves everything about sex. He may not prefer anal sex or using salad dressing along with foreplay, but he's willing to experiment with whatever pleases his partner. He is a nervous sort, though, and he does worry about birth control so he'll appreciate his lover taking care of that.

"I can't weigh one sex act versus another. I like it all."

"Oral sex, intercourse, mutual masturbation, fondling, and group sex . . ."

"Intercourse, kissing, cuddling, foreplay, and nursing at lover's breast."

"Intercourse and foreplay . . . combination of them all . . ."

A Memory

"The two of us on a catamaran sail-boat in Key West, Florida. The sun was setting, the wind was warm and gentle across our nude bodies. We were both salty from swimming. We caressed each other and licked the salt from each other's neck[s] and shoulders. We touched and explored each other all over our bodies. We became one and got lost in the sunset. It was so awesome and intense."

AS A LOVER, WHAT'S YOUR BEST SKILL?

As the Sign of Gemini rules the hands, this man is gifted at pleasuring his partner with them. He also loves to use sex toys, thrilling her with his manipulation of a wide range of them. The lover who brings Gemini the latest vibrating dildo or electrical stimulant will make him a very happy camper. Gemini at a fetish fair is like a kid in a candy store.

WHAT SMELLS AND TASTES ON YOUR PARTNER DO YOU ENJOY?

Gemini is a Sign that loves to experience all things, tastes and smells included. It fits, therefore, that he has no problem with his partner's aromas and tastes. In fact, the smell and taste of her secretions are aphrodisiacs for him.

"I am turned on by the smell of my lover's skin and sweat, baby powder, and clean skin."

"I love the summer, sweat, the smell of her hair, underwear, and some perfumes."

"Her saliva, vaginal fluids, sweat, and lips . . ."

"Her sweet breasts, their smell and taste [are] heaven to me."

FOR SOME PEOPLE THE TASTE OF THEIR PARTNER'S CUM OR SECRETIONS IS UNPLEASANT. IF THIS IS TRUE FOR YOU, WHAT DO YOU DO ABOUT THE TASTE?

As he has no problem with her secretions, Gemini has no need to do anything about them except savor them.

"Doesn't bother me . . ."

"When going down on a girl who is clean, I enjoy it."

A Memory

"I visited a girlfriend who was house-sitting. We were really going at it and in the middle of it all, we realized that the owners had come home. I ran into another room and hid in a closet naked for a full half hour. After my girlfriend found me, we had sex while they were in the other room. The intrigue, the whole night, was great. Afterward, they never talked to her again."

DO YOU ENJOY WATCHING YOUR PARTNER DURING SEX AND ORGASM? DO YOU ENJOY BEING WATCHED?

He loves to watch his lover during sex and orgasm, and it's a high for Gemini to have his partner watch him as well.

The Big "O"

HOW DO YOU REACH AN ORGASM AND HOW OFTEN?

Gemini reaches orgasm comfortably in any number of ways. He loves to have oral sex to the brink of orgasm and to finish with intercourse.

"Ninety-five percent of the time, and usually twice . . ."

"Intercourse all the time; oral sex if she is good at it . . ."

WHAT'S YOUR FAVORITE POSITION?

He loves sitting up, so that he can watch, while oral sex is performed on him to the point of near climax. Then he wants to mount his partner in either the doggie position or missionary style.

SOME PEOPLE ARE CONCERNED ABOUT BRINGING THEIR PARTNER TO CLIMAX BEFORE HAVING AN ORGASM THEMSELVES. OTHERS STRIVE TO REACH ORGASM TOGETHER. WHICH IS TRUE FOR YOU?

Watching, feeling, smelling her orgasm all heighten his, so Gemini prefers to bring his partner to climax before cumming himself.

"I prefer her to have multiple orgasms before I have mine."

"I think orgasm together is the best, but I would like to see her orgasm first, to experience it fully focused on her."

ARE YOU VOCAL DURING SEX?

He is vocal during sex, enjoying a bit of conversation. More than that, the Gemini man likes to let his lover know how he feels with appreciative moans.

"The more verbal the better . . . I prefer it when we openly express our pleasure."

"I used to not be, [but] now I certainly am."

 A Memory

"*We were in my art studio. I had a lovely model and one night we got to fooling around. She started to masturbate me and she wouldn't stop. She kept it up until I came all over my shoes, my trousers, and everything. It was great. Another time after she posed for me, when she left she forgot her panties. The next time I saw her, I said I had them and she wanted them back. I told her I was a fetishist and wouldn't give them to her. I married that woman and still have those [panties].*"

AFTER SEX WHAT DO YOU LIKE TO DO?

After sex Gemini prefers to stay home. If he is not tired, he enjoys lounging around and talking with his lover.

"I like to listen to music, cuddle, share food, laugh together, watch romantic movies."

"Perhaps shower together, but mostly cuddle up and sleep."

"After we make love in the daytime, I like to hang out and relax. At night, after sex I like to sleep."

CANCER

June 21–July 22

THE CRAB

Water Sign Cancer, nurturing and sensitive, is concerned with home, family, and food. Ruler of the breasts, stomach, and chest, Cancer is turned on by sharing food, emotional closeness, and feeling loved. Cancers like to have sex in the woods or by a body of water.

She says: "I feed him, make sure he is okay. I am a mom."

He says: "I remember a wonderful sexual encounter with my wife on our honeymoon. We made love in the water, out in the hot sunshine in the Florida Keys, the waves rhythmically aided my thrusting."

"As life's pleasures go, food is second only to sex."
—Alan King

The Cancer Woman in Her Own Words

A Memory

"Late at night, walking along a dark, deserted street in Mexico, dogs barking in the background. It was hot. I was wearing a short skirt without underwear. I was looking downward to ensure my footing when my boyfriend started tugging at my skirt. He licked his fingers and began fingering me right there in the street. The stars were plentiful. We went off the road, against a wall. He was behind me, his shorts around his ankles. No words were said."

Attraction and Dating a Cancer

WHAT ATTRACTS YOU TO SOMEONE?

A man's eyes, his general overall grooming, and his smile are the first elements that attract Cancer's attention. He needn't have the physique of a bodybuilder.

"I can be attracted to almost any man if his personality is right. I don't care about size or hair. The first things I notice are smiles, his eyes, a kind face, his thighs, his butt."

"Energy, maybe it's pheromones. Physique is not really important to me; it is more the person himself."

"Physical attributes don't factor into what turns me on. It's usually behavior that gets to me."

WHAT MIGHT TURN YOU OFF?

She is turned off by a man who pays little attention to his teeth or who bites his nails, as well as by aggressive behavior. In addition, as she cares enormously about family, it is disconcerting to her if a man is distant from his relatives.

"If he has bad teeth that can be fixed [or if he] has bad style that can be fixed. It is negative or crude behavior that turns me off."

"What turns me off most is a man who is overly materialistic, putting too much emphasis on fancy clothes or expensive cars, or [who] thinks he is better than everyone else."

WHAT DO YOU ENJOY DOING ON A DATE?

The Cancer woman enjoys active dates, doing things like bowling or playing miniature golf, especially at the start of a relationship when she may be feeling a bit unsure of herself. One thing is always indispensable: sharing food.

"I enjoy going out to dinner and participating in interactive activities that allow you to get to know your date. Bowling is good."

"A good date would start with going out to dinner. Maybe we would take in a movie or do something athletic like hiking or biking."

A Fantasy

"We meet on campus between classes and go into a classroom that seems to be closed off from the world. I walk into the room and he surprises me from behind and whispers in my ear things that almost turn my skirt inside out. Then we just go for it."

ARE YOU FLIRTATIOUS?

She can be somewhat flirtatious, but not overly so. Especially in a new situation, Cancer is cautious, somewhat shy. Once she is comfortable with a man or in a group, she can be quite flirtatious.

"I'd say that I am, but subtly. I am a bit shy."

"My flirting is subtle. I come across as generally friendly, and happily there is something about me that men find attractive."

ARE YOU JEALOUS?

"I feel" are her key words. She is emotional by nature and the feelings that she experiences include jealousy.

"Definitely, and of most living, breathing women . . ."

"I am very territorial, but not insanely jealous."

HOW DO YOU FEEL ABOUT PUBLIC DISPLAYS OF AFFECTION?

Given Cancer's somewhat possessive nature, when her partner hugs and kisses her in public, she feels reassured about his affection for her.

"I think they are healthy. If you care about someone you shouldn't hide it."

"Holding hands is okay, hugging and little pecks are okay. But I don't like to see people making out everywhere."

"They are fine if kept minimal and within the realm of good taste."

 ### A Memory
"*Doing it in a DJ booth at a night club with one-way windows. We could see out on the dance floor while everyone danced around us. It was very erotic. The music really got me going, the secrecy of it, and the high emotion between my partner and me.*"

Sexual Attitudes and Behaviors

HOW OFTEN DO YOU THINK ABOUT SEX AND HOW OFTEN PER WEEK DO YOU WANT TO HAVE SEX?

Cancer is a very sexual Sign, and she thinks about sex to the point of almost being preoccupied with it. She might want sex more frequently, but she'll be content with four encounters per week.

"In my mind I can turn almost any situation into a sexual one, even business."

"I want it any time my teenage kids are out for the evening!"

"I will take it whenever I can get it."

HOW LONG DO YOU LIKE TO SPEND HAVING SEX AND HOW MUCH OF THAT TIME IS FOREPLAY? DO YOU ENJOY QUICKIES?

She likes to spend 30 minutes to an hour having sex. A man who shortchanges her in the foreplay department, especially in terms of fondling and sucking on her breasts, won't be around very long. Quickies are okay on occasion.

"I like both. If I could only have one, I'd choose two to three hours over a quickie."

"Thirty minutes or more of foreplay is just right. After eating and shopping, my favorite activity is foreplay. I enjoy that even more than intercourse."

"I love quickies and slow buildups, but when the actual intercourse happens, I like the guy to go crazy and cum pretty fast. I like that take charge and ram it home feeling."

 ### A Memory
"*It was October, cold and windy. We climbed to the top of an observation tower. He had told me not to wear underwear. At the top he lifted my sweater. The wind touched my nipples, making them hard. He was behind me, lifting my skirt. I heard his zipper. He grabbed my nipples, pushed me over and entered me. It was hard, fast, exciting, and wonderful. I could smell the ocean in the wind. I could see the lights on the bridge. It was a clear night. Perfect.*"

WHAT TIME OF DAY DO YOU PREFER TO HAVE SEX?

She loves mornings but her preference is apt

to change now and then. The moon rules Cancer, so perhaps her pleasure changes with the phases of that moon.

"Eleven [in the morning] or early in the night before I get too tired . . ."

"I like the morning, because I am rested and relaxed."

"Anytime is fine, but mornings seem to be especially intimate for some reason."

"Anytime, but I really do like the morning."

HOW OFTEN PER WEEK DO YOU MASTURBATE?

She usually masturbates two or three times weekly, more if her lover turns her on with a phone call but can't make time to see her.

HOW LONG DO YOU WANT TO KNOW SOMEONE BEFORE GETTING SEXUAL?

Cancer is highly intuitive and trusts her instincts. When she's interested in a man and believes he returns the feelings, she becomes sexual. This could be as early as a second date. In some cases she wants to wait a while, but seldom longer than one month.

"As I see it, sex doesn't equal love. Getting sexual depends on the mental connection and how safe I feel with the person."

"It's usually the first or second date. I don't want to get emotionally involved until I've had sex. If it isn't good, why bother with the relationship?"

"It varies: a night, a month. [It] depends on the amount of physical and emotional connection I feel with the person and what I want at that moment."

 A Memory

"I took my clothes off and sprawled myself out under the dark sky. It was so much a world all to ourselves. The highway lights became stars. His body covered me. My legs wrapped around his. Kissing and kissing. I opened my eyes and

saw tattered clouds whizzing by behind his shadowed face. We were interwoven and flying. I was holding on for life."

WHAT'S YOUR ATTITUDE TOWARD CASUAL SEX?

Even though she may get sexually involved with a new man in short order, Cancer makes a distinction between that and anonymous sex. Sex, just for physical release, doesn't appeal to her. She considers it unsafe and does not find it at all satisfying.

"I need some emotional connection or deep desire to get really turned on."

"It's risky, less satisfying."

"I don't agree with casual sex. Personally, I get too emotionally involved for that."

DO YOU BELIEVE IN MONOGAMY?

Cancer cares enormously about family and, as a result, she values monogamy highly. Nevertheless, sex is tremendously important to her and an unsatisfactory sex life will be detrimental to her relationship.

"Seventy-five percent of sex is mental. Therefore, you can control yourself if you choose to. Also, I feel monogamy adds to the feeling that we are in our own special world."

"I have been faithful to the same guy for twenty-six years, and I can't imagine being with anyone else."

"Sex is emotional for me. Therefore, I don't sleep with someone unless I feel a bond. I only sleep with one person at a time, and I expect that in return."

 A Fantasy

"I have a fantasy of my wedding day. I'm in a beautiful white lace and satin gown with a sheer veil. I feel like a princess. My new husband takes me and then wraps me like a present. The love is tender, with lots of kisses and declarations of his love for me. The bed is huge with lots of fluffy pillows. Soft light filters through the balcony doors. I feel safe, like his love for me can never die."

DOES SEX HAVE A SPIRITUAL SIGNIFICANCE FOR YOU?

The core of her being is love and family. When the Cancer woman promises to be faithful, she is making a sacred vow. The idea that a commitment is sacred feeds into her sexuality and brings a spiritual connotation.

"It is an exchange of intimate energy, and it is the ultimate way one can do this."

"It does when you and your partner are in love. If not, though, sex can still be excellent, but that super satisfaction is not there."

"Sometimes it feels like you are seeing into each other's souls, experiencing something out of this world, feeling so good that it is not of this plane."

ARE YOU COMFORTABLE INITIATING SEXUAL ACTIVITIES?

Cancer is shy in the initial stages of a relationship and won't be the one to introduce the subject of sex for the first time.

HOW DO YOU COMMUNICATE TO YOUR PARTNER YOUR SEXUAL WANTS AND NEEDS?

While Cancer is very responsive emotionally, she is hesitant to express herself verbally. She trusts that her partner will be tuned in to her sufficiently to read her body language.

"Mostly by gestures . . . I move his hands or body where I want them."

"My eyes explore and reflect my inner emotions."

"I am not very good at communicating. I guess I just do it."

"With my hands, rarely with words . . ."

DO YOU THINK OF YOURSELF AS BEING IN THE MAINSTREAM SEXUALLY, MORE EXPERIMENTAL, OR OPEN TO ANYTHING?

Cancer is an experimental lover and open to a range of experiences that nearly always includes the use of food, preferably sweets such as chocolate, whipped cream, and sweet melons more likely than tart strawberries. She will also try dominance and submission, bondage, sex in public places, spanking, and wearing sexy lingerie. Her use of sex toys is generally limited to dildos and vibrators.

"I can be mild or wild; depends on the moment and the man."

"I will definitely try a variety of things to spice the action up."

"I am pretty open to anything if I am in the right state of mind or mood."

Her fantasies frequently incorporate sex with another woman, a ménage à trois, bondage, and being spanked.

Fantasies

"I am a submissive being humiliated by a dominant man who verbally humiliates me, then farms me out to his male friends to make sure that I know I am his slut, to be used any way he wishes."

"I am a machine and many men come up to me, deposit a quarter, and my legs open. Then they stick their dicks in me, satisfy themselves, and move on."

"Having sex in a public place without fear of getting caught. Having a penis for a day and allowing my boyfriend to perform fellatio on me so I know what it feels like for him when I do it."

HOW DO YOU DEMONSTRATE AFFECTION FOR YOUR PARTNER?

Cancer is a nurturing Sign for whom the focus of life is the home, the family, and food. She shows her regard for her partner by cooking for him and tending to his needs.

"I feed him, make sure he is okay. I am a mom."

"Cooking for him (I know . . . how typically Cancerian.)"

"By making a special dinner, sitting on the sofa and reaching over to give a soft touch or kiss."

"We touch each other a lot. As I was typing this, my husband walked by to get a cup of coffee. He touched my shoulder and gave it a gentle squeeze. We hardly ever pass by one another without touching."

The Five Senses

HOW IMPORTANT TO YOU IS THE SEXUAL ENVIRONMENT?

Considering that Cancer is the Sign that rules the home, it is a bit surprising to find that the setting for sex is not of great importance to her. Passion matters far more. Beyond cleanliness, the overall environment does not concern her much at all.

"If I am really in the mood, I don't think about that."

"Sometimes I like to have a nice atmosphere: clean, orderly, low lights. Once in a while it is nice to just go for it without concern for the surroundings."

"Dim lighting is always nice, and a clean place shows that he takes good care of himself."

A Memory

"Candlelit bathroom, warm water in the tub, bottle of champagne waiting, [my] lover in a towel greeted me at the door, undressed me, lowered me into the tub. We bathed with scented soaps. We drank wine and lay together in the tub. Then he carried me to the bed. I was still wet and our lips never left each other."

WHERE DO YOU LIKE TO HAVE SEX?

While she may not want to be observed, Cancer does love sex in public places, such as on a stretch of secluded beach, a dark rooftop, or in a car parked on an isolated road. Her number one thrill is having sex in the woods with the sounds of crickets and birds and smells of the earth and the trees.

"Outdoors in a public place can be exciting as long as no kids or grandparents might stumble along."

"I prefer to be in bed or somewhere warm and comfortable, but I would love to have sex on a private stretch of beach somewhere."

WHAT PUTS YOU IN THE MOOD FOR SEX?

Emotional Water Sign Cancer is turned on by almost anything relating to water and by gentle loving actions, romance, and by all things that signify the closeness—the emotional connection—she shares with her partner.

"I am always in the mood. I love it if he brings over a small gift, candles, or flowers. Then I put on jazz, touching me while we are relaxing, especially my nipples. I love a massage. I like it if he showered with a fragrant soap."

"Showering together, watching or reading sexual material, dancing, and ice cream."

"I get turned on by being joined in the shower or sitting on the sofa and cuddling."

"I get excited hearing romantic music. I like being massaged or tickled, and I like to touch and rub my partner."

A Fantasy

"A foursome with my husband and a friend and her boyfriend. My husband isn't allowed to touch anyone else, but I can and I do. I make out with my friend and it's so hot, caressing her chest and touching her where it drives her boyfriend crazy, but he can't touch her either—until I let him. They drool watching us until we share each other with them. Maybe we blow one of them at the same time until it drives the other one crazy, and then we switch. But actual sex will be reserved for our partners. Everything else is up for grabs."

WHAT'S YOUR ATTITUDE TOWARD PORNOGRAPHY?

The Cancer woman has very little interest in pornography, especially as a part of foreplay. After all, why watch someone else do what she is perfectly willing to do herself? She may use pornography privately for self-stimulation, but even this is rare.

"I enjoy erotica. To me porno is just a lot of naked bodies with no text or creativity, boring within ten minutes."

"I used to dislike it and felt threatened when my boyfriend used pornographic materials. Recently I have become more accepting of it, but still have only slight interest."

"I like erotic photographs and reading adult porno literature. I find pornographic films to be crude. A movie like *9 1/2 Weeks* is more exciting for me."

HOW MUCH CUDDLING DO YOU ENJOY, ASIDE FROM SEX?

Touching people is part of Cancer's nature. She hugs and kisses friends naturally. With a lover, she wants signs of affection frequently: cuddling, a touch on the shoulder, holding her arm when walking. For her, being close is not always a prelude to sexual activity.

"Sometimes cuddling is more satisfying than sex."

"I love to cuddle with no strings attached."

"I like to cuddle in front of the TV or read with my partner, especially in bed at night before sleeping."

HOW TACTILE AND HOW ORAL ARE YOU?

Cancer loves to explore every inch of her lover's body with her hands. She enjoys kissing her partner's lips, neck, chest, and arms. She is likely to withhold oral sex until she feels secure in a relationship.

"I love deep kissing almost more than sex. I perform oral sex only if very involved with someone."

"I like to feel every inch of him and I love oral sex, but only when it is not expected of me. Deep kissing is awesome."

"I like the feeling of closeness and touch during lovemaking. I enjoy deep kissing and light kissing on my lover's body. I do not like oral sex as a rule."

"I am very oral. Give and you shall receive."

 A Memory

"In a hot tub, warm water [and] out in the cold night air. We had sex in about ten different positions and he kept telling me how beautiful I was. The water jets were bubbling all around and I felt kind of like a mermaid. I came four times that night. The next day I was exhausted."

WHAT SEX ACTS DO YOU LIKE MOST AND LEAST?

As Cancer is the Sign that rules the breasts, they must always be attended to—caressed lovingly and sucked with passion. They make a perfect place to paint on a dollop of honey. She dislikes anal sex or anything that causes pain.

"I always love kissing and intercourse, oral sex sometimes, and my breasts. Yes, always touch them."

"I like intercourse, oral sex, mutual masturbation all while fondling my breasts and kissing them too."

"I've never tried anal sex and never want to."

AS A LOVER, WHAT'S YOUR BEST SKILL?

Cancer is by nature nurturing, and she strives to satisfy her man. Her most important skill is her ability to understand what her lover needs.

"I think my best skill is being tuned in to my partner. I strive to adjust to what he is responding to."

"What works best for me is showing the proper attitude toward my partner."

"My skill is how I follow my partner's gestures, as if I were reading his mind."

WHAT SMELLS AND TASTES ON YOUR PARTNER DO YOU ENJOY?

Cancer loves her partner's natural smells, fresh sweat, and also his cologne if it's light and a bit woodsy. She likes the taste of her partner's lips and nipples, and she enjoys mixing food with sex.

"I love the way his face smells after he has shaved."

"I like the smell of his skin, his cologne, and his smell after sweaty sex."

"I love the smell of clean hair, the smell of soap, and as far as tastes go, a little sweat."

"I enjoy the smell of him and the taste of whipped cream."

FOR SOME PEOPLE THE TASTE OF THEIR PARTNER'S CUM OR SECRETIONS IS UNPLEASANT. IF THAT'S TRUE FOR YOU, WHAT DO YOU DO ABOUT THE TASTE?

Cancer performs oral sex because she wants to please her partner. She may find the taste of cum unpleasant, and she prefers that her partner not cum in her mouth. Flavored oils or even a flavored condom help.

"The taste is unpleasant so he doesn't cum in my mouth. But if he should, I spit and brush my teeth."

"I don't care too much for the taste, but I grin and bear it."

"I don't enjoy the flavor of cum. I usually let it drip out of my mouth and give a quick lube job to drive the final pleasure home."

"The taste is no problem for me. I swallow if I have known the guy for some time. Otherwise, I just have him unload on my breasts."

A Fantasy

"I would love to be surrounded by men, like Cleopatra, being able to have power and get fucked all day without worrying about my reputation. I'd love to see any man's penis I wanted to, whenever I wanted; and do whatever I wanted with it without dealing with societal bullshit and guilt. I want to be overwhelmed by a man's fucking abilities to the point of tears, where I lose control and forget everything except what is happening in the moment. Pure pleasure."

DO YOU ENJOY WATCHING YOUR PARTNER DURING SEX AND ORGASM? DO YOU ENJOY BEING WATCHED?

In a new relationship Cancer is likely to feel self-conscious, so she tends to close her eyes during much of the sexual experience. Over time, both watching and being watched will prove a turn-on for her.

"More than watching, I listen. I love hearing moans of pleasure. It makes me feel like I am doing it right and he likes it. I don't mind being watched if the mood is right. Other times I feel pressured."

"I love watching his eyes get glossy when he is about to cum."

"I think mirrors are important in sex. Watching heightens my pleasure."

The Big "O"

HOW DO YOU REACH ORGASM AND HOW OFTEN?

After being very turned on by her partner fondling her breasts, Cancer reaches orgasm almost every time she has sex with a combination of masturbation and intercourse.

"I reach orgasm usually through good foreplay completed by intercourse. I cum most often when I am on top."

"I cum almost all the time with oral sex, always with masturbation, but almost never with just intercourse . . ."

A Fantasy

"I encounter a stranger who is very well endowed. He grabs me and forces me on my knees to suck him. I do. Right as he is about to cum he makes me stop. He then tells me to lie down and [he] gets between my thighs. He teases me, licking every part of me except my clit. Finally he slowly licks it and then sticks a finger in me. He brings me close to orgasm many times but then backs off. Then he sucks on my clit slowly, nipping it with *his teeth until I cum. While I am cumming he is still sucking, sending me into multiple orgasms.*

WHAT'S YOUR FAVORITE POSITION?

Top, bottom, side by side, or spooning, all are pleasurable to the Cancer woman. She has absolutely no exclusive favorite position.

"I can reach orgasm just by lots of foreplay, especially [on] my nipples."

"For me it doesn't matter. It depends on how much foreplay and how deep he is in me."

"My husband on his side, facing me, me on my back, legs intertwined."

"I like doggie style because I can tickle my clit at the same time."

SOME PEOPLE ARE CONCERNED ABOUT BRINGING THEIR PARTNER TO CLIMAX BEFORE HAVING AN ORGASM THEMSELVES. OTHERS STRIVE TO REACH ORGASM TOGETHER. WHICH IS TRUE FOR YOU?

Ms. Cancer loves the intensity of achieving orgasm simultaneously with her partner, but if this is not possible, she is content as long as they both climax.

"I am not concerned about who cums first as long as we both have orgasms."

"It's nice to climax together, but either way the job will get done."

"The ultimate is reaching it together; however, sometimes this doesn't happen and it doesn't really matter."

ARE YOU VOCAL DURING SEX?

The sounds that Cancer makes during sex are mostly low moans and soft whispers.

"My husband is very vocal. I am not but try to be because I know it turns him on."

"I am quite vocal. I like my partner to know that I enjoy what he is doing."

 A Fantasy

"*I am by nature dominant, yet when I fantasize I am almost always submissive—often being humiliated by a dom who verbally humiliates me, then farms me out to his male friends to make sure that I know I am his slut to be used any way he wishes.*"

AFTER SEX WHAT DO YOU LIKE TO DO?

After sex most often Cancer prefers to stay in, to cuddle, and to relax together. About the only thing she enjoys doing beyond sleeping is sharing food.

"After sex I enjoy cuddling, talking, and watching a movie."

"I love it when we cuddle and fall asleep holding each other."

The Cancer Man in His Own Words

A Memory

"Lying inserted under warm covers, quiet and long, and eventually we're floating and there is this hot light coming through my back, through my penis, and filling her belly. I don't even feel my penis; it is just this fast flow of light between us. It goes on and on, as orgasmic waves come and go."

Attraction and Dating a Cancer

WHAT ATTRACTS YOU TO SOMEONE?

When it comes time for a committed relationship, the Cancer man wants a woman with certain traditional family values. It pleases him if she likes to cook and tend the garden, and he loves watching her with children. After all, Cancer is the Sign that represents home and family. Initially, however, he notices a woman's smile, her weight, her looks in general, and especially her breasts. Beyond that a woman's behavior and energy are important in holding his attention.

"Weight and beauty are important to me, but I would not say that I am into body worship, not one bit. A woman's smile, energy, and behavior matter to me more."

"First attraction: large breasts and a good-sized butt. After that, it is how she moves."

"The first thing I notice is femininity. I like curves; then lots of hair, nice hands, well-tended fingernails and toenails, lovely skin, and full lips."

"I am attracted to a woman who comes across as self-assured and strong. Nice breasts and great eyes are a definite plus."

"I must admit that I first notice a woman's breasts, and [I] prefer them large. A sense of humor is important to me, and I like a woman who is not too thin."

WHAT MIGHT TURN YOU OFF?

Cancer has a fair amount of pride. He wants his partner to look good, to stay near him, and he loves having other people notice her. As a result, her presentation in public—the way she dresses, carries herself, and behaves—all matter to him. He dislikes a woman who is loud or narrow-minded, and he may be turned off if she smokes. In addition, even though he likes a lot of physical attention, hugs, and holding hands, he does not like a woman to be too clingy.

A range of personal behaviors that will turn Cancer away includes smoking, and being overly possessive, loud, or narrow-minded.

"The behaviors I dislike include talking too much about herself, being too clingy, being loud, or lacking discretion or respect."

"Generally I get along with all people, but bitchiness and obnoxious behavior turn me off."

"When I see a woman wearing sloppy clothing [and] who is generally unkempt, even if she is beautiful, I am not interested."

WHAT DO YOU ENJOY DOING ON A DATE?

In the human body, the Sign of Cancer rules the stomach. This is the man for whom the adage that "the best way to a man's heart is through his stomach" was written. From dining out to a wine, cheese, and bread picnic, buying chili dogs at a kiosk in the park, or preparing a home-cooked meal, sharing food is indispensable for a successful date with Cancer. In addition to that he enjoys many outdoor activities.

"I enjoy eating out together and doing something quiet like taking a walk or a drive by the water."

"For me a good date might include conversation, hand holding, laughing, dancing, a good meal together, spending time in nature."

"Dinner, movies, long conversations, and long drives . . ."

A Fantasy

"I visualize women in positions indicating that they are about to have sex. They might be lying nude on a bed, or seated with legs apart and not wearing underwear, or bending over exposing thong undies. Sometimes I imagine absurd situations such as a secretary up on the desk baying like a hound while the UPS guy pokes her from behind. Some of these images come to have an iconic status in my mind."

ARE YOU FLIRTATIOUS?

Cancer has a warm personality, a way of drawing people out. Men and women find themselves opening up to him, telling him perhaps more than he wants to know about their lives. This quality attracts women to him. Is it flirtatiousness? He says yes.

"Yes. Paying that kind of attention to people makes them feel better about themselves and perhaps about me, too."

"I like to be flirtatious when I feel confident."

"I think by nature I am flirtatious, but I am also a bit reticent."

"I can be very flirtatious."

"It seems to me that I am a little flirtatious, but so subtly that most people do not even notice."

ARE YOU JEALOUS?

His nature is not inherently jealous, but Cancer will acknowledge that he is possessive.

He wants his mate to stay by his side when out in public, and his insecurities are triggered if she behaves too flirtatiously with others.

HOW DO YOU FEEL ABOUT PUBLIC DISPLAYS OF AFFECTION?

Cancer is highly sexual. He is very into touch and he craves affection. Nevertheless, there is a proper time and place for everything and when it comes to displaying ardor, Cancer thinks that place is away from the eyes of others. He is embarrassed by anything beyond a casual hug in public.

"So-so. Keep it limited, please."

"I do not like them. I get a little embarrassed."

"I enjoy holding hands, but I prefer to maintain decorum wherever I am."

"I disapprove of them unless in an environment specifically designed for them. I have been to fetish clubs where there are sex scenes being acted out and that's fine. But out on the street, in front of people of all ages, that's not for me."

Sexual Attitudes and Behaviors

HOW OFTEN DO YOU THINK ABOUT SEX AND HOW OFTEN PER WEEK DO YOU WANT TO HAVE SEX?

Being a highly sexual Sign, Cancer thinks about sex frequently each day. Triggers include aromas that remind him of his partner, but not necessarily the scent of her shampoo or cologne. It might be coffee or cinnamon that will bring her to his mind. The Cancer man enjoys having sex about four times per week.

"I think about it a lot, at least daily. Some weeks it is on my mind throughout the day."

"Sometimes it seems to me that I am preoccupied with it and go through periods when I want sex seven times a week."

HOW LONG DO YOU LIKE TO SPEND HAVING SEX AND HOW MUCH OF THAT TIME IS FOREPLAY? DO YOU ENJOY QUICKIES?

Overall, time is not an important variable for Cancer. He enjoys sessions that last from 15 minutes to two hours, depending on the situation and the mood. Sometimes he enjoys having a quick encounter followed by a longer session that might include a slower buildup, say with an hour for foreplay. Quickies are not particularly appealing to Cancer.

"I will perform foreplay as long as she likes and spend as much time as I can having sex."

"Both quickies and maybe two hours . . . we lose all sense of time."

"I enjoy quickies, 15 minutes, half hour, whatever."

"Not into the fore and after idea. It is all sex. When do I poke? Depends . . ."

"I spend three hours at a time having sex. I don't enjoy quickies."

WHAT TIME OF DAY DO YOU PREFER TO HAVE SEX?

Cancer is unlikely to say no to sex at any time of the day or night, but he does have some preference for evening.

"My preference is late afternoon when the sun has gone down some."

"I like to have sex in the afternoon or evening. I meditate in the morning."

HOW OFTEN PER WEEK DO YOU MASTURBATE?

The Cancer man masturbates on average four times a week.

 A Memory

"I had been watching a sex animation video and was feeling really turned on. I went to a local bar where I met a very pretty woman and got into [a] conversation with her. No more than five minutes passed before we started kissing. She invited me to her place. We left the bar immediately, got to her place quite quickly, and had repeated urgent sex, both oral and intercourse. All I remember about her apartment was the dim lighting. The sex was rough and fast and mutually satisfactory."

HOW LONG DO YOU WANT TO KNOW SOMEONE BEFORE GETTING SEXUAL?

Given the highly sexual nature of this Sign, it stands to reason that Cancer expects to become physical very quickly, possibly on the first date.

"Five minutes."

"Very quickly . . . first date sex is best for me."

"As soon as I am comfortable with a woman's body, I think it is okay to get physical."

"I know right away whether I want to or not."

WHAT'S YOUR ATTITUDE TOWARD CASUAL SEX?

Food and sex go hand and hand for Cancer, and both are usually part of an evening. He is smart enough to practice safe sex with women he does not know well.

"It is cool as long as boundaries are set and understood. It is never my intention to mislead a woman or [to] hurt her feelings."

"I am aware that anonymous sex can be dangerous, but I am not foolhardy about it and find it fun."

DO YOU BELIEVE IN MONOGAMY?

For Cancer monogamy is not a sacrosanct value. He may be faithful in a committed relationship for the sake of family stability, but his sex drive is very strong and his appetite has to be sated at home or he will go out for a side order.

"Monogamy is a choice. I think people make it for non-sexual benefits, home life stability, children, et cetera. Some people are more in need of diversity."

"No, I am married and have two additional partners."

"No, it is boring."

"I think that it works for people who deeply desire it, but I am not sure that it suits me."

"Monogamy may not be right for me, but I think couples can make their own choices. I believe in whatever works for the adults involved."

DOES SEX HAVE A SPIRITUAL SIGNIFICANCE FOR YOU?

Cancer may be the most emotional Sign in the zodiac, and when his feelings are deeply touched during sex, the sensation goes far beyond any merely physical gratification. It creates a bond with his partner that transcends the earthly plane.

"It has warmth and intimacy and implies a mental and physical soulful connection."

"When there is openness between the two of us there is an exchange of energy, of light and ecstasy."

"Big time . . . for me sexual ecstasy creates a feeling that reconnects the male and female to oneness with a sense of one divine energy."

"I am not sure that I would call it spiritual, though it may be, but sex certainly has great emotional as well as intellectual significance."

ARE YOU COMFORTABLE INITIATING SEXUAL ACTIVITIES?

In the early days of a relationship he enjoys initiating sex. For one thing he is very physical, sensual, as well as sexual. He loves to touch, to hug and cuddle. With him, this usually progresses to sex. It does please Cancer, however, over time, to have his lover take on the role of the aggressor.

"Yes, it is a turn-on to be dominant at first, then become submissive."

HOW DO YOU COMMUNICATE TO YOUR PARTNER YOUR SEXUAL WANTS AND NEEDS?

This is a man who often uses touch to communicate. He expresses tenderness with a hand on the shoulder or by putting an arm around his partner's waist. In bed he may use a combination of words and body language to express his desires, but with greater emphasis on gestures.

"I am very intense, but say little. I hardly ever talk. I project my wishes and am surprised how well people hear me."

"Mostly gestures, but it usually just happens."

DO YOU THINK OF YOURSELF AS BEING IN THE MAINSTREAM SEXUALLY, MORE EXPERIMENTAL, OR OPEN TO ANYTHING?

His range of sexuality is fundamentally mainstream, from kissing and fondling to oral sex and intercourse. Venturing a bit beyond vanilla sex, Cancer explores light bondage and using food. He might enjoy licking jams or chocolate syrup or whipped cream off his lover's body. The experimental Cancer will try anal sex and bondage, hot wax, and ice cubes but he uses few toys other than perhaps a vibrator.

"I think of myself as mainstream, but definitely sensual, romantic, and into lovemaking rather than having sex."

His fantasies generally reflect his own range of sexual behaviors with images of intense, long, satisfying sex. Sometimes he imagines having sex with two women. More extreme images include aggressive sex, rape fantasies, and an orgy with four or five women.

 Fantasies

"*I imagine that I am a lesbian about to get a new girl in bed for the first time. Just the thought of being a woman and the excitement of the first time is very arousing.*"

"*Currently my most common fantasy is watching my wife [being] pleasured by other men.*"

"*I have rape fantasies or those involving rather rough sex with mutual intensity, arousal, and interest.*"

HOW DO YOU DEMONSTRATE AFFECTION FOR YOUR PARTNER?

When he cares for a woman, Cancer demonstrates his regard for his partner by being protective, complimentary, and perhaps giving her a massage. He may also prepare wonderful meals for her as he loves his home and is often an accomplished cook.

"I show my regard with kisses, hand holding, compliments, and petting."

"With massages, touching, compliments, helping out, being interested in her day and her thoughts. I cook for her and make her laugh."

"I shop for her, I call her, I try to take care of her and keep her safe."

The Five Senses

HOW IMPORTANT TO YOU IS THE SEXUAL ENVIRONMENT?

The environment for sex is not important to the Cancer man. Okay, he will notice it if a woman has gone to some effort to light scented candles or spread out satin sheets. But it is likely that the smell of home cooking will turn him on more than low lights and sexy music.

"Any environment has its perks."

"It is not particularly important but I do enjoy a clean atmosphere."

"Messy is okay, but not smelly. I prefer it dark with mood music."

"It is nice if it is clean with candlelight, incense, some order. But, on the other hand I like spontaneity, so whatever and wherever is great too."

"The sexual setting is somewhat important. I think that orderliness and cleanliness count for a lot."

WHERE DO YOU LIKE TO HAVE SEX?

In addition to having sex at home, in bed, or in other parts of the house, Cancer loves having sex outdoors, in a car, or in a dark pine forest.

And, being a Water Sign, his sexual pleasure is always heightened if he is near water, on a secluded beach, by a lake, or close to a waterfall.

"Bed, outdoors in a secluded area that might not be necessarily a comfortable environment . . . The park picnic table with just a tablecloth was a bit hard but also exciting."

"Bedroom, bathroom, laundry room, outdoors, but not in a place where we might be seen . . ."

"I really have no preference as long as the setting is not offensive."

 A Memory

"Making love in the water while in the hot sunshine in the Florida Keys on my honeymoon. The waves rhythmically aided my thrusting. It was a wonderful place for my Pisces wife and me, a Fish and a Crab, to make love."

WHAT PUTS YOU IN THE MOOD FOR SEX?

Cancer is a highly sexual and emotional sign. He wants to hear "I love you." His sex drive is triggered by feelings of closeness to his lover, whether by her touch, the scent of her perfume or clean hair, or an image in a film. Any of these sensations will put him in the mood.

"A massage, erotic wrestling, my lover's breath on my neck, or seeing her sexy lingerie turn me on—as well as looking at her nude body or watching her undress."

"When my lover and I talk about deep psychological secrets in a warm, hidden bedroom . . ."

"Just being with someone sexy or someone you want."

"Noticing my girl's hips, flirting, relaxing . . . it can be very sudden."

"For me just about anything will put me in the mood . . . thinking of an attractive female will do it. I might say, being awake is about all it takes."

"Aromas are a strong turn-on for me . . . the smell of vanilla or scented candles."

WHAT'S YOUR ATTITUDE TOWARD PORNOGRAPHY?

Cancer has a love/hate relationship with porn. It turns him on and he may admit that he loves it, but at the same time he sees it as something not quite right. Certainly he will prefer using it alone as a masturbation stimulus unless his partner introduces it.

"It's a really base but enjoyable thing."

"I like the stimulation, but I am uncomfortable with it because it is pure sex without divine love."

HOW MUCH CUDDLING DO YOU ENJOY, ASIDE FROM SEX?

It pleases Cancer to feel his partner's hand on his arm when out walking. He likes to run his hand across her shoulders when he passes. Touch is a constant reminder of his affection for her. In truth, however, most of the time cuddling leads to sex.

"If there is no rush to go somewhere, I love to just hang around and enjoy being together."

"I love it but do not get anywhere near enough of it."

"I enjoy it sometimes but I don't want a woman hanging all over me when we are out."

HOW TACTILE AND HOW ORAL ARE YOU?

He is a very tactile lover with soft, but forceful, hands. He can excite a woman immeasurably in the way he fondles her breasts. He is less oral, though he performs cunnilingus because he wants to please his partner.

"Women tell me I have magical hands. They are always very hot."

"I show my affection by my touch."

"I am quite fond of feeling my partner, kissing her, and of oral sex."

"I guess this is unusual but I don't like receiving oral sex, and yet I love to give it."

WHAT SEX ACTS DO YOU LIKE MOST AND LEAST?

Cancer has a strong sex drive and the success of a relationship is tied to satisfaction in his sex life. He thoroughly enjoys kissing, oral sex, and intercourse. Beyond that, looking at and fondling and kissing a woman's breasts are of greatest pleasure.

"I haven't experienced a bad sex act yet."

"I like kissing, oral sex, intercourse, anal sex, fondling breasts, rimming, cum play. I like just about everything."

"There are things I have not tried but I like everything that I actually do."

AS A LOVER, WHAT'S YOUR BEST SKILL?

Cancer is an intuitive Water Sign. His best sexual skill reflects his sensitivity. It is his ability to sense and attend to his lover's needs.

"She tells me it is how attentive I am to her and my sensuous touch."

"The passion of my approach and overall lovemaking, kissing, intercourse . . ."

"I think it is my oral skills and how I use my hands."

 A Memory

"It was aggressive. I was dominating my partner, taking complete control. We were in a hotel room that had an interesting décor. The day was warm and she was sweating and when she reached orgasm, she came loudly."

WHAT SMELLS AND TASTES ON YOUR PARTNER DO YOU ENJOY?

He is a sensual man. He loves all things as they are in nature, such as the smell of pine forests or an ocean breeze. When it comes to sex, colognes and perfumes aren't necessary to enhance the pleasure he finds in the aroma of his lover's skin or secretions. A light scent is okay, but her body, just as it is, will excite him most.

"Natural body tastes and fruity flavored oils appeal to me."

"I love to look at panties. I love to smell the sweat on her lower back."

"I love to taste her pussy."

"Natural odors are attractive, any cologne or perfume is distracting and not good. I enjoy the taste of her natural secretions."

"I love the smell and taste of her skin when sweating, her vagina when wet, and her perfume if it is very light."

FOR SOME PEOPLE THE TASTE OF THEIR PARTNER'S CUM OR SECRETIONS IS UNPLEASANT. IF THAT'S TRUE FOR YOU, WHAT DO YOU DO ABOUT THE TASTE?

For many Cancer men, a woman's secretions may be quite pleasant. For those that find them a bit unpleasant, foods such as whipped cream or sex oils with minty flavors will prove most useful.

"Most of the time her secretions taste fine. When the taste is off, I avoid it."

"The taste is fine."

"I am quite fond of the taste of her ejaculate."

"This is true for me and I try not to taste it, but as I wish to please my lover I put up with it."

"I love the taste."

DO YOU ENJOY WATCHING YOUR PARTNER DURING SEX AND ORGASM? DO YOU ENJOY BEING WATCHED?

Cancer is comfortable with intimacy and eye-to-eye contact, and he enjoys watching his partner during sex and orgasm. He may not be equally enthusiastic about being watched, but he does not object to having her look at him.

"I am very voyeuristic. I enjoy seeing her pleasure. I'm fine with her watching me, too, but not as much as I like to look at her."

Memories

"My glasses were off. There was a nice song playing on the radio. We were lying on the grass and the afternoon sun was falling on my lover's defocused pink face surrounded by what seemed to be a bright green wall. I remember us lying there together after cumming. All of these sensory experiences together were fabulous."

"Perfect music, wanting each other, lots of foreplay. Doing it again and again, all over the house, until we were both drained."

The Big "O"

HOW DO YOU REACH AN ORGASM AND HOW OFTEN?

The Cancer man reaches orgasm every time he has sex. For him, anything works: masturbation, oral sex, and intercourse. As long as he feels close emotionally, he climaxes with ease.

"I cum all the time until I'm tired or I have had a few orgasms."

"I will reach an orgasm every time I have sex and by using any means necessary."

"I always have an orgasm. Oral sex and masturbation are the best ways."

WHAT'S YOUR FAVORITE POSITION?

He might get into a routine for sex and orgasm but variety pleases him as well, and if his partner initiates novel positions, he will be very turned on. Cancer has no favorite position for reaching orgasm. He enjoys being on top, having his partner on top, sixty-nine, and doggie style.

"All positions will work. Doggie style is fast and sharp. Other ways are more about the foreplay buildup with my partner."

"Anything goes but I love being on top, with my girl's legs high in the air."

SOME PEOPLE ARE CONCERNED ABOUT BRINGING THEIR PARTNER TO CLIMAX BEFORE HAVING AN ORGASM THEMSELVES. OTHERS STRIVE TO REACH ORGASM TOGETHER. WHICH IS TRUE FOR YOU?

Consistent with his desire to please his partner and his inclination to be in control, Cancer prefers to have her achieve orgasm before he does.

"I try to let my partner experience the same satisfaction I do. I know full well that a satisfied partner is a happy partner."

"Cumming together is best. It is easiest to achieve simultaneous orgasm through intercourse and I try not to go alone. In other positions it is not so important to cum together."

"I like to bring my partner many orgasms before I achieve one myself."

ARE YOU VOCAL DURING SEX?

Cancer is not particularly vocal during sex, but he does make his feelings known with sighs and moans.

"I am not verbal, but I do make my pleasure known with sound. I enjoy moaning."

AFTER SEX WHAT DO YOU LIKE TO DO?

After sex the Cancer man enjoys some cuddling, perhaps a massage, and then he prefers to sleep. If it's earlier in the day he enjoys quiet activities such as taking a walk or having something to eat.

LEO

July 23–August 22
THE LION

Fire Sign Leo has a sunny, generous disposition, is flamboyant and enthusiastic, and loves having an audience. Ruler of the spine and heart, Leo is a romantic for whom setting the stage for sex is important. Cleanliness, a candle or two, and some flowers enhance the Lion's sexual pleasure.

She says: "Save the clitoris for last. Don't go to it right away."

He says: "Don't be afraid to talk about sex before, during, or after. And if you aren't laughing you aren't having fun."

"I never miss a chance to have sex or appear on television."
—Gore Vidal

The Leo Woman in Her Own Words

A Memory

"A four-hour sexual encounter that started with him lighting candles and playing soft music. He gave me a complete body rub that seemed to last forever. I returned the favor and did some oral sex, too. We then slid around on the bed for a while before he picked me up, pushed me against the wall, and took me there. After he climaxed we moved to the kitchen table, cleared that off, and proceeded to go at it like bunnies again."

Attraction and Dating a Leo

WHAT ATTRACTS YOU TO SOMEONE?

Leo has considerable energy and wants a partner who matches her. She wants to be the center of his attention. He needn't be exceptionally handsome, but she prefers a man who is fairly slim.

"I don't really pay attention to physical attributes. I notice a man's smile, attitude toward life, behavior toward me and other people."

"I look for someone with physical energy, who feels confident about who he is."

"Physique, I prefer a lean build: muscular but not huge. I'm more turned on by a sense of humor and by romance, consideration of what might make me feel good."

"Penis size is not an issue with me, unless a guy likes me to give him oral sex. Smaller guys are great then, as you can really make them moan. But so long as he knows what to do with it, I don't care about size. I care more about endurance and rebound, lasting longer and starting over later after some cuddling and touching."

WHAT MIGHT TURN YOU OFF?

Leo is a woman who is exuberant about life, so a man who lacks a sense of playfulness or who has little sense of humor will not hold her interest. Also, arrogance and disrespect for others turn her off.

"I am turned off when a man does not appreciate me or when a man feels I am lucky to be with him, and also when a man discusses other women with me."

"Boorishness, rudeness, ignorance, substance abuse, poor hygiene, bad teeth, self-neglect . . ."

"The biggest turnoff is rushing me to perform before I am ready; that and being unclean. Other than that I can find something to like about anybody."

WHAT DO YOU ENJOY DOING ON A DATE?

Talking, laughter, and food are the top three ingredients for a successful night out with Leo. She loves movies and theater and beyond that she enjoys doing active things, from water-skiing to kayaking, playing miniature golf to bowling.

"Good conversation, wining and dining, exploring and laughing, dancing, a moonlight stroll, bathing, lovemaking."

"Dinner, going to sports events, outdoor activities such as hiking or bicycling."

Fantasies

"I would like to watch a porn video and do as they do. Then I'd like to make a videotape of my partner and me in the kitchen using all fruits and whipped cream and chocolate."

"Acting out a romance novel, telling my lover [exactly] what and how to do everything, having total control, bordering on being [a] dominatrix."

ARE YOU FLIRTATIOUS?

Leo is outgoing and frequently effusive, often making her the center of attention, and yet her behavior is not flirtatious per se. Her behavior is much more about performance, about the size of her personality, rather than about trying to get any one man's attention.

"Not too much, only to enhance a feel-good atmosphere . . . I love life and will always have a twinkle in my eyes."

"I have been told I am. I just think I am interested in people, who they are and how they got there."

ARE YOU JEALOUS?

Given the fact that Leo is self-assured, outgoing, and dynamic, one would not expert her to be jealous. But she is, and this is true even when she's in a very long-term relationship.

"I have been married for thirty-two years, but I pay attention if someone is touching or leaning too close to my husband."

"I can be jealous if I don't feel completely adored by my partner."

"Not murderous or harping, but it makes me insecure to think that my guy is looking elsewhere, makes me wonder if something is missing. I won't tolerate infidelity."

"I am a green-eyed monster."

HOW DO YOU FEEL ABOUT PUBLIC DISPLAYS OF AFFECTION?

Exuberant, open, enthusiastic, charming, Leo is very comfortable having her lover hug her, kiss her, and hold her close in public. She is equally comfortable observing other couples in love.

"I think we should get over our phobias and behave like the French in that regard."

"I do it all the time in a quick style. Big, fat kisses and quick strong hugs around the waist."

"I completely endorse public displays of affection, just not grossly physical ones."

 ### A Memory

"I went out to a blues bar alone and asked a sexy-looking guy to dance. He moved rhythmically in sync with my body. We talked between dances and laughed a lot. When the bar closed, we walked to his car and talked a little. I bent over to kiss him, he got so excited that we kissed and fondled each other very passionately in his car for ten minutes before driving to his place, where we had incredible sex. He sixty-nined with me. At one point he held my arms down, totally turning me on even more, and he made love to me in all the major positions. I screamed so loud [I] woke up his roommates."

Sexual Attitudes and Behaviors

HOW OFTEN DO YOU THINK ABOUT SEX AND HOW OFTEN PER WEEK DO YOU WANT TO HAVE SEX?

Leo enjoys frequent sex, perhaps five times per week. When she thinks about it, she wants to get to it.

"I'd say approximately six times."

"As much as my body allows it . . ."

"Every day would be wonderful, but three to four times a week would be okay."

"When in a relationship, as often as possible: a minimum of four or five times a week."

HOW LONG DO YOU LIKE TO SPEND HAVING SEX AND HOW MUCH OF THAT TIME IS FOREPLAY? DO YOU ENJOY QUICKIES?

When time permits, the Leo woman enjoys long sexual sessions. Generally 15 to 30 minutes is just right for foreplay. She also derives pleasure from the occasional quickie.

What matters most to Leo in any sexual experience is the feeling that she is appreciated by her partner and that her behavior thoroughly pleases him.

"I take it whenever I can get it, however long it takes. Yes, I enjoy an occasional quickie."

"I prefer to draw out pleasure. Quickies are okay if followed by slow sex."

"All day if time allows, otherwise 15 minutes will do."

"I like variety. Some days I'd like just foreplay and other days I'd like immediate sex."

WHAT TIME OF DAY DO YOU PREFER TO HAVE SEX?

Whenever her partner is appropriately adoring and regardless of the time on the clock, Leo enjoys having sex.

"Anytime, but I do enjoy nights better."

"Lovemaking is fine anytime we both agree on and want it."

HOW OFTEN PER WEEK DO YOU MASTURBATE?

Attention turns her on, so self-stimulation doesn't do much for Leo. She masturbates rarely, on average once or twice a week.

A Memory

"After a party my boyfriend and I were resting on a couch. We took our clothes off and necked lazily. Then he got up and knelt between my legs and began slowly caressing my thighs and between my legs, staring the whole time between my legs. He slowly leaned forward and began performing oral sex on me. I came immediately and wildly."

HOW LONG DO YOU WANT TO KNOW SOMEONE BEFORE GETTING SEXUAL?

Leo has an enthusiastic and spontaneous nature. If she feels a connection with a man, she is apt to get involved physically quite soon. In such cases it is because she truly believes there is the potential for a significant relationship to develop.

"The length of time depends on the other person and how we click with each other."

"It depends on the person. If there's good rapport, immediately is okay as long as precautions are used . . . condoms."

"It depends. For some the connection may be instant, for others it may be a month or two."

"As long as it takes me to be comfortable . . . there is no set time frame."

WHAT'S YOUR ATTITUDE TOWARD CASUAL SEX?

Without the potential for a relationship to develop and for a man to become more than just a sex partner, the Leo woman has no interest in engaging in intimacy.

"It's unsafe, but I'll resort to it after months of celibacy if I'm in the mood."

"I think that it is unsafe and I would prefer to be in a committed relationship."

"It is unsafe and unhealthy for your mind and body."

"For me there's no use in having a sexual relationship that is not going to be a meaningful one. I'd rather be single than have meaningless sex, which I find self-deprecating."

DO YOU BELIEVE IN MONOGAMY?

Leo is a Fixed Sign, meaning that once she makes up her mind about something she maintains that position. In other words, when she commits to someone she sticks to that commitment. Monogamy is a matter of trust and connection with her partner.

"If you are in love, you don't need to go out and cheat. It is respect."

"Yes. It deepens the pleasure to know that what we share is just for us."

"Yes. Why be in a relationship at all if one partner is not enough?"

DOES SEX HAVE A SPIRITUAL SIGNIFICANCE FOR YOU?

For Leo all the world's a stage, and sometimes sex is almost like a performance, one for which she appreciates applause. But sometimes, when she feels exceptionally close to her partner, sex is more than merely physical.

"Sex is sex, but I believe there is a difference between sex and lovemaking. When you love someone, you are involved emotionally and physically, whereas sex is physical only."

"Yes. When I am with my partner I feel like we are one . . . it makes me feel as though I am better connected to God."

Fantasies

"I'm out in the evening and a very good-looking stranger approaches me. There isn't much talking and we proceed to his house. He is dominant and I'm very submissive. Everything he does to me is more incredible than I've ever known. After a delicious night of raw sex I go home and never see him again."

ARE YOU COMFORTABLE INITIATING SEXUAL ACTIVITIES?

Self-confident and rarely self-conscious, Leo is completely comfortable initiating sex. There is no doubt, however, that her mate must be a strong and independent man who knows to take charge most of the time.

"I will so long as I'm not the only one to do it."

"I will initiate in the beginning, like kissing and stuff, but then he has to get to the real sexual stuff."

"Very, as long as he initiates more often than I do . . ."

HOW DO YOU COMMUNICATE TO YOUR PARTNER YOUR SEXUAL WANTS AND NEEDS?

Reflecting her nature as an active Fire Sign, during the sex act Leo will communicate more with gestures and body language than with words.

"It's fun to demonstrate what pleases me."

"I communicate through vocalizations: moans and groans."

"Both, but mostly with body language . . ."

"I communicate any way possible. It is very important that he knows what pleases me and that I know the same about him."

DO YOU THINK OF YOURSELF AS BEING IN THE MAINSTREAM SEXUALLY, MORE EXPERIMENTAL, OR OPEN TO ANYTHING?

Leo is open to anal sex, bondage, dominance and submission, and having sex in public places. She may be willing to use sexy underwear, wear costumes, shoes and boots, and incorporate food in her sex play. She will also enjoy trying out accoutrements such as dildos, vibrators, and anal toys. Overall her range of sexuality is fairly experimental.

She is the star in her sex fantasies, a superwoman figure whose mere presence, body, and voice drive her lover wild. In fact, a Leo woman wants to be worshiped.

A Fantasy

"My partner is so obsessed with me that he calls at all hours of the night and day. In fact, the sexual attraction is so intense that when I call him at his office he can't help touching himself as soon as he hears my voice. He gets so excited that he has to beat off before he can carry on a normal conversation. I make him speechless! Ha! And vice versa!"

HOW DO YOU DEMONSTRATE AFFECTION FOR YOUR PARTNER?

Showing her Fire Sign nature, Leo extends herself for her lover with her actions. Without waiting to be asked for her help, she volunteers to run errands for him; for example, she might pick up the dry cleaning or mail off packages.

"I cook, get his clothes ready for him every day, buy things for him that I think he will like, send him flowers, touch and kiss him frequently during the day."

"Give him cards and handmade items (photo collages, poems), buy clothes for him— including sexy undies for me or both of us."

"Give massages, fulfill fantasies, read books aloud, support dreams, hold hands, and give personal space."

The Five Senses

HOW IMPORTANT TO YOU IS THE SEXUAL ENVIRONMENT?

In keeping with her theatrical flair, with her sense of being the center of attention, Leo cares about the sexual environment. She strives to make the setting appealing not only to please her lover but also for her own gratification.

"I love to keep my own bedroom looking beautiful. It turns me on to show off my taste in décor, my artistic flair, and to be appreciated."

"If it is not a quickie, the environment has to be clean, comfortable, well scented, and preferably lit up with candles."

"I like to be comfortable if possible. If we are in a public place then the environment does not matter, the man matters."

"It's important. I can't get my libido moving well in filth, and I hate a messy place."

WHERE DO YOU LIKE TO HAVE SEX?

Given her concern about the setting, Leo prefers to have sex at home, primarily in the bedroom. The creative man might set up a comfortable array of bedding and pillows in the living room just for a fun alternative. Leo is seldom interested in much of anything more adventurous than that.

"Anywhere that is clean [and] where we can have privacy."

"Outdoors, under the trees and the stars. . ."

"Anyplace sheltered from view: a locked restroom, camping, outdoors in a secluded spot . . ."

A Fantasy

"*The complete romantic experience: soft lighting, bubble baths, and nice music, with him lovingly washing my hair and body, teasing the appropriate places, then him drying off, drying me off, then brushing out my hair. Through it all he is praising my beauty and sexiness, then he lays me on the bed and makes my every sexual wish come true 'til I orgasm at least twice. Then he comes with me the third time.*"

WHAT PUTS YOU IN THE MOOD FOR SEX?

Above all, that which is crucial to put Leo in the mood is making her feel that she is adored. Her lover may do this with a smile, a hug, or a word. It may be the way he looks at her, holds her a bit more forcefully than necessary for a kiss or, most effectively, the way he rubs her back.

"Knowing how much the other person desires me. Material things and activities are not that important to me."

"How the guy talks to me and touches me."

"My partner puts me in the mood. Watching him shave and a massage always make me want to make love."

"I am only stimulated by the person himself. If he does something cute or sweet, or just smiles at me, I get in the mood."

WHAT'S YOUR ATTITUDE TOWARD PORNOGRAPHY?

Leo is the star, the center of attention. How could she possibly get much pleasure out of watching some other woman engaging in sex? The only kind of pornography that Leo might enjoy is fetishistic, going into areas of sexuality that reflect only her fantasy life.

"Most of it bores me, entirely lacking in emotional content on any real level."

"No interest and would prefer that my partner have no interest."

HOW MUCH CUDDLING DO YOU ENJOY, ASIDE FROM SEX?

Considering her effusive nature and the way that she envelops people with her personality, hugging and other indications of regard are always welcome. Leo enjoys being close to her partner and appreciates loving touches without sex ensuing.

"When my husband and I were dating, we took every opportunity we could to be alone and make out. Sex was out of the question at that time, but it was pretty heavy petting."

"Cuddling is what turns me on most, having a guy hold me, giving me the time that I feel I deserve. Absolutely love cuddling; it is a requirement."

"Lots: hand holding, hugs, hair touching, feet stroking, love it."

 ### Fantasies

"*In one I am strung up and teased with sensual toys. In another I dominate, tying him down, pouring raspberry honey all over him and licking it off, or dripping hot wax on him while having sex, and then pushing him against the wall and demanding that he meet my needs.*"

"*He is standing. I go down on him. He wants me to stop. I don't. He yells with delight and shakes all over. I completely dominate him.*"

HOW TACTILE AND HOW ORAL ARE YOU?

Leo loves all aspects of sex. When her lover is appropriately appreciative of her, she proves to be an expressive lover both in terms of touch and oral aspects of sex. In return, she loves having her partner explore her body with his hands and mouth.

"I love running my hands over my partner and exploring his body and discovering the spots that make him moan the loudest. I am also very oral. I cannot picture sex without the oral aspect."

"On the oral scale of 1 to 10, I think I'm about a 12, except for anal stuff. That is only a turn-on if I'm really emotionally enthralled with the person."

"I am very oral. I enjoy making my lover gasp whatever way I can."

"I have done and enjoy all, except taking a load of cum in my mouth and rimming. I love kissing, licking, and having the same done to me."

"I love to kiss. I could kiss all day. I do not lick rectums. I would give the right man anything except suck his toes or lick his anus . . . but I like having my anus licked."

 ### A Memory

"*Nighttime, the room was dark. He was lying on his back and I was on top of him, with my legs between his and my chin on his chest. We were just looking at each other, listening to a Barry White CD, breathing together. I asked him to make love to me. He kissed me, rolled me over, and made love to me so slowly and beautifully while looking into my eyes and kissing me softly. It was the most beautiful and memorable experience.*"

WHAT SEX ACTS DO YOU LIKE MOST AND LEAST?

On a regular basis, Leo prefers to stick with mainstream sexual behaviors: kissing, fondling, oral sex, and intercourse. For longer sex play, when time allows, she broadens her perspective into the experimental range by enjoying dominance and submission and incorporating food. If a lover is skillful and sensitive, she also enjoys anal sex.

"Kissing, oral sex, intercourse, fondling breasts, and licking [the] body."

"Kissing, intercourse, oral sex performed on me if the man knows how, and being touched. I also like to have my toes sucked."

"I love to kiss and to have my breasts fondled during intercourse."

"I enjoy it all, but I've never had anal sex. With the right partner and moment, I'm willing to explore the possibilities."

AS A LOVER, WHAT'S YOUR BEST SKILL?

The Leo woman is strong and independent.

She loves to perform and she appreciates praise. This woman takes charge, gives her lover a great blow job, and is only satisfied when he acknowledges her mastery.

"I am very good at oral sex: the way I use my hands, mouth, and tongue together."

"The ability to give an amazing blow job using my mouth and hands . . ."

WHAT SMELLS AND TASTES ON YOUR PARTNER DO YOU ENJOY?

She enjoys the smell and taste of her partner's skin either just showered or with a hint of sweat. If she likes to mix food with sex, Leo prefers sweets like melted chocolate and raspberry jam.

"Mmmm . . . I like the smell of his skin, hair, mouth, genitals, underarms; love male musk; and the taste of his mouth, penis, fingertips, butt cheeks, neck."

"I like the way certain people smell naturally. I also like cologne. Some people taste good sweaty."

"I love the smell of his skin and breath and the taste of his kisses, his skin, his cum—all of it."

 A Memory

"It was the first time I inhaled his scent and touched his lips; it was the most erotic sensation. The room was so quiet we could hear our hearts beating. I knew I just couldn't wait much longer to give myself to him."

FOR SOME PEOPLE THE TASTE OF THEIR PARTNER'S CUM OR SECRETIONS IS UNPLEASANT. IF THAT'S TRUE FOR YOU, WHAT DO YOU DO ABOUT THE TASTE?

Leo loves to bring her lover to the point that he is writhing in ecstasy and she does this best with oral sex. The taste of his cum may not be her favorite thing, but most often she swallows willingly.

"It's slightly unpleasant, but making him feel good overrides any bad taste."

"I don't love it, but I don't hate it. I swallow or he cums externally; or I hop on before he orgasms."

"I let him cum in my mouth, but I let it ooze out and he is none the wiser."

DO YOU ENJOY WATCHING YOUR PARTNER DURING SEX AND ORGASM? DO YOU ENJOY BEING WATCHED?

Being a performer at heart and loving to be the center of attention and wanting to please, the Leo woman considers watching and being watched important turn-ons for her during sex and orgasm.

The Big "O"

HOW DO YOU REACH AN ORGASM AND HOW OFTEN?

Leo almost always reaches orgasm in every sexual encounter, mainly through oral sex and masturbation. She seldom climaxes during intercourse.

"Oral sex and masturbation . . . I have yet to reach it through intercourse."

"Never have through intercourse, every time through masturbation . . . Usually through oral sex if the man is patient and follows directions."

"Through oral sex, him masturbating me during, or before intercourse . . ."

WHAT'S YOUR FAVORITE POSITION?

Leo enjoys a variety of sexual positions, especially missionary style with the man on top. When it is time for her to cum, the Leo woman can achieve orgasm best in a position that allows for oral or digital stimulation of her clitoris.

SOME PEOPLE ARE CONCERNED ABOUT BRINGING THEIR PARTNER TO CLIMAX BEFORE HAVING AN ORGASM THEMSELVES. OTHERS STRIVE TO REACH ORGASM TOGETHER. WHICH IS TRUE FOR YOU?

Given the fact that Leo seldom climaxes during intercourse, it does not matter to her who reaches orgasm first. She does want to cum and she also wants her partner to be satisfied. The sequence is irrelevant.

"I don't orgasm during sex, so I usually orgasm first during oral, and then he orgasms after he enters me."

"Reaching orgasm together would be crazy. I would love that. I don't have to have an orgasm to be fulfilled with sex. I just need for the man to be satisfied . . . If he wants me to have an orgasm, all the better."

"Not too many men are capable after their own orgasm, so I strive to reach orgasm with him or climax before him."

 Memories

"My first sexual encounter with my boyfriend. We were in his room. He had lighted some incense and there was reggae music playing. He was gentle, but not too gentle. He was singing the songs to me during sex. It was very special."

"My best lover was great at cunnilingus and loved watching me cum. One night after he climaxed, he enjoyed seeing me climax so much he told me to pleasure myself again and again."

"An all-nighter with an almost complete stranger, in front of a fireplace, in the still of the night, with the sparks, heat, sound, and sight of the fire."

ARE YOU VOCAL DURING SEX?

Leo prefers body language to words during sexual encounters, and she is most likely to express her pleasure with moans.

"A little vocal; I am tender and romantic."

"Somewhat vocal; depends on the man. If I know that he likes for me to talk then I will talk."

"I can be quiet if the situation calls for it; otherwise, I am rather vocal."

AFTER SEX WHAT DO YOU LIKE TO DO?

After sex the Leo woman enjoys luxuriating in her lover's company, just lying back, taking it easy, cuddling. She may like a shower before going to sleep.

"Cuddle, stay in bed, share food, laugh together, good conversation, sleep."

"It depends on the time of day. At night, I like to sleep. In the morning I like to shower. Midday, I like to lie around and gear up to do it again."

"Hold hands in the silent dark, enjoying the feeling in body and mind."

The Leo Man in His Own Words

A Memory

"The first time my wife and I had sex before we were married. She came over to my apartment for dinner. We ate by candlelight, [with] soft music in the background. After dinner we talked, held hands, [and] began kissing and caressing each other. In no time we were lying on the couch. She was on top of me, her skirt around her waist and her blouse and bra undone. Her nipples were red and distended, and we were both panting. We went into my bedroom. I gently pushed her onto the bed, lay down beside her, [and kissed] her mouth. I ran my tongue down her body to her pubic hair. She had the fullest blonde bush I'd ever seen. The smell coming from between her legs was driving me wild. I licked and sucked for a few minutes and then asked her to straddle my head and hold onto the headboard. I caressed her breasts: pulled, twisted, and pinched her nipples while licking and sucking her. She reached orgasm within minutes, wanted to stop, but I held her hips and asked her to relax. I continued to lick and suck and she came again."

Attraction and Dating a Leo

WHAT ATTRACTS YOU TO SOMEONE?

Leo is a dynamic Sign and is, therefore, first attracted by a woman's personality. Beauty and body proportions are important, but second to who the woman is inside.

"I am attracted to intelligent, energetic, dynamic women with definite ideas about things. Whether I agree or not is irrelevant."

"Honor thy body, the temple for the mind, breasts, butt, teeth, hair, facial glow, energy, smile, looks, interests."

"I look for a woman who is easy to get along with, warm, friendly, and personable. Physical characteristics are secondary."

WHAT MIGHT TURN YOU OFF?

Leo is self-confident, perhaps to the level of being a tad egotistical. Maybe there is a little projection involved, but he is turned off by a woman who is arrogant. He is also very independent and doesn't like women who are weak or clingy.

"What turns me off is arrogance, rudeness, pushiness, wanting to always be right, then finally rigidity."

"Being selfish, insensitive, smoking, being too clingy, overbearing, [and] always needing to be right."

"Turnoffs include stupidity, excessive weight, [and] dependency."

WHAT DO YOU ENJOY DOING ON A DATE?

Leo is a performer and loves to be entertained. He enjoys going out, not idly driving around, but rather attending events such as a museum, the theater, or a concert. He also loves movies and prefers seeing them on the big screen.

"Comedy shows, dinner and drinks, movies, sometimes walks in the park are good too, as well as various sightseeing activities."

"Museums, movies, theater, food, sightseeing . . ."

"I love catching a live band or a theater presentation. I also enjoy taking long walks around the city, window shopping, café cruising, and the occasional pint at the local tavern."

A Fantasy

"Most of my fantasies involve bondage. My partner is standing in the middle of the room wearing only a pair of black tights. I slip a remote-controlled vibrator into her tights and nestle it in between [the folds of] her labia. I pull her tights back up and help her to get into a corset. I put a belt around her cinched waist with leather cuffs dangling on a short chain behind her back. I apply the cuffs to her wrists and lock them with small, brass padlocks. A pair of slender ropes hangs from her cuffs to her ankles. I bring these ropes up between her legs to trap the vibrator in place and tie them to the front of her belt. Now, any movement of her hands will tug on the ropes. Next I cuff her ankles together with more leather straps and have her kneel on the floor in front of a chair. Last I blindfold her and ball gag her, and then sit in the chair [and tease] her with my touch and the vibrator for a while. Then I carry her to the bed, untie the crotch rope, cut a hole in her tights, and fuck her into bliss."

ARE YOU FLIRTATIOUS?

Leo is a flirt, overtly so and with charm. He is not trying to manipulate and, in fact, he does not expect to be taken seriously. To the Leo man, flirting is a fun part of almost any interaction with a woman.

"Too much; I have a difficult time staying away from flirtatious conversation."

"I am friendly and open, and I think that that sometimes comes off as flirtatious."

ARE YOU JEALOUS?

Not often. Leo is far too self-confident to be jealous, perhaps in part because he has a healthy opinion of himself. He expects that any woman who is with him will be proud to bask in his light. He is equally appreciative of his partner.

"I am not usually jealous and, when I am, I deal with it by finding someone else to talk to."

"I'd say I have occasional flashes that quickly succumb to common sense."

"I have never been a jealous person but I caught myself acting jealous recently. It was a very specific circumstance, but [it] showed me I could have such feelings."

HOW DO YOU FEEL ABOUT PUBLIC DISPLAYS OF AFFECTION?

A little public display of affection goes a long way. Even though Leo is a generally outgoing Sign, he doesn't like seeing or participating in displays that go much beyond being considerate and attentive to his partner.

"I hold my partner's hand, put my arms around her waist or shoulder, or kiss her."

"I stand close to her and observe her, and let everyone know I am with her and only with her."

A Memory

"The other night when I arrived at my girl's house, she came to the door wearing a skirt, stockings with garters, big black boots, and a satiny smooth blouse. The lights in the house were low and there were candles lit all around the room. As I drew near, I smelled the sweet scent of her hair and buried my face in the nape of her neck and kissed it softly. She closed the door behind me and told me to lie on the floor, which I did. She removed my shirt and open mouth kissed my nipples, flicking the rings with the tip of her tongue.

"She removed my shoes, socks, slowly [peeled] away my pants and straddled me. I reached up to remove her blouse but she said, 'Uh uh.' I touched her breasts and her nipples came to full attention, and she slipped herself onto me. She rubbed my chest and dragged her nails across it as she was grinding back and forth and up and down on me. We rolled over into various positions: her on top, me on top, me kneeling with her straddling my lap, doggie style, scissors style. The delicate scent of her perspiration filled the room. I'm sure that she smelled mine as well. She asked me to cum and we synchronized our rhythms. We became louder and louder until we climaxed nearly in unison."

Sexual Attitudes and Behaviors

HOW OFTEN DO YOU THINK ABOUT SEX? HOW OFTEN PER WEEK DO YOU WANT TO HAVE SEX?

Leo's sunny disposition draws women to him with ease. A woman with a friendly smile and charming personality is all that it takes to get him thinking about getting it on. Of course, if he has a partner, his thoughts focus on her. He enjoys having sex about three or four times per week.

"Unless there is something especially heavy on my mind, I think about sex several times daily."

HOW LONG DO YOU LIKE TO SPEND HAVING SEX AND HOW MUCH OF THAT TIME IS FOREPLAY? DO YOU ENJOY QUICKIES?

He enjoys spending from 20 minutes to an hour during a sexual encounter with foreplay encompassing about one-half that time. Leo is an active Fire Sign who does most things fairly quickly and, as a result, quickies are fine too.

"Forty-five minutes to hours, and yes, I like quickies; foreplay, as long as my partner wants it."

"I enjoy all kinds of sex."

"[I] like to spend as much time as I can having sex. Yes, I do enjoy quickies, but not nearly as much."

"Yes, quickies are great but sometimes time is needed to enjoy sex fully."

WHAT TIME OF DAY DO YOU PREFER TO HAVE SEX?

Leo is something of a night owl, and while he enjoys sex at any time of day and night, he has some preference for nighttime encounters.

"Anytime, from before I go to sleep to the first thing when I wake up and any time in between."

HOW OFTEN PER WEEK DO YOU MASTURBATE?

The Leo man masturbates on average twice a week.

 A Memory

"I took her clothes off and tied her spread eagle to the bed. Using various toys I played with her until she came with me inside her. Then staying inside her, I became erect again and brought her to orgasm again. I repeated this until she passed out from cumming so hard and so many times."

HOW LONG DO YOU WANT TO KNOW SOMEONE BEFORE GETTING SEXUAL?

Leo would prefer a relationship to become sexual within a few weeks, but he is not pushy and takes his lead from his partner.

"Personally, I would like to know a woman for three to four weeks."

"At least a couple to a few weeks . . ."

"Once I know she is free of AIDS and STDs, and I am turned on by her signals."

"A while, until I know they are cool and don't have any diseases."

WHAT'S YOUR ATTITUDE TOWARD CASUAL SEX?

Leo is not judgmental, but sex without some sort of relationship in place doesn't suit him.

"It is okay for others. I would rather know the person before getting involved."

"It's just not my cup of tea. I see sex as just part of a relationship, but I don't think less of others who are more casual about it."

"Anonymous sex is not good for me, psychically or physically."

"There's nothing wrong about it, but it's not for me."

A Fantasy

"I would love to see my wife undress in front of a complete stranger. I envision her stripped down to just a pair of high heels, and then I let him fondle her breasts and ass. In another fantasy, I watch my wife have sex with at least two other men."

DO YOU BELIEVE IN MONOGAMY?

Leo is a fundamentally honorable Sign. When he makes a commitment to love, honor, and cherish, he strives to keep his word. He admits that monogamy isn't easy, but he does believe in it.

"Yes and no. I believe in marriage, but [I] also believe that threesomes would add to our relationship."

"I think it is difficult to be in a loving relationship without monogamy for jealousy reasons. But I have a very difficult time settling on one person."

"Sure, I would rather have monogamy overall."

"Ideally yes, [though] exceptions abound."

"I believe it is possible, but I have not managed to find that one yet."

DOES SEX HAVE A SPIRITUAL SIGNIFICANCE FOR YOU?

Leo is, at heart, a very responsible man who does not take relationships lightly. As such, he does not often become involved sexually without some sense of emotional tie. When the feelings are deepest, sex has a spiritual connotation for Leo that is almost sacred.

"Yes, it puts me in touch with the real me and the real person in my partner."

"Yes, sharing emotions with another in a sexual way when truly in love. In a deeper sense, it's the unity of two coming together as one."

"Yes, I believe that sex is sacred and private. The act is creating sacred grounds."

ARE YOU COMFORTABLE INITIATING SEXUAL ACTIVITIES?

Leo is a self-confident man and quite at ease initiating sexual activities, though he doesn't rush into this aspect of a relationship.

HOW DO YOU COMMUNICATE TO YOUR PARTNER YOUR SEXUAL WANTS AND NEEDS?

Leo isn't shy. He is comfortable being in control, as he wants to please his partner. A woman will easily understand how to satisfy him because he'll make his desires known through words, gestures, and sounds of contentment.

"I think it is important to talk about sex before, during, or after. And if you aren't laughing, you aren't having fun."

"Usually by controlling her hands to show her how and where I like to be touched . . ."

DO YOU THINK OF YOURSELF AS BEING IN THE MAINSTREAM SEXUALLY, MORE EXPERIMENTAL, OR OPEN TO ANYTHING?

Leo's sexual practices extend from the mainstream to the experimental and may include anal sex, some light dominance and submission, and hot wax. He enjoys incorporating food and costumes in his sex play and is turned on by sexy underwear, shoes, and boots. Given that he is by nature a performer, Leo is likely to try sex in public places.

In his fantasies, Leo often envisions multiple partners and scenes in which he observes and directs as his partner engages in sex with other men.

A Fantasy

"I fantasize about women being tied up and fucked to the point of exhaustion. Sometimes I am watching the scene. At other times, I am a participant. I fantasize about spending an entire day devoted to the exploration of each other and about sex with two partners."

HOW DO YOU DEMONSTRATE AFFECTION FOR YOUR PARTNER?

Leo sees himself as the traditional gentleman. He wants a woman to let him open the door for her, and on a date he usually prefers to pick up the tab. On occasion, Leo will allow his partner to treat him, but preferably by preparing him a meal at her place rather than by her paying for dinner at a restaurant. He is romantic and sends his partner flowers and cards.

"I say 'please' and 'thank you.' I open and close doors for her. I touch her and kiss her gently in passing. I call her at work to see how her day is going."

"I send flowers, cards; do the dishes; open doors for her; and buy tampons at the store."

The Five Senses

HOW IMPORTANT TO YOU IS THE SEXUAL ENVIRONMENT?

For the most part, the setting is not of overriding concern for Leo. His own place may be a mess, but when he comes to a woman's home, he prefers that it be at least somewhat orderly. Cleanliness and soft lighting clearly add to his sexual pleasure.

"Ideally, I would like the environment to be clean, neat, smell good, with few if any distractions such as loud noises, and no people around to interrupt us."

"It should always be clean, softly lighted, and nicely decorated."

WHERE DO YOU LIKE TO HAVE SEX?

Leo is not above taking chances and he loves excitement, but he prefers privacy and comfort. Any place where those criteria can be met is fine for sex. Otherwise, the bedroom is Leo's preferred place to be romantic.

"At home as well as in airplanes, on boats, and in the office. . ."

"Anywhere that is legally permissible."

"At home, but in all the rooms at one time or another . . ."

 A Fantasy

"*Most of my fantasies are pretty typical, male dominant fantasies . . . several men with one woman, anal pounding, and deep throat. It doesn't get more typical than that.*"

WHAT PUTS YOU IN THE MOOD FOR SEX?

Leo is an action Sign. Physical acts—movement and touch—are his primary stimuli. All his lover needs to do is hold his hand, hug him, rub his shoulders, or especially massage his back and he will want her.

"Holding hands and touching, her sexy lingerie. I especially get excited when she is wearing nylons and a garter belt."

"Sensually eating foods, smell of a showered women, sexual body language, foreplay."

"I am always in the mood as long as I am with someone I am attracted to. Cuddling or any kind of physical contact gets me aroused."

WHAT'S YOUR ATTITUDE TOWARD PORNOGRAPHY?

Leo likes some pornography, but he gets bored with a steady diet of the all-too-familiar scenes and cum shots. Instead, he prefers films that are more erotic in nature.

"If a movie has a nude scene in it, I enjoy it; but if it is straight porn, no interest."

"It is often fun and relatively harmless."

"I think porn can be fun and invigorating, especially when enjoying it with a partner as a way to set a frisky fun mood, but I am picky about it."

HOW MUCH CUDDLING DO YOU ENJOY, ASIDE FROM SEX?

Cuddling is great in the right place and at the right time. Leo, out in public, wants attention from the group. That is one time when he would not want his lover holding on too closely. In other words, he loves cuddling but he does not like to feel smothered.

"I hold and protect her, make her feel needed and safe."

"I really enjoy cuddling, holding hands, gentle touching, soft caresses."

"I love it when watching a movie and maybe while riding in the car."

Fantasies

"I would live to have sex with two women at the same time, one sitting on my face, one sitting on my penis, [and] then the two women are kissing each other and we all climax together."

"I like to think of myself as the king of the world and my fantasy is to sit on my throne and have fifty or sixty whores run a dick sucking marathon on me."

HOW TACTILE AND HOW ORAL ARE YOU?

Leo is a passionate lover who takes pride in thrilling his partner. He is very tactile and enjoys exploring her body with his hands.

"Women get wet from my touch."

"I love to explore her whole body with my hands."

"Physical exploration is essential to my love-making."

He also loves kissing, performing cunnilingus, and receiving oral sex.

"I have an oral fixation, which is why I spend two-thirds of sex time in foreplay."

"I am able to get women to [achieve] many orgasms from cunnilingus. I am very good at this: drives women wild, their bodies shake. I could do it all day and night."

"I am very oral. I enjoy giving my partner oral sex as much as she can handle."

WHAT SEX ACTS DO YOU LIKE MOST AND LEAST?

His favorite sex acts include just about everything from kissing and cuddling through intercourse and oral sex. For some Leos, anal sex is especially satisfying.

"I love soft touches, caresses, licking and sucking the breasts, vagina—especially the lips and clitoris. Anal sex is fantastic."

"I love receiving and giving oral sex, and mutual masturbation. Something that really turns me off is a tongue inside the ear."

"I like it all: oral, intercourse, mutual masturbation, exploring each other's body, using strap-ons."

There is little the Leo man doesn't like when it comes to the mainstream range of sex acts.

"I don't like to worry about birth control, be rushed, or interrupted situations."

AS A LOVER, WHAT'S YOUR BEST SKILL?

Leo has a lot of pride in his basic nature. He sees himself as a very responsible man, and when he is involved sexually, this sense of responsibility extends to pleasing his partner. He does this with the touch of his tongue and the use of his hands.

"Hands and tongue are tools [for making] my partner happy."

"My massage ability; and my last serious relationship taught me much about making my partner cum with my tongue."

"My touch, hands, conversation, creating a sacred place, tongue, then doggie style . . ."

"Touch[ing] the lip with hand, fondling her breasts with my tongue, and kiss[ing] her body."

A Fantasy

"A very attractive masseuse massages my arms, chest, legs, and finally slides her hand down to my cock. I stroke her inner thighs, kiss and lick her nipples. She strokes herself, and takes me in her other hand.

She climbs on top straddling my cock, rubbing herself on it, moving her breasts within reach of my tongue. We're sweating, our skin a little slick. Smells intensify, time slows, and she lifts my cock and I slide into her. Her muscles are tight and firm. I taste salt on her nipples as I lick them, then she sits up again and I can take a breast in each hand. She uses her hands to stroke my belly. We're getting close. My hips push into her and she sits down firmly, her thighs tight around me. We stare at each other as one of her hands moves to her clit and begins stroking. Her eyes shine, then she shudders as I come inside . . . long, deep breaths and strokes . . . intensity . . . striving to get further inside and finally touching her cervix."

WHAT SMELLS AND TASTES ON YOUR PARTNER DO YOU ENJOY?

Leo relishes all senses during sex. He watches, he listens, he smells, and he loves to taste. If he enjoys mixing food with sex play, he prefers sweets flavors. Bring on the whipped cream, honey, or a bit of chocolate. It could get messy; it will get exciting.

"The most enjoyable smell is her vagina. If I could bottle that aroma, I could make a million dollars. I also love the taste of her vagina before, during, and after we have both reached orgasm."

"I thoroughly enjoy the smell and taste of her vagina when she is fully excited."

"I play with syrups, whipped cream, and honey sometimes."

FOR SOME PEOPLE THE TASTE OF THEIR PARTNER'S CUM OR SECRETIONS IS UNPLEASANT. IF THAT'S TRUE FOR YOU, WHAT DO YOU DO ABOUT THE TASTE?

Given that Leo loves to taste everything, his partner's secretions are not a problem for him.

DO YOU ENJOY WATCHING YOUR PARTNER DURING SEX AND ORGASM? DO YOU ENJOY BEING WATCHED?

For a man who can be a performer in public, who enjoys center stage so often, Leo prefers the behind-the-scenes role in bed. As the director, he gets to watch; however, he may not enjoy being watched anywhere near as much.

"I don't really know about having my lover watch me; probably not as much as I like watching her."

The Big "O"

HOW DO YOU REACH AN ORGASM AND HOW OFTEN?

Leo has no trouble climaxing, but he likes to be in control, so intercourse works better for him than oral sex.

"Most often through intercourse, the rest of the time through anal or oral, and sometimes through mutual masturbation . . ."

"What works for me is a combination of intercourse, some oral sex, and masturbation—though least during oral sex."

WHAT'S YOUR FAVORITE POSITION?

He prefers to achieve orgasm during intercourse. Leo enjoys any position that allows him deep penetration, usually being on top of his lover and often in the doggie style.

"I blindfolded my wife, ran my hands over all parts of her body, and then took her from behind doggie style. It was a complete turn-on."

"I reach orgasm easily when my partner lies on her side and pulls one leg up toward her chest. I straddle her bottom leg, insert my penis, and reach orgasm within minutes. The other position I enjoy is doggie style, but it takes a lot longer for me to reach orgasm that way."

"Doggie style is my favorite, but it depends on the person. I achieve orgasm in many different positions."

"I have my most powerful orgasms when she is on her back with her legs in the air together on one of my shoulders and I am kneeling."

SOME PEOPLE ARE CONCERNED ABOUT BRINGING THEIR PARTNER TO CLIMAX BEFORE HAVING AN ORGASM THEMSELVES. OTHERS STRIVE TO REACH ORGASM TOGETHER. WHICH IS TRUE FOR YOU?

The Leo man wants to bring his partner off—perhaps more than once—before cumming himself.

"I have an orgasm fetish. It turns me on to see her cum."

"I want my partner to experience two or three orgasms before I have mine. I try to make this happen as often as possible."

"Being able to give someone else an orgasm is a point of pride for me. I get nervous, however, if I suspect that they are faking."

ARE YOU VOCAL DURING SEX?

Leo is not overly vocal during the sex act itself, but much more so as he reaches climax.

"I'm fairly vocal, but my body does most of the talking."

AFTER SEX WHAT DO YOU LIKE TO DO?

After sex what matters most to the Leo man is sharing quiet time with his partner.

"Shower together, cuddle, stay in bed, have dinner cooked for me or share a meal, laugh together, sleep."

"Cuddle, hold hands; I clean her by licking and sucking her."

"Sleep; I am usually exhausted."

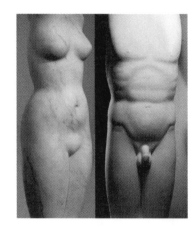

VIRGO

August 23–September 22

THE VIRGIN

Earth Sign Virgo is straightforward, a devoted friend, and works hard at everything including sexually fulfilling a partner. Ruler of the abdomen and bowels, health and hygiene, in bed Virgo prefers an orderly approach. Start at A, progress through B and C and you wind up at "O."

She says: "How vocal I am during sex depends . . . a little if it's bad, a lot if it's good."

He says: "I love the taste of her neck, her vagina, her skin in general."

"Cleanliness is next to Godliness."
—Proverb

The Virgo Woman in Her Own Words

A Memory

"In a freshly cleaned house, we showered and washed each other, [and] then he carried me to the bed. There were scented candles going, adding enough light to see and be flattering. There were flowers in a vase placed where I could look at them from the bed. He smelled so fresh and his skin was soft. We rubbed lotion on each other. Then we made love. Very soft, very romantic."

Attraction and Dating a Virgo

WHAT ATTRACTS YOU TO SOMEONE?

Virgo is very particular. Penis size does matter: too big may be a problem, too small will disappoint.

"What attracts me is confidence and a dominant attitude. Physique counts: I hate flabby men. His hands must be sensitive in sex."

"First a man's smile, eyes, looks, energy, intelligence, warmth, humor. Physical attributes important to me, height, not too skinny, not bald, penis size not tiny."

"Eyes, definitely, overall outward appearance, and the way he dresses. Penis size is important to me."

WHAT MIGHT TURN YOU OFF?

Virgo looks so impeccably neat, as though she could repel lint, and expects the same from her man. Inattention to hygiene will always turn her away.

"No sense of humor, bad hygiene, no goals in life, always complaining, obesity."

"Poor choice [in] clothing, bad teeth or breath, sloppiness or messiness, poor hygiene (I am a Virgo, after all) . . ."

"I like a man who is squeaky clean—good and clean enough to eat—so bad breath, not being well-groomed, or a man who is unshaved all repel me."

WHAT DO YOU ENJOY DOING ON A DATE?

Most often the Virgo woman appreciates quiet time with her partner. On occasion she enjoys hiking, sailing, and attending county fairs. She also likes to go to bookstores, art galleries, and antique shops.

"Something different, like a carnival or a zoo; something other than a movie, which is so boring; a chance to talk and laugh, get to know each other, even if it's just driving."

"Ice skating, dinner, concert, theater, museum, movies, maybe a boat ride, sit and have coffee, walk."

"Dinner and dancing, then going parking . . . Sex in the car or giving head on the highway."

"Anything out of the ordinary is better, like 4-wheeler mudding, but a movie is okay."

A Memory

"A party at a high rise. We went up several floors in the service elevator. My boyfriend hit the stop button, pushed me against the wall, pulled my skirt up, hoisted me to his waist, and shoved his extremely hard cock into me. He fucked me hard, grinding

against my clit. I came almost immediately. He kept his hand over my mouth to keep me from screaming. He didn't cum, but [then he] took me up to the roof, bent me over the railing, and fucked me from behind for a good hour. He made me cum over and over before cumming himself."

ARE YOU FLIRTATIOUS?

Surprisingly, the reputed "Virgin" is a flirt. She may be coy about it, but she turns on the charm with ease almost anywhere and almost anytime.

"Very flirtatious. I am married but not dead. I can read the menu; I just can't eat off it."

"Yes, I frequently make sexual jokes and comments with people who respond positively to me."

"I like to 'car flirt' with cute guys driving next to me."

"I know when not to be or when enough is enough."

ARE YOU JEALOUS?

Virgo is an analytical Sign. Within her relationships, she is attentive and aware of what is going on. She is more likely to be angry than jealous if she thinks her man is paying inadequate attention to her or too much attention to some other woman.

"A little, but not to the point of being psycho . . . I like my possessions and am cautious about who I allow to play with them."

"I couldn't be in a relationship with someone who would put me in the position of having to act jealous. It is a very undignified feeling and behavior."

HOW DO YOU FEEL ABOUT PUBLIC DISPLAYS OF AFFECTION?

Subtle public displays of affection are always fine to Virgo. Sometimes even going a bit beyond that is also pleasurable.

"I'm very open to it: good for me and the public. I think people enjoy seeing it. I know I do. It is exciting and a turn-on for me."

"I love showing public affection. I want the world to see how much he means to me."

"Less is more. Too much is just gross. I can't stand having a man all over me in public."

"I think they are great, as long as they are measured. Holding hands is okay, but not getting too physical."

Sexual Attitudes and Behaviors

HOW OFTEN DO YOU THINK ABOUT SEX AND HOW OFTEN PER WEEK DO YOU WANT TO HAVE SEX?

The Virgo woman may not think about sex every day, but she'd like to make love daily. She'll settle for three or four times per week.

"I like sex as often as possible, but I don't want to climax every time. I enjoy being desired sexually."

"Always . . . I am not kidding."

HOW LONG DO YOU LIKE TO SPEND HAVING SEX AND HOW MUCH OF THAT TIME IS FOREPLAY? DO YOU ENJOY QUICKIES?

Foreplay doesn't have to be lengthy, just long enough to get her very turned on. She is expressive and so responsive that she expects her partner to know when it is time to move from the preliminary to the main event. Quickies suit her fine occasionally but she prefers taking her time.

"What is most important to me is how much time is available. Quickies are okay, but longer [sessions with] more foreplay are better."

"Any amount of time: quickies or long sessions. I enjoy the closeness, intimacy, being wanted by a man, quickie or not. As to foreplay, a half hour would be great, but 10 to 15 minutes will suffice."

"Thirty minutes or so depending on feelings at the time and, yes, quickies can be good fun."

Fantasies

"*A man who really loves me approaches me with loving kindness, talks to me, appreciates me verbally, and handles me. I am fully comfortable with him. We find a quiet bedroom for foreplay and intercourse. We live together forever.*"

"*Sex with men I don't know, with more than one man, with other women, being watched during sex or masturbation, and having that person be turned on. My fantasies often feature receiving oral sex rather than intercourse.*"

WHAT TIME OF DAY DO YOU PREFER TO HAVE SEX?

She'll make herself available at any time. "I'll take it whenever I can get it," she says, but she really does have her preferences. As far as sex in the morning, Virgo prefers coffee first please. If at night, before she gets too tired.

"Not first thing in the morning and not too late at night when I'd rather be sleeping."

"As long as I am awake . . ."

HOW OFTEN PER WEEK DO YOU MASTURBATE?

She believes that sex is good for her health so if she has no lover, she takes care of herself. Virgo usually masturbates about three times a week.

HOW LONG DO YOU WANT TO KNOW SOMEONE BEFORE GETTING SEXUAL?

Her answer almost always begins with, "It depends." The determining factor in Virgo's mind is developing some sense of emotional closeness. What's tricky is that she will want some indication from a potential lover that he's interested in her before signaling that she has such an interest herself.

"It depends on how long it takes for us to be in love. I don't like being sexual unless there is love."

"It depends on the person and how comfortable I feel with him."

"That depends on the kind of relationship I want with a man."

A Memory

"*Candles lit in a white room. A king-size bed. The blinds are up and it's not yet dark. We play some gentle music and get out the plastic bed cover and sundae ingredients. We take turns being a sundae and scream while getting licked free of the most delectable sweets.*"

WHAT'S YOUR ATTITUDE TOWARD CASUAL SEX?

Casual sex isn't appealing to Virgo, mainly because this Sign has a streak of hypochondria and she is afraid of contracting a sexually transmitted disease.

"It's unwise to have multiple partners, for physical and emotional reasons."

"It is unsafe and leaves you feeling empty."

"I am not into casual sex. I have to have some feelings for a man before I can be intimate."

DO YOU BELIEVE IN MONOGAMY?

Absolutely. Being health conscious, as well as a woman who takes a little while before allowing a relationship to become intimate, one lover at a time is it for Virgo.

"I can't bring myself to share."

"Yes, I think in order to fulfill one's wildest fantasies, there can only be one lover."

"I give and expect monogamy in a committed relationship."

DOES SEX HAVE A SPIRITUAL SIGNIFICANCE FOR YOU?

Virgo regards the intimacy of sex as extremely important and fulfilling, good for one's health and to be engaged in regularly. The sexual experience rises to the level of spirituality.

"I wouldn't call it spiritual, but I believe it is very special between two people who care deeply about each other."

"Yes, I feel it brings us together in a way that no other action can. It unites us as one."

"I think that sex is an act of sharing your soul, a sacred energy exchange that shouldn't be abused or taken too lightly."

ARE YOU COMFORTABLE INITIATING SEXUAL ACTIVITIES?

With her analytical nature and her ability to understand her partner, Virgo knows when the topic is appropriate. Nevertheless, she is more likely to signal her willingness, and then wait for the man to take the initiative.

A Memory

"*At our beach house in the spa, mid-afternoon, blue sky, sun beating down, birds chirping, and the smell of fresh[ly] mowed grass. We started kissing, stripped off our clothes. He was caressing my body and sucking on my nipples, driving me crazy. He turned off all but two jets and positioned me so that one was on my clit and one was on my anus. It felt like he was in me both ways at the same time. He turned the pressure up to maximum. I exploded.*"

HOW DO YOU COMMUNICATE TO YOUR PARTNER YOUR SEXUAL WANTS AND NEEDS?

Let's face it; Virgo wants to get it right. She may be a tad reticent initially but in short order, she will be specific, telling her lover how to please her, letting him know what's working and what isn't.

"Both. I will say it first and if that doesn't work, I will move his hands where I want them, then moan to let him know that that is right."

"I used to do to my partner what I wanted him to do to me, thinking that he would pick up the hint. I have learned to be specific with words to get what I need."

"I use words most of the time. My partner and I have great communication. We always check in with each other about likes, dislikes, and trying new things."

DO YOU THINK OF YOURSELF AS BEING IN THE MAINSTREAM SEXUALLY, MORE EXPERIMENTAL, OR OPEN TO ANYTHING?

The traditional Virgo, the Virgin, is mainstream in her range of sexuality, which includes fondling, oral sex, and intercourse. She likes long sex and is very physical, and goes out of her way to satisfy her partner. But in addition to the Virgin, the ancient symbol for Virgo was the Nymphet, lovely and highly sexual.

While both types of Virgo women are very proper in public, the Nymph is a tigress in motion and sound effects, and all in the privacy of the bedroom. This Virgo wants a man who is well endowed. She'll enjoy bringing him off through oral sex and then work like hell to get him ready for a second round.

This Virgo's range of sexual behaviors goes from just beyond vanilla sex all the way to kinky. She may be willing to try bondage, dominance and submission, role-playing, wearing costumes and boots, using hot wax, incorporating food, being spanked, and being shaved. For sex toys she'll try vibrators, dildos, handcuffs, paddles, and anal beads.

"My favorite summer treat [is] filling a condom with water and freezing it. The cold of that and the warmth of his penis are great."

"I like to use cucumbers and hand-carved dildos."

Virgo's fantasies include having multiple partners, voyeurism, and elements of dominance and submission.

A Fantasy

"*A wonderful dinner in a candlelit room with a hooded man dressed in leather. Dinner finished, he grabs a handful of my hair and tells me that the training will commence now. A night on my knees, in a cage, hanging, being flogged and tortured— followed by his wonderful raping of my bound and gagged body. Afterward, he cradles me and looks deeply into my eyes and tells me how happy he has been with everything."*

HOW DO YOU DEMONSTRATE AFFECTION FOR YOUR PARTNER?

Virgo shows her affection primarily with attentiveness, by extending herself for her lover. She strives to maintain an impeccable home and to serve tasty, well-balanced meals. Her intention is to make him feel comfortable, relaxed, and attended to.

"Soft kisses, cooking, massage, compliments, even doing things I don't want to [do in order to] accommodate him."

"When my husband comes home from work, I make him a gourmet dinner and wait on him hand and foot. I enjoy making him happy. I derive great pleasure from this."

"Making sure that he is taken care of in any way and listening to him is important."

The Five Senses

HOW IMPORTANT TO YOU IS THE SEXUAL ENVIRONMENT?

Virgo says she isn't overly fussy about the setting for sex, but then she goes on to list the elements that do matter. As it turns out, the environment matters quite a bit, especially that it be clean and warm.

"I don't care too much about the setting for sex but clean, crisp, new sheets are a decided turn-on."

"I don't care about the décor but if it's not clean, that's a deal breaker."

"It's not too important, once you are at ease with a person. Candlelight preferred, temperature comfortable and, of course, a clean environment."

 Memories

"It was about 95 degrees and we were outside on a blanket. It was so hot, from both the sex and the

weather, that we were completely drenched in sweat and were licking it off each other's [bodies] and rubbing our sweaty bodies together."

"Nighttime, full moon, swimming pool, candles. [We] started out skinny dipping. Night insects, aggressiveness, our own talking in whispers and being watched by some high school boys."

"Outside on the grass, under the stars on a warm summer's eve, we started kissing and fondling each other. After a half hour I couldn't take it anymore and I had to have him in me."

WHERE DO YOU LIKE TO HAVE SEX?

Her favorite place for sex is the bedroom, but Virgo says she's open to making love anyplace that meets her criteria. So, provide a clean and comfortable place at the beach or in a car and she'll say okay.

"Anywhere that is not physically uncomfortable and [is] fairly private."

"Bedroom mostly, but the other parts of the house are fair game . . . Also the woods on a nice summer day or night."

"Bedroom, shower, kitchen, and out on the deck."

WHAT PUTS YOU IN THE MOOD FOR SEX?

Touch is the short answer. Virgo wants all of her senses and her entire body involved in setting her mood for sex. Going straight at her erogenous zones may be okay for the occasional quickie, but not for getting her all worked up for a night of wonderful sex. That requires more care, appreciation of the curve of her thigh, the spot at the base of her neck, the cleft in her chin, or the inside of her elbow.

"Seeing my husband toweling off after a shower does it every time. He still turns me on like a light switch."

"Seeing sex in movies, thinking of sex, bathing, talking dirty, using a vibrator."

"I love it when we are both clean and fresh smelling, music, fresh sheets, pretty scenes like a vase of flowers next to the bed, or a good-smelling candle."

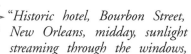

A Memory

"Historic hotel, Bourbon Street, New Orleans, midday, sunlight streaming through the windows, comfy bed with big pillows, quiet, smells of clean laundry. We'd just bought a vibrator system for couples. WOW! My partner used it and oral sex to keep me on the edge of climax for so long [that] my lower abdominal muscles ached the next day. Usually our sex is mostly about him. This day it was all about me and he indulged me very well."

WHAT'S YOUR ATTITUDE TOWARD PORNOGRAPHY?

Virgo likes some pornography. She admits that it's a turn-on but she also finds it occasionally unpleasant. The pornographic films she prefers have something of a story line, maybe some romance—or at least some intrigue. They are more than sex scenes and cum shots.

"It can be hot, but it can also be incredibly tawdry and/or repulsive. It depends on what is done and how it is done."

"I like to watch it, but on the other hand I can see how it can be destructive."

"I hate to admit it, but I like the soft or mainstream stuff. Playboy and Penthouse are intriguing. I like a good porn movie now and then, but nothing kinky or weird."

"Occasionally I like it. I find the more gentle images appealing."

HOW MUCH CUDDLING DO YOU ENJOY, ASIDE FROM SEX?

Virgo loves to touch and be touched at rather specific times and in specific places. She's too busy most of the time to have a lover grabbing for her while she's getting things done. But she very much appreciates indications of his love for her in the form of cuddling in the evening—whether or not that leads to sex.

"I love to cuddle. That is one of my favorite things. Every night when we get the kids to bed and watch a little TV, he lays his head in my lap. I stroke his hair. And in bed we cuddle and watch TV and fall asleep."

"I love to be held before and after sex. The feeling of being embraced by someone you love is awesome."

Memories

"A great dinner at a beautiful restaurant. Back home, he lit candles. We took a long bath together, made love in the bathtub, and then in the bedroom, where the only light came from moonlight and a single candle. It was slow and gentle, then rough and wild."

"In the Outback, at about midnight, those wonderful country smells, almost full moon, lots of stars, [we did it] on the hard red earth on a blanket."

HOW TACTILE AND HOW ORAL ARE YOU?

Almost everything about sex is good to the Virgo woman. She loves to kiss. But most of all, she has wonderfully sensitive hands. She loves exploring his body with her fingers and gets very turned on when her lover takes time to move his hands around her body as if discovering it for the first time.

"I am very tactile. I especially love running my fingers through his hair."

"Very. I love to touch and move my hands all over him and me."

"I enjoy all: deep kissing, oral sex, even rimming as long as it's clean."

"I love all of it. My husband says I have an educated tongue. My favorite activities are fellatio and rimming."

WHAT SEX ACTS DO YOU LIKE MOST AND LEAST?

In addition to kissing, oral sex, and intercourse, Virgo enjoys a variety of other sex acts: having her breasts stimulated, cuddling, feeling skin against skin, and mutual masturbation. Some Virgo women are uncomfortable with oral sex but may be open to it with time and patience. Anal sex is of little interest.

"Oral sex makes me nervous. I worry that I'm not doing things correctly."

"I don't enjoy slow intercourse. I prefer rough, hard sex."

"I don't like anal sex, but I do like to be touched there."

AS A LOVER, WHAT'S YOUR BEST SKILL?

Virgo's got it all together, organized, and analyzed. She knows exactly what turns him on and what moves to make. Beyond her wonderful hands, she's proud of her ability to excite her lover with all parts of her body.

"Using my hands and tongue together, hip moving and grinding skills . . . I'm also good at seducing someone and bringing him to ecstasy before we even have sex."

"Being able to switch positions with ease and without pulling off . . ."

"Using my body to get my boyfriend off in the shower . . ."

WHAT SMELLS AND TASTES ON YOUR PARTNER DO YOU ENJOY?

When it comes to sex, cleanliness matters to Virgo, not only in the environment but also on her lover. Skin and hair, newly washed, is her aphrodisiac. She also likes a slight aroma of body lotion or a touch of cologne.

"Skin, colognes, and outside smells like grass or wood smoke, clean smells like soap or fresh laundry, sweat if it is clean sweat."

"His personal smell . . . The combination of his cologne, deodorant, and body . . ."

"Chocolate, whipped cream, anything sweet. I like real foods, not the fake body sprays and oils and stuff."

"After shower taste, combined with his body during sex . . ."

"All of him."

Fantasies

"Rough sex, double-penetration, role-play (master/slave). Being punished, through sexual acts, a little roughness, physical abuse, [but] not to hurt me seriously; being tied up, being 'raped' by my partner."

"My favorite is a threesome, watching my husband bend over a gorgeous woman with big, beautiful breasts, with a clean shaved vagina, while I am tied down and made to watch. Then when he is done with her, I am forced to do both of them. You can use your imagination from there and, oh, put some rough stuff in."

FOR SOME PEOPLE THE TASTE OF THEIR PARTNER'S CUM OR SECRETIONS IS UNPLEASANT. IF THAT'S TRUE FOR YOU, WHAT DO YOU DO ABOUT THE TASTE?

Many Virgo women, including those who enjoy oral sex, don't like the taste of cum. She never wants to hurt her lover's feelings and appreciates it if he ejaculates in her vagina or outside her mouth.

"I'll generally spit it out. I find it unpleasant, salty, and gooey."

"Normally if I'm giving him oral sex we use some other form of stimulation for the last little bit before ejaculation."

"It helps if he watches what he eats during the day."

DO YOU ENJOY WATCHING YOUR PARTNER DURING SEX AND ORGASM? DO YOU ENJOY BEING WATCHED?

Considering that Virgo puts effort into the moves she makes in order to excite her lover to the fullest, it stands to reason that she would want to watch the effects of her actions. She is equally comfortable being observed by him.

"I am definitely fascinated with watching him masturbate."

"I like being watched by my partner when I am getting dressed or undressed, and I am comfortable masturbating in front of him."

"Yes to both. I love to hear him and watch him be pleased."

"We always look each other in the eyes."

Fantasies

"Having sex in public places where being caught is probable."

"I think of my partner in latex outfits, and then using handcuffs and having sex in unusual positions such as the 'wheelbarrow.'"

"In the kitchen, cooking a delicious dinner, then smearing it all over my lover and having sex on the table."

The Big "O"

HOW DO YOU REACH AN ORGASM AND HOW OFTEN?

Virgo cums "All the time, damn it," or at least almost every time she has sex through oral sex, masturbation, or intercourse with clitoral stimulation.

"I climax almost all the time through intercourse or masturbation, occasionally with oral sex on me. I once had an orgasm from kissing alone. It was amazing."

A Memory

"We wanted each other so much. We were parked in a remote area and couldn't help ourselves. We stripped off our clothes and made love in the car. A loud thunderstorm hit the area. It was incredible: the feeling of safety in his arms, the sounds of the downpour, my partner sweating, hot, with very strong thrusts and then gentle and sweet."

WHAT'S YOUR FAVORITE POSITION?

What's not to like? Spooning makes her feel enveloped by her partner and sixty-nine is always fun. If the Virgo woman has favorites,

they include sex in the missionary style or being on top of her partner.

SOME PEOPLE ARE CONCERNED ABOUT BRINGING THEIR PARTNER TO CLIMAX BEFORE HAVING AN ORGASM THEMSELVES. OTHERS STRIVE TO REACH ORGASM TOGETHER. WHICH IS TRUE FOR YOU?

She loves the high of climaxing simultaneously with her lover and will work with him to make that happen.

"Together. It's awesome."

"We try to come together; if not, we make sure each other is satisfied before finishing."

"I love having orgasms together, but my spouse usually makes sure that I have one or two before he does. Cumming together is my favorite."

ARE YOU VOCAL DURING SEX?

Virgo can be fairly vocal; in fact, her partner can measure the success of his lovemaking by the volume of her response.

"A little, if it's bad . . . a lot if it's good."

"Yes, very loud moans and words."

AFTER SEX WHAT DO YOU LIKE TO DO?

After sex, cuddling is paramount. The Virgo woman wants a little time to relax against her partner. What happens next depends upon the time of day.

"Touch each other gently, breathe in his skin, linger in the feelings."

"I like to lie around and talk or snooze a little; then get up and get on with the day."

"Something together, it doesn't matter what."

The Virgo Man in His Own Words

A Memory

"Waking up on a Sunday morning beside my woman while she still slept. The sun poured in through the windows. A pleasant scent filled the room. I touched and kissed her gently. She had a look of utter contentment on her face. I got on top of her and the lovemaking began. It continued into the afternoon. What a wonderful day we had together."

Attraction and Dating a Virgo

WHAT ATTRACTS YOU TO SOMEONE?

The Virgo man cares a lot about a woman's looks; not that she be drop-dead gorgeous, but that she is neat, clean, and in good shape. It shows that she puts an effort into being appropriate and Virgo cares about that kind of public appearance.

"First, the body; weight isn't that important as long as she isn't too skinny or terribly obese. After the physical, intelligence and a decent sense of humor, social awareness, and candor matter most."

"A youthful look, nice skin; all weights acceptable except human skeletons and the morbidly obese . . . I like a lot of curves, [and] a nice face, eyes, and smile. I prefer a high level of sexual responsiveness."

"Weight matters, which is not to say super fitness is required. Energy, behavior, and intelligence absolutely . . ."

WHAT MIGHT TURN YOU OFF?

Virgo values looking neat and clean. Whether he is meeting a woman for the first time or going out with someone he has been seeing over time, the Virgo man will be turned off if she is less than impeccably put together.

"I'm turned off by a woman who shows disregard for her body, who is obese, or [who] doesn't take good care of her teeth."

"Some physical traits, such as badly tended-to teeth, turn me off but negative attitudes and rude behavior have much more impact. For example, I was dating a truly beautiful, smart woman. One day a man of color cut us off in traffic, and wow, prejudice to the core. That was our last date."

"I want a woman who is real, not flashy. I don't like dyed or permed hair, and I am turned off by a woman who is materialistic, too talkative, or [who] laughs nervously."

WHAT DO YOU ENJOY DOING ON A DATE?

Virgo enjoys spending time in quiet activities: going for walks or seeing a movie. He appreciates a woman who will go to the effort of making a meal and serving it by candlelight. He will be kindly and thoughtful, though not overly romantic. Interestingly, though, he loves it when she makes romantic gestures.

"I prefer quiet activities, an opportunity to get to know a woman rather than going to a dance club or rock concert."

"Dinner, looking at the stars, going for a swim . . . any activity that allows us to become closer and more comfortable together . . ."

"Talking, discovering common interests, having fun, outdoor activities on nice sunny days. I like to get to know a woman without a lot of extraneous activities in the way. I like to keep it simple."

A Memory

"One summer night my girlfriend and I wanted to have sex, but we were far away from our homes. We couldn't think of anywhere to go to be alone but as we wandered around we came upon a school that had a small yard behind it. I love having sex in the moonlight. We made love in several positions and then just sat there talking afterward."

ARE YOU FLIRTATIOUS?

He comes across as straightforward and matter-of-fact, but he has a way of coming on to a woman that makes her feel as though she is in control. More than being a flirt himself, he loves being the object of flirtation.

"I love to make women smile and to feel important and special."

"Innocently . . . I hug a lot, but not with the intention of getting a woman into bed. I just like to love people."

"Not overly, but I have occasional moments. I look for a woman with whom I feel compatible and then take the direct approach."

ARE YOU JEALOUS?

Virgo has a jealous streak. If his lover goes out of her way to trigger that emotion, he will react briefly, dislike that feeling in himself, and then he's apt to vanish with the sunset.

"It depends somewhat on the situation, but I would have to say yes. Perhaps possessive would be a more accurate word in my case."

"I would love to say 'absolutely not,' but I have twinges, which I strive to get over. If someone wants to be with me, that's great. If they don't, so be it."

HOW DO YOU FEEL ABOUT PUBLIC DISPLAYS OF AFFECTION?

Virgo sees sex as a positive thing, good for one's health. When it comes to showing his feelings in public, he won't go so far as foreplay, but he is comfortable with public displays. He enjoys hugging his woman, holding her close, and pulling her toward him for a kiss.

"Sometimes when you are deeply involved, everyone else just goes away and you forget they are there."

"I love them."

"I like them a lot. Giving and receiving public affection is flattering and feels really good."

A Memory

"We were out dancing, surrounded by other people in a dimly [lit] room. I pulled down the zippers on her slacks and on my trousers and started having sex with her in the middle of the dance floor. The music stopped, the lights came up, and we had to stand there for the longest time with my dick still hard against her, waiting for the next song to start."

Sexual Attitudes and Behaviors

HOW OFTEN DO YOU THINK ABOUT SEX AND HOW OFTEN PER WEEK DO YOU WANT TO HAVE SEX?

Should Virgo be accused of being preoccupied with sex? Label it any way, but Virgo thinks about sex daily and would like to have sex at least five times a week. Why not? It is good for the body and the spirit.

"Sex is on my mind every five minutes."

"Many times per day . . . almost constantly when [I was] in my teens and early twenties."

"Frequently throughout the day . . . Excuse me, my hand is tired."

HOW LONG DO YOU LIKE TO SPEND HAVING SEX AND HOW MUCH OF THAT TIME IS FOREPLAY? DO YOU ENJOY QUICKIES?

Virgo is in no hurry. He would enjoy having several encounters throughout the night, with periods of sleep in between. When that is not possible, his preference is for about 45 minutes to an hour, with about 30 minutes of this time in foreplay. He enjoys quickies only on occasion.

"I love to take as long as I can . . . as long as she will let me. I love watching the woman I am with as I give her pleasure. I only enjoy quickies if the alternative is no sex at all."

"Quickies are okay, but I prefer longer. Two to four hours is typical. I have never had a partner who would go longer than that."

"Foreplay as much as she allows . . . I like to tease. Overall, two to three hours on average and I enjoy quickies, too."

WHAT TIME OF DAY DO YOU PREFER TO HAVE SEX?

He is available to make love anytime, though Virgo has a preference for evening and night.

"When daylight falls, the dark knight rises."

"Time really doesn't matter. For me sex does not work with time."

"Any time . . . how about now?"

HOW OFTEN PER WEEK DO YOU MASTURBATE?

The Virgo man masturbates approximately five times a week.

A Memory

"They're all good with my partner and each time is slightly different in the sensations I experience. But I also enjoy solo sex, behaviors my lover doesn't necessarily enjoy. I find wearing plastic a big turn-on, cross-dressing as well. The plastic I like reminds me of the diapers I wore as a child, soft, vinyl. I bought some and tried peeing in them, but then I had to clean it up and do the laundry.

I found that a big price to pay. In my fantasy someone else cleans everything up. On rare occasions I enjoy breath play alone. I know this can be dangerous, but I use hoods that leak a lot of air so I won't suffocate. I don't even get close, but I'm very excited by the fantasy of it from the material against my face."

HOW LONG DO YOU WANT TO KNOW SOMEONE BEFORE GETTING SEXUAL?

The Virgo man will take his time in developing an affair, as he wants to know a woman pretty well before becoming sexual. If he believes a new relationship has the potential to become truly serious, he will take even more time.

"Becoming sexual is a very important step with me. There is no set time, but I wait until I feel comfortable with a woman."

WHAT'S YOUR ATTITUDE TOWARD CASUAL SEX?

Virgo is not overly fond of casual sex. It may be all right occasionally, but only if handled cautiously.

"It is just not my thing. I like to share sex with a loved one."

"I don't respect people who do it frequently though I've done it on occasion, usually with the intent of it developing into something a bit more serious."

"It is fine if you are smart about it."

DO YOU BELIEVE IN MONOGAMY?

Many Virgos think that monogamy enables them to develop greater intimacy with their partners. If their sex life is not satisfactory, however, Virgo will seek fulfillment elsewhere because he truly believes that being sexually active is part of being fit.

"I can only handle one relationship at a time."

"I believe it is beneficial in raising children. In other circumstances it is a potential death trap."

"Only one percent of all species is monogamous . . . I don't believe we're part of that one percent."

"I believe that monogamy is great when you have committed to someone."

A Memory

"My best lover was innocent and believed in positive things, like happiness, goodness, and fairy tales. The best sex we had was in the dark, a little moonlight, under the stars, and there was no one around but the two of us."

DOES SEX HAVE A SPIRITUAL SIGNIFICANCE FOR YOU?

Virgo is an Earth Sign: pragmatic and concerned with wellness. He eats carefully, stays physically fit, and regards sex as part of a complete healthy lifestyle. Beyond that, sex in a loving relationship enhances life and is spiritual.

"It is where I feel most alive. I see a connection between high spiritual energy and a powerful orgasm."

"I often feel as though I am in direct contact with a woman's essence or energy. It is highly intimate. When this sort of connection exists during sex, this feeling goes far beyond the mere physical sensation. It is something that is sacred to me."

"Meaningless sex is just that. It leaves me empty. When I am with someone to whom I feel connected, the sex is spiritual."

ARE YOU COMFORTABLE INITIATING SEXUAL ACTIVITIES?

Virgo is not likely to pursue a potential lover in a predictable fashion. He prefers to keep the other person guessing, but when he feels confident, he will make sexual advances comfortably.

In an early stage of a relationship it is unwise for a woman to be the sexual aggressor with Virgo. Subtlety counts significantly with him. In other words, he needs a sign from a woman that his advances will be welcome, but he does not want her to be the initiator until he returns the signal that he is drawn to her. Coyly, once he's sure the object of his affection is available,

he is apt to maneuver her into initiating sex. His partner never realizes that Virgo is in fact the seducer, not the seduced.

HOW DO YOU COMMUNICATE TO YOUR PARTNER YOUR SEXUAL WANTS AND NEEDS?

Virgo is an Earth Sign, as are Taurus and Capricorn. All of these Signs are very physical, very into touch. As a result, he is more comfortable communicating about sex through the use of his hands rather than with words.

"I am most comfortable with gestures and use words only if the gestures are not successful."

DO YOU THINK OF YOURSELF AS BEING IN THE MAINSTREAM SEXUALLY, MORE EXPERIMENTAL, OR OPEN TO ANYTHING?

Virgo comes in two distinct sexual types: the mainstream and the experimental. The former has a modest sex drive, is not particularly interested in trying sex toys, and his sexual practices rarely extend beyond kissing, fondling, oral sex, and intercourse. The experimental Virgo enjoys dominance and submission, bondage, using hot wax, spanking, and having sex in public places. He isn't likely to use many sex toys, but he does find anal beads fascinating.

"With my wife, my sex life is mainstream. When I am alone masturbating, I am far more experimental."

"I would call myself experimental, as I have tried dominance and submission, bondage, [and have] used sex toys such as floggers, restraints, blindfolds, and gags. I have a pretty good handle on what I want in my sex life."

Virgo's fantasies range from bondage and submission to sadomasochism.

A Fantasy

"I see myself encountering severe bondage with leather, rubber ropes, nylon webbing, and sensory deprivation. I am compelled into extreme postures. In

some instances there is [a] cock and ball and nipple torture as well as orgasm control. Sometimes I fantasize that I'm the 'top' inflicting domination on a 'bottom' . . . master/slave stuff."

HOW DO YOU DEMONSTRATE AFFECTION FOR YOUR PARTNER?

While he is not overly demonstrative in public and may not verbalize his regard very much, in the early stages of a relationship Virgo will send romantic gifts on the appropriate occasions. When the relationship becomes long term, his gifts are likely to be more practical in nature.

"I use my imagination to create large surprises on special days and small ones on random days, just so that my lover understands her importance to me."

"I surprise her by doing chores in the house that she did not expect and by leaving love notes."

"When I feel really good about a relationship, I hug and touch a lot. I am probably not as expressive as a lot of people."

A Memory

"Once my girl brought a friend over and they both jacked me at the same time. I didn't know they were going to do this and I had just masturbated, which I don't do all that often, so I didn't cum for about 12 minutes. I remember seeing the cum going all over her friend's face and my girl licking it off."

The Five Senses

HOW IMPORTANT TO YOU IS THE SEXUAL ENVIRONMENT?

In a clash between his desire to have sex daily and his natural regard for cleanliness, the sex drive will win out—at least for a while.

"The environment doesn't matter. You can have bombs flying off if I'm getting my nut."

But over the length of a relationship, the setting will take on more importance.

Cleanliness is necessary. The smell of freshly laundered sheets is an aphrodisiac.

"I appreciate a room being clean and neat. Sometimes it's fun to have a special scene décor with candles and soft music."

"It's important to me; the environment sets a mood. I like it to be clean and sensuous. As to lighting, from bright to almost dark or ample sunlight all suits me. Pleasant natural scents and sounds are a plus."

WHERE DO YOU LIKE TO HAVE SEX?

"Take me. I'm yours." That about sums it up for this man: anywhere, anytime. Virgo just wants to be comfortable and private. One special place is the office, after hours.

"Just let it be: here, there, everywhere,"

"In private; other than that anything goes."

"The bedroom, living room, or any private natural setting,"

WHAT PUTS YOU IN THE MOOD FOR SEX?

Kissing and talking about sex will certainly put him in the mood, but more than that, for this Earth Sign man, aromas are the triggers. He prefers a slightly musky perfume, something that has a spicy rather than a sweet tinge to it. In addition, his lover's hands exploring his body really turn him on.

"Just being awake . . . I like to kiss, hold hands, massage, give back rubs."

"Before sex, with all her clothes off, watching her from behind; she bends over with legs open and I am looking at that pretty sight."

"Aromas . . . God yes, some perfumes are awesome, a slow dance in the house. Ummm, sometimes just walking hand in hand . . ."

WHAT'S YOUR ATTITUDE TOWARD PORNOGRAPHY?

Erotica is always a turn-on for Virgo, but pornography only works in specific circumstances. Many Virgos find it uninteresting, while some admit that pornography has its use at least as a masturbation tool.

"It's what I make love to every night. Kill porn and you kill my girlfriend."

"I look at things on the Web . . . of the fetish world, not the conventional stuff."

"I like it but find that it desensitizes me to the real thing, so I do not use it frequently."

 ### A Memory
"I had on my pony outfit, dressed with horse ears, bridle and bit, butt plug tail and mitts, and horse boots from Australia. My 'mistress' (wife) was dressed in a leather corset. She was cruel and demanding as she forced me to strut and prance and stand in these boots. I could only grunt and squeal due to the bit tightly in my mouth. I had to pleasure her with my mouth, lips, and arms. It was arousing especially because it was the first time she tapped into my pony boy fantasy."

HOW MUCH CUDDLING DO YOU ENJOY, ASIDE FROM SEX?

He loves to hug and caress extensively. Although he doesn't expect his lover to hang by his side at all times, he wants a lot of cuddling nightly before drifting off to sleep.

"I like cuddling and talking even more than sex."

"A lot . . . I like being touchy-feely."

HOW TACTILE AND HOW ORAL ARE YOU?

With Virgo it's a tie. He gives great pleasure and derives equal satisfaction from both the oral and tactile elements of sex. He is very good with his hands and he loves to please his partner with his mouth and his tongue.

"I love to feel, squeeze, slap. Oh boy, I love it."

"I am very oral, as long as my woman enjoys it,"

"I love licking, kissing, [and] eating the pussy because I know they love it."

WHAT SEX ACTS DO YOU LIKE MOST AND LEAST?

His favorite acts include cunnilingus, fellatio, and intercourse. He also enjoys fondling a woman's breasts and teasing her. Though many Virgo men enjoy anal sex and become very adept at it, others have no interest in it at all.

"I dislike anal sex. If I have to use a condom it has no feeling. If I go without a condom I get sick. Forget anal."

"I enjoy intercourse, touching and kissing the breasts and nipples, [and] giving and receiving oral sex. I don't enjoy mutual masturbation, rimming, or anal sex."

 ### Fantasies
"I'd like to have my own harem girl. She would ask how to please me, and I'd have her dance for me."

"One of them is being transformed into a woman."

"To have several sex slaves, all of whom live to obey me in any and all ways. To be able to take any liberty with them and push their limits."

"Morning sex and waking my partner orally, slowly, waking her body before her mind. Kissing her softly all over until she is hot for me."

AS A LOVER, WHAT'S YOUR BEST SKILL?

Take his orderly nature, add in his sense of fair play, and Virgo becomes the kind of lover any woman would appreciate. He is as concerned about pleasing her as he is about deriving pleasure himself. He takes his time and is responsive to her cues. Overall, Virgo's desire to satisfy his lover is his best skill.

"My partner loves the way I use my tongue, so I really do my best for her."

"Teasingly slow penis entry, pulling out a little, then back in a little, then into the vagina a little more."

"I know how to give a multiple orgasm. It's like I know my partner's body better than my own."

WHAT SMELLS AND TASTES ON YOUR PARTNER DO YOU ENJOY?

Keep it simple. He prefers the smell of his lover's skin unadorned by artificial scents. Sniffing panties is a real turn-on for him; in fact he enjoys all of his partner's natural aromas and tastes.

"The scent of a woman, period . . ."

"I would rather put my tongue and mouth between her legs than on her lips."

"I like the natural scent of a woman; her panties if pleasant and mild. I also like the scents of food such as vanilla, coffee, cinnamon, cloves, and spice."

"I do not like the taste of perfume, makeup, or anything synthetic but some foods are a turn-on—flavors like cinnamon, vanilla, chocolate, sometimes whipped cream."

FOR SOME PEOPLE THE TASTE OF THEIR PARTNER'S CUM OR SECRETIONS IS UNPLEASANT. IF THAT'S TRUE FOR YOU, WHAT DO YOU DO ABOUT THE TASTE?

His partners' secretions are usually appealing to Virgo men. If he finds the smell or taste somewhat unpleasant, he still aims to please.

"I do whatever makes her happy . . . it's no worse than tuna fish."

"The musk and taste of my partner is the biggest turn-on to me."

"I love those juices if clean, and I swallow happily."

 Fantasies

"I imagine a guy with breasts dressed in a sexy woman's outfit looking very much like a pretty girl, and we have sex all day long."

"I dream that I am naked on a deserted island and five hot women come along. One gives me a hand job while another has her pussy in my face; one licks my ass while the other two do a commentary, [a] play-by-play, of what is going on."

DO YOU ENJOY WATCHING YOUR PARTNER DURING SEX AND ORGASM? DO YOU ENJOY BEING WATCHED?

He enjoys watching his partner during sex and orgasm. It adds to his pleasure enormously to observe the effect his efforts are producing, but he doesn't necessarily want to return the favor.

"I love the way she looks when she cums."

The Big "O"

HOW DO YOU REACH AN ORGASM AND HOW OFTEN?

Except when he chooses to hold back, the Virgo man achieves orgasm virtually every time he has sex, whether through intercourse alone or intercourse in combination with masturbation.

"I can climax through intercourse and masturbation about 90 percent of the time. Maybe ten percent of the time I get aroused but can't cum."

"Sometimes I hold back from cumming because I want to prolong the experience."

"I usually have an orgasm during sex. Sometimes I choose not to."

WHAT'S YOUR FAVORITE POSITION?

Primarily because he wants to watch his lover, Virgo prefers positions that put him on top of her. Occasionally he likes to switch off, putting her on top of him.

"Most of the time, I am on top. Once in a great while her on top and rarely doggie style . . ."

"Missionary with one or both legs held up in the air and sometimes with a pillow under her butt."

"I like them all but sixty-nine least because I like to do one thing at a time."

SOME PEOPLE ARE CONCERNED ABOUT BRINGING THEIR PARTNER TO CLIMAX BEFORE HAVING AN ORGASM THEMSELVES. OTHERS STRIVE TO REACH ORGASM TOGETHER. WHICH IS TRUE FOR YOU?

As he enjoys taking his time and because feeling her sensations is an important part of the experience for him, Virgo likes to have his partner achieve orgasm before he cums.

"I like to give before I receive. I really can't have pleasure unless she does."

"It doesn't matter: she cums, I cum . . . no problem. You cum first or after me, I don't care."

"She cums first almost always. I love seeing and feeling her build. Then it is my turn and she can enjoy mine."

ARE YOU VOCAL DURING SEX?

During sex he is only moderately vocal, as he communicates his pleasure more with body language than with sound.

"Only a little, once intercourse has started."

"I am, but mostly [in] whispers. Sometimes I can be loud."

"A little, [like] saying 'I love you.'"

AFTER SEX WHAT DO YOU LIKE TO DO?

After sex, Virgo likes to spend a little time talking. On occasion, he takes a shower and then goes to sleep.

"Sleep, sometimes just lie there with her and share a little quiet conversation."

"Quiet things: cuddle, kiss, have more sex, go for a nice walk."

"I like to talk, [lie] around and bask for a while, shower, take a walk . . . something nice and intimate."

LIBRA

September 23–October 22

THE SCALES

Air Sign Libra—romantic, good-natured, and courteous—strives for harmony and hates discord. The Sign of marriage and partnership, Librans find fulfillment through their relationships. Ruler of the kidneys, loins, ovaries, and lower back, a sensual massage and attention to the backside add to their sexual pleasure.

She says: "My best skill is knowing how to arouse my partner from head to toe, [in] all his special places. That is the ultimate gift to him."

He says: "I prefer to have sex in a place where we have no distractions, where we can really explore each other's desires. I find it fun in the shower."

"In love the paradox occurs that two beings become one and yet remain two."

—Erich Fromm

The Libra Woman in Her Own Words

A Memory

"I was at my boyfriend's house, in his room. The room smelled of him, a sweet smell. The lights were low. He started to undress me. There wasn't a part of my body that his lips didn't touch. I couldn't wait to have him in my mouth, inside of me. Then I did the same to him. When we were both ready, he said to me 'take a seat,' meaning get on top of him. The feeling of him inside me was wonderful. As I was on top of him we looked into each other's eyes, and that was amazing. The night went on for seven hours. I have to stop here, because I am getting very turned on and he is not with me at this moment."

Attraction and Dating a Libra

WHAT ATTRACTS YOU TO SOMEONE?

Libra is the Sign of the arts, of beauty; thus it is that a man's looks are a prerequisite to getting her attention. After that, as Libra is concerned with communication, his ability to hold her interest will stem from the world of ideas.

"Physical attraction first; sad to say, but if someone is not pleasing to the eye, it is sometimes as far as [my] interest goes. Inner beauty comes through, and if there is no inner beauty even Adonis may not be appealing."

"Slender, quick, gleeful smile, winks, an upbeat character, plus has to be decent-looking, maybe even handsome. I won't be seen with anyone [of] whom I am not proud in looks."

"Physical chemistry, confidence, a nice physique, deep, sexy voice, sexiness (someone who is sensual, passionate), an agile mind, charm, chivalry . . ."

"Looks first, then the ability to speak/write well . . . Above average intelligence is especially dreamy."

WHAT MIGHT TURN YOU OFF?

Libra, like all Air Signs, focuses on conversation. She notices not only a man's ideas but also the lips and teeth they pass through.

"Rude behavior turns me off, and yes, ugly teeth too."

"First, bad teeth; then if he's a slob, lazy, dresses ugly, is conceited or arrogant."

"What bothers me is a lack of a sense of humor, bad teeth, having a mean streak, not having a social circle of his own."

"Ignorance is a turnoff and a man who has poor grooming or is overweight."

A Memory

"On a beautiful day my lover and I took a ride on a motorcycle to the country. We stopped and bought a couple of beers and went to the park to sit and talk. It was quiet except for the birds and the crickets. We looked at the lake, and then started kissing. He leaned me back onto the picnic table and pulled my pants down, and proceeded to do oral sex on me. Then after I came, I went down on him. It was very sexy and very romantic."

WHAT DO YOU ENJOY DOING ON A DATE?

Almost anything can be a part of a fun night out: from dining in a beautiful restaurant to a picnic on the beach, from movies to country fairs. The indispensable element is conversation.

"What matters most is being in an atmosphere that allows me to communicate with a date. Sometimes a distraction is okay, such as going to a movie or a club."

"I enjoy intimate conversations as well as sharing fun activities."

"Eating, conversing, being affectionate, doing varied things such as horseback riding or going camping."

"Just spending time with him, talking, dinner, shopping, dancing . . . A good date is sometimes staying home, watching a movie and ending with good sex. What's better than that?"

ARE YOU FLIRTATIOUS?

Libra gets the best press of all the Sun Signs, primarily because she is genuinely nice. Her affable ways and her ease in conversing with all people may be perceived as flirtation, but there is no underlying motive. She is simply being her friendly self.

"I think so, but in a very easy-going, comfortable way."

"People think I am flirtatious and really friendly, but I don't think I flirt. I just like to talk and be social."

"I am fairly flirtatious, in a good-natured way."

ARE YOU JEALOUS?

Libra's key words are "I balance." As a result, she always tries to be fair in assessing a situation. She has a possessive trait when it comes to her man, but jealousy is not a major problem for her.

"I can be so, but I try to control my wrong emotions."

"I am jealous about my man only. I don't care what others do."

"I can be. It depends on the person, the situation, and my state of mind."

HOW DO YOU FEEL ABOUT PUBLIC DISPLAYS OF AFFECTION?

Libra, the Sign of love, of marriage and partnership, is a romantic woman. She enjoys having her partner hold her hand, give her a hug and, kiss her when they are out together. In general, she is always comfortable with public displays of affection.

"I like showing affection as long as it remains decent."

"A little public affection can't hurt. I will hug and kiss anywhere."

"I love it, makes me feel that my man is proud to have me next to him."

"I like . . . receiving them and seeing them. It shows that the rest of the world doesn't matter to that couple."

A Memory

"It was simply at home, just a night when we were both really horny. We [lit] candles, played sensual music. I had a blast dressing up: fishnet stockings, a black leather dress, sexy wig. I felt like a different person and my husband loved it. We had a few drinks, and it took off with some incredible foreplay using ice cubes and some flavored lotions. My husband knows where all my zones are and he hit every one that night. I must have cum at least three times."

Sexual Attitudes and Behaviors

HOW OFTEN DO YOU THINK ABOUT SEX AND HOW OFTEN PER WEEK DO YOU WANT TO HAVE SEX?

Libra is the Sign of physical love, so sex crosses her mind daily. It pleases her to have sex as often as five times weekly.

HOW LONG DO YOU LIKE TO SPEND HAVING SEX AND HOW MUCH OF THAT TIME IS FOREPLAY? DO YOU ENJOY QUICKIES?

Libra enjoys spending at least 30 minutes having sex, and sometimes up to two hours. Foreplay lasts from 15 minutes to an hour and a half. Because romance is important to her, quickies are only okay when there's no time for anything else.

"I like to take as much time as possible. Quickies can be okay, but not as the rule."

"Quickies are boring. I like sex to take more than an hour, [and] most of that is foreplay."

"I prefer about 30 or 40 minutes for sex, very little time on foreplay, and I only like quickies when it is eight minutes before work."

WHAT TIME OF DAY DO YOU PREFER TO HAVE SEX?

Libra doesn't like to make little decisions and, in fact, doesn't care whether she has sex in the morning, afternoon, or night. Anytime when there is quiet and opportunity she is content.

"Sex is a pleasure whenever my partner is here; anytime, whether day or night."

"Mornings are nice, but so are nights."

HOW OFTEN PER WEEK DO YOU MASTURBATE?

She rarely masturbates. When with a partner, she may not do so at all. When alone, Libra masturbates as little as once or twice a week.

A Fantasy

"I am in the kitchen cooking when he comes through the door and says, 'Sexy, I'm home.' He comes behind me and puts his hands down my trousers. He spins me around, whips off my shirt, runs his lips down my neck to my breasts, to my nipples. Then bends me over the table, pulls my trousers down, the thong to the side, and [he] takes me as hard as he can from behind. Then we go to the bedroom to carry on."

HOW LONG DO YOU WANT TO KNOW SOMEONE BEFORE GETTING SEXUAL?

Libra is a highly sexual Sign and may be well aware of physical chemistry with a man in short order, but she prefers to take some time to feel

secure in a new relationship. If pressed, she'll admit she doesn't like to engage in sex with a man she's known less than three weeks.

"As long as it takes for me to be assured that there is a real connection between us: days, weeks, months."

"How long depends on the person. With one man I might feel safe and close sooner than with another."

"I can't say how much time because each situation is different, but it is very important for me to know him well before having sex."

WHAT'S YOUR ATTITUDE TOWARD CASUAL SEX?

Sex without some amount of love and romance doesn't fit Libra's personality. Without knowing a man at least well enough to be treated to a dinner or two, she isn't likely to get involved sexually.

"It's unsafe. I prefer to be with someone I know and feel close with rather than a casual fling."

"I think it is harmful emotionally, physically, [and] psychologically."

"I have enjoyed it but have recognized that it can be unsafe."

DO YOU BELIEVE IN MONOGAMY?

Libra strives for balance in all aspects of her life. More than one lover at a time would be unbalanced in her estimation. In addition, the best sex for her requires a strong emotional tie, and that connotes monogamy for her.

"If two people are truly in love, there is no need to look further. For me, I am then content and satisfied with my one partner."

"Monogamy is not necessarily important when you are young and single, but I believe that when you are married or committed to one partner, you should definitely be faithful."

"For me monogamy builds trust and a greater emotional connection, which makes the sex better."

"Monogamy is important to me because

beyond the physical connection, the best parts of the sexual act are the mental and emotional bonds."

A Memory

"My fiancé and I had just brought a Christmas tree back to his place in Boston. We spent the afternoon decorating it. We talked about nothing special and laughed about everything. We sent out for our favorite Chinese food and ate on cushions in front of the tree and admired our handiwork. Later, in front of the fire, we made slow, passionate love. I felt safe and warm and very loved."

DOES SEX HAVE A SPIRITUAL SIGNIFICANCE FOR YOU?

Maybe yes, maybe no. This Sign is ruled by the planet Venus, which represents physical love, so it's difficult for a Libra to connote spirituality with sex. In spite of that, love and good sex go well beyond the mundane.

"Sex is the highest form of interpersonal connection, the melding of two people. At its best it encompasses absolute trust, openness, and vulnerability."

"There are times when I feel so close and so connected to my partner that having sex with him is like getting closer to God."

"Sex can bring with it joy that transcends the self: a profound, intimate connection with another human being."

ARE YOU COMFORTABLE INITIATING SEXUAL ACTIVITIES?

Librans are certainly comfortable initiating sexual activities in an established relationship. With a new partner, however, it is highly unlikely.

HOW DO YOU COMMUNICATE TO YOUR PARTNER YOUR SEXUAL WANTS AND NEEDS?

Libra is a Sign of communication. During sex she is comfortable using both words and body language, though her emphasis is on words.

"Purring, sighing, 'Oh Honey,' saying his name . . .'"

"Sometimes we read something erotic and discuss our fantasies."

"I give him attention with sexual touches and whisper in his ear that I desire him."

DO YOU THINK OF YOURSELF AS BEING IN THE MAINSTREAM SEXUALLY, MORE EXPERIMENTAL, OR OPEN TO ANYTHING?

For Libra women, most sexual experiences are likely to encompass anal sex along with the traditional range of kissing, fondling, oral sex, and intercourse. When there is adequate time she enjoys participating in role-playing scenes of dominance and submission with bondage, spanking, perhaps wearing sexy underwear or incorporating costumes, and using food.

She is something of a voyeur and is open to exhibitionism and sex in public places, done discreetly, of course. Libra rarely uses sex toys other than dildos and vibrators. In her fantasy life, she imagines sex with a woman, multiple partners, and being submissive or raped.

A Fantasy

"I am a virgin bride-to-be. My fiancé and I are kidnapped by an oversexed motorcycle gang. They tie my fiancé up and strip him naked. Then one or two women suck on him while he watches me being fondled by the gang members. I am naked and tied up on a cold slab of rock. Then in comes the leader of the gang, who has a giant hard-on, and who is going to rape me. We are surrounded by a dozen naked men with hard-ons. I am scared and I begin to scream because he is too big, but he rapes me anyhow, and then I really begin to enjoy it and start begging for more as my fiancé watches."

HOW DO YOU DEMONSTRATE AFFECTION FOR YOUR PARTNER?

Libra has a kind and loving disposition, which is apparent in all of her relationships. With the man she loves, she is consistently attentive to his desires and aims to please.

"Try to be kind and caring always by cooking great foods, listening, and paying attention—even when bored."

"I anticipate things he might need or appreciate, and surprise him with unasked-for attentions."

"Listen, don't judge, be present when I am with him, reflect back his feeling toward me, show respect."

The Five Senses

HOW IMPORTANT TO YOU IS THE SEXUAL ENVIRONMENT?

Libra is a romantic, ruled by Venus, goddess of love. Certainly a clean, sensual environment will enhance her mood and so she creates such a setting for her partner. A bit of music, a hint of perfume, and a well-placed mirror all enhance the total experience.

"I like it to be romantic: candlelit and with music playing."

"It's very important to me: cleanliness, privacy, or darkness sufficient to mask our activities, and set the mood."

"No doubt about it, sex is better in a prettier environment, but sometimes one has to deal with what one has available."

Memories

"Having intercourse in a hotel room by the ocean. The windows were open and I could hear the waves crashing on the rocks. The smell and sound of salt water are a real turn-on."

"We were staying at a friend's [house] in a wonderful room full of plants—tall, small, exotic, all shapes and sizes. There was a thunderstorm and we watched the lightning. Against this background, we played soft music and lit candles. We had a great night of sex . . . one of my best nights."

WHERE DO YOU LIKE TO HAVE SEX?

Ideally sex is in a bedroom, at home or in a four-star hotel, and on a large bed with plush pillows. In addition, creating a romantic setting, outdoors but private, with comfort, maybe a candle will satisfy the Libra woman's desire for variety.

"Usually in the bedroom or on the couch . . . Less frequently underwater and in the woods . . ."

"Beside the bedroom, living room in front of the fire or outdoors under the stars . . ."

"In addition to the bedroom, I like to have sex on the kitchen table, in the car, at the beach, and on picnic tables at the park."

WHAT PUTS YOU IN THE MOOD FOR SEX?

Libra is an Air Sign and so she is turned on by gentle, wordless sounds: sexy music, the patter of rain, the lapping of waves, an erotic movie in the background, reading poetry aloud. These and other sounds build passion in her heart and pave the way to wonderful sex.

"Spending time with my boyfriend; romantic movies; wild weather like snow, heavy rain, hurricanes; gourmet food . . ."

"Favorite music is number one, [also] dancing, lots of kissing."

"Slow rhythm-and-blues music, sometimes porn, candles, showering together."

"Whatever triggers my sexual awareness; it could be music, aromas, movies, stories, porn, or just remembering a previous sexual session with my love."

WHAT'S YOUR ATTITUDE TOWARD PORNOGRAPHY?

Pornography seldom interests Libra. She is too much of a romantic to find sex scene after sex scene after sex scene particularly stimulating. She is also, however, somewhat of a voyeur, so pornography such as videos of two women together, a woman with multiple partners, or scenes of dominance and submission turn her on.

"It is okay. It gets old fast."

OKOKOKOK

"I would rather read a good erotic story than look at photos or films."

"We use it occasionally to stir things up."

Memories

"We kissed and fondled for at least 30 minutes and then had intercourse for two and a half hours. I came three times. The only light came from my open window and Bjork was playing on the stereo."

"A lot of candles burning, Sarah McLaughlin playing on the stereo, lots of slow passionate kissing and touching."

HOW MUCH CUDDLING DO YOU ENJOY, ASIDE FROM SEX?

Since the Libra woman is comfortable with public displays of affection, she enjoys having her lover show his feelings for her with hugs and kisses and by holding hands, whether they are alone or out in a crowd. Cuddling isn't necessarily a prelude to sex for her.

"I like a lot: hand holding, kisses, and hugs."

"A light touch in public, curling up together on the couch, watching a movie . . ."

HOW TACTILE AND HOW ORAL ARE YOU?

Air Sign Libra uses her lovely lips not only to talk with her lover seductively, but also to turn him on with the passion of her kisses and her approach to oral sex. And while she is good with her hands, the oral aspects of sex are more pleasurable to her than touching.

"I love oral sex and when I satisfy my partner that way it also turns me on."

"I love kissing his mouth and parts of his body. I also enjoy cunnilingus."

"I am very oral. My tongue goes everywhere except the anus."

"I love to touch my lover's body. For me the most fun is getting him aroused."

WHAT SEX ACTS DO YOU LIKE MOST AND LEAST?

As Libra is primarily a mainstream lover, her favorite sex acts are kissing, oral sex, and intercourse. Variety is less important to her than just taking enough time to enjoy the special intimacy sex brings. A fair number of Librans will experiment with anal sex, and many enjoy it.

AS A LOVER, WHAT'S YOUR BEST SKILL?

Beyond her oral skills and expressive kisses, Libra is also genuinely loving and attentive to her partner. It is her responsiveness to him that makes her a good lover in all regards.

"My best skill is knowing how to arouse my partner from head to toe, all his special places. That is the ultimate gift to him. The next morning he can't stop thinking about it."

"If I want to express love it comes through all over."

"I think it is my total enjoyment of him, his touch, his taste, and my responsiveness to him."

Memories

"An aggressive rape scene, where my lover held my arms back and fucked my ass hard for almost an hour."

"My living room sofa, a friend stopped to visit, started trying to kiss me. I pushed him away calling him a pig. He then tore my skirt off. I pointed to the door and then yelled, 'Out!' He lunged at my knees and threw me to the floor. I spread my arms and yelled, 'Take me!' We made love all night, laughed all night, and both fell madly in love."

"It was the first time with my boyfriend. We ran into each other at college and ended up cutting class to go eat and watch a movie at his house. We didn't quite see a movie; instead, he gave me a full body massage and we had sex for four hours straight."

WHAT SMELLS AND TASTES ON YOUR PARTNER DO YOU ENJOY?

She relishes all natural smells and tastes of her partner, his lips, and his body, as well as his cologne. Her senses of smell and taste are critically important to the success of the sexual experience for her.

"I like the smell of him and his sex organs."

"He smells so good to me. It is the animal thing, amazing. I love all his tastes; his skin is like sugar cookies."

"I love the feel, the smell, and the tastes of his manly, firm body."

FOR SOME PEOPLE THE TASTE OF THEIR PARTNER'S CUM OR SECRETIONS IS UNPLEASANT. IF THAT'S TRUE FOR YOU, WHAT DO YOU DO ABOUT THE TASTE?

For most Libra women, the taste of a partner's cum is no problem and most often she will swallow it. Should she find it unpleasant she is likely to keep a glass of water or soda nearby or to ask her partner to withdraw before cumming.

"I don't like the taste. I keep a Coke nearby. I swallow his cum sometimes, but mostly I either rub it on myself or spit it out."

"I have no problem with the taste, but he usually cums inside me. If I make him cum by a blow job, I swallow."

"I don't like the taste, but I am quiet about it and I wipe it on the sheets or rub it off on anything but me."

Fantasies

"Having another woman, roughly the same build as me, in an intimate situation with my boyfriend watching."

"Multiple partners, having sex with four or five men, one at a time, all different ages, being submissive, not domineering."

"Since I am into dominance and submission, the best is a punishment fantasy: 'Daddy' punishing me, then fucking my ass."

"I imagine my boyfriend taking control and me being submissive. I fantasize about him telling me what to do and spankings, about him tying me up and blindfolding me."

DO YOU ENJOY WATCHING YOUR PARTNER DURING SEX AND ORGASM? DO YOU ENJOY BEING WATCHED?

Libra thoroughly enjoys watching her partner, but is a little less sure about being watched. As the Sign ruled by the scales, seeking balance she admits that this is a tad unfair of her.

"I like to see him enjoying himself. It is okay to be watched if that pleases him."

"I like watching him, but I don't really like being watched unless he asks me."

The Big "O"

HOW DO YOU REACH AN ORGASM AND HOW OFTEN?

Libra can generally achieve orgasm through intercourse when the position allows for simultaneous clitoral stimulation. She also cums easily via oral sex and masturbation.

"I enjoy orgasm when I am on top of my partner and ride him."

"I reach orgasm by clitoral stimulation, G-spot stimulation, and anal."

Memories

"One night in the pouring rain we went out on the deck where others could have seen us. The cold rain fell on my back and body as he bent me over the rail and took me from behind. The leaves on the trees blowing in the wind. It was awesome."

"We had sex in the window of our apartment [during] a freak April snowstorm. I was leaning with my upper body out in the swirling wind, looking at the orange sky. My boyfriend was behind me, his hands on my hips. The thrill of being so cold externally, while being so hot internally [and] the rarity and wildness of the storm made the experience memorable."

WHAT'S YOUR FAVORITE POSITION?

In addition to enjoying being on top or having him on top of her, Libra loves the doggie position because it turns her on to have her lover thrust against her backside.

SOME PEOPLE ARE CONCERNED ABOUT BRINGING THEIR PARTNER TO CLIMAX BEFORE HAVING AN ORGASM THEMSELVES. OTHERS STRIVE TO REACH ORGASM TOGETHER. WHICH IS TRUE FOR YOU?

Libra is easy to please. If her partner wants her to cum first she will. She also loves reaching orgasm simultaneously, but her real objective is to make her partner happy.

"Orgasm is not the specific goal for me. Climaxing together is illusive and phenomenal when it happens."

"My orgasms stimulate my partner, causing multiples for me and exciting him all the more."

"I want him to be so happy; that fulfills my desire. For me orgasm can be tomorrow."

ARE YOU VOCAL DURING SEX?

The Libra woman is moderately to quite vocal during sex. When her partner lets her know that he likes hearing her expressions of pleasure, she is very responsive.

"I am vocal during sex. I don't hide my emotions."

"I have a big mouth."

 A Memory

"Away for the weekend at a ski resort: big feathered bed, comforter, lots of pillows, low light, lots of touching and kissing. We just had regular missionary sex, but [I had] the most extraordinary, multiple orgasms."

AFTER SEX WHAT DO YOU LIKE TO DO?

Except after a quickie, Libra wants to go to sleep. If it is early in the day, she likes to doze a while. She appreciates hearing a "thank you" from her partner.

"I like to be flattered, massaged, to watch romantic movies and stay in bed a while or listen to music, laugh together, have good conversation and then sleep."

"We talk and then we fall asleep and wake up for a steamy morning."

The Libra Man in His Own Words

A Memory

"We woke up one morning and began kissing, fondling, and masturbating each other. I knew her so well that I could make her achieve climax with a few movements. We kept making each other climax and then we would hold each other and start all over again. We did this for twelve hours and never left her house. We did not even eat that day. Above all, it was the intimacy, the passion, and the tenderness that made it one of the best days of my life."

Attraction and Dating a Libra

WHAT ATTRACTS YOU TO SOMEONE?

Libra is the Sign of the arts, of decorating, and beautiful things. Thus, it is a pretty face that first gets his attention. In addition, since Libra rules the lower back he will notice a woman's posture and butt.

"I first notice a woman's eyes, her face, energy, intelligence, hips, ass, behavior, spirituality, and her boobs."

"Beauty, energy, behavior, firm body, eyes, hair . . ."

"I like a pretty face. I also want a person who is a good person on the inside; the body type is not as important."

"Her physical attributes, eyes, butt, laughter, hair, and the way she carries herself."

WHAT MIGHT TURN YOU OFF?

Libra has a refined disposition. A woman who is loud or crude, in public or in private, will turn him off. He also cares about style. A woman who has little interest in how she dresses and does her hair or makeup won't hold his attention.

"I don't like rude people or anyone who makes a scene. I'm more of a laid-back type of person."

"A woman whose behavior is ignorant or crude turns me off."

WHAT DO YOU ENJOY DOING ON A DATE?

Libra is an Air Sign and the Air Signs are all good conversationalists. Whatever else Libra might do on a date, he always makes time for talking. He enjoys treating his woman to a lovely evening and is likely to bring her flowers, but he is not necessarily a big spender. Dinner will be good, but not at a five-star restaurant. The flowers will be lovely, but not necessarily long-stem roses. His gestures will be loving and charming but never ostentatious.

"I like movies, theater, the ocean, music, and just driving around talking. I think the best date is time set aside to get to know the other person better."

"Being together, talking. What we do isn't important. It is the person that is important."

"Stimulating conversation, trying a new restaurant or place . . ."

"Holding hands, talking, dinner, movies, time to spend together . . ."

A Memory

"The first time we had a threesome with a new woman I will call 'Kim.' There was an instant sexual chemistry among the three of us. To see my partner and Kim kissing while I penetrated Kim—first vaginally, then anally—was so erotic. To have *them willing to do whatever I asked of them was such a strong exchange of power that the atmosphere was incredible."*

ARE YOU FLIRTATIOUS?

Libra is a friendly, relaxed man. He is comfortable talking with people in all kinds of settings, and his natural charm has a flirtatious quality. It is unlikely that he will be pushy or will behave in a manner that would make a woman uncomfortable.

"I do flirt . . . just enough to get me in trouble."

"I'm more of a quiet type. I do like to flirt."

"I flirt on a pretty regular basis. I mean nothing by it—it just helps get though the day."

ARE YOU JEALOUS?

The Libra man is capable of feeling jealousy, but it is by no means a problem of any consequence in his disposition. He is far too independent to be possessive.

"I do feel that emotion but strive to keep it under control."

"If a woman doesn't want to be with me and would rather be with someone else, it's her loss. I don't want to be made a fool of and I don't have time for games."

"I would say no. I do not covet what others have and I am not angry if another man finds my partner beautiful and flirts with her."

HOW DO YOU FEEL ABOUT PUBLIC DISPLAYS OF AFFECTION?

Libra is romantic, loving, and at ease showing affection. Observing other people is also pleasurable. The couple kissing in a gondola in Venice or engrossed only in each other outside the Louvre Museum is a moment he remembers forever.

"Love it. I love to hold hands, kiss, hug . . . and whether it is in public or private it does not matter."

"Holding hands, kissing is just fine. Of course, some awareness of the effect a couple is having on others is important."

"Public displays are okay within limits. Kissing is okay, short caresses okay, sex is not okay."

 ## Memories

"It was a rainy, hot, and humid day. We made love in my car. I remember hearing thunder, seeing lightning strike as our nude bodies [were] intertwined as one. Sweat was dripping off my face, onto my partner's. I continued thrusting my cock hard into her pussy for at least an hour."

". . . Being thrown down on the bed by a woman I was dating but hadn't seen for a while. She was completely aggressive, which was a major turn-on for me."

Sexual Attitudes and Behaviors

HOW OFTEN DO YOU THINK ABOUT SEX AND HOW OFTEN PER WEEK DO YOU WANT TO HAVE SEX?

Libra is a very sexual Sign. This man thinks about sex at least once every day and would be very happy, if time permitted, to have sex seven times a week. As that is often not possible, he will be content with three or four encounters weekly.

"I'd like it every night, but work gets in the way sometimes."

"I would like it at least once a day, preferably more."

HOW LONG DO YOU LIKE TO SPEND HAVING SEX AND HOW MUCH OF THAT TIME IS FOREPLAY? DO YOU ENJOY QUICKIES?

Libra would prefer having at least two hours devoted to sex, but one hour is the average time that he spends. Sometimes foreplay is almost all of that time, but it may be as brief as 15 minutes. He likes quickies to some extent, though not often.

"For sex, about an hour and a half . . . Foreplay as long as possible—that is what sex is all about. Quickies are okay, just not as enjoyable."

"Two to three hours is my preference, but quickies are fine in a different way. I like spending a lot of time on foreplay. It is my favorite part."

"I enjoy as much time as we have, preferably a couple of hours. Unfortunately, real life intrudes sometimes and that is not always possible."

WHAT TIME OF DAY DO YOU PREFER TO HAVE SEX?

Libra enjoys some daylight streaming through the windows. Beyond that, the time of day is irrelevant to him.

"It can happen anytime."

"Afternoon delight is best."

"Any time of the day when I can get it . . ."

HOW OFTEN PER WEEK DO YOU MASTURBATE?

He masturbates on average four times a week, more often when he is not in a relationship.

HOW LONG DO YOU WANT TO KNOW SOMEONE BEFORE GETTING SEXUAL?

Libra seldom gives a simple, definitive answer to a question and so it is regarding the timing of sexual encounters. He may decide to approach a woman about sex on a first date or he may wait a few months. A woman who tries to short-circuit his process of reaching this decision may be more likely to become a casual relationship than a long-term one.

"That varies with every person: a few hours to a few months. Generally, I want to have a good feeling about her before any sexual activity."

"It can happen right away if it is right."

"As long as it takes until we are both comfortable with it."

"Depends on the woman, but it is better when I have known someone for a few months."

WHAT'S YOUR ATTITUDE TOWARD CASUAL SEX?

Casual sex is not usually his choice, but he is a diplomatic man and not likely to judge others by his own standards.

"Been there, done that. Not for me anymore."

"Haven't done casual sex more than twice . . . It's unsafe . . ."

"For me it is not okay, for others it is fine."

DO YOU BELIEVE IN MONOGAMY?

Monogamy is okay but it's a matter of choice within any relationship. Yes, monogamy is important to the Libra man if two people have promised to be faithful. On the other hand, he considers multiple partners just fine when in an open relationship.

"A person's feelings are not to be used. If you want a partner to be monogamous then you have to treat her as you would want to be treated."

"I believe in monogamy only with the woman I truly love. Every fantasy is fulfilled by my mate."

"If you choose to be monogamous that's great; if not, that is great, too."

DOES SEX HAVE A SPIRITUAL SIGNIFICANCE FOR YOU?

If the term "spirituality" is seen as connoting some religious aspect, then sex isn't spiritual in Libra's view. However, the intimacy of sex does take it to a level that transcends the physical plane.

"I wouldn't say it's spiritual. Intimacy is more than physical, but not religious or spiritual."

"Perhaps, to the extent that sex can bring two people closer together."

"Sex is spiritual to the extent that I feel like we both become one."

ARE YOU COMFORTABLE INITIATING SEXUAL ACTIVITIES?

He is quite open about approaching a partner for sex when he is ready. Libra is far too diplomatic and considerate to ever be pushy or aggressive. As he is always welcoming, he appreciates it when his partner initiates.

"Most of the time I let her. She knows I will always go for it."

HOW DO YOU COMMUNICATE TO YOUR PARTNER YOUR SEXUAL WANTS AND NEEDS?

As an Air Sign, Libra is usually comfortable expressing what he has on his mind. On the topic of his sexual needs, however, he may hold back. Worse yet, he may assume a woman will just know what he wants in bed. A smart lover asks her Libra partner whether he likes "this" or "that" better. When Libra is given a choice of two options, he's quite at ease making a decision.

"I tend to be more concerned with getting my partner off more than myself."

"My partner knows what I need and when I need it."

"I use both: sometimes a whisper in her ear, otherwise a handful of hair."

DO YOU THINK OF YOURSELF AS BEING IN THE MAINSTREAM SEXUALLY, MORE EXPERIMENTAL, OR OPEN TO ANYTHING?

Libra's range of sexuality goes from mainstream to experimental. On the mainstream end he is likely to perform anal sex. He may be something of an exhibitionist and likes to have sex discreetly in public places. He enjoys having his partner dress up in sexy lingerie, leather and latex, and boots or high heels. Sometimes he finds it fun to incorporate food with sex.

On the experimental end he may try bondage, dominance and submission, spanking, and role-playing during which his partner wears costumes. He enjoys a fair range of sex toys such as glass dildos, vibrators, body clips, butt plugs, and bondage accoutrements.

"We love toys. We have several glass dildos that are our new favorites. Being involved in the BDSM lifestyle, we have a huge assortment for these activities: whips, floggers, chains, cuffs, canes, paddles, feathers, furs, vampire claws."

In his fantasy life he envisions multiple partners and being in the dominant role.

A Fantasy

"I imagine myself dominant over a group of female prisoners. Some of the women will be punished, some praised, some made to perform sexually for me, and some made to perform sexually with me. I want to be the center of the group in the end, with my cock being worshipped by all of them."

HOW ELSE DO YOU DEMONSTRATE AFFECTION FOR YOUR PARTNER?

Libra is a kind and affectionate Sign. He is also a romantic and loves to give small gifts of candy or flowers. He appreciates receiving token gifts and love notes as well. He does his best to tune in to his partner and please her. He will appreciate a woman who is straightforward in describing what makes her happy; in return, he won't disappoint her.

"I bring her small gifts, a touch just to let her know I am there supporting her and doing things that are important to her, and by making a phone call during the day just to say hello."

"I tell her how much I love her, call during the day to ask if she needs anything."

"I send flowers and cards, hug her, or give her a nice soft kiss for no reason."

The Five Senses

HOW IMPORTANT TO YOU IS THE SEXUAL ENVIRONMENT?

He claims that the setting is not extremely important beyond cleanliness, but in fact, Libra is the Sign of luxury and he appreciates a pleasant environment, a cool space, an open window, nice sheets, and a soft comforter.

"Cleanliness is very important, an orderly environment; lighting is secondary."

"I need a clean place where we won't be interrupted or distracted."

"I like the place to be comfortable. It does not have to be immaculate, but it does need to be clean enough so that it is not a distraction."

WHERE DO YOU LIKE TO HAVE SEX?

Libra is seldom interested in having sex outside the most traditional places. He doesn't want to be rushed. Any quiet, clean spot in the house or in a motel is his preference.

"I prefer a place where we have no distractions, where we can explore each other's desires. It's also fun in the shower."

"Mostly in the bedroom or other rooms in the house, but I am open for other suggestions."

"Bedroom, shower, car, outdoors, anyplace my lover is interested in trying."

A Memory
"A wonderful first date with a woman who was full of surprises. First, I never expected to have sex with her that night. But after dinner she invited me to her place and before I knew it we were in bed. Not only did that take me off guard but also there was a second surprise. Her vulva was completely shaved!"

WHAT PUTS YOU IN THE MOOD FOR SEX?

It takes very little stimulus to put Libra in the mood, but he is truly turned on by femininity. He loves to watch his partner moving, the contours of her body silhouetted beneath her dress. He finds the smell of gentle perfume on her neck or in her hair exciting.

"I am a man. Pretty much anything puts me in the mood."

"Being awake is usually enough, but I like making love to rock and roll, to Jimmy Hendrix, and to groups such as The Grateful Dead and Yes."

"Any woman with a heartbeat excites me."

"The woman I am with."

WHAT'S YOUR ATTITUDE TOWARD PORNOGRAPHY?

Libra likes pornography. When he knows his partner fairly well he will want to watch it with her. He also enjoys a wide range of videos such as those that explore fetishes, dominance and submission, and multiple partners.

"I think pornography is fantastic when it is done well."

"It's got me through life. Sometimes I think it helps."

"Love it; naked people are beautiful."

HOW MUCH CUDDLING DO YOU ENJOY, ASIDE FROM SEX?

Libra is a highly independent Sign, but it is also the Sign of marriage and partnership. He wants closeness and loves to cuddle, at least for a while every day. Cuddling is satisfying for a sense of connection.

"A lot! We set aside at least an hour a day and just sit on the couch, watch TV, and talk about our day and things that are happening in our lives."

"I like to cuddle when watching TV or a movie. But if I'm really tired—I have a demanding physical job—I may not be as willing to cuddle."

"That depends on the partner, but with the right person I like it a lot."

A Memory
"A few years ago I ran into the mother of a childhood friend, first at a supermarket, a little later at a local restaurant, and then later again at another store. I had not seen her in a number of years. When I was a teenager, I thought she was so hot.

She had put on a few pounds but she still looked great. We started to talk and about an hour later she invited me over to see her new apartment.

"*We had some wine and listened to music. Before I knew it we were making out. She went down on me and then I went down on her. We moved into the bedroom. I started to fuck her missionary style. She was very flexible; her legs could go way back. She was really into it. We moved into doggie style. This is when I blew my load.*

"*We continued seeing each other for a while. I did things with her that I had never done with anyone else. She did things to me that no one has done ever since. She turned me on to anal sex which I had always wanted to do. One night she started to lick my ass. Before long she had her finger up my ass and eventually we progressed to her using a vibrator on me. We also got into other sex toys: nipple clamps, cock rings. I used double-dildos on her, love beads. Amazing.*"

HOW TACTILE AND HOW ORAL ARE YOU?

While he is quite a tactile lover, Libra is even more oral. He loves to kiss his partner: her lips, her breasts, and every part of her body. Performing oral sex is nearly as exciting to him as it is to her. He enjoys virtually everything about oral sex except, perhaps, rimming.

"I am quite tactile, but especially as part of cuddling as opposed to when we are having sex. During sex I am highly oral and I enjoy kissing, licking, but no rimming."

"I am very oral . . . love kissing, sucking nipples, oral sex, and rimming."

"I am very tactile, but even more oral. I enjoy kissing her mouth, her breasts, and all parts of her genitals."

"I am a total toucher. My hands never leave my lover's body. And as to oral sex, I love it all."

WHAT SEX ACTS DO YOU LIKE MOST AND LEAST?

True to the nature of his Sign, Libra has a hard time choosing what he likes most. Oral sex is wonderful, whether giving or receiving.

And then again, intercourse is such a thrill. Does he really have to choose a favorite? He hopes not. The least pleasurable act for the Libra man might be anal sex.

"I like sex, pure and simple."

"I enjoy kissing, oral sex, and touching naked. I don't like anything that I consider too extreme, such as sex with animals or golden showers."

"Favorite acts: kissing, intercourse, oral sex, rubbing breasts and ass, as well as mutual masturbation. I don't like anal sex."

"I enjoy receiving oral sex, performing anal and vaginal intercourse, breast intercourse and masturbation. I can't think of anything I really like least."

AS A LOVER, WHAT'S YOUR BEST SKILL?

Here again, Libra has a hard time choosing one of many. He says his best skill is both this and that, what he does with his mouth and tongue, how he uses his hands. In fact, Libra does have a wonderful touch and a gentle way of bringing his lover to ecstasy.

"I believe it is a combination of everything working together that makes me a skilled lover."

"A combination of kissing, how I use my hands, and how I move my cock inside her."

"Being able to assess my partner's needs and map out her erogenous zones quickly."

"How I use my body. It is a whole body experience."

 A Memory

"*The fireplace was blazing in the bedroom. Through the sliding glass doors we could see snow falling. My beautiful woman [was] dressed in lace [and] waiting for me on top of the bed. There were candles [lit] all around the room and soft music playing. I don't remember any words being spoken or needed.*"

WHAT SMELLS AND TASTES ON YOUR PARTNER DO YOU ENJOY?

He is romantic by nature and enjoys the scent of gentle body lotions, shampoos, and perfumes, and the basic scent of his lover's skin.

"I love the smell of her skin and her natural tastes."

"She uses lotion on her skin and hair. She always smells great."

"I like the smell of her skin, perfume, shampoo, vagina, and the taste of her clean skin and her vaginal juices."

"The smell of her hair and body turn me on, and I love the taste of her lips and pussy."

FOR SOME PEOPLE THE TASTE OF THEIR PARTNER'S CUM OR SECRETIONS IS UNPLEASANT. IF THAT'S TRUE FOR YOU, WHAT DO YOU DO ABOUT THE TASTE?

Most of the time, Libra enjoys his partner's taste. On occasion, if he doesn't like it, he might have some sex oils nearby to rub on to her clitoris and vagina.

"It is not unpleasant to me. I swallow it and will lick my lips."

"When I am pleasing my partner orally, and she cums in my mouth, and I feel that warm gush it seems to make me harder. It definitely makes me horny."

"Grin and bear it. If you love them for who they are, you do it."

"It is not a problem, but if it were, I would suggest a scent for her to douche with to be more appealing."

DO YOU ENJOY WATCHING YOUR PARTNER DURING SEX AND ORGASM? DO YOU ENJOY BEING WATCHED?

He loves to see his lover's ecstasy, but he isn't enthusiastic about being observed. When a room is dimly lit and he isn't totally aware that she's watching, he's more likely to relax.

"Watching my lover is a major turn-on."

"Being watched isn't something I've really thought about, I guess it doesn't matter to me overall."

 Fantasies

"Two women having sex with me, one giving me oral as I perform oral on the other."

"I imagine watching my lover strip nude on the beach, and then making love to her with everyone else looking on."

"The image I have is of my partner and [me] encased in rubber, alternating [between] having sex and lying next to each other all day."

"I get hot thinking about having a threesome with my wife and her best friend."

"There was this woman I found tremendously attractive. I imagine that she is a nurse and services me while I am in the hospital."

The Big "O"

HOW DO YOU REACH AN ORGASM AND HOW OFTEN?

How often Libra reaches orgasm depends upon the nature of the relationship with his partner. When he is deeply involved with his lover, he always cums. When a relationship is new, he may not cum every time.

"I cum most of the time when my partner performs oral sex."

"How often depends on the method: nearly always through masturbation, sometimes by intercourse, sometimes by nipple play."

"I cum all the time from a combination of masturbation, oral sex, and intercourse."

WHAT'S YOUR FAVORITE POSITION?

Libra enjoys several positions, including either man or woman on top. But as one who admires a beautiful butt, Libra's favorite position is doggie style.

SOME PEOPLE ARE CONCERNED ABOUT BRINGING THEIR PARTNER TO CLIMAX BEFORE HAVING AN ORGASM THEMSELVES. OTHERS STRIVE TO REACH ORGASM TOGETHER. WHICH IS TRUE FOR YOU?

The Libra man is divided between bringing his partner to climax first and striving to reach mutual orgasm. For him an ideal sexual encounter includes satisfying his partner first and then in a second go-round, striving to cum together.

"I need to bring my partner to climax multiple times before I can climax."

ARE YOU VOCAL DURING SEX?

Libra expresses pleasure during sex and orgasm very subtly by making only a little sound, usually some moans of pleasure.

AFTER SEX WHAT DO YOU LIKE TO DO?

He enjoys having sex in the late afternoon, or early in the evening followed by going out. Only if it were quite late would Libra prefer to go to sleep right after sex.

"If it is at night, cuddle [in] bed. During the day, shower and go on with the day."

"Talk, sleep if there is time, shower, and go to dinner."

"Sleep or go out if it is early enough."

"Hold each other until we fall asleep, or pay the bill and leave."

SCORPIO
October 23–November 21
THE SCORPION

Water Sign Scorpio is powerful, emotional, intense, and secretive. Ruler of the genitals, Scorpio is the Sign of sex. Rushing to the heart of the matter—his penis, her clitoris—will turn off Scorpio. Some teasing and buildup make the experience far more passionate for this Sign.

She says: "I got his cock hard and used it to make myself cum on him, then made him lick my pussy clean of all the cum. Then I let him have his way with me."

He says: "I enjoy kissing, Frenching, and sucking on neck or ears. I love eating pussy. I can suck nipples until I sleep."

"I love thee to the depth, and breadth and height / My soul can reach"
—Elizabeth Barrett Browning

The Scorpio Woman in Her Own Words

A Memory

"The first time we kissed I felt like I was floating. I wanted to kiss every part of him. There were no beds left in the condo, so we went into the bathroom. We teased each other for a couple hours, until we couldn't take it anymore. He lifted me up and fucked me against the bathroom wall. I climbed up a ladder that was attached to the wall and we had incredibly crazy animalistic sex there. Then he sat on the toilet while I climbed on top of him and we had sex really slowly, taking in every minute. Finally we had sex on the counter until we were so tired we could hardly move and I could hardly walk. I remember the way he tasted, the way he smelled, the way he looked at me."

Attraction and Dating a Scorpio

WHAT ATTRACTS YOU TO SOMEONE?

Brains, an aura of mystery, and the ability to make eye contact to hold her attention are among the qualities most attractive to the Scorpio woman. Her partner should also be in reasonably good shape.

"I am attracted to intelligence. Good looks might draw my eyes, but it is a man's mind that turns me on."

"Intelligence and humor first and foremost; the physical usually takes care of itself. My mother used to say, 'when you love someone they become beautiful to you' and I have found that to be true."

WHAT MIGHT TURN YOU OFF?

Behaviors that she dislikes turn away the Scorpio woman much more than any specific physical characteristics. In fact, she'll overlook a lot if a man can hold her interest and is competent in his field of endeavor.

"It doesn't matter how hot he is; a negative attitude will make him ugly to me."

"Being too clingy, low self-confidence, takes himself too seriously, dishonesty."

"Not listening to me, being cheap, no sense of humor."

WHAT DO YOU ENJOY DOING ON A DATE?

Scorpio prefers quiet evening-out activities, especially when in a new relationship. She doesn't rush to get to know a man and may not trust her first impressions. Attending large parties is okay on occasion, but such outings are by no means her preference.

"I like a variety of things: hanging out at home or at the beach, maybe going out with friends as a group, or doing something outside. I love being outdoors. I like guys who will just go with the flow and see where the date will take us."

"I try to just open up and let what's going to happen, happen. If it's not working you can't force it. The chemistry has to be there. If it is, you are swept away by it."

A Fantasy

"I have this fantasy of going to my husband's office, locking the door, and sucking his cock while he's typing on the computer. And every time someone knocks on the door, I run my lips right down to the bottom of the shaft and suck harder. And when he is on the phone, I tease that head even more. His only hope is that when he finally comes, he won't make a sound."

ARE YOU FLIRTATIOUS?

The Scorpio woman loves being noticed and makes sure that she is. Her method of flirting is subtle, more through body language than with conversation. Her way of watching a man—that unflinching eye contact—makes it clear that she's interested in him.

"I am more of a tease. I like guys to chase me, not me chasing them."

"I am the most flirtatious person I know . . . sometimes more than is acceptable in some situations."

ARE YOU JEALOUS?

Scorpio's key words are "I desire." If she thinks for a minute that her lover desires another woman, he'll find out that "hell has no fury like a woman scorned."

"I expect a man's undivided attention. If he openly looks at other women I will feel jealous and the relationship won't last long."

HOW DO YOU FEEL ABOUT PUBLIC DISPLAYS OF ATTENTION?

Perhaps because her sex drive is so strong and acts of affection trigger it, a little loving in public is fine, but more than that is not. Also, Scorpio is a very private woman and doesn't like to advertise anything about herself.

"A very little bit is okay. I don't like it when people hang off each other."

"I don't like it when other people do it, but I like to."

"I prefer them to public displays of aggression."

A Memory

"Smell of clean clothes, in a closet with the lights out and the door ajar. There is not much room and we struggle to take off our clothes, stepping all over them. Another time, we were on a train in the handicapped bathroom; going down on him and being excited at making him excited because we knew we shouldn't be in there doing this."

Sexual Attitudes and Behaviors

HOW OFTEN DO YOU THINK ABOUT SEX AND HOW OFTEN PER WEEK DO YOU WANT TO HAVE SEX?

Scorpio thinks about sex daily and would enjoy having sex at least five times per week. With a good lover, the more she gets of it the more she wants.

"I go through phases, sometimes thinking about sex constantly, sometimes not at all."

"I've never been with a man who wanted sex more than I did."

"The more often I have sex, the more likely I am to want it."

HOW LONG DO YOU LIKE TO SPEND HAVING SEX AND HOW MUCH OF THAT TIME IS FOREPLAY? DO YOU ENJOY QUICKIES?

The optimum time for sex is approximately one-half to three-quarters of an hour, with 20 minutes to a half hour of foreplay. Quickies are fine because the central theme in sex for Scorpio isn't time—it's passion.

"When time isn't an issue, I like to keep it going for as long as I can. If I'm tired or need to get up early for work I like to get right down to business."

"Foreplay: just enough to make me very horny."

Memories

"He was dangerous, mysterious, older. It was spontaneous. He complimented me on my skills. We had fun with each other. We both climaxed. He was very cuddly afterward."

"Being in a remote jungle lodge in Belize, in a canopy bed with an animal print canopy, candles ablaze, and soft music playing. Making love with the person I adored and knowing he loved me."

"We used to meet for a quick encounter at

lunch times. It was also urgent and hot. We called it 'Funch.'"

WHAT TIME OF DAY DO YOU PREFER TO HAVE SEX?

Scorpio believes that sex is too important to do when fatigued, so it's much better before an evening out than afterward.

"Evening, especially before going out to a party or with friends . . ."

"It's usually at night, but morning is also nice when we sleep in and don't have to be anywhere."

"At night usually, but it's fun all the time."

HOW OFTEN PER WEEK DO YOU MASTURBATE?

She masturbates about three times weekly, but by no means consistently. There are times when she'll masturbate seven times a week, and then go for a couple of weeks without masturbating at all.

HOW LONG DO YOU WANT TO KNOW SOMEONE BEFORE GETTING SEXUAL?

Chemistry is a factor and some Scorpios are philosophic about this; however, most want to take their time despite physical attraction. She isn't convinced that you can judge a book by its cover and she doesn't always trust the first impression she gets of a man. So, she wants to spend some time getting to know him before deciding whether a relationship will become sexual.

"Time isn't an issue. It's about really knowing a man."

"I'm trying to get better and stretch it out, to get to know someone first, but sometimes I can't help myself."

 A Memory

"We had not seen each other in a month. The minute we got together, the feeling was so intense that we

went straight to his bedroom. The room was all white and smelled like him, a mixture of sweat and cologne. The bed was soft and small. He was both gentle and yet aggressive. The only sound was our breathing. We just needed each other and wanted to be physically joined."

WHAT'S YOUR ATTITUDE TOWARD CASUAL SEX?

Part of her resistance to becoming sexual quickly stems from Scorpio's attitude toward casual sex. As Scorpio is the Sign of sex, it is too important to her to treat lightly.

"Anonymous sex is unrewarding and self-destructive . . . unsafe . . . maybe it's fine for others, but it's not for me."

"It is immoral. It cheapens and dissipates relationships."

DO YOU BELIEVE IN MONOGAMY?

She values monogamy but is not above having an affair. She's highly secretive and can keep things to herself. As such, Scorpio would rather suspect than know for sure if her partner has had a side order.

"I have been married for three years and even though I might desire other men, I don't act on it out of love for my husband."

"I do, but it is very hard to do."

"It's the only way a relationship can be. You need trust and you won't have that with someone who is having sex outside the relationship."

DOES SEX HAVE A SPIRITUAL SIGNIFICANCE FOR YOU?

Perhaps because Scorpio is the Sign of sex and perhaps because her libido is so strong, she looks at sex as an almost religious practice.

"It's a coming together as one, a melding. We almost switch places—feel our essences going into the other body."

"It is an incredible bond between partners."

"It is an emotional connection that enhances everything in a relationship."

A Fantasy

"I am an actress in a film being shot on the beach. I'm with several other actors. We take a break and head down toward the water. We wind up performing oral sex on each other, having intercourse . . . all with the sound of the roar of the surf in the background."

ARE YOU COMFORTABLE INITIATING SEXUAL ACTIVITIES?

A Scorpio woman has no difficulty taking the lead in sexual advances. This is not to say that she'll be aggressive in this manner; rather, as she approaches a man, her behavior will make it obvious that she's interested and available.

"Yes, provided I am with a partner I can trust not to be cold and rejecting. It is okay if he says 'No thanks,' but it must be done with kindness."

HOW DO YOU COMMUNICATE TO YOUR PARTNER YOUR SEXUAL WANTS AND NEEDS?

Generally speaking, Scorpio is equally at ease telling her partner how to please her and demonstrating that with body language, but she loves to hear her partner verbalize his reactions.

"Saying 'no' is an art."

"I use mostly gestures, but when we talk about what we want during sex, it's a turn-on."

A Fantasy

"I am a dominant personality in daily life. My fantasies are a counterpoint to that and I am always submissive in them. I imagine sexual scenes in which I am ordered around by my boss, college professors, other men, and even other women."

DO YOU THINK OF YOURSELF AS BEING IN THE MAINSTREAM SEXUALLY, MORE EXPERIMENTAL, OR OPEN TO ANYTHING?

She is intrigued by experimental sex and will try anything once or twice. Her experimentation is likely to include anal sex, bondage, dominance and submission, sex in public places, being shaved, being blindfolded, being spanked, using food, wearing sexy lingerie or costumes, and trying out sex toys such as dildos and vibrators. Given her secretive nature, however, she is not into exhibitionism and is not much of a voyeur.

Overall, she is not likely to make many of these behaviors a regular part of her sexual routine. In her estimation mainstream sexuality at its best is as good as it gets.

"I am open to anything that is not painful, degrading, or boring."

Scorpio's fantasy life usually involves something hidden and secretive, too.

A Fantasy

"Being initiated into a sex cult, blindfolded in a tent. Others can see everything that goes on. Fires burning, the air is warm. A man cradles me against him. The cult chief enters carrying a long, thick dildo. He pushes it into my vagina. There is chanting as I receive this large totem. The man holding me from behind uses his hand to masturbate me while the totem is thrusting in and out until I cum."

HOW DO YOU DEMONSTRATE AFFECTION FOR YOUR PARTNER?

She wants to be the center of her partner's life and thus treats him as the center of hers. When he wants something, whether that is help with a project or simply her attention, she is there for him. Of course, she expects the same in return.

"I'll do little chores that show I am thinking of him like putting things away that he may have left out, and I leave him notes that say I love him."

"By anticipating his needs, helping without waiting to be asked, drawing a hot bath and scrubbing his back after a long day, buying small gifts."

"I watch the baby while I let him nap, or take her out so he can be alone."

The Five Senses

HOW IMPORTANT TO YOU IS THE SEXUAL ENVIRONMENT?

With Scorpio, the environment for sex is not of great consequence. She gets so involved with the feelings that her emotions completely overpower her other senses. She does not see, hear, or feel distractions.

"The setting isn't important. I remember one lover who made me feel like a cat in heat. His place was atrocious, but I didn't care."

"Cleanliness might be important, but other things are secondary to the person himself."

A Memory

"In a cozy cabin with a fireplace and candles lit all around. Some music and a nice heavy blanket on the floor. Lots of kissing and fondling on the floor in front of the fireplace, making nice love all night [and] until morning, cuddling and smooching."

WHERE DO YOU LIKE TO HAVE SEX?

You name it, she's there. Ask a Scorpio to describe the most unusual places she's done it and expect an entertaining list to follow. While some of the locations may be commonplace, one or two of them will undoubtedly be surprising.

"Anywhere, anyplace: changing room in a department store, on the beach, in a ski gondola sitting on his lap (we were coming down, others going up). Once we dug a hole in the snow and put our coats down. Skinny dipping in Yellowstone then [doing it] right there on the shore."

"Sex is great at the office, in a car, on the beach, anyplace secret and sneaky."

"I love taking chances. We had sex once in the front seat of a two-seater car in broad daylight. I still don't quite understand how we managed to fit."

A Memory

"The best sex is when we have no time restrictions, are really in tune with each other, and have been flirting for hours. We go at it all night. It starts romantically and we go down on each other and lick each other from head to toe. I like to get him so turned on that he forces himself into me hard."

WHAT PUTS YOU IN THE MOOD FOR SEX?

With Scorpio, one might ask, "What doesn't?" She is a powerful woman. When it comes to sex, she wants her femininity affirmed. It pleases her when her lover remarks about the softness of her skin, the lines of her body, and the aroma of her hair.

"When I am in love, I am in the mood all the time."

"Being with someone who treats the body as a feast for the senses is wonderful."

"Touch me and kiss me the right way. Basically it's touch, then caress, then kiss."

"Talking about sex over dinner, the smell of the person I love, sappy movies."

"Showering or bathing together, talking dirty."

WHAT'S YOUR ATTITUDE TOWARD PORNOGRAPHY?

Scorpio gets bored by almost anything that's done too often or is used too repetitively. If her lover never tries to change things, surprise her, approach her a bit differently, even sex will get boring. She responds to pornography the same way. A little is fine but a steady diet is not.

"Like it if I am alone, but not as a stimulant if I am with a partner."

"I find it stimulating and it's nice now and then, but I would rather have the real thing."

HOW MUCH CUDDLING DO YOU ENJOY, ASIDE FROM SEX?

Scorpio likes being hugged and cuddled but not to the point where she feels confined. A little will go a long way. More often than not she interprets certain actions—such as her partner sitting close to her and hugging—as the first stage of foreplay.

"I love to cuddle, but I don't like anyone hanging on me. I like to hold hands and I like to lie close to him before falling asleep."

"I enjoy it on my own terms."

"I like cuddling a lot if I really like the guy. If I am only kind of into him then I don't feel right cuddling a lot for some reason."

 ### A Fantasy

"It's summer, hot and sticky, late afternoon. I am walking a nature trail, the air smells like wet leaves. I come face to face with a tall stranger, his bare chest shimmers with sweat. His jeans hide a strong, suggestive bulge. He is masked. His hands touch my cheeks and lift my chin. The tip of his tongue traces my lips, then teases the tip of mine. His tongue coerces mine, weakens my knees. In a matter of minutes his fingers find their way under my skirt (no undies) and feeling my wetness, he slides a hot, hard cock inside. The intensity is outrageous."

HOW TACTILE AND HOW ORAL ARE YOU?

Given that Scorpio is the Sign of sex, it is to be expected that she would be comfortable with and enjoy all aspects of sex equally. She is an exceptionally tactile lover.

"I like to feel his chest, lower back, and butt."

"I love knowing every inch of his body."

"I love touching everywhere, every single place on the body."

Scorpio is also highly oral, loves to give her partner a blow job but only likes receiving oral sex if he's good at it.

"Tongue and lips on every part of the body . . ."

"I enjoy kissing very much, when the other person is a good kisser. I enjoy cunnilingus but fellatio more."

"Fellatio; I enjoy his pleasure. Deep kissing: yummmmm!"

WHAT SEX ACTS DO YOU LIKE MOST AND LEAST?

Her favorite sex acts are deep kissing, oral sex, and intercourse. Anal is okay sometimes. The lover who pleases her most knows to use his finger to stimulate her G-spot while performing cunnilingus. Nothing excites her more than that.

"I enjoy foreplay and intercourse, kissing, and oral sex. A favorite would be hard to pick."

"Good old-fashioned hot and heavy intercourse and sixty-nine."

"Fast and deep intercourse . . ."

 ### Memories

"I came home and found my honey in bed sleeping. I took a shower, [snuck] into bed, and pounced on him. I got his cock hard and used it to make myself cum on him. Then [I] made him lick my pussy clean of all the cum. Then I let him have his way with me."

"We had just returned to our hotel room. I was wearing a short skirt. He pushed me face down onto the bed and devoured me from behind. Then we had intercourse in this same position. It was amazing: his power, taking me over, his mouth ravishing me, and his fingers probing."

AS A LOVER, WHAT'S YOUR BEST SKILL?

Sex is her domain. Her skills are broad, so much so that many men let her take control. She'll enjoy that for a while because she wants to please him, but in time she expects him to reciprocate and to show that he understands her needs, too.

"My tight pussy, my dirty talk . . . I can make him cum by the dirty things I say."

"I am told I am highly skilled—to the point that some men are intimidated."

"Enjoying my lover with all my senses and letting him know of my pleasure."

WHAT SMELLS AND TASTES ON YOUR PARTNER DO YOU ENJOY?

The Scorpio woman likes musky-smelling or spicy colognes, but they should be kept to a minimum as they interfere with her lover's distinct smell. She enjoys the taste of her partner's penis, lips, and neck.

"I love the way a healthy man smells. I can tell if he eats well, drinks a lot, or smokes by his smell."

"I love the smell of his skin when he sweats during sex. It is HOT!"

"There is a particular taste to his kisses when he is aroused that I love."

Fantasies
"My ultimate experience that I dream of is spiritual, finding someone who I connect with on such a deep level that we transcend the sex act itself."

"I am in the office, tied to a chair with no power over what happens to me, submitting to the experience.

"Having him being in total control, being spanked . . . someone sitting in a dark corner watching us."

FOR SOME PEOPLE THE TASTE OF THEIR PARTNER'S CUM OR SECRETIONS IS UNPLEASANT. IF THAT'S TRUE FOR YOU, WHAT DO YOU DO ABOUT THE TASTE?

She doesn't like the taste of her partner's cum and prefers that he not climax during fellatio, but her desire to satisfy him takes over so she looks for creative solutions. For example, she might keep a tissue or a glass of water beside the bed.

"I put some toothpaste in my hand and masturbate him before performing fellatio."

"My current partner has such a pleasant taste, I love it. But in the past I used to imagine that I was swallowing strawberries and cream."

"I try to swallow it without it touching my tongue or mouth, straight down my throat. I hate the taste."

DO YOU ENJOY WATCHING YOUR PARTNER DURING SEX AND ORGASM? DO YOU ENJOY BEING WATCHED?

Scorpio loves seeing how her partner responds during sex and orgasm and is almost as comfortable having him observe her. The whole experience works better if the room is dimly lit.

"I like to watch his face."

"I really enjoy it a lot."

"It's okay when he watches me, but I prefer to be the one doing the watching."

The Big "O"

HOW DO YOU REACH AN ORGASM AND HOW OFTEN?

Given the importance Scorpio places on sex and her single-mindedness, she has no difficulty achieving orgasm. It's irrelevant to her whether her partner favors oral sex, masturbation, or intercourse.

"I can orgasm by any means available and possible."

"I reach orgasm often and easily through intercourse, mutual masturbation, and oral sex."

A Memory
"My partner asked me to dance in my underwear for him. Afterward, he touched me gently and fed me some food then he danced with me, [rubbed] against me. We kissed and went to the bedroom. He finished undressing me and gently touched me everywhere, then his tongue licked me all over and he made love to me. Everything was for me. He played with me intensely, and then gently, and kept it up until he made me cum."

WHAT'S YOUR FAVORITE POSITION?

Variety is critical to keeping Scorpio happy in and out of bed, so it's no surprise that she enjoys a range of different positions. Perhaps her favorite is doggie style because she loves the feeling of deep thrusting.

SOME PEOPLE ARE CONCERNED ABOUT BRINGING THEIR PARTNER TO CLIMAX BEFORE HAVING AN ORGASM THEMSELVES. OTHERS STRIVE TO REACH ORGASM TOGETHER. WHICH IS TRUE FOR YOU?

She says it's not critical to her to cum at the same time, but Scorpio is a controlling sign and she'll strive to reach orgasm with her partner.

"I love to do it together, but I'm not goal oriented during sex."

"We are very much in sync and usually climax together."

"I keep my hand on the small of his back. I can feel when his orgasm is coming. Then I let myself go."

ARE YOU VOCAL DURING SEX?

Some Scorpios are very vocal during sex. Others reflect the more secretive nature of the Sign and aren't very vocal at all.

"I am the queen of dirty talk."

"I am not one to scream out. I just like to concentrate on how good it feels."

"By nature, I'm not very vocal, but if I sense that my partner wants me to be, I am."

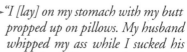

A Memory

"I [lay] on my stomach with my butt propped up on pillows. My husband whipped my ass while I sucked his cock. He then poured oil all over my back and ass and continued to massage it while penetrating my ass with his finger. I got up on my knees and my husband pounded into me from behind. He then rolled me over onto my back and began thrusting in me while we kissed and I twisted his nipples until he came."

AFTER SEX WHAT DO YOU LIKE TO DO?

The Scorpio woman loves sex before an evening out. A warm shower and watching her lover get ready to dress for the evening turn her on. Later at night after sex she enjoys relaxing at home, cuddling a bit, and sleeping.

"I love having sex before we go out for the evening. We're both showered, not yet tired. For me that sets the mood for a lovely evening."

"Shower together, listen to music, talk, cuddle, stay in bed, dance, eat, sleep, just be."

The Scorpio Man in His Own Words

A Memory

"We met at a small bar, and she was dressed so sexy. Her clothing and attitude seemed to say 'take me' yet her eyes said 'not yet.' We had some drinks and food. We flirted and made sexual gestures. We were aware that others were watching. I felt myself getting excited. We went for a walk under a bright moonlit night, touching each other. The erotic tension built. I believed that everyone who saw us was jealous. We talked about what we would do to each other when were alone. The heat was growing. We found a private place and acted out our conversation."

Attraction and Dating a Scorpio

WHAT ATTRACTS YOU TO SOMEONE?

What Scorpio notices first about a woman is her general physical fitness. He appreciates someone who takes care of herself, a woman with style, someone who carries herself with a sense of self-assurance. Someone who comes across as insecure, even if very beautiful, will not appeal to him.

"I notice her proportions, confidence, and inner beauty."

Once he is physically attracted to a woman he will begin to notice the specifics.

"I am first attracted by eyes. I care that a woman makes direct eye contact. Then I notice her proportions, and look for nice-sized breasts. Perky nipples are a turn-on, and being clean and pretty."

"Physical attributes: breasts, behind, hair, teeth, smile."

"Nice hair, skin tone, good communication skills, the sound of her laughter."

"I notice a woman who seems to be all together, ladylike, feminine. I notice whether she is a good listener, intelligent and is current with what's going on in the world."

"What first attracts me is confidence, humor, an easy feel for joy in things. Physical attributes take second chair to the above."

But more than anything physical, it is a woman's intelligence that is indispensable to the Scorpio man. He isn't all that interested in small talk. He wants his partner to be someone with whom he can share confidences and from whom he may get a different perspective. Passion is important to him not only in bed but also in his approach to life. A woman who is deeply involved in her work or her community is intriguing to him.

WHAT MIGHT TURN YOU OFF?

His list focuses on behaviors far more than looks. One thing stands out, however. While he likes his partner to look appealing in public, he doesn't want her to reveal too much flesh. A suggestion excites him more than everything hanging out and he doesn't want her to expose too much in front of other men.

"A woman who is fresh, in your face, tries too hard to be cool, into wisecracking."

"Not listening to me, low self-confidence, no sense of humor, and smoking . . ."

"Negative attitude, rude people, disinterest, snobbish women, game players . . ."

"Smoking, grossly overweight, or an unkempt person . . ."

WHAT DO YOU ENJOY DOING ON A DATE?

Whatever else he might enjoy, dinner is always on Scorpio's list. It provides him two important opportunities, the chance to talk with a woman at length and to look her in the eyes across the table. He intimidates many people with his unblinking gaze—think of the eyes of Pablo Picasso—so he wants to be with a woman who can meet that gaze comfortably.

"Dinner, movie, and alone time . . ."

"Eating out, moonlight walk, talking, getting to know the person."

"Feeling comfortable with the person, good communication sharing food . . ."

"I like quiet evenings with dinner, taking a drive, going for a walk, sitting and talking."

 Memories

"*Anonymous sex with another over-sexed person.*"

"*An afternoon rendezvous at a motel, then taking a day off and resting.*"

"*Sex with my wife when she was nursing our child. Breast milk was awesome.*"

ARE YOU FLIRTATIOUS?

Scorpio is flirtatious, but subtly so. His energy is quiet and full of intrigue. It isn't usually his style to be obvious. Instead, he has a way of lowering his head, seeming to appraise the woman he's studying, and looking at her until he has her attention.

"Yes. Flirting is like playing a game. It is fun."

"If I am attracted to someone, I certainly do flirt with her."

"I can be very flirtatious, especially if I see a potential for some kind of relationship."

ARE YOU JEALOUS?

Scorpio can be jealous—especially those in their twenties and early thirties. He watches how his lover behaves in social settings with other men. There is no question that he will be displeased if he thinks she's flirting with them in anything more than the lightest fashion.

HOW DO YOU FEEL ABOUT PUBLIC DISPLAYS OF AFFECTION?

Being secretive is a fundamental Scorpio trait, so public displays of affection need to be kept to a minimum both in frequency of occurrence and depth of passion displayed. Holding hands is comfortable, but having a partner hang all over him is not to his liking.

"I do not believe anyone just walking around should be exposed to another person's animal instincts."

"Rather not in front of friends and family; okay out and about."

"On occasion it is okay as long as it is minimal."

"I like them in the right setting."

Sexual Attitudes and Behaviors

HOW OFTEN DO YOU THINK ABOUT SEX AND HOW OFTEN PER WEEK DO YOU WANT TO HAVE SEX?

Scorpio is the Sign of sex and desire, and he has sex on his mind often. It is when he has a few moments alone, apart from noise, even music, that his mind will turn to things he finds most gratifying. Sex is always on that list. He might want sex more frequently but three times per week will satisfy him.

"Oh, daily please. Well, maybe every other day and a half."

 A Memory

"*Dancing in a club . . . it was our first date. We went straight to the dance floor and wrapped ourselves around each other—eyes looking longingly into the*

other's—and then [we] started kissing. We held hands all night long and were always touching each other. We danced to techno music, and were both sweaty. I loved the way the sweat glistened on her body. She bit my tongue and that was highly arousing."

HOW LONG DO YOU LIKE TO SPEND HAVING SEX AND HOW MUCH OF THAT TIME IS FOREPLAY? DO YOU ENJOY QUICKIES?

He enjoys lengthy sex on occasion, but his preference is from a half hour to an hour. Quickies can be a lot of fun as well. With Scorpio, foreplay is likely to last from five to 30 minutes.

"Depending on the mood, I enjoy both long and quick sessions. Quickies can be a perfect means to an end . . . or a beginning."

"I would like more than we usually do. Most of the time, after about ten minutes my lover tells me to 'put it in.'"

WHAT TIME OF DAY DO YOU PREFER TO HAVE SEX?

No way can Scorpio make a choice here. Sex is great whenever he can get it.

"I love afternoon, but we usually have sex late at night."

"Oh . . . A.M., P.M., evenings . . ."

HOW OFTEN PER WEEK DO YOU MASTURBATE?

When he is single, the Scorpio man masturbates five to seven times weekly. When he is in a relationship, he does so rarely—perhaps once or twice a week.

"I am married and have sex whenever I want to, so at this point I do not masturbate. When I was single, I masturbated at least seven times a week."

 Fantasies

"I imagine my wife on the dance floor wearing thigh-high boots . . . that is all she is wearing."

"My fantasies include having sex in an airplane and anonymous sex with strangers."

"If I see an interesting woman on the streets, I imagine I am doing her in an adult video."

"Woman with blonde hair, makeup, jewelry, satin night gown, perfume, satin sheets. I can have a huge erection and do it all day."

HOW LONG DO YOU WANT TO KNOW SOMEONE BEFORE GETTING SEXUAL?

While he may not be in a mad dash to get a woman into bed, Scorpio prefers that a relationship become sexual in short order. When he is seriously interested in a woman, he will wait until she makes it clear that she returns the feelings before broaching the subject.

"I prefer to have sex with a woman I really like. I want us to have talked about it . . . probably about a month or two."

"That depends, I want to feel comfortable. It could be one hour. It could be several months."

"It does not take long, maybe a week or two."

"I am not impatient the way I was in my twenties so it depends on the situation. It could be momentary . . . it could be weeks or months . . . I can wait."

WHAT'S YOUR ATTITUDE TOWARD CASUAL SEX?

Anonymous sex has its drawbacks and Scorpio acknowledges that it is not safe. All in all, though, he likes it.

"It is unsafe, but I don't complain about others having it."

"It's fine, but I know it is risky and I do worry about STDs."

"In some ways fun; in others, [it's] emotionally unsafe."

"It is fine as long as there is at least some connection between us."

DO YOU BELIEVE IN MONOGAMY?

Scorpio is a fixed Sign. When he gives his word to be faithful he intends to abide by it. But if he is unhappy with his partner he is likely to seek sexual gratification outside of the relationship.

"Once in a committed relationship you should stay that way."

"Yes, if that is the understanding between two people, honor it. If both agree to other possibilities, that is okay too. I would like to try an encounter with another couple."

"I do. I am a damn romantic. I believe in the possibility of total satisfaction with one partner."

DOES SEX HAVE A SPIRITUAL SIGNIFICANCE FOR YOU?

Perhaps he remains open-minded to the possibility of a spiritual connection with sex, but for most Scorpio men sex is rewarding and fulfilling on its own.

"No, but it is beautiful to meet a girl, talk, and love."

"I figure this is the Garden of Eden and while you are in the garden you may as well eat some fruit."

 A Fantasy

"Two exceptionally attractive women ask me to make love to them. The three of us entangled, kissing, stroking, sucking, caressing, fucking, and after we're done, showering together."

ARE YOU COMFORTABLE INITIATING SEXUAL ACTIVITIES?

Scorpio has a considerable libido and his partner is always aware of his sexual interest in her. There are Scorpios who are quite overt in their approach to this subject, while others rely more on that sense of chemistry. Either way the Scorpio man is not likely to be shy about initiating sex.

"I'm the spark, but I also enjoy taking a lead from my partner."

"I am always horny, so yes, I am the initiator."

HOW DO YOU COMMUNICATE TO YOUR PARTNER YOUR SEXUAL WANTS AND NEEDS?

Scorpio is not necessarily at ease stating his preferences. He relies mostly on body language. On the other hand, Scorpio wants to satisfy his lover, so he dearly appreciates having her guide his hand or tell him how to satisfy her.

"I wish I were comfortable using words, but I normally make gestures instead."

"I usually just go with the flow."

DO YOU THINK OF YOURSELF AS BEING IN THE MAINSTREAM SEXUALLY, MORE EXPERIMENTAL, OR OPEN TO ANYTHING?

The traditional Scorpio enjoys kissing, fondling his lover's breasts, oral sex, and intercourse. On the more experimental end he is likely to have sex in public places, try some bondage, or play around with food during sex. Sexual pleasure for him is much more about the intense involvement with his partner rather than the use of sex toys or any peripheral accoutrements.

"I am mostly mainstream but with some experimental behaviors, definitely not open to 'anything.'"

Images prevalent in Scorpio fantasies involve sex in public places and being dominant over his partner.

 A Fantasy

"She is in an upright position, bound with arms and legs extended. She is blindfolded. Candles are lit. She is wearing little clothing that I . . . remove. I caress her body; maybe use the vibrator to excite her. Then I shave her pubic hair. She struggles against the ropes but is held. I lick her body and bring her off. I bite (little) her nipples and excite her more. Finally I untie her, put her on the bed, and make love."

HOW DO YOU DEMONSTRATE AFFECTION FOR YOUR PARTNER?

He demonstrates his attentive and romantic nature by doing things such as household chores, bringing his partner flowers, and sending her cards. He enjoys being helpful when there is need and can be relied on to be supportive when his partner is having a difficult time emotionally. He prides himself on being a good listener.

"By doing things such as housework, sending flowers."

"I help her when she needs me, caress her, and listen to her."

"Spontaneous giving of special gifts and surprises . . . I try to keep her happy."

A Fantasy

"In my fantasy, I encounter my wife unexpectedly, run into her somewhere out of the ordinary. Unbeknownst to her, I follow as she is shopping or just walking around. She doesn't see me, but I get off looking at her without her knowing that I am there. Then I go over to her and tell her I have been watching her and that I find her very sexy. We head off to some secluded place and have passionate sex."

The Five Senses

HOW IMPORTANT TO YOU IS THE SEXUAL ENVIRONMENT?

In all aspects, Scorpio is a very sexual person and he appreciates a woman who makes an effort for him with a clean and comfortable environment. Romantic music, candlelight, and a hint of perfume will be noted and much appreciated.

"Cleanliness is important, lighting and décor matter only if planning something special."

"Very important. Candlelight helps. If we are in a room, it has to be clean."

"I like it clean. Ambiance matters. I set the scene, as if I did nothing to prepare, yet I cleaned the house and adjusted everything just a few degrees to my liking."

"Cleanliness and orderliness are important, softer lighting can be more romantic but is not necessary."

WHERE DO YOU LIKE TO HAVE SEX?

As the sexual environment is important to Scorpio, he prefers the comfort and privacy of the bedroom or other rooms in the house. Apart from that, Scorpio is a Water Sign and if he is involved in sex outdoors, water often figures in.

"Bedroom, house, outdoors, in a lake or pond . . ."

"Indoors, anywhere it is unlikely we'll be seen."

"Bedroom, beach, car, whenever it happens . . ."

"Sex in a car is fun, as well as on a blanket spread on a mountainside."

WHAT PUTS YOU IN THE MOOD FOR SEX?

Everything! Scorpio is the Sign that rules sex. Very little is required to get his mind on the subject, and once he starts thinking about it, he is ready. Focusing on things such as touching his lover, talking about sex, or watching X-rated videos all put him in the mood.

"Back rubs, front rubs, erotic touching."

"Caressing, sensual conversation or eating, watching porn videos, or some Internet sex will put me in the mood."

"Showering, porn, lover's breath on my neck . . . just about anything . . . I am always in the mood."

"I do not need help to get in the mood."

"My girl in satin lingerie, the smell of perfume, jewelry, staying in bed."

A Memory

"One of the best sexual experiences I ever had was in a small, dingy, motel room on vacation. It was very aggressive and unplanned."

WHAT'S YOUR ATTITUDE TOWARD PORNOGRAPHY?

Scorpio likes pornography, not only for self-stimulation, but also as an art form. On occasion he enjoys watching it instead of network television. He likes to use pornography both when he is alone and with a partner.

"I like porno if it is not trashy."

"I like it and believe that it has its place for adults."

"Just to keep my sexual stimulation, it's useful."

"It's rousing . . . amusing . . . artful at times, even inspiring."

"I like some pornography if it is done well, such as films by Andrew Blake."

HOW MUCH CUDDLING DO YOU ENJOY, ASIDE FROM SEX?

While Scorpio is the Sign of sex, this man is extremely self-controlled. At the same time he longs for intimacy. He enjoys holding hands, cuddling, and kissing—often without it leading to a full sexual encounter.

"I like making out, kissing, touching. I enjoy being held."

"I can cuddle for hours . . . days, work permitting."

HOW TACTILE AND HOW ORAL ARE YOU?

The Scorpio man has a way of looking at a woman that can make her feel almost like she's being physically touched. His hands seem to be a continuation of that intensity. They are highly sensitive and it is obvious that he loves to touch. Amazingly, he is even more oral than he is tactile.

"I like to feel her body. I love to squeeze her breasts and nipples."

"I will massage until melting point . . . I have time on my side."

"I enjoy kissing, Frenching, and sucking on neck or ears. I love eating pussy. I can suck nipples until I sleep."

"Kissing is great and I love how women respond to cunnilingus."

"Very oral . . . I dream about kissing and sucking . . . I'm dreaming of my partner's taste right now."

"It's all great. Sensual touching really turns me on and I love kissing everywhere on her body."

 Fantasies

"The ultimate: three women. Enough said."

"Masturbating on my lover's face."

"I fantasize about sixty-nine, and I also like to imagine us wearing costumes and getting into some casual and even silly role-playing to lighten the mood."

WHAT SEX ACTS DO YOU LIKE MOST AND LEAST?

Scorpio doesn't hesitate long in answering this question. His favorite sex acts are intercourse and oral sex. He doesn't like anal sex. In addition, although Scorpio is the Sign of reproduction, he does not want to assume responsibility for birth control.

AS A LOVER, WHAT'S YOUR BEST SKILL?

He is particularly proud of his oral skills, deep kissing, nursing at his lover's breasts, and cunnilingus. He has great self-control and will hold himself back from orgasm until he has thoroughly satisfied his lover.

WHAT SMELLS AND TASTES ON YOUR PARTNER DO YOU ENJOY?

Scorpio does not want any of his partner's smells covered up by chemicals. Shampoos, deodorants, or perfumes that interfere with his ability to smell her as she really is will diminish his pleasure, not enhance it.

"Her skin (neck) and her pussy . . ."

"She smells good all over."

"The smell of clean right after a shower . . ."

"It can even be what others consider odor if it is coming from someone I am fascinated with . . . the smell of her feet. In the absence of my partner, her panties will have to do."

Memories

"Recently when we returned home after a concert, my partner played with me hard, then slowed down and it became sensual. After a while she pulled me on top of her for a fantastic mutual orgasm. Afterward we cuddled, showered, and went out for an excellent dinner."

"It was the first time that my future wife and I were together and it was awesome. The day was extremely hot and humid and we were sweating and sliding all over each other. I remember how great it was as we explored each other for hours."

FOR SOME PEOPLE THE TASTE OF THEIR PARTNER'S CUM OR SECRETIONS IS UNPLEASANT. IF THAT'S TRUE FOR YOU, WHAT DO YOU DO ABOUT THE TASTE?

Scorpio is very matter-of-fact about his partner's sex juices. Generally, he finds the taste pleasant, especially when she is clean and her secretions are fresh.

"I'm all for taste, and will take it as it comes."

"I like the taste and apply honey or other liquid."

"Normal secretions taste great. If unpleasant, I do something else."

DO YOU ENJOY WATCHING YOUR PARTNER DURING SEX AND ORGASM? DO YOU ENJOY BEING WATCHED?

It may seem a bit puzzling that Scorpio, Sign of sex, doesn't much like to be watched; however, keep in mind that this Sign is somewhat inhibited. Put a blindfold on him and watch him relax.

"For the most part I don't like being observed."

"It is very pleasurable to watch, but being watched depends on the confidence and trust I feel with the right person in the right situation."

A Memory

"I entered a hotel room for a BDSM scene. Two big, beautiful women were being dominant over me, making me call them [both] 'Mistress.' I was standing, blindfolded, tied up with my wrists behind my back. I was paddled and flogged with leather tassels, as well as with various brushes and some kitchenware. I was kissed and touched for a very long time. When my hands were untied I was allowed to fondle one woman's breasts, though not permitted to suck on them. At the same time the other woman lubed my asshole with her finger. They put me on my knees and while one woman stroked my cock, the other fucked my ass with a strap-on. I came in her hand and she wiped my cum on my tongue."

The Big "O"

HOW DO YOU REACH AN ORGASM AND HOW OFTEN?

He achieves orgasm with ease virtually every time he makes love in almost any position. "It doesn't take much," intercourse, masturbation, oral sex, or a combination of these for the Scorpio man.

"I can cum from any act and I like to reach climax at least once, maybe twice."

WHAT'S YOUR FAVORITE POSITION?

He's not fussy about the position for most satisfying sex, as he finds that they all work. He is a bit controlling and likes to get his partner all worked up with oral sex before backing off and allowing her to please him.

"I love to look at her face when she is on top. It feels good when I'm on top and it's satisfying face to face. I guess I like all positions: mutual oral sex, doggie style . . . they all work."

"They are all excellent, but my partner likes doggie style least and I really enjoy it when I can get it."

 Fantasies

"*I never used to fantasize during sex. When I was alone, masturbating, I would imagine a powerful woman dominating me, having her way with me. Now that we are into BDSM I live my fantasy every time we play. She can use me any way she wants.*"

"*I fantasize about sex with two women. After perhaps an hour of foreplay, I am blindfolded, then I mount one woman missionary style while the second one takes me from behind with a strap-on.*"

SOME PEOPLE ARE CONCERNED ABOUT BRINGING THEIR PARTNER TO CLIMAX BEFORE HAVING AN ORGASM THEMSELVES. OTHERS STRIVE TO REACH ORGASM TOGETHER. WHICH IS TRUE FOR YOU?

It is so important to Scorpio to satisfy his partner that he enjoys sex most when he brings her to climax before cumming himself. He has the stamina to go on and on, and he enjoys achieving mutual orgasm after his partner has had her first climax.

"I prefer to bring my partner first, in order to make sure that she is satisfied."

"I bring her first, and then I usually cum immediately after."

"Partner first. I aim to please, then you aim to please, too."

"Her first, then me, but together is okay for our second time."

ARE YOU VOCAL DURING SEX?

As Scorpio communicates about sex primarily with body language, it is rare for him to make much noise during sex and orgasm.

"I am only a little vocal. I think about being more so. I was with an uninhibited Leo once and she wanted me to be vocal. It was some of the best sex I've ever had."

AFTER SEX WHAT DO YOU LIKE TO DO?

The time after sex is important to Scorpio. He will want to go to sleep, but not right away. This is a man of considerable mystery who desires intimacy and the intense feeling of closeness that sex brings. So after sex he wants to prolong that sensation.

"My ideal scenario is to talk for a while, then take a shower, have more sex, and fall asleep."

"Hold hands, listen to music, cuddle, talk, shower together, stay in bed, eat, sleep."

"Cuddle, smoke, eat, laugh, prepare for more."

SAGITTARIUS

November 22–December 21

THE ARCHER

Fire Sign Sagittarius is mellow, laid back, generous, friendly, and forthright. They speak bluntly, without awareness that their words can hurt, striking home like the Archer's arrows. Ruler of the hips and legs in the physical body, Sagittarius loves the outdoors for hiking, camping, and having sex.

She says: "The environment for sex must be clean, although natural scents are okay. Lighting and décor have nothing to do with it. Is there décor in the woods?"

He says: "We went for a walk on a mountaintop, and made love on a hilltop. The smell was mushrooms and salt sea air. The extra thrill was realizing that in the distance another couple was watching us."

"Float like a butterfly, sting like a bee."
—Muhammad Ali

The Sagittarius Woman in Her Own Words

A Memory

"I was at my parents' house and my boyfriend was visiting. He was staying on the sofa bed in our guestroom, directly underneath my mother's bedroom. We started making out and fooling around on the sofa bed, but it began creaking noisily and I swear I heard footsteps upstairs. We moved to the floor and made sure that the door to the guestroom was shut. He had already started going down on me and when he went to go down again, I had to have him inside me. Once we were having sex, he was on top and grabbed my hands, pushing them over my head and holding them there. He got really into it, almost rough, but it was amazing. I had to try very hard to keep from screaming. I did not want to wake anyone up, but then again, the fact that I might get caught was a total turn-on."

Attraction and Dating a Sagittarius

WHAT ATTRACTS YOU TO SOMEONE?

Sagittarius is a strong woman, active and straightforward in nature. She is attracted to men who are energetic and self-confident. While there are certain physical attributes that catch her eye—a nice butt and muscular legs, and she does care about penis size—it is a man's intellect and behavior most of all that attracts Sagittarius.

"What attracts me to a man is an overall sense: chemistry. As to looks, his physique and height make no difference to me. It's his heart, sensitivity, and energy that matter."

"I love guys that are bigger than me: tall and bulky is great. I love big, hardworking hands. Aside from the physical aspects, I am attracted to understated confidence, maturity, friendliness, humor."

"Beautiful hands, clean and self-confident, sense of humor."

WHAT MIGHT TURN YOU OFF?

A man who pays no attention to style—for example, thinks it is okay to go out for the evening in sweat pants—is out of shape, and either arrogant or insecure won't hold Sagittarius' interest for long.

"Dull conversationalist, no sense of humor, bad hygiene, clothes [that] don't match, too clingy, stuck in a time warp."

"Lack of polite manners; willful ignorance; being rude, crude, or socially unacceptable . . ."

"Low self-confidence, being insensitive, no sense of humor, putting others down . . ."

WHAT DO YOU ENJOY DOING ON A DATE?

Sagittarius, being an energetic Fire Sign, enjoys evenings out that involve activities from simple walks to exploring caves, rock climbing to canoeing. She loves a man who challenges her by expanding her range of experiences.

"I love to do things outside like walk or kayak, or go to the driving range, the beach, or amusement park."

"Sightseeing, movies, eating, picnics, museums, amusement parks, dancing; listening to live music . . ."

A Fantasy

"I am asleep at the stern of a boat drifting on the ocean. He wakes me up with kisses and by rubbing his

lips over my cheek and jawbone. We kiss slowly and gradually build in depth and intensity. We walk into the cabin where I rub my hands over his shoulders, back, and chest. I unbutton his shorts, while he slides my swimsuit straps from my shoulders. We lie on the bed. The rocking of the boat on the waves, the smell of the warm sunshine and ocean lend a slow, sleepy pleasure to the leisurely pace of our exploits."

ARE YOU FLIRTATIOUS?

She is a Fire Sign, loves attention, and even though she is not aggressive, consistent with her direct approach (after all, she is the Archer letting fly her arrow), Sagittarius is highly flirtatious. Any man on whom she sets her sights will be well aware of her interest.

"I am generally pretty friendly and I can flirt like hell if I want to, but only if I am really interested in someone."

"Yes, I am always flirting. I have to get attention from men."

ARE YOU JEALOUS?

Sagittarius is a self-confident woman. She speaks her mind and confronts situations when they surface rather than let them fester. As a result, she is not overly possessive or by nature jealous.

"If I am feeling jealous then it is a red flag that the relationship isn't right."

"I get very involved in trusting, probably too much for my well-being. I know jealousy is never good."

"I didn't find out I was jealous until twenty years of marriage [when] a waitress touched my husband's shoulder. I saw red."

HOW DO YOU FEEL ABOUT PUBLIC DISPLAYS OF AFFECTION?

Sagittarius isn't exactly an exhibitionist, but she does believe that tasteful public displays are just fine. In other words, she welcomes her lover's affection but doesn't want to attract negative attention from onlookers.

"I think [they are] great. [They] really show how comfortable the couple is together."

"They are great, but not to the point of being sickening."

"I never used to like them, but now, seeing older adults walking down the street holding hands and stealing a kiss is wonderful."

Sexual Attitudes and Behaviors

HOW OFTEN DO YOU THINK ABOUT SEX AND HOW OFTEN PER WEEK DO YOU WANT TO HAVE SEX?

The Sagittarius woman would enjoy having sex daily. Only time constraints put a damper on her sexual appetite.

"Three times is nice, two times is okay; less is frustrating, more is fine."

"Every day if I could, twice even . . ."

"I could have it seven days a week."

 A Fantasy

"*My sex fantasies usually take place by the ocean or a bubbling stream and involve someone famous or an athlete. He is strong but gentle, kind and considerate, and takes charge. He's thoughtful and completely enamored with me. We are perfect for each other. Our bodies mold together perfectly.*"

HOW LONG DO YOU LIKE TO SPEND HAVING SEX AND HOW MUCH OF THAT TIME IS FOREPLAY? DO YOU ENJOY QUICKIES?

Plan on devoting at least 45 minutes for sex with Sagittarius, and more time is even better. Time for foreplay varies from ten to 30 minutes, preferably on the longer side especially if a new sex toy is part of the mix. Quickies are okay, but not as a steady diet.

"I love spending an afternoon or a couple of hours, including a nap at the end, but I also enjoy quickies."

"I like romantic foreplay, a long slow buildup to climax, romantic cuddling afterward. Quickies, not really . . ."

"I enjoy quickies, but prefer more time with foreplay, dining, humor, innuendoes, and discussion of what is to come."

 ### A Fantasy

"I'm on vacation or in a club, approached by a couple with whom I have been making eye contact. The wife tells me her husband would like to have sex with me. She says she would like to watch. I agree. We go to their hotel room. Her husband is taking a shower. She has me undress and lie on the bed. I end up having sex with the husband several times during vacation, frequently including the wife. We do not exchange numbers but everyone has a memorable vacation."

WHAT TIME OF DAY DO YOU PREFER TO HAVE SEX?

Just about any time is fine for sex, though Sagittarius does have some preference for mornings and mid-afternoon.

"Anytime of day is good, but sex in the morning makes my entire day a good one."

"Afternoons are great, morning too. Sometimes at night I am too sleepy."

"I like mornings, but any time is good."

HOW OFTEN PER WEEK DO YOU MASTURBATE?

She's far too independent to rely on a man to take care of her sexual needs. When she feels sexy, she masturbates—perhaps as often as five times a week.

HOW LONG DO YOU WANT TO KNOW SOMEONE BEFORE GETTING SEXUAL?

Any man who hopes for a sexual relationship with Sagittarius better make up his mind to be patient. She is blunt and to the point about this; she won't be rushed.

"I need to reach a comfort level with someone, get to be friends, however long it takes. That could be in one month, maybe more."

"I really have to love the person before I get sexual with him."

"I take my time. I don't share my body with someone unless he deserves it."

WHAT'S YOUR ATTITUDE TOWARD CASUAL SEX?

For Sagittarius, sex and love—or at least some amount of emotional connection—are bound together. Casual sex isn't usually among her behaviors.

"It is not for me. My heart and body are linked together. I need to be in a somewhat committed partnership to enjoy sex with a man."

"I prefer being in a relationship and I think casual sex is unsafe, too."

"It is unsafe. I have to be in love to give myself to someone."

DO YOU BELIEVE IN MONOGAMY?

Honesty, trust, and being candid with her partner are very important to Sagittarius. In most cases, she prefers monogamy; however, an open relationship might be okay with her. Having a clandestine affair or learning that her lover has been cheating would not be acceptable to this Sign.

"I believe in finding that one true partner, and having the relationship last for life."

"If you love someone, why would you want to hurt them by being with someone else?"

DOES SEX HAVE A SPIRITUAL SIGNIFICANCE FOR YOU?

Sex is much more than a physical experience for Sagittarius. The connection that sex enables her to make with her partner, especially at the height of the sexual experience, is transcendent.

"Sex leads to a deeper connection with the universe and the Creator."

"There is something about looking into each other's eyes during sex that is amazingly spiritual."

"Absolutely. Sex is soul energy exchange. That is why an emotional connection is essential for me to be sexual."

ARE YOU COMFORTABLE INITIATING SEXUAL ACTIVITIES?

Given her flirtatious nature, her bluntness of speech, and her innate self-confidence, Sagittarius is quite at ease suggesting sex.

"I am plenty comfortable when I know it is welcomed."

"Of course! Men like it, though it depends on how well I know a person."

 A Fantasy

"I fantasize about the UPS man coming to deliver a package. I'm not completely dressed. He picks me up and puts me on the counter and gives me oral pleasure. I return the favor and we have sex all over the house in different positions."

HOW DO YOU COMMUNICATE TO YOUR PARTNER YOUR SEXUAL WANTS AND NEEDS?

Known for being direct, Sagittarius is forthright in expressing her desires and responses. She uses a combination of signals to indicate her wants and needs.

"Gentle words and gestures . . ."

"I try to be subtle, using more gestures than words, but I will ask if I have to."

"I tell him in plain English."

"I use words, sounds, and gestures."

DO YOU THINK OF YOURSELF AS BEING IN THE MAINSTREAM SEXUALLY, MORE EXPERIMENTAL, OR OPEN TO ANYTHING?

Sagittarius is an experimental lover who is likely to explore a range of sex acts, including anal sex, dominance and submission, spanking and bondage, wearing costumes, and using chains. She is willing to have sex in public places and incorporate foods such as fruits and chocolate. She doesn't use a wide range of sex toys other than vibrators, dildos, and some bondage accoutrements.

"I will try anything once, maybe twice."

"I own three vibrators. The Jack Rabbit is God's gift to women."

Her fantasy life reflects her actual behavior. It may include images of dominance and submission with strangers or multiple partners, and often takes place in or near water.

 A Fantasy

"I get picked up off the floor and brought to the Jacuzzi, and as he lifts off my thin dress, he realizes I am wearing nothing underneath. He follows me into the Jacuzzi and moves to the front and starts biting my neck and shoulders, then starts to caress my vagina with his two fingers under the water. As he feels my body begin to move into his hand he slips his fingers inside me and moves them about as he grabs the back of my neck and pulls me to him for a deep passionate kiss. He then slides his fingers out and his enlarged penis in. My body trembles as he begins to pump in and out. He tells me how tight I feel and starts to pump faster and faster. I cum and just as I peak I feel him explode inside me. We melt together as one and cuddle without a sound, under the stars."

HOW DO YOU DEMONSTRATE AFFECTION FOR YOUR PARTNER?

Words of love don't cut it with Sagittarius unless they are backed up with action. Therefore, she is more likely to demonstrate her regard for her partner through her behavior than through cards and gifts. In return, she respects the man who is competent and who makes himself useful around the house and with joint responsibilities.

"Small gestures like bringing dessert home or planning a surprise, massages, doing his laundry, folding it."

"Cooking, buying gifts, holding hands, picking events or items that I know will make him happy."

"I make his favorite dinner and go places willingly that he enjoys even if I don't."

The Five Senses

HOW IMPORTANT TO YOU IS THE SEXUAL ENVIRONMENT?

While she is not overly concerned about the environment, soft lights, quiet music, fresh clean smells, and a comfortable bed are very appealing to her. She also likes to have sex in a variety of locations where setting the stage may not be possible. In these cases, cleanliness is the only factor that matters.

"It must be clean, although natural scents are okay. Lighting and décor have nothing to do with it. Is there décor in the woods?"

"Cleanliness and lighting are important. I like my bedroom to be comfortable and private, with curtains, and soundproof if possible."

 ### A Fantasy
"I would love for my partner to drive down a dark alley and get out of the car and walk around to my side and grab me out of the car and throw me up against the wall. Him talking naughty to me the whole time. Whispering in my ear how bad he wants me. Then he lifts my skirt and we have hot, steamy, aggressive sex."

WHERE DO YOU LIKE TO HAVE SEX?
Sagittarius rules the woods, open plains, and fields. She finds such settings exciting turn-ons for sex. She would love to have her partner take her for a drive, surprise her with a blanket and

perhaps some wine and a light picnic, and park in a quiet dark forest.

"Outdoors is fine or on a boat or in a car as long as it is not likely that we would be caught or heard. That is not a turn-on for me."

"River, lake, ocean, swimming pool, on a boat, on a private beach . . ."

"I have done it all. No place is off limits as long as you do not hurt anyone or expose yourself to unsuspecting people."

"The bedroom is nice, but I have explored other places also. My worst experience was in my boss's office with my ex-husband, late at night. I kept thinking 'What if there are hidden video cameras?' Totally ruined the moment . . ."

WHAT PUTS YOU IN THE MOOD FOR SEX?
She has a busy life and an active mind. Quiet time, a sort of stop-the-world feeling, and cuddling all put Sagittarius in the mood for sex. She also has a romantic streak and is somewhat of a daydreamer. Thus it is that creating a setting, real or imagined through erotica, helps to turn her on.

"The environment sets the mood for me, like being outside at night or on the beach or a dark bar. Sometimes just mid-morning does it."

"Candles, elegant settings, music in the background, cuddling up watching movies . . ."

"Cuddling, a glass of wine, lit candles and soft music; sometimes watching porn videos; putting on something sexy."

Memories
"At the beach in a semi-secluded area; we had sex on a large rock with the sound and the smell of the ocean in the background. Later we realized that at this little encounter we had conceived our daughter."

"In an alcove in the rocks, overlooking the beach, with people walking around and above us but unable to see."

"On a private beach during the day behind a small clump of bushes."

"We used to have sex in the soft grass outside a cabin in the woods in Vermont."

WHAT'S YOUR ATTITUDE TOWARD PORNOGRAPHY?

Porn is okay sometimes. Her preference is for videos that reflect the kinds of settings that turn her on, that trigger memories of wonderful personal encounters, especially in out-of-the-way places. As a steady diet or a substitute for foreplay, though, pornography turns her off.

"Some of it is good. Some of it sucks . . . pardon the pun."

"It's okay. I wouldn't mind porn that is more loving and less kinky."

 Fantasies

"A man with a large penis; someone who can do me well from behind without me having to arch my back as much as I have had to in the past. Someone who will hold my hands back or put them in handcuffs while he fucks me."

"My latest sexual dream is that my favorite man who lives out of state comes in through my window, sees me in bed with another man, ties him [up] and then makes him watch as we make our usual wild and wonderful sex."

HOW MUCH CUDDLING DO YOU ENJOY, ASIDE FROM SEX?

At night on the couch, in bed while saying goodnight, or when walking cuddling is great but Sagittarius is a Sign that needs her space. Too much holding on becomes cloying and puts her off.

"With someone I know well, I like it a lot; otherwise, almost none."

"Physical contact is very important to me, being held, holding hands, frequently but not on a constant basis."

"On many occasions, cuddling is as good as sex."

HOW TACTILE AND HOW ORAL ARE YOU?

She is more oral than tactile in her approach to sex, preferring kissing to fondling and oral sex to having her partner masturbate her.

"I have an oral fixation: love oral sex, deep kissing, and licking."

"I love it. I start at the toes and work my way up."

"I love kissing, can never get enough, long and hard or soft and sweet. I enjoy giving oral sex or receiving [it]."

"I love deep kissing and often judge my partners by their kissing. Oral sex is wonderful."

 A Memory

"I was once seduced by a friend who took complete control of my pleasure and drove me wild. It was daytime, on a bed, my legs in the air, his hands holding my legs; and he really knew what to do with his dick."

WHAT SEX ACTS DO YOU LIKE MOST AND LEAST?

She enjoys most everything in the mainstream range of sexuality, from kissing and fondling to oral sex and intercourse. She especially loves deep penetration during vaginal intercourse.

"I enjoy anal sex, mutual masturbation, kissing, oral sex, and being controlled during sex."

"My favorites are cuddling and kissing. When it is with someone I love, oral sex is exciting and fun. I enjoy both performing and receiving it."

"I enjoy kissing, both giving and receiving oral sex, and intercourse. I have tried anal sex, but I am not sure if I am interested in it."

"All of them are part of the sex act. I am not fond of anal sex, but will consent at times."

AS A LOVER, WHAT'S YOUR BEST SKILL?

Fire Sign Sagittarius is a confident lover who puts energy into pleasing her partner with her hands and even more so with her mouth. Perhaps her best attribute is her willingness to experiment and move beyond traditional sex acts.

"How I use my hands and mouth. It is all pressure and timing,"

"I bite. People seem to like that. As a skill I am very good at, kissing mouth and body parts."

"Everything I do drives him crazy. I think I am great at everything I do."

"My partner tells me that it is my response to his actions that is the real turn-on."

WHAT SMELLS AND TASTES ON YOUR PARTNER DO YOU ENJOY?

Sagittarius is responsive to her partner's smells and tastes fresh from the shower or dabbed with cologne. When it comes to adding flavors to sex, she prefers fruit and sweet tastes.

"The smells I enjoy include clean skin, ocean salt, soft scents like Bay Rum cologne. For food tastes: chocolate, wine, Irish Mist."

"Smells: skin of his neck, his colognes, the inner elbows and his hands. Tastes: chocolate, whipped cream, and strawberries."

"I love Curve cologne. Lucky You is nice, too. Tastes: Cool Whip with the little bit of salt I can taste on him after a round of rowdy sex."

A Fantasy

"It's hot and humid, and I'm at an outside dance place near water. I'm wearing a short skirt and no underwear and a tight, sheer top. I'm dancing very closely with some man, and he has his hands all over me even under my skirt. Men around start to watch and then start to touch me, too. I have hands all over me. Then someone takes me from behind while I start to suck someone else. Still hands everywhere. I take as many men in me as I can at one time. After, I just go lie on the beach on a blanket, naked, while someone touches me gently."

FOR SOME PEOPLE THE TASTE OF THEIR PARTNER'S CUM OR SECRETIONS IS UNPLEASANT. IF THAT'S TRUE FOR YOU, WHAT DO YOU DO ABOUT THE TASTE?

Being such an oral lover, Sagittarius accepts handling cum as part of the experience. The greater the love she has for her partner, the easier it is for her to swallow his cum.

"It is unpleasant and I try to block out thinking about it. I do swallow."

"I tolerate it and swallow as fast as I can."

"My partner tastes great. I take turns swallowing and rubbing it all over myself."

"If it is unpleasant, I make sure I have something to spit it in."

DO YOU ENJOY WATCHING YOUR PARTNER DURING SEX AND ORGASM? DO YOU ENJOY BEING WATCHED?

She likes to see her partner's expressions during sex and orgasm but she has mixed feelings about being watched. This is a bit unexpected, considering that she is so open in most other ways. When she's comfortable with her partner it gets easier.

The Big "O"

HOW DO YOU REACH AN ORGASM AND HOW OFTEN?

She reaches orgasm often during intercourse, more frequently via oral sex and always by masturbation. She isn't shy about taking care of her own orgasm.

"Reaching orgasm depends on the partner but I believe it is important, so if my current partner can't do it I will masturbate. He likes to watch. I can cum through oral sex as well as intercourse."

"I reach climax by oral sex performed on me [but] not through intercourse."

WHAT'S YOUR FAVORITE POSITION?

The Sagittarius woman enjoys being on bottom or top. If the latter, she enjoys a particular variation—she faces away from him.

"I like to be on top, facing away from my partner."

"Being on the bottom, maybe on my tummy . . ."

"Woman on top, sitting on the man's lap, facing away from him . . ."

 A Memory

"It was during an orgy, a man started fondling me while in a hot tub and when we emerged we had sex, including anal penetration. He was very gentle and asked permission to cum inside me when having anal sex. During a second orgy, I was having sex with one man, while another man was lying beside us watching TV. He watched us the entire time and was so turned on [he] took his turn having intercourse with me when the first guy was finished. They alternated having sex with me, including using toys, throughout the night and [the] following morning."

SOME PEOPLE ARE CONCERNED ABOUT BRINGING THEIR PARTNER TO CLIMAX BEFORE HAVING AN ORGASM THEMSELVES. OTHERS STRIVE TO REACH ORGASM TOGETHER. WHICH IS TRUE FOR YOU?

Sagittarius loves to achieve orgasm with her partner. If this isn't possible, she prefers to cum first because she derives greatest pleasure from the penetration.

"We try for togetherness."

"I can orgasm several times before my partner and [I] like to orgasm again after him."

"It's nice if it is together, but I'm not too concerned about timing as long as we both climax."

"My favorite partner makes certain that I have several orgasms, then we do it together."

ARE YOU VOCAL DURING SEX?

People always know where they stand with Sagittarius because she expresses herself freely on all topics. This is true also during sex. The Archer's lover will surely know when he's pleasing her.

"I am extremely vocal during sex."

"My partner would say I never shut up. Talking is arousing as long as the topic is not the kids, house . . ."

"I am somewhat vocal; not a screamer."

AFTER SEX WHAT DO YOU LIKE TO DO?

Since Sagittarius likes to take her time during sex, whatever activities might come later, she prefers to take a nap or to at least relax a while, just after sex.

"Cuddle for a while, shower together, wait a while, and do it again."

"Immediately after sex, sleep cuddled up. Later, it depends on the time of day and where we are."

"Just relax. It's sort of like having ridden a horse for a long time. I need to rest."

The Sagittarius Man in His Own Words

A Memory

"I was on a visit to Ireland. I was in a group. I had my eye on one woman, but another made a serious pass at me. We went for a walk on a mountain, and made love on a hilltop. The smell was mushrooms and salt sea air. The extra thrill was realizing that another couple was watching us."

Attraction and Dating a Sagittarius

WHAT ATTRACTS YOU TO SOMEONE?

Sagittarius is an even-tempered, fairly easy-going man. He appreciates a woman with a gentle disposition and who doesn't get overly upset about trivialities. Intelligence certainly counts, but the Sagittarius man never underestimates the importance of a nice pair of legs and lovely hips

"Eyes, hair, smell, stance, and gap between thighs with skin tight pants."

"A combination of a woman's mind and athletic body . . ."

"I would call myself a leg man. I am turned on sexually by short skirts, with or without panty hose, and high heels. I like leather skirts, also."

"A woman's form, breasts that aren't overly large, intelligence . . . She must be energetic and have a free spirit."

WHAT MIGHT TURN YOU OFF?

A woman who is loud and boisterous and tries too hard to be the center of attention will turn off this laid-back man. Style and grace are also important to him.

"Sour attitude, crude language, bitterness, any extreme attitudes, such as racism, homophobia . . ."

"A woman who is too conventional and anti-intellectual, and too fat . . ."

"Someone who doesn't take time to look nice, a profane mouth, acting too tough, someone who is cold."

WHAT DO YOU ENJOY DOING ON A DATE?

He is somewhat of a gambler and enjoys the occasional night at the track or at a nearby casino. Sagittarius loves sports and a woman who comes up with tickets to the local farm team's baseball game will score with him. He also likes a good debate, even a very heated one. That's all part of the fun for him.

"I have enjoyed dining out, movies, amusement parks, visiting friends, and going out with another couple."

"Intelligent conversation, walking on a beach, going to a fine restaurant . . ."

"Dance, drink, talk, movie, dinner, a walk through the park . . ."

"Talking, learning about the person, long drives . . ."

"Movies, eating out, cooking together, sports events, cuddling and holding hands . . ."

Memories

"*Romantic: a girlfriend once asked me over on the first day it snowed in order to sweep the snow off her car. She was only 5' 1" and was having a hard time reaching across the top. We ended up making love in the back seat, something I hadn't done before. I have no idea why that one stands out with me so much . . . something about the cold snowy air, warm car, unexpected quality of it all, I guess.*"

"*My nineteenth birthday. My girlfriend did not say a word to me when I came to her house. She just grabbed me and proceeded from there.*"

ARE YOU FLIRTATIOUS?

Of course he is flirtatious. Sagittarius is a friendly and fairly outgoing Sign. He is relaxed and mellow, but when in conversation with a woman his focus is completely upon her. Flirting is fun.

"To the point where it is a problem, yes . . ."

"I am not a conscious flirt, but I am told that my eyes attract."

"Somewhat, probably just enough so I [won't] get into trouble . . ."

ARE YOU JEALOUS?

Sagittarius isn't a possessive sign. He has a fun-loving disposition and is open and forthright. When he is in a relationship, he expects the same from his partner. If both parties are being honest, what could possibly provoke jealousy?

"I am not naturally jealous, unless I have cause to suspect my love, and I am not the type to make a scene."

HOW DO YOU FEEL ABOUT PUBLIC DISPLAYS OF AFFECTION?

For the Sagittarius man, the rules are simple: affection, yes; sex, no. A loving kiss is fine, Frenching isn't. Sitting close and embracing, absolutely. Dry humping never.

"I was somewhat shy about it when I was younger, but I am more comfortable now. I still don't like to see tongue kissing."

"It is great so long as it doesn't become really sexual."

Sexual Attitudes and Behaviors

HOW OFTEN DO YOU THINK ABOUT SEX AND HOW OFTEN PER WEEK DO YOU WANT TO HAVE SEX?

Sagittarius has a playful side. He wants to have fun, to enjoy himself. Pleasures for him include traveling, sports, perhaps gambling, and certainly sex. In fact, sex is never far from the surface of his mind and he would enjoy having sex three to four times a week.

"I probably think about women several times daily, as well as the thought of sex itself."

"I think about it daily, several times a day."

"I am preoccupied with it."

A Fantasy

"*I fantasize about a celebrity I want to please with champagne and soft music: to lie beside her warm, beautiful body. I undress her slowly, savoring every moment. We take a romantic bath by candlelight. I give her a sensual massage, stimulating all her erogenous zones. I caress her breasts, buttocks, and mouth. My tongue and lips artfully explore her entire body. I move my head between her legs, feeling silky smooth thighs on my cheeks.*

"*I lightly lick her clitoris. I am very careful and sensitive with this beautiful little bud of excitement. She is writhing with ecstasy, anticipating the joy that is about to come. Looking at her beautiful vagina makes me very hot and I can't resist licking her love juices from my fingers and looking into her soulful eyes. I bring her to . . . climax as many times as she wants.*

"*Then she performs oral sex on me, stopping right before I cum. She climbs on top and rides me. After cumming, I rest a few minutes, until my body stops vibrating, and [then] I am ready to make love to her again."*

HOW MUCH TIME DO YOU LIKE TO SPEND HAVING SEX AND HOW MUCH OF THAT TIME IS FOREPLAY? DO YOU ENJOY QUICKIES?

Sagittarius enjoys spending about an hour having sex, sometimes even more, with at least 30 minutes for foreplay. Quickies are all right, but they are not his preference. In fact, if there is only time for a quickie, he might not want to have sex at all.

"I like to take my time, with as much foreplay as my partner requires. When she's ready, I am . . . I hope."

"Forty-five minutes to an hour for sex, and a half-hour on average of foreplay. Quickies are okay, but I wouldn't want to rely on them."

"For sex, I want at least two to three hours [of] listening to music, changing positions, and withdrawing many times before climax."

"I like spending no less than one hour for sex. If there is only time for a quickie, why bother?"

"I usually spend several hours, foreplay is the best part. Quickies are fun sometimes."

WHAT TIME OF DAY DO YOU PREFER TO MAKE LOVE?

He will rouse himself most any time, but his preference for having sex is from morning to early evening.

"Days are nice for quickies, but we generally get together after 8 or 9 P.M."

"Mornings, but anytime with the right person . . ."

HOW OFTEN PER WEEK DO YOU MASTURBATE?

Sagittarius masturbates on average three times weekly, more often when he doesn't have a sex partner. When single, he may do so on a daily basis.

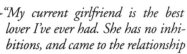

A Memory

"My current girlfriend is the best lover I've ever had. She has no inhibitions, and came to the relationship four years ago with a list of all the things she wanted to do before she died. I've never seen the list but she tells me we are working our way through it."

HOW LONG DO YOU WANT TO KNOW SOMEONE BEFORE GETTING SEXUAL?

He has no set time before becoming sexual, but Sagittarius is not a pushy or aggressive Sign and he takes his lead from his partner. From his point of view, sooner is better than later. This might be at once, after three dates, or up to four weeks after beginning to date.

"This is entirely dependent on the woman. It could be a week, it could be 15 minutes."

"For me it would be easy to have sex right away, but the woman needs to be ready. I wouldn't lie to a woman to have sex, and if I cared for her, I wouldn't like her to give herself too quickly."

"There is no set time. When it is right, it is right."

"It depends on the chemistry; if it is the right person, the sooner the better."

WHAT'S YOUR ATTITUDE TOWARD CASUAL SEX?

Imagine a waitress walking by with a tray of exquisite hors d'oeuvres. Why not take one? This is how Sagittarius regards casual sex.

"It is okay if done responsibly."

"Casual sex is mostly fine. It is only unhealthy if it becomes a lifestyle."

"It is fine. You know you got it if it makes you feel good."

"I know it is risky, but honestly, if it is available it is okay."

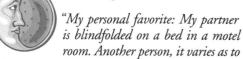

A Fantasy

"My personal favorite: My partner is blindfolded on a bed in a motel room. Another person, it varies as to whom, joins us and we both pleasure her. I video-tape this and play this tape back to my partner later. I am particularly fond of threesome fantasies, either with another man plus a woman or two women."

DO YOU BELIEVE IN MONOGAMY?

Sagittarius is in no rush to get into a monogamous relationship. When committed to a woman, he will be faithful. However, if she is accepting of a more open relationship, he might prefer that.

"Monogamy is unnatural but is sometimes possible. Serial monogamy is a much more realistic lifestyle for me."

"I believe in monogamy, mostly; but I am not opposed to multiple partners if the circumstances are right and no one gets hurt."

"Yes. There is a sense of loyalty that must be honored with your partner."

"I believe in monogamy when you are in a permanent relationship."

DOES SEX HAVE A SPIRITUAL SIGNIFICANCE FOR YOU?

Sagittarius is a spiritual Sign, though one who frequently resists traditional religion. Because he connects spirituality with religion, he does not see sex as spiritual per se. If you call it lovemaking, then sex becomes more than physical gratification to him.

"When you truly love and care for someone, there can be a feeling as though the relationship were heaven sent."

"Yes, I worship my partner."

"It is the key to self-liberation."

"In a way, it is like bonding with another's soul."

A Memory

"My first date with my girlfriend. We went out for Chinese food then back to my workplace. As I was showing her around, she poked me in my ass cheek. She swears that she didn't do it, even to this day, but for me it was like getting a 'go' sign pinned across my butt. I walked her into another part of the building. As we entered the hall I told her the light switch was at the other end of the hallway. I walked in front of her a few feet, turned and let her walk into me. We made love right there in the hallway."

ARE YOU COMFORTABLE INITIATING SEXUAL ACTIVITIES?

Sagittarius is the gambler of the zodiac, highly unlikely to be the least bit reticent about initiating sex. Not only that, but he is the stallion, known to be well endowed and always eager to show a woman how well he can please her.

HOW DO YOU COMMUNICATE TO YOUR PARTNER YOUR SEXUAL WANTS AND NEEDS?

Sagittarius is very straightforward. He is usually quite direct in speech and although he isn't aggressive, neither is he shy about making his needs known. When it comes to communicating about sex, he is comfortable letting his partner know how to please him with a combination of words and gestures, and with some emphasis on body language.

"Communication about sex is not a problem, as my primary need is to satisfy my partner."

DO YOU THINK OF YOURSELF AS BEING IN THE MAINSTREAM SEXUALLY, MORE EXPERIMENTAL, OR OPEN TO ANYTHING?

Sagittarius is known for being well endowed, and his main objective as a lover is to please his partner in the most traditional range of sexuality. Beyond the boundaries of the bedroom, he does enjoy sex in public places—secluded, of course—such as in a pine forest or on an isolated stretch of beach. Occasionally he will get a kick out of having his lover wear costumes, or he may want to participate in a certain amount of dominance and submission using hot wax. Now and then he might be interested in sex toys such as dildos and body clips.

In his fantasy life, images range from the aggressive to the romantic. Sometimes he imagines multiple partners. Occasionally he plays the part of submissive and at other times he takes total control.

Fantasies

"My sex fantasies involve random, unprepared rear entry of a woman over the dining room table. I would love to act that one out."

"Taken against my will to a dominatrix or a doctor where I am stripped and put in stirrups. I am then probed and shaved completely."

HOW DO YOU DEMONSTRATE AFFECTION FOR YOUR PARTNER?

Sagittarius uses touch to convey awareness of his partner's needs and his willingness to be supportive. He is also attentive and quite aware of his partner's state of mind. If she is upset, he knows how to let things ride, to keep things light.

"Holding hands, putting my arm around her, touching, writing cards, and calling . . ."

"Flowers for no special occasion, a meal prepared for her when she arrives home tired."

"Gifts, back rubs, getting things on request, generally tending to [her] needs."

"Just being there for her; listening well."

The Five Senses

HOW IMPORTANT IS THE ENVIRONMENT TO YOU?

Easy-going Sagittarius likes his sexual environment to be clean and softly lighted, but such details are not particularly important. As long as he can be comfortable, which means no crumbs in the bed and preferably no dog hair, he'll be content.

"In bed it is the woman, not the surroundings, that matters."

"Cleanliness counts; otherwise, the setting is not the major stimulus."

"I care about the environment, but with the right person it is not important."

"It really doesn't matter to me as long as it is clean."

A Fantasy

"Watching my girl have sex with another man. We go out for drinks at a restaurant. A man walks by. They exchange glances. I dare my lover to strike up a conversation. She invites him to our table and we talk.

"Her hand is on my thigh. I start to get hard. She strokes me. Her eyes are closed. She's breathing heavily. I reach over to touch her and a hand is already there. We decide to return to our hotel room. Once there, we turn the lights off. It's almost completely dark. I feel hands on me and hands on her. I'm not sure whose hands are where. We work our way to the bed, rip off the covers, and strip off our clothes.

"The heat is steaming. We are moaning. She climbs on top of him. With my hand I guide him into her. I lean in to watch his penetrating strokes. When it's unbearable for me I get back on my knees, spit on my dick, and work it into her ass. I can feel his cock driving into her through the skin that separates us. The sensations, the moaning, the electricity are all in sync as we explode into frantic orgasm. He thanks us and leaves. She falls asleep in my arms as I stroke her hair."

WHERE DO YOU LIKE TO HAVE SEX?

He will say that his favorite place is the bedroom, but a quiet area in a forest is always a turn-on. Sagittarius also enjoys having sex in a car, while camping, and in other rooms throughout the house.

"Bedroom, car, under the stars . . ."

"Privately, otherwise it doesn't matter."

"The edge of a bar stool at a house, not in a bar, on the couch or a chair, in the car, even standing up at times."

WHAT PUTS YOU IN THE MOOD FOR SEX?

Sagittarius is turned on by a wide range of romantic sounds, such as gentle rain and love songs, by seeing his partner in silk lingerie or revealing clothes, and by the aromas of food and subtle perfumes. In other words, stimulate his senses and he is in the mood for sex.

"Food, candles, rain, showering, videos, nice smells, clothing or lack of it . . ."

"Music, sexy clothing, talk, walk, erotic videos . . ."

"Rainy days and evenings, soft music . . ."

"My partner looking beautiful, some drinking, music, environment, scented candles, black lights and a nice room and bed . . ."

WHAT'S YOUR ATTITUDE TOWARD PORNOGRAPHY?

In his estimation, pornography is okay but nothing great. Considering the gentle and subtle things that turn him on, it fits that the Sagittarius man's preference is for eroticism in films and literature rather than anything overly graphic.

"It's okay. I don't think it reflects reality. I think many porn users forget this."

"I have not found explicit sex in X-rated movies very interesting. I enjoy eroticism, looking at a picture of a pretty nude woman."

"I like it, but 90 percent of it doesn't turn me on."

 A Memory
"My partner tied me up and beat my cock and balls. I was helpless to move and watched her as she positioned her fists over me. She beat my testicles until they swelled and my glands were very bruised. Then she positioned herself over me and masturbated herself to orgasm with my cock. She stroked my entire body and rubbed my cock until I came."

HOW MUCH CUDDLING DO YOU ENJOY, ASIDE FROM SEX?

Sagittarius is the "don't fence me in" Sign of the zodiac. He may love with great passion, but he does not respond well if a woman clings to him. For Sagittarius, cuddling is sexual. A little goes a long way when it is not a part of sex.

"Cuddling is fun and a form of sex."

"A lot before sex; a little after."

"Cuddling is fine at the right time and place."

"A lot. That is the beginning of sex."

HOW TACTILE AND HOW ORAL ARE YOU?

Sagittarius loves the feel of his partner's skin. Foreplay, for him, incorporates time to study her with his hands. On the oral side, he enjoys kissing his partner's lips, body, and genitals.

"I love to perform oral sex. In fact, I enjoy everything oral except rimming."

"I love to run my hands over her rear and down her legs."

WHAT SEX ACTS DO YOU LIKE MOST AND LEAST?

Sagittarius loves it when a woman goes down on him or rubs his penis between her breasts. He more than shows his appreciation in the way he responds with kissing and performing oral sex, and he is a master at intercourse. He often enjoys anal sex, though he might list that as his least favorite sex act.

AS A LOVER, WHAT'S YOUR BEST SKILL?

He prides himself on the use of his hands and tongue, but in fact, Sagittarius is especially skillful at intercourse. Sagittarius is called the stallion of the zodiac. He has great endurance and is often well endowed.

"I have great staying power. I can go for three hours and put it away without cumming, then take it out and start again the next morning."

"I think it is probably my hands, but many women have commented that I am well hung and they seem to appreciate that."

A Memory

"I knew a couple who performed sex as theater for voyeurs. One time I participated. We all took off our clothes. First he gave her oral sex and had intercourse. Then he invited me to have sex with her. At one point we were all going at it . . . he performed oral sex on her while I did anal sex on him. Then I lay down and she performed fellatio on me, then she blew her husband and he was eating her while I was doing him. I came twice and left exhausted."

WHAT SMELLS AND TASTES ON YOUR PARTNER DO YOU ENJOY?

Sagittarius is easy. He will be happy with his lover if she dabs on perfume or uses none at all, or if she wants to bring strawberries, champagne, and mint juleps into the act.

"Her vaginal smells are pleasant and I like the saltiness and fishiness of her secretions."

"I like the smell of her skin, perfume, and hair; and it is fun to incorporate mint flavors and chocolate with sex."

FOR SOME PEOPLE THE TASTE OF THEIR PARTNER'S CUM OR SECRETIONS IS UNPLEASANT. IF THAT'S TRUE FOR YOU, WHAT DO YOU DO ABOUT THE TASTE?

This is no problem for Sagittarius. He genuinely likes it all.

"I like fishiness unreservedly."

"I like the taste of a woman."

"I love the taste."

DO YOU ENJOY WATCHING YOUR PARTNER DURING SEX AND ORGASM? DO YOU ENJOY BEING WATCHED?

Sagittarius is comfortable with intimacy—both watching and being watched. He wants his

lover to take a good look at his penis moving in and out of her, and he loves watching her ecstasy.

A Memory

"An acquaintance invited me home to meet his wife. When we got there he showed me pictures of her nude. She was beautiful. She came out of her bedroom naked. He asked me if I wanted to have sex with her while he watched. He sat in the doorway masturbating as I kissed her breasts and pussy. I had intercourse with her, pulling out at her request to cum all over her bush so her husband could clean it up. I watched him do that and then went back for a second round. This time he kept his head on her thigh, watching as I pumped in and out. Again I withdrew at the end, came all over her and he licked up my cum."

The Big "O"

HOW DO YOU REACH AN ORGASM AND HOW OFTEN?

Sagittarius has no trouble achieving orgasm. Any method or combination, from intercourse to oral sex, masturbation to anal sex, works for him.

"I always achieve orgasm and if I am really stimulated, any method will work: oral sex, intercourse, and any number of combinations."

"I enjoy all kinds of sex acts and easily reach orgasm every time."

WHAT'S THE BEST POSITION FOR YOU TO ACHIEVE ORGASM?

All positions satisfy him, as long as they allow deep penetration. Sagittarius loves to hear his partner react to the size of his penis and then to ask for more. He has some preference for doggie style.

"Doggie is good, woman on top is good if she is not too fat, missionary always works. I have tried them all."

"The edge of a couch, up close and face to face; doggie is nice; also man sitting on edge, woman riding up and down."

SOME PEOPLE ARE CONCERNED ABOUT BRINGING THEIR PARTNER TO CLIMAX BEFORE HAVING AN ORGASM THEMSELVES. OTHERS STRIVE TO REACH ORGASM TOGETHER. WHICH IS TRUE FOR YOU?

He prefers to bring his partner to climax first. He may keep on going for a few seconds after she climaxes to intensify her reactions. Then he allows himself an orgasm.

"The partner always cums first, unless it can be done together."

"Ladies first . . ."

"I love bringing my partner to orgasm multiple times first."

"I want my partner to cum first, multiple times. The last thing we do is my climax. I love satisfying a woman. That is my biggest turn-on."

A Fantasy

"I know a woman who is all too often on my mind. I fantasize that I am standing in front of her and letting her look at me, to see how she excites me. I imagine that I am playing nice and slow, sucking her beautiful breasts, licking her cunt, and fucking her until she can't cum anymore."

ARE YOU VOCAL DURING SEX?

He makes his desires and pleasures clearly known verbally, but he is not overly talkative during the act, especially as he nears climax.

AFTER SEX WHAT DO YOU LIKE TO DO?

After sex he would prefer to lounge around and cuddle a bit. On occasion, he might enjoy having something to eat or watching TV or a video. Generally he is not ready to go directly to sleep.

CAPRICORN
December 22–January 19
THE GOAT

Earth Sign Capricorn—thoughtful, practical, ambitious—has great integrity. Ruler of the knees in particular and the whole skeletal system, Capricorn loves exploring all of the body with hands and tongue. The hardest workers in the zodiac, they put effort into everything they do, including being great lovers.

She says: "My best sexual skill is how long I can tease and prolong my partner's fulfillment."

He says: "I'll do whatever turns her on. I like to push her to her limits, and then even surpass them."

"Sex is like money; only too much is enough."
—John Updike

The Capricorn Woman in Her Own Words

A Memory

"I was masturbating on my bed. A local contractor arrived early. (My bathroom wall was removed for an addition.) He walked down the hall to my bedroom to see if anyone was home and caught me in the act. I saw him standing in my doorway . . . he came in, sat on the edge of my bed, and watched me bring myself to orgasm. No words were exchanged and he [then] returned to the bathroom to wait for the carpenters to show up."

Attraction and Dating a Capricorn

WHAT ATTRACTS YOU TO SOMEONE?

Capricorn is fairly demure in front of others and cares about how she is perceived, so the way a man behaves in public is important to her. She also has a dry wit and wants a man who likes to laugh.

"I am attracted by a great smile, confidence, intelligence and quick wit, good manners."

"Mentality, conduct . . ."

"Great sense of humor, intelligence, easy going, assertive, flexible, nice looking, takes reasonable care with appearance, open-minded."

"Personality first; pleasing to the eyes also needed, honesty, sense of humor . . ."

"Intelligence, common sense, sense of humor is a must."

"He needs to be a gentleman, conservative by nature and of a similar religious faith."

WHAT MIGHT TURN YOU OFF?

Consistent with her concern about what other people think, the qualities in a man that turn her off include poor grooming, poor hygiene, being loud or rude, or behaving in any manner that would draw negative attention in public.

"Egotistical behavior, superficiality, dysfunctional behavior, being drunk and out of control."

"Bad teeth are a huge turnoff. Also, mean people and smokers."

"Poor dental hygiene, bad breath, sloppy, closed-minded, set in ways, overbearing, controlling."

"Radically prejudiced opinions, lack of chivalry, dogmatic attitude, unappealing physically."

A Fantasy

"I've always wanted to make love on the beach during the day. The warmth of the sun is very stimulating to me. In my fantasy there are people all around, but no one seems to see us. After that a great swim in the waves."

WHAT DO YOU ENJOY DOING ON A DATE?

An ideal date for Capricorn is a quiet evening, dinner in a small dimly lit bistro, picnic in a remote field, or sharing a meal in front of the fireplace. She does appreciate her date showing up with some token gift as a sign of appreciation for the efforts she makes on his behalf. Daisies will do, long-stem roses are not always necessary.

"Connecting, being listened to, flirt, food, fun, some physical contact, cemeteries, nature, art, lots of talking."

"Talk in a neutral environment, dancing, and a couple of drinks."

"A relaxed meal with a great connection; the food can suck if the conversation flows."

"A nice dinner, a great bottle of wine, and great conversation with a lot of laughs . . ."

"Holding hands, taking a walk, and just getting to know one another."

ARE YOU FLIRTATIOUS?

This is a woman who is guarded about her behavior in public and is only mildly flirtatious. Her method is so cautious many a man may miss her signals. It is her body language that indicates her interest. She will face a man squarely and listen to him attentively.

"Occasionally I flirt . . . with both sexes in socially appropriate situations."

"I've been told I am a flirt, but in my opinion, it is deeper. It is real. It is about wanting to know the other."

"I am, but only in the right environment, I'd say 'mildly flirtatious.'"

Memories
"In the Waldorf Astoria Hotel. My husband was on the phone checking in with his office. He looked so sexy. I just could not wait for the call to end. I started to undress him and fondled him until he hung up. Then we made love for the whole afternoon."

"We were on the beach, alone at night, wrapped in a blanket. It was wonderful, smelling the ocean and listening to the sounds of the surf. Afterward we lay there watching the sun come up."

ARE YOU JEALOUS?

The Capricorn woman can be jealous, and she dislikes this quality in herself. As she sees it, the feeling is only generated when there's good cause.

"Jealousy is a waste of time, but if one feels that way it's important to recognize why and work it out quickly."

"I can imagine being jealous if I were in a committed relationship and found out that my partner was cheating or trying to date other women."

HOW DO YOU FEEL ABOUT PUBLIC DISPLAYS OF AFFECTION?

Because Capricorn is concerned about the opinions that others have of her, public affection is fine in its mildest forms. Not only does she want them kept to a minimum for herself, but also because she dislikes observing more than the subtlest displays.

"Discreet public displays are okay. As long as it isn't grossly sexual, I have no problem with it."

"There is a line of appropriate behavior that should be followed, gay or straight."

Sexual Attitudes and Behaviors

HOW OFTEN DO YOU THINK ABOUT SEX AND HOW OFTEN PER WEEK DO YOU WANT TO HAVE SEX?

Thoughts of sex may cross her mind every day, but she doesn't have a sexual appetite to match that. Sex two or three times per week will suit Capricorn perfectly, though she might like to have more than one round per session.

A Memory
"One night I was with a male friend; we were just good friends. He gave me a ride home from a pub and walked me to my door. I gave him a goodnight peck on the cheek. We ended up having the best sex I have ever had, right there in the hallway of my apartment, standing up against the wall. It was incredible sex. My sweat, along with my perfume, could be smelled for two days after."

HOW LONG DO YOU LIKE TO SPEND HAVING SEX AND HOW MUCH OF THAT TIME IS FOREPLAY? DO YOU ENJOY QUICKIES?

From a half hour to a full hour is just the right amount of time for sex. Once things heat up and the mood is set, the normal time for foreplay is from 15 to 30 minutes. Marathon sex may not be her thing, but she also doesn't want to feel rushed. The process itself should be slow and steady. Quickies are also a lot of fun.

"With foreplay, I enjoy spending time as much as I can get; certainly enough to get us both hot."

"For me, foreplay is normally an on-and-off activity all day."

"I like to spend an hour altogether for sex, with foreplay lasting as long as I can take it. Foreplay and after play are as important to me as the sexual act itself."

WHAT TIME OF DAY DO YOU PREFER TO HAVE SEX?

Her sex drive is at its greatest from late afternoon until the early nighttime hours, say 3 to 10 P.M.

"My preference is after dinner, when I'm a little tired and gently burning."

HOW OFTEN PER WEEK DO YOU MASTURBATE?

Capricorn masturbates infrequently, some weeks not at all and others once or twice.

 A Memory

"I had not seen him for several years. When we met, it was electric. We talked and went out to dinner, then just sat looking into each other's eyes. And then it started. We couldn't stop kissing. We kissed in a parking lot. People must have been staring at us. He had been out on the range earlier; I could smell the smoke from his hand. We reached for each other's private parts. We drove off to a secluded place and went the whole way in a pickup truck."

HOW LONG DO YOU WANT TO KNOW SOMEONE BEFORE GETTING SEXUAL?

Maybe any woman will throw caution to the wind once in a while, but it is truly the rare Capricorn who gets into a sexual relationship within a short period of time. She is simply not a woman who goes home with a guy on a first date.

"Does he know my mother's maiden name? Quite a while . . ."

"A month, give or take; it depends on the person."

"When I know we really have a relationship, that he will honestly call me the next day, and if we are attracted to each other, then I will be sexual."

"Three to four months preferably . . . If things feel very intense, maybe in two weeks . . ."

WHAT'S YOUR ATTITUDE TOWARD CASUAL SEX?

After a brief flirtation with casual sex, what she finds out is that her emotions get bruised. Capricorn regards it as a measure of her inner strength and self-assurance to remain alone rather than engage in what she considers to be meaningless sex.

"Sex requires emotional feelings for me to engage in it."

"I find it confusing and depressing. After the thrill and the buildup that leads to the act, the actual sex is often horrible."

DO YOU BELIEVE IN MONOGAMY?

Capricorn tends to be quite conservative in outward appearance and traditional in the values she holds. She is most likely to let her defenses down in an intimate, committed relationship. As a result, monogamy is very important to her.

"That kind of commitment is vital for depth, intimacy, and growth: for truth and honesty."

"If you have promised your partner; for me it is a must."

"Yes, even in dating. I believe in dating one person at a time."

A Fantasy

"My partner is a doctor. I go into his office as a patient: short skirt, no undies. He has sex with me while I sit on the exam table. I then strip completely and he probes every part of me. He does a complete gynecological and rectal exam, and then has intercourse and then anal intercourse with me."

DOES SEX HAVE A SPIRITUAL SIGNIFICANCE FOR YOU?

Consider that Capricorn values herself too much to get sexual quickly—to do more than dabble briefly in meaningless sex—add the importance she places on monogamy, and you'll find a woman who regards sex as spiritual. There is a core of loneliness in Capricorn that the intimacy of sex dissolves.

"Occasionally a real connection between souls and God happens in sex. It transcends emotion."

"It's a wonderful feeling when two people come together in the closest way possible."

"It's a meeting of hearts, minds, bodies, and emotions on a level that transcends just about any other human behavior."

ARE YOU COMFORTABLE INITIATING SEXUAL ACTIVITIES?

The Capricorn woman is not likely to initiate sex in the early stages of a relationship. When she has been with a man for a while, she will help him understand the rhythm of her sexual desire and initiate it on a regular basis.

HOW DO YOU COMMUNICATE TO YOUR PARTNER YOUR SEXUAL WANTS AND NEEDS?

Capricorn is a supremely competent woman at everything she does. She wants to please and be pleased in sex. As a result, she uses words when they are appropriate and gestures when they fit the situation better.

"I use both. We communicate well."

"Quietly: words and gestures."

"Gestures; he really knows what I need and when."

"Facial gestures and hand motions. I don't talk too much during sex."

A Memory

"A bondage and domination scene. We were at home. He was on the floor, hands and feet bound, dark groove music playing. He was naked except for leather cuffs, nipple clamps, and [a] cock ring. I was dressed in a dom outfit: leather, heels, and stockings. Made up and feeling sexy. He adored the scene. I had been doing some cock and ball teasing and really had him straining and sweating. I began to whip him in time to the music, and the scene took on a life of its own. I realized it was really turning me on to see my partner in this state. After some time and intense whipping, he came without any stimulation to his penis. Wow! It blew my mind that we could both get so turned on by this. It was a very intimate and wonderful act with someone I loved."

DO YOU THINK OF YOURSELF AS BEING IN THE MAINSTREAM SEXUALLY, MORE EXPERIMENTAL, OR OPEN TO ANYTHING?

Many Capricorns are mainstream in their range of sexuality, satisfied with oral sex and intercourse. However, consistent with the value she places on pleasing her partner and the respect that she has for romantic relationships, she puts considerable effort into satisfying him. Therefore, if her partner is interested in exploring beyond vanilla sex, he will find a willing partner in Capricorn.

She will experiment with anal sex, bondage, dominance and submission, spanking, having sex in public places, wearing costumes, and using food and some sex toys such as vibrators. Some Capricorns practice sadomasochism: being spanked and using chains, whips, and paddles. Her fantasies frequently involve being punished, bound, and dominated.

A Fantasy

"An authoritative male spanks me. I am a teenager. I deserve the spanking and it is not cruel or harsh, but it is bare bottom, over the knee with his hand, and it is very hot. I like to have intercourse following."

HOW DO YOU DEMONSTRATE AFFECTION FOR YOUR PARTNER?

Her fundamental nature—determined, centered, practical, and a bit romantic—is apparent in the way she attends to her lover. Along with little gifts or love notes, Capricorn shows her regard for him with acts of thoughtfulness such as doing errands for him, providing a quiet environment to come home to, and keeping the house in good order.

"Patience, tolerance, touch, food, compliments, hugs, kisses, keeping house . . ."

"Surprise him with dinner after a hard day's work."

"The small things in life, thoughtfulness . . ."

The Five Senses

HOW IMPORTANT TO YOU IS THE SEXUAL ENVIRONMENT?

The environment matters, not excessively so, but as a reflection of the regard she has for her partner and as an indication of the respect he has for her. Comfort and cleanliness are paramount. When her lover goes a bit beyond that, with décor and lighting, she'll be more relaxed.

"Lighting, natural or evening, dim."

"I like soft lighting but mostly it just has to be clean."

WHERE DO YOU LIKE TO HAVE SEX?

She does not seek a lot of variety when it comes to the location for sex. Because she has a strong sense of propriety, any possibility of being seen is a decided turnoff. Overall, the bedroom suits her fine. As to the outdoors, she has a strong opinion, either very much in favor of or completely opposed to it.

"In bed, in front of the fireplace, safe places, not too public . . . It's fun on the dance floor, and I love outdoor sex—privately like when we've gone camping."

"Bedroom or any room that is comfortable . . . not outside: bugs, sand, and bears turn me off."

A Memory

"I was being kind of aggressive. We were on a pond, on a floating tube. The sun was setting. We could hear all kinds of bugs, crickets, and frogs. I love the fresh smell of the outdoors so that was great. The idea that someone else might see us was very exhilarating."

WHAT PUTS YOU IN THE MOOD FOR SEX?

For Capricorn, competence and achievement are sexy. The man who is going somewhere with his life is the one she finds fascinating. Overall, there's no one magic thing that turns her on. It's much more about treating her like the very special person she is, about showing regard for her in all ways.

"Feeling a connection; we're talking and I feel like the guy is the most interesting person I have met in forever. I'm tingly, and impatient for his move."

"Intellectual stimulation, lover's nude body . . ."

WHAT'S YOUR ATTITUDE TOWARD PORNOGRAPHY?

Capricorn's response to pornography is somewhere between boredom and disinterest. Erotica in film and literature, reading sexy passages in romance novels, or exploring descriptions of sexual experiences found in fetish magazines is much more of a turn-on for her.

"Hard-core porn is ignorant and fake. I prefer mainstream films with explicit scenes of a couple making love."

"Other than mild spanking videos, porn is boring, repetitive, unimaginative. It is all body parts: zzzzzzzzzz."

Memories

"A sore neck; rubdown turned into animalistic aggressive, room to room, clothes flying; a complete frenzy, and all this with someone I should not have been with."

"I was dressing, combing my hair in the bathroom. My lover came up behind me, gently turned me around, and began kissing me. He slowly took off my clothes then we stood against the bathroom wall and had intercourse right there."

HOW MUCH CUDDLING DO YOU ENJOY, ASIDE FROM SEX?

She loves to cuddle, just not when she's involved in a project. But holding hands, hugs, and a touch on the shoulder please her. More contact than that and she anticipates that her lover is looking for sex.

"A lot; I am very affectionate."

"Cuddling gets me in the mood. It shows me how affectionate my mate can be."

HOW TACTILE AND HOW ORAL ARE YOU?

She's an Earth Sign, an earthy lover who enjoys giving and receiving the full range of oral and tactile experiences. The resulting smells and tastes make her partner crazy and heighten her pleasure.

"I love touching and caressing every part of him."

"I love to kiss, and I love oral sex with my boyfriend."

"I enjoy oral sex; giving and getting turns me on immensely."

"I really enjoy all kinds of kissing; kissing my lover's body. I love cunnilingus and doing fellatio."

WHAT SEX ACTS DO YOU LIKE MOST AND LEAST?

Intercourse is great but it should never be the first course. Rushing into it will turn off Ms. Capricorn. Some Capricorn women enjoy anal sex on occasion. Mutual masturbation is probably her least favorite sexual behavior.

"Kissing, fondling genitals, intercourse, mutual masturbation, in that order."

"Oral sex and kissing are number one, followed by intercourse."

"I don't like a guy cumming on my face."

A Memory

"My first sexual encounter with my boyfriend, at a party with friends. There were people in rooms all over the house and we were on the foldout couch. Very quiet. We started kissing and touching one another. He turned me on my stomach and began kissing my back. The room was full of electricity. Between having to be quiet and the intensity and sensuality of his kisses, it was amazing. It was the most romantic, sensual, and exciting experience I ever had."

AS A LOVER, WHAT'S YOUR BEST SKILL?

She is sure of herself in bed, trusting her abilities to please her partner, and why not? Capricorn works hard to excel at all her endeavors, both public and private.

"Everything is great about me. I get told all the time. Tongue, body, hands, eye contact, and energy . . ."

"How long I can tease and prolong my partner's fulfillment, especially in a BDSM scene."

Fantasies

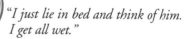

"I just lie in bed and think of him. I get all wet."

"Two guys and me dressed up in fetish clothing, latex, and rubber. And all this for the pleasure of our voyeur, my husband."

"I imaging having sex with characters that I

have found hot in movies. Other times I just lie there and remember a former boyfriend in Puerto Rico. He was so gentle and loving."

WHAT SMELLS AND TASTES ON YOUR PARTNER DO YOU ENJOY?

An earthy Sign, Capricorn enjoys her partner's body smells and tastes, unadorned by colognes or deodorants. Foods are not often part of sex play, but flavored oils can be fun.

"My lover's sweat and natural body smells are exciting to me."

"I love the smell of his skin on his chest, neck, and shoulders, and the smell of his hair and cologne."

"The taste of gourmet food applied to his fingers, [and] then fed to me."

"Hot, sweaty skin and the smell of sex along with the taste of his lips and nipples . . ."

A Fantasy

"I have two fantasies of anonymous sex. In one, we are making love in the back of a pickup truck in the woods during a thunderstorm. In the other, a sexy stranger pulls me into a dark room at the back of a club. You can barely hear the music; breathing hard and heavy. He strips my clothes off, pins my hands to the wall and slowly starts to make love, then holds me tight. It gets harder, deeper, and a bit forceful until we reach orgasm. Then he leaves. We never see each other again."

FOR SOME PEOPLE THE TASTE OF THEIR PARTNER'S CUM OR SECRETIONS IS UNPLEASANT. IF THAT'S TRUE FOR YOU, WHAT DO YOU DO ABOUT THE TASTE?

Most of the time, she doesn't object to the taste of her partner's cum. If it's at all a problem for her, she handles it very matter-of-factly. She might keep a drink beside the bed or use some mouthwash shortly after his climax.

"I don't think it's that unpleasant. I swallow."

"It's not a problem for me. The taste is salty. I swallow and rub it all over my chest and my privates."

"The taste is mildly unpleasant. I spit it out."

"I find it unpleasant and I don't swallow cum. A little is okay. I usually rub it on myself, or help clean it up."

"I am not thrilled with cum in terms of ingesting it but I like it as a skin moisturizer."

DO YOU ENJOY WATCHING YOUR PARTNER DURING SEX AND ORGASM? DO YOU ENJOY BEING WATCHED?

Capricorn takes pride in everything she does, including sex. So she loves watching her partner during sex and orgasm, but in truth, she isn't as content being observed.

"Watching him is wonderful. It is sometimes amazing and spiritual."

"I'm somewhat uncomfortable when I know he's watching, but it is okay."

"I'm not really comfortable being watched, but who cares when that moment comes?"

A Memory

"The first time my boyfriend and I kissed, [and] then made love. The kiss was pure pleasure with immense passion, soft and gentle yet hard and secure. His touch was serving, yet confident, and I melted in his arms.

"In the process of taking our clothes off to have sex, he ripped my underwear from my body. It was just a very hot moment that made me feel like he wanted me so badly. He couldn't even take the time to remove my panties, like that would have taken too long."

The Big "O"

HOW DO YOU REACH AN ORGASM AND HOW OFTEN?

Capricorn is a goal-oriented Sign. She achieves orgasm most of the time she has sex.

When she is sufficiently excited and wants to climax, she does so and the method is irrelevant.

"When I want to, I can get off alone. With a partner a good intercourse session sends me, but it is trickier. Too long and I am sore; too short and I am hungry."

"I climax all the time: multiple orgasms, through oral sex, intercourse, and with my partner fondling me."

"I cum often; sometimes through oral sex, but usually with intercourse and masturbation."

WHAT'S YOUR FAVORITE POSITION?

They all work for Capricorn, and she likes a variety of positions. In order of favorites, she might prefer doggie style first, woman on top second, and man on top third.

 A Memory
"A party, spanking is the theme. I am dressed in a variety of clothing: some vintage, some skimpy, some fashionable. All show off my attributes to best advantage. In front of a group of like-minded spankos, I am taken over my lover's knees, panties pulled down, and given a long, slow, hand spanking. I am very hot from this. He lets me up. Bids adieu to the crowd, and [then he] takes me back to the privacy of his room and fucks me doggie style, pulling my hair back, causing my back to arch, fucking me slowly, teasingly, roughly, rudely, sensitively, callously, all ways."

SOME PEOPLE ARE CONCERNED ABOUT BRINGING THEIR PARTNER TO CLIMAX BEFORE HAVING AN ORGASM THEMSELVES. OTHERS STRIVE TO REACH ORGASM TOGETHER. WHICH IS TRUE FOR YOU?

She is not always in control, but when she is, Capricorn is pretty good at timing her orgasm to match her partner's. Overall, however, who cums first is not important to her. That they both achieve orgasm is what matters.

"I like to orgasm together, but what's most important is that both our needs are usually met."

"He likes me to orgasm first; most of the time we cum together."

ARE YOU VOCAL DURING SEX?

Whether Capricorn expresses herself with words or simply with sounds, they are low in volume.

"Yes, lots of moaning and sounds—mostly monosyllabic."

"Some, but not too loud . . ."

"It varies in volume, but I'm usually at least a little vocal."

 Fantasies
"Androgyny fantasies, both heterosexual and gay. My clothes come off and voilà, you get quite a surprise. The sex is always great."

"To have sex in a graveyard."

"I am on a beach and kissing and hugging and loving my husband. That scene [in] From Here to Eternity *keeps playing in my head."*

"Brief images: having sex in a bathroom stall or on a golf course, role-playing of various kinds like being dressed up in a maid's uniform."

AFTER SEX WHAT DO YOU LIKE TO DO?

The closeness that Capricorn feels for her lover after sex is precious to her. She wants to take time to cuddle before sleeping.

"Cuddle, stay in bed, sleep."

"We cuddle even if we cannot stay the rest of the day or night."

The Capricorn Man in His Own Words

A Memory
"Over a period of time I became friends with a woman who lived 1,800 miles away. We had exchanged pictures and talked at great length on the phone about sex and all the attributes and behaviors that turned each other on. At long last, business brought me to her hometown.

"We met at the airport and were so anxious to be together that we went directly to a nearby hotel. We made love for nearly 24 hours, trying all sorts of interesting and exciting experiences that grew out of our extensive conversations."

Attraction and Dating a Capricorn

WHAT ATTRACTS YOU TO SOMEONE?

The Capricorn man has great pride and cares about what other people think. He's taken by a woman who is self-confident enough to be flirtatious. Looks do matter to him. It is not necessary for her to be a ten on a scale of one to ten, but the way she dresses and carries herself is important. In fact, being with a woman who attracts attention by the way she looks and moves makes Capricorn feel very proud of himself.

"Physique, beauty, energy, and behavior . . ."

"Body and attitude (good person), physical characteristics: nice ass, firm tummy, and proportional breasts, pretty face."

"It does not take a large breast size to please me. I am turned on by women who are spiritual, positive, smiling, happy, and intelligent, and by women who take the initiative for sex and relationships."

WHAT MIGHT TURN YOU OFF?

A lovely woman who makes no effort to look good for him, to fix herself up when they are going to be together, will lose this man. Extremes of any sort will turn him off.

"Too showy, too wild, too much makeup, too fake."

"Egotism, wrong attitude . . ."

"Women who do not keep themselves clean, smoke too much or drink too much. Women who think very little of themselves or see themselves as inferior."

"Women who constantly complain about life and take no responsibility for the life they make."

WHAT DO YOU ENJOY DOING ON A DATE?

Capricorn is perfectly capable of being both sociable and charming. He handles himself well in large groups and intimate settings. A concert or a county fair can be a lot of fun, but for the most part, he far prefers time to relax and enjoy simple pleasures, such as dining out or having a picnic with his partner.

"Good dinner, talk, playful teasing."

"Going for a walk, hugging, kissing, sitting on a couch and talking, watching a good movie on the VCR, taking a hike . . ."

"Just being together with the one I love in any way at all."

"I like being in social situations where we can talk."

ARE YOU FLIRTATIOUS?

The Capricorn image is the man in a three-piece suit, white shirt, and conservative tie. He's business-like and to the point. Underneath it all, though, he has a playful disposition and sees himself as a flirt.

"I am incredibly flirtatious."

"Yes, playfully . . ."

"I will stare right at girls for a while."

 ### A Memory

"We had been friends for a long time but had not yet started a sexual relationship. We were staying in a cabin with a bunch of friends. The weather was cold and the cabin was unheated. We were cuddling to stay warm, [and] then started to kiss. It was awkward at first, but then we began taking turns being aggressive. She had the sweetest moan I had ever heard. Part of the turn-on was the sense that our friends could hear what we were doing."

ARE YOU JEALOUS?

Would anyone expect Capricorn to be jealous? He is. Capricorn understands human nature. He knows that people have hidden motives and can be manipulative. As a result, he has a suspicious streak.

"Absolutely yes . . ."

"Yes, when the relationship has led to commitment."

"Hmm . . . Is suspicious better than jealous? Okay, I get a little jealous."

HOW DO YOU FEEL ABOUT PUBLIC DISPLAYS OF AFFECTION?

Signs of affection in public with some limits please Capricorn. He isn't apt to like it if his partner clings to him in a group or goes out of her way to prove that he is her property. When the gesture is a natural expression of feeling at a given moment, he thinks it's just fine.

"No problem, though time and place is important; and no petting around children."

"As long as they are not done too often they are fine."

"I enjoy them as long as they are appropriate."

"When it is natural it is okay; not as a way to mark territory, though even that can be okay."

"I think it is great. Love should not have any bounds."

Sexual Attitude and Behaviors

HOW OFTEN DO YOU THINK ABOUT SEX AND HOW OFTEN PER WEEK DO YOU WANT TO HAVE SEX?

Never underestimate how often Capricorn thinks about sex. He has a very strong sex drive and while he may not get what he wants, he would love to have sex virtually every day of the week.

"I think about sex with every breath, every day."

"Preoccupied . . ."

"Daily, sometimes preoccupied."

"I think about sex several times per day, although I don't feel I am preoccupied with it."

"Twenty-four hours a day, seven days a week."

"When I am living with a woman, I like to have sex about four to seven times a week."

"As often as possible . . ."

"Seven days . . . at least once a day if it were possible . . ."

HOW MUCH TIME DO YOU LIKE TO SPEND HAVING SEX AND HOW MUCH OF THAT TIME IS FOREPLAY? DO YOU ENJOY QUICKIES?

Time is of little importance to Capricorn when it comes to sex; however, it is his intention to please his lover and he is by nature indomitable in pursuing his goal. Sex will go on and on until she is thoroughly satisfied.

"I can go for an hour approximately and I enjoy many forms of foreplay. I am kind of kinky."

"As long as it takes . . . Quickies, yes and no . . ."

"When I am in a committed relationship, I do not enjoy quickies. I like to spend hours in foreplay and regular sexual intercourse."

"With the right person, I want as much time as possible, with foreplay to the point of no return. I enjoy quickies if that is all there is time for."

"Her pleasure is what matters. I prefer to take my time to ensure that she is satisfied."

"I will go on for as long as it is erotic for her and sometimes a little longer just to turn her on more, but I can enjoy a quickie too."

WHAT TIME OF DAY DO YOU PREFER TO HAVE SEX?

The Capricorn man just loves sex. Time on the clock is of no significance when it comes to having sex.

"Evening and night . . ."

"Anytime is the right time."

"Morning, midday, and night . . ."

HOW OFTEN PER WEEK DO YOU MASTURBATE?

Capricorn masturbates a minimum of three times weekly.

"Three to four times . . ."

"Three to five times . . ."

"Every other day . . ."

HOW LONG DO YOU WANT TO KNOW SOMEONE BEFORE GETTING SEXUAL?

With Capricorn, sex might be part of a first date or after a week or more. It is hardly likely that he will be going out with a woman much longer than that before becoming sexual. Overall, the answer is dependent upon the chemistry and the mood.

"A name is good . . . Just enough time to be sure that she is into it."

"A few hours . . . It depends on the mood and the person."

"Sometimes a week, sometimes a day, given the chemistry . . ."

WHAT'S YOUR ATTITUDE TOWARD CASUAL SEX?

Capricorn has a pragmatic attitude toward casual sex. It is fine for someone who is single, but it is certainly no match for sex within a loving relationship.

"Fine if one isn't married and if it's done safely."

"I am not too interested in casual sex. It is fine for others."

"It is an individual decision."

"I know it is not all that safe, so one has to be careful."

DO YOU BELIEVE IN MONOGAMY?

He is, by nature, very faithful and devoted to his family; therefore, Capricorn places value on monogamy. It is important to him that sex with his partner remains fulfilling and he enjoys both adding variation and having his lover bring new elements into their lovemaking.

"The problem is that sex with one person becomes routine, no matter the emotions."

"I believe monogamy is the most wholesome form of male/female relationships."

"If you make a commitment, then you honor it. If not, do as you please."

"I believe that if you find the right person, monogamy is awesome and the sex is never boring. I am open, however, to the occasional threesome."

DOES SEX HAVE A SPIRITUAL SIGNIFICANCE FOR YOU?

He sees sex as mainly physical though not exclusively so, primarily because of the connection he feels with his partner. Casual sex is not likely to be spiritual. Within a committed relationship it can be to Capricorn.

"People relating sexually should feel a spiritual bond."

"Only with my soul mate . . ."

"Yes and no. It's very physical, but connections can be strong spiritually."

"With the right woman, sex can bring you highs—even spiritual—that you can't get anywhere else."

 ### Memories

"We had sex in a movie theater. The look of euphoria as my partner came is one I'll always remember."

"Having sex with two women at a private retreat surrounded by ten to 15 other couples having sexual intercourse at the same time. It was in a dimly lit room with intense primitive music playing in the background."

"I was very turned on at a fetish flea market listening to a stranger who squealed with paddle impact."

ARE YOU COMFORTABLE INITIATING SEXUAL ACTIVITIES?

In addition to the fact that Capricorn is a straightforward and pragmatic Earth Sign, he is also remarkably astute and a very good reader of other people. When the signals are clear, he has no problem initiating sex and he also responds well when the woman takes charge.

"I am, but I like it when she is the one to initiate as well."

"Yes, although I do have sensitivity to rejection. Not in a bad way; I just may wait a while before going back to try again if I have been turned down recently."

HOW DO YOU COMMUNICATE TO YOUR PARTNER YOUR SEXUAL WANTS AND NEEDS?

For Capricorn, there's a time and a place for both words and gestures. During the act of sex itself, he finds words more intrusive than helpful.

Interestingly, though nobody likes criticism, Capricorn takes it better than most other Signs. When a lover says that she wants something done differently, he will not take offense. Instead of taking it personally, he understands that he will please her more by taking cues from his partner.

"I use words and explanations; if needed, tips and pointers at a later moment."

"Mostly I like to communicate with words before sex. I don't like talking a lot during sex."

"Sometimes during sex side by side if I really love a woman deeply. I like telling of my deep feeling for her, but not about how we are to move or act during sex."

"During sex I use gestures mostly. I love everything my partner does to and for me."

DO YOU THINK OF YOURSELF AS BEING IN THE MAINSTREAM SEXUALLY, MORE EXPERIMENTAL, OR OPEN TO ANYTHING?

Most Capricorn lovers are conventional in their sexual practices; they like to take their time. When moving beyond the most mainstream activities, he may have anal sex, sex in public places, enjoy having his partner shave her genital area. Finally, while he typically wants his partner to go easy, it turns him on to be spanked.

"I have used a vibrator, anal plugs, and beads."

"I like using a short dildo in a woman's ass during intercourse. I like having a dildo in my ass while kissing and other foreplay."

"Toys include a dildo, anal probe, [and] wrist and ankle restraints."

The more experimental Capricorn is open to dominance and submission play, and may want to add some food to the mix. Some participate in the sadomasochistic lifestyle. For these Capricorns, bondage and the use of restraints and paddles add excitement. Capricorn's fantasies frequently involve anal sex.

Fantasies

"I imagine a woman putting her asshole down around my penis while she faces me and masturbates her own clit. I would like a woman to sit her asshole on my mouth while I lay down on my back [and] masturbate her clit for her."

"Taking someone to that most erotic place, where she is completely vulnerable and trusting and I don't let her down with the level we achieve. Anal sex, of course."

HOW DO YOU DEMONSTRATE AFFECTION FOR YOUR PARTNER?

Capricorn enjoys doing things for his partner; being close physically, giving hugs and holding hands, taking her to dinner, and buying little tokens of affection. It is almost a measure of pride for him to demonstrate his feelings with such actions.

"I'll take her out to a candlelit dinner, send cards and small gifts."

"I give her a full body massage and call her by pet names."

"A hand around the shoulder, holding of hands . . ."

"Do the things that matter when she doesn't expect it, massages, kisses."

"With constant touching and verbal affirmations as well as lots of sex . . ."

The Five Senses

HOW IMPORTANT TO YOU IS THE SEXUAL ENVIRONMENT?

Capricorn likes his intimate space to be fairly dark and at least somewhat clean, but some surprise element in the environment such as sex toys or costumes has more effect on him than incense, rose petals, or candlelight.

"It just needs to be clean."

"I like dark, quiet music or absolute silence."

"There are places I wouldn't want to do it, but it is not super important."

"It's not really important; depends on mood."

"Cleanliness is always good. Other than that not much matters."

 Memories

"She blindfolded me and touched me with things of different textures, all the while talking to me in a sweet and sensual voice."

"My girl was on top and it was deep. She said it hurt, but held me against her and said 'Don't stop. Don't stop.' That was hot."

WHERE DO YOU LIKE TO HAVE SEX?

With a slight preference for the bedroom, Capricorn is open to having sex in several other locations. Let it be dark. If he can find a way to be discreet, doing it with other people nearby is exciting.

"In the woods, on the beach with a blanket, in the shower or wherever . . ."

"Bedroom is my favorite, nice and private. It's fun in a tent when no one is near."

"Anywhere, but not where someone might actually be offended by finding us."

WHAT PUTS YOU IN THE MOOD FOR SEX?

Capricorn strives to achieve his ambitions in all areas of his life. He does what it takes to get what he wants. And when it comes to sex, he wants his lover to want him. He will go out of his way to turn her on with dinner, music, and romance. When she is turned on, so is he.

"A sensual woman dressed for the occasion, thigh high stockings, and a seductive smile."

"I'm always in the mood. All I need is her willingness."

"The mood is set by the cologne she wears and good conversation before sex, which indicates how we are attuned to one another intellectually, spiritually, and emotionally."

"If I am with the person I love, anything puts me in the mood."

"Just being around my girl and doing things together, planning for the future. When I feel secure . . ."

"Almost anything! Just looking at my girl-friend, especially when she bends over . . ."

WHAT'S YOUR ATTITUDE TOWARD PORNOGRAPHY?

Capricorn's attitude toward pornography depends upon his range of sexuality and his partner's openness to experimentation. The most mainstream Capricorn lover has little interest in XXX-rated videos. Capricorns who delve into the BDSM lifestyle enjoy it far more.

"Love it, whether alone or with my mate. It's erotic and exciting."

"I can take it or leave it, although I tend to have a distaste for the raunchy."

"It is pretty cool."

A Fantasy

"I have several: showering with two blonde women, lap dance sex. In another I am watching my significant other give oral sex to several men while they fondle her and she is straddling me."

HOW MUCH CUDDLING DO YOU ENJOY, ASIDE FROM SEX?

Beyond sex, cuddling is Capricorn's way of demonstrating the depth of his feelings for his partner. He loves being close when out in public, hugging on a park bench, or sitting side by side at a restaurant.

"Love it. It adds meaning to a physical relationship."

"Just being close is fine."

"I like a lot of cuddling, holding hands."

HOW TACTILE AND HOW ORAL ARE YOU?

Earth Sign Capricorn is highly tactile. He

runs his hands gently and sometimes forcefully over his lover's skin. The woman who knows how to use her hands well excites him to fever pitch. The earthiness of Capricorn's nature extends to the pleasure he gets from taste: oral sex ranging from kissing to sucking and cunnilingus.

"I love to touch, to give a full body massage."

"I like to use my hands a lot. I like to use my hands, my fingers all over a woman's body. I put my hand around her anus and rub. I put it over her clit and rub. I put my fingers on her feet, her hair, and her ears."

"I love to taste her every being. The tongue is a wonderful muscle."

"I am very oral. If it is a part of the body, it is in my mouth."

"I like rimming if she keeps clean before lovemaking. I like deep, slow kissing during intercourse. I kiss a good woman's body from head to toe, her back. I lick her thighs, her vagina, her clit. I love being kissed all over and licked."

"I'll do whatever turns her on. I like to push her to her limits, and then even surpass them."

Fantasies

"I just have to think about us spending quality time together to get turned on. I imagine us just eyeing each other in public or private, not knowing or caring about anything else. For me that is the perfect fantasy."

"I fantasize about sex with older women, including my partner's mother. I imagine her seducing me, and then I give her the best sex that she has ever had—the kind of sex that she needs and deserves."

WHAT SEX ACTS DO YOU LIKE MOST AND LEAST?

What's not to like? Capricorn men, in general, like all sex acts. In fact, beyond the mainstream acts—from cuddling to oral sex and intercourse, both vaginal and anal, all of which Capricorn enjoys—he may also like to delve into the BDSM lifestyle.

"If there is anything I do not like, it is not having sex."

"I have not found anything that I do not like."

"The whole thing is important. Anal sex is erotic because of the amount of trust it takes and how much a woman is surprised by liking it."

"I really don't have a favorite. I like them all."

"I like intercourse, but I would not like it nearly as much without kissing and fondling breasts, and other acts during and before intercourse."

"I do not like anything that involves pain. That is completely out of my agenda."

AS A LOVER, WHAT'S YOUR BEST SKILL?

Capricorn is the hardest worker in the zodiac, and true to form he works hard to satisfy his partner. He is a skillful lover in the full scope of sexual activities, whether within the mainstream or beyond that, including various fetishes.

"Paying attention . . . Knowing what my partner wants, responding to suggestion."

"My best skill is the use of my fingers, hands, and tongue during intercourse. My hips move very rapidly and vigorously during intercourse, but I keep them moving slowly when appropriate."

"Using my imagination to find new ways to pleasure my partner . . ."

"I think I am equally adept in most areas."

WHAT SMELLS AND TASTES ON YOUR PARTNER DO YOU ENJOY?

Capricorn is earthy by nature and a sensual lover. He is very much into smells and tastes, all of them. On occasion, sex might be stimulated by bringing in food, especially in the somewhat spicy range; a little honey mustard, something more toward cinnamon than sugar or something with a lemony flavor. But most of the time he is fully satisfied with his partner, just as she is.

"During sex I love the smell of her body. For tastes, all of it . . ."

"I enjoy the aroma of her colognes, sweat under the arms and skin as well as the tastes of her skin between the thighs, the vagina, the anus, the mouth, her underarm sweat, and even her feet."

 Fantasies

"To be tied up and blindfolded, then pleasured endlessly by my partner."

"Having sex with the female postal worker when she delivers the mail."

"Rough (not brutal) sex, S&M, multiple female partners, bondage, being in control, playing with her feet and legs, oral sex."

"Group sex with my partner and some of my close female friends."

FOR SOME PEOPLE THE TASTE OF THEIR PARTNER'S CUM OR SECRETIONS IS UNPLEASANT. IF THAT'S TRUE FOR YOU, WHAT DO YOU DO ABOUT THE TASTE?

As he enjoys all of his partner's flavors, her secretions never bother him and he has no need to do anything about handling the taste.

"It has not been a problem. If it is good I just enjoy and wipe it off my mouth . . . intercourse so I can kiss nicely during intercourse."

"No problem for me. I love the way my girl tastes."

DO YOU ENJOY WATCHING YOUR PARTNER DURING SEX AND ORGASM? DO YOU ENJOY BEING WATCHED?

Capricorn is analytical, maybe even calculating. What's wrong with that? It's all about pleasing his partner, so he loves to watch the effect he's having on her.

"Yes, I like to know what she is feeling and [to] watch what she is doing."

"Yes, absolutely . . ."

The Capricorn male is not so enthusiastic about her watching him, however.

"Somewhat."

"Sure, I guess."

The Big "O"

HOW DO YOU REACH AN ORGASM AND HOW OFTEN?

Capricorn is goal oriented in everything he does. When it comes to orgasm, his goal is at least one for her and at least one for him.

"All that a woman has to do is touch my penis, any way at all."

"I reach orgasm from a variety of means: oral sex, mutual masturbation, intercourse, and any combination of these."

"I climax all the time. If it is hard, it is pumping."

WHAT'S YOUR FAVORITE POSITION?

There is absolutely no one position that tops Capricorn's hit parade. Her pleasure dictates his choice.

"There is no best. They all work for me."

"It depends on what is more erotic at the time. Is she into getting me off or does she want me to give it to her hard and deep and fast? Back or front? Whatever fits the occasion works for me."

SOME PEOPLE ARE CONCERNED ABOUT BRINGING THEIR PARTNER TO CLIMAX BEFORE HAVING AN ORGASM THEMSELVES. OTHERS STRIVE TO REACH ORGASM TOGETHER. WHICH IS TRUE FOR YOU?

Climaxing together is great, but not at the risk of her missing an orgasm. This is where that Capricorn pride plays a role in his sex life. He will satisfy his lover no matter what, preferably more than once.

"[My] partner should climax several times, then [us] together."

"I like a woman to get two or three orgasms before I cum."

"Partner first, which brings me to full orgasm."

"I try to bring my partner to orgasm before myself. I don't last as long as she does, and I want her to be satisfied."

"Her first a few times, then together if possible."

ARE YOU VOCAL DURING SEX?

Moans and sounds that indicate pleasure, along with body language, will let his partner know how he is responding to her actions.

"I like a woman to be somewhat vocal. I say a little, but not much."

AFTER SEX WHAT DO YOU LIKE TO DO?

Capricorn works hard at everything he does and since this includes his activity in bed, most often he just wants to go to sleep after sex. If it is early in the day, he will feel invigorated and will enjoy going out with his lover.

AQUARIUS

January 20–February 18

THE WATER BEARER

Air Sign Aquarius is the Sign of brotherhood. Aquarians are diplomatic, friendly, and generous. They find intelligence sexy and they're great communicators. Ruler of the ankles and circulation, sexy talk and anything that gets the blood moving—sports, a workout, or a massage—gets Aquarius set for sex.

She says: "Am I flirtatious? Very much so . . . verbal banter . . . I will take it to the level right before physical contact starts to take place."

He says: "Nice music, mental activity, and anything in the porn line puts me in the mood for sex, as well as passionate kissing, my lover's nude body, and [the] sound of rain."

"Seduce my mind and you can have my body. Find my soul and I'm yours forever."
—Lilly Nomad

The Aquarius Woman in Her Own Words

A Memory

"It was Valentine's Day and my boyfriend took me to a hotel. He blindfolded me and I had no idea where I was going or what the night had in store. He led me down a flight of stairs. I heard a key in a lock. I heard the door open and felt a sudden rush of warm air. The room was very hot and there was a smell of lavender in the air. Then my boyfriend led me through the door and told me to stay there. I heard the door close and what sound[ed] like footsteps. I thought that maybe someone else was [there].

"There was a sudden flash of light and my boyfriend's voice telling to take off the blindfold. When I did I saw a path of rose petals starting at my feet [and] leading to an upstairs room. I followed the petals and as I came up the final step I saw that the bed was covered with rose petals and surrounded by candles. As I got closer to the bed, music started to play. My guy came up behind me and put his arms around me and told me that he loved me very much. That was the best night of my life. He did everything right and made me feel very special."

Attraction and Dating an Aquarius

WHAT ATTRACTS YOU TO SOMEONE?

Air Sign Aquarius is turned on by the mind, ideas, and words. It is a man's intellect and even the sound of his voice that first attract her attention. She also stresses being truthful and having good manners. Good looks don't hurt either.

"The inside of a person, his behavior and character, is what makes him attractive. I love a sense of humor, intelligence, and a person who is honest."

"I'm usually attracted to someone's eyes. If I feel a connection, then I begin a conversation with him. I also need someone who is fun, likes to do new and different things, is honest with me, and cares about my family."

"I notice his eyes, energy, behavior, intelligence, sense of humor, and good manners."

WHAT MIGHT TURN YOU OFF?

Lack of confidence tops this list for the Aquarius woman, along with narrow-mindedness, disinterest in current affairs, and an overall lack of curiosity about the problems facing people in other societies.

"Vulgarity in speech or action and unclean, smoker, sarcasm, hostile nature, negativity, doom and gloom personality . . ."

"Ignorance, rudeness, being insulting or uneducated, bad energy, someone without confidence."

"Rudeness, head games . . ."

WHAT DO YOU ENJOY DOING ON A DATE?

Aquarius enjoys being out and about. Active dates and doing things a bit out of the ordinary—going to demolition derbies, viewing the stars at an observatory, consulting a psychic—all please her more than the traditional dinner and a movie.

"Horseback riding, walking in the woods or city, listening to my favorite group playing music or any classic rock band, dancing . . . I like to try new things of interest to my partner."

"Taking a drive and seeing the country, petting zoo, corny plays, short outings."

"Doing something spontaneous, from a sports activity to dinner and theater . . ."

A Fantasy

"I fantasize that my partner is a stranger to me. We encounter each other in a bar. Our eyes meet and there's a smile and a wink. He sends a drink over. I thank him by sending one to him. He comes over to thank me in person and we begin the getting-to-know-you-stage. There is light touching on the shoulder and slowly going to the arm and finally to the leg. Once my hand is on his leg I slowly rub it back and forth, letting him know that I'm interested in him. He starts to whisper in my ears things like, 'I've never done this before,' 'there is something different about you, don't know what it is.' I tell him that I'm ready to leave and he is more than welcome to join me in leaving. We leave together and at the car we begin to kiss like high school kids do on their dates. He is kissing my neck and sucking on my earlobe, getting me ready to have him. I start to rub his back and I kiss his ears slowly, blowing into them. We find a hotel and make passionate love and leave at separate times, still going with the game of being strangers."

ARE YOU FLIRTATIOUS?

Aquarius is flirtatious, but in a unique way. She is a wonderful conversationalist and the way that she listens, the way that she questions a man and gets him to open up about his life and his work, is her form of flirtation.

"Very much so, verbal banter . . . I will take it to the level right before physical contact starts to take place."

"I feel that when I flirt it is subtle and sometimes guys don't pick up on it."

ARE YOU JEALOUS?

For Aquarius the key words are "I know." Her relationships are based on open communication. Her confidence in her ability to know someone results in her being fairly trusting. Nevertheless, she has somewhat of a tendency to be jealous.

"Yes, when I see a girl showing interest in my

boyfriend. But, when I'm with someone I trust, then I realize that I have nothing to worry about."

"Sometimes I get jealous, especially with someone I care about. I do have a spiritual side and tell myself if it wasn't meant to be then let it go."

"Yes, I have that trait and I used to be jealous but now I have a boyfriend I can trust."

HOW DO YOU FEEL ABOUT PUBLIC DISPLAYS OF AFFECTION?

Aquarius is the Sign of diplomacy and she is naturally well mannered. She also considers affection, love, and sexuality to be wholesome experiences. As a result, she enjoys only subtle forms of public displays of affection.

"How nice . . ."

"Hand holding or putting your arm around your partner is fine, but other than that it should be kept private."

"A hug is okay, but for anything further, there is another time and place."

Fantasies

"Having sex with another female while my partner watches and is turned on."

"Making love to my boyfriend in a pool, on the Fourth of July, with fireworks overhead. A little boring perhaps, but it has always been my fantasy."

"I fantasize about attractive men, sometimes about one of the guys I work with. They come to my door. I welcome them in and tell them to make love to me."

Sexual Attitudes and Behaviors

HOW OFTEN DO YOU THINK ABOUT SEX AND HOW OFTEN PER WEEK DO YOU WANT TO HAVE SEX?

Sex is on her mind a couple of times a week.

The Aquarius woman is content to have sex just that often.

"I think I am preoccupied with sex, but I'm happy having it once or twice a week."

"I think about it maybe once a week. How often we have it depends on our schedule, but usually at least twice."

HOW LONG DO YOU LIKE TO SPEND HAVING SEX AND HOW MUCH OF THAT TIME IS FOREPLAY? DO YOU ENJOY QUICKIES?

The ideal time spent on sex for Aquarius is less than 30 minutes. Lots of time is devoted to foreplay, but not necessarily in bed. Foreplay of the verbal sort, from the hint over breakfast of things to come at night to phone sex in the middle of the day, is the major turn-on for Aquarius. Quickies can also be a lot of fun for her.

"Foreplay is sometimes the best part of making love."

"Foreplay, all day, in small ways . . . anticipation is really important."

WHAT TIME OF DAY DO YOU PREFER TO HAVE SEX?

Anytime will be okay if the mood has been set, but Aquarius is primarily a nighttime lover.

"At night or in the morning; a nooner is good, too. Hell, any time of the day."

HOW OFTEN PER WEEK DO YOU MASTURBATE?

For the Aquarius woman, masturbation is only fun when she's having phone sex with her lover.

Memories

"My partner shaved my pubic hair and then performed oral sex. It was really amazing because he loved it as much as I did."

"The first time I made love with my current boyfriend. He made me feel special and he worried about what I wanted. It was magical to me. His skin smelled amazing. The room was quiet, with the moonlight coming in the window."

HOW LONG DO YOU WANT TO KNOW SOMEONE BEFORE GETTING SEXUAL?

Aquarius is not a woman who wants to include sex as a first date activity. Far from it. She really wants to know a man and be clear about future prospects before getting sexual.

"Ideally I want to meet a man, ask him to speak to my family members about marriage, and then jump in bed with him after that meeting to see if we are really a pair."

"On average it is about six months."

"I want to know someone about three to six months before getting sexual."

WHAT'S YOUR ATTITUDE TOWARD CASUAL SEX?

Aquarius is not interested in anonymous sex. Her basic nature, needing verbal stimulation to get turned on, depends upon having a fairly solid connection with a man before she can get much pleasure out of sex.

"It's unsafe and not for me."

"It is unsafe and self-destructive."

A Memory

"It was outside in the woods. We walked to a restaurant with our friends and had dinner. Seven of us all sat around, had some drinks, and chatted for a while. We were all on our way home and he said, 'I have to piss,' so he walked into the woods. The next thing I knew he grabbed my arm and pulled me in with him. He threw me up against [a] tree and we did it against the tree until we came together. Then we walked back to our friend's house and got picked on, but it was great."

DO YOU BELIEVE IN MONOGAMY?

For Aquarius, sex is far from being the most important part of a relationship.

Communication, the world of ideas and the plans she shares with her partner matter much more. The bonds that grow out of all of these attributes give her sexual energy. Aquarius cannot form such a connection with more than one man at a time.

"Yes. When you commit yourself to someone, that commitment is both sexual and emotional."

"I believe that monogamy is the basis for a relationship in terms of trust. The shared experiences, that special communication with exclusively one other person, makes for a much healthier relationship."

"Yes, for the sense of trust. You know he may look at another and think about it, but he won't have sex with anyone else."

DOES SEX HAVE A SPIRITUAL SIGNIFICANCE FOR YOU?

Aquarius is a woman of ideas and inspiration. The world of emotion is more difficult for her to handle. Sex at its best is emotional, intense, and passionate. In the bond that sex helps her to experience with her partner, it becomes a spiritual act.

"Yes. I believe that when you are having sex with someone you love, both souls are coming together as one."

"When I have sex with a man, it is like giving him a piece of my soul, an invisible attachment to him."

"Definitely. I view sex as the bonding of two souls, which makes it much more satisfying than merely a physical experience."

ARE YOU COMFORTABLE INITIATING SEXUAL ACTIVITIES?

Aquarius is a bit reticent about taking the initiative and it takes verbal foreplay to get her started. Considering these aspects of her nature, it makes sense that Aquarius is more comfortable when her partner begins the conversation about sex.

"Sometimes I get scared that my guy will think I'm not a 'good girl' if I'm the aggressive

one, but there are times that I just want him so badly I forget that I'm shy."

"No, let the man see how lovely I am and take appropriate action."

HOW DO YOU COMMUNICATE TO YOUR PARTNER YOUR SEXUAL WANTS AND NEEDS?

Aquarius is a verbal Sign. Words turn her on, keep her going, and add to her stimulation. Granted, words are most important before the experience is actually taking place; in the throes of passion she won't be doing a lot of talking. Overall, she is comfortable using words along with gestures to express her sexual desires.

"Sometimes I tell him. Other times I move any part of him where I want him."

DO YOU THINK OF YOURSELF AS BEING IN THE MAINSTREAM SEXUALLY, MORE EXPERIMENTAL, OR OPEN TO ANYTHING?

Her range of sexuality is primarily mainstream: kissing, fondling, and intercourse. Beyond that, Aquarius enjoys wearing sexy lingerie and will have sex in public places as long as there is no risk of being seen. On rare occasions she may be open to using food in sex play, specifically strawberries, chocolate, and whipped cream. She has little interest in sex toys other than vibrators. Her fantasies are based on actual events and tend toward the romantic.

Fantasies

"I remember my wedding night. Closing the hotel door, seeing him already undressing, in anticipation of what's to come. Just the indescribable feeling of that first sexual encounter and loving him so much is all the fantasy I ever need."

"All I do is imagine making love gently with the man I love."

"My fantasies are very romantic and cultured: violins playing, candles, et cetera."

HOW DO YOU DEMONSTRATE AFFECTION FOR YOUR PARTNER?

Two things dominate in the list of ways Aquarius shows her regard for her lover: she cooks for him and she listens attentively. Her remarkable skill in all areas of communication is apparent when she leaves him messages, sends him cards, and responds to him in conversation.

"Remember the things we talked about and fulfill those desires, getting things he especially likes for dinner, checking his horoscope and forgetting mine."

"I leave him poems, letters; give him a kiss; cook his favorite meal."

"Cook from scratch his favorite meals, give rubdowns for aching muscles."

"Pick up things I know he likes when I am out, send cards and small gifts, cook food he likes, help him out, be his friend."

 A Memory

"He brought flowers and helped with the dinner cleanup. On the way to the bedroom, we were all over each other with kisses and soft caresses. He rubbed his hands between my legs and we had intercourse. During the evening there was more going down on each other and more intercourse. He brought me a warm wash cloth and helped clean off some of his sperm, and then continued some of his sweetness for a while. We slept."

The Five Senses

HOW IMPORTANT TO YOU IS THE SEXUAL ENVIRONMENT?

For Aquarius, all of the elements that affect her senses are important. As a result, she cares about the condition of the sexual surroundings. Being in a pleasant place, one that is warm, comfortable, and clean, certainly adds to her pleasure.

"The environment elevates the whole thing. It is primo number one and it should be [at] the top of the list in sex education."

"Very important: a clean place and I like candles burning."

"I like a clean environment. It's important to me."

WHERE DO YOU LIKE TO HAVE SEX?

Aquarius says that sex in different locations is fun and that she likes variety. In truth, though, variety wears thin in short order. She likes the predictability, safety, and comfort of her bed, his bed, a motel, or a B&B.

"Mostly in the bedroom or elsewhere in the house like the living room, kitchen, and the bathroom; but we have had oral sex in a car and in a playground."

"Anywhere, as long as we don't get caught by someone else . . ."

"Any comfortable clean place, in the red rocks with a large blanket, or anywhere where the kids couldn't come across us . . ."

"Anywhere. I am up for new things, but usually not public places."

WHAT PUTS YOU IN THE MOOD FOR SEX?

Sounds, from music to the ocean to her lover's voice, all contribute to setting the mood for Aquarius. When her lover talks about what he wants to do to her, how he wants to savor her body, where he wants to put his hands, in her mind she feels all the things he is describing. That, for her, is the ultimate turn-on.

"Being around someone who triggers that special chemistry, fragrances, music, showering, and baths get me turned on."

"Favorite songs, nature of the environment, where I am after a day of having fun with my partner—no kids around."

"Music, quiet place, clothes, sometimes just the sight of his naked chest and body . . ."

 A Memory

"After a warm, beautiful sunny day [of] lying on the rocks by the ocean at Beavertail listening to the sounds of the ocean and birds, and gently touching each other's back. We came home and had a wonderful experience in bed. My boyfriend [was] very gentle and loving. He slowly and gently touched my body and brought out incredible sexual feelings I had never before experienced."

WHAT'S YOUR ATTITUDE TOWARD PORNOGRAPHY?

Because it is words that turn her on, the most exciting part of pornography for Aquarius is the soundtrack. Turn off the image and leave just the panting, the moaning, the "Yes, yes. Oh God" and she will respond.

"I wouldn't want to watch it every day but once in a while it can spice up your sex life."

"It depends. If it is hard core, no; if it is soft core it may enhance the relationship."

"Sometimes intrigued, sometimes disgusted . . ."

"It is okay, once in a while but I don't need it or love it."

A Fantasy

"I wish my man would come in, throw me down, and rip off all my clothes. He would push me down, cuff me to the bed, and do whatever he wants like eat me out until I cum on his face and lift my whole body and fuck my brains loose. I wouldn't even mind if we both had bruises when we were done."

HOW MUCH CUDDLING DO YOU ENJOY, ASIDE FROM SEX?

When they are home alone, the housework is out of the way, and dinner is over, Aquarius loves to have her partner sit close to her and hold hands. The feeling of closeness matters. Sex doesn't have to follow.

"I like to cuddle when I'm watching a movie with my guy, or just watch TV with him."

"My partner and I cuddle all the time. Yes, he really enjoys it."

"All that I can get, which works in my favor because my boyfriend likes it also."

HOW TACTILE AND HOW ORAL ARE YOU?

Most of all Aquarius wants to feel things profoundly. When it comes to sex, it doesn't matter whether her lover turns her on with his hands or his mouth. Similarly, she is equally comfortable using tactile and oral acts to stimulate her partner. Intensity matters, not method.

"I love to caress and touch. I run my hands over my guy when he is on top."

"I love touch: doing it very lightly and plenty of it, rather like a ballet."

"I love anything that will make him feel good, from deep kissing and kissing his body to fellatio. I am very oral."

"I love giving oral sex to him because he is very appreciative. When we are having sex in the missionary position, I enjoy deep kissing."

"I enjoy deep kissing on the mouth and light touching of the tongues."

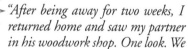 A Memory

"After being away for two weeks, I returned home and saw my partner in his woodwork shop. One look. We were both horny. We started kissing softly, then deeper. Hungry for more, we began undressing each other. Sunlight streamed through the skylight. The muskiness of his body and the smell of pine on his hands turned me on. We explored each other, standing and kneeling, until we couldn't take it anymore. Our bodies became one on the floor. We could hear nothing except each other and then slowly, very slowly, I could hear the birds in the trees and the waterfall and other signs of life as I lay there next to my best friend."

WHAT SEX ACTS DO YOU LIKE MOST AND LEAST?

Staying mostly in the mainstream range of sex acts, the Aquarius woman loves everything from kissing and fondling to vaginal intercourse. Aquarius has little to no interest in anal sex.

"I do not like anal sex, mutual masturbation, or anything uncomfortable."

"I enjoy foreplay and intercourse. Anal sex is out. We will never try that."

"Oral, intercourse, fondling body parts with clothes on to get him in the mood. I don't enjoy mutual masturbation."

AS A LOVER, WHAT'S YOUR BEST SKILL?

More than what she does with her hands or tongue, it is the way Aquarius moves that most thrills her partner. This includes the sexy way that she undresses to the way she responds in bed.

"My best skills as a lover [are] knowing how to move my body and knowing what to say."

"My motions, the way I move."

"I am very flexible and strong, and like to move a lot."

WHAT SMELLS AND TASTES ON YOUR PARTNER DO YOU ENJOY?

Keep it simple to satisfy Aquarius most. The smells that she likes include scented soaps and spicy colognes. The tastes of his kisses will turn her on more than using foods or body oils and gels.

"Aftershave, clean hair, and skin smells, and the taste of his mouth when we kiss."

"Sometimes I like the taste of his sweat when I know we have been enjoying ourselves."

"I like the smell of a man's skin and his cologne, and the taste of anything sweet."

 Memories

"One New Year's Eve my boyfriend and I had sex in front of the refrigerator. I had candles burning all over the house and his cologne smelled sexy and we had romantic music playing."

"In a hotel room with ocean view: sexy lingerie, slow foreplay, smell of his body, the look in his eyes; no outside interference; and lying beside him, snuggling my head on his shoulder; talking or just relaxing."

FOR SOME PEOPLE THE TASTE OF THEIR PARTNER'S CUM OR SECRETIONS IS UNPLEASANT. IF THAT'S TRUE FOR YOU, WHAT DO YOU DO ABOUT THE TASTE?

Most often Aquarius is turned off by the taste of cum and she does not want her partner to reach orgasm during oral sex. Precum is no problem for her as she enjoys oral sex.

"I don't like the taste so I have him take chlorophyll tablets. They're good for breath and everything else."

"I don't let him cum in my mouth. I have a weak stomach."

"I think people should keep their bodily fluids to themselves."

DO YOU ENJOY WATCHING YOUR PARTNER DURING SEX AND ORGASM? DO YOU ENJOY BEING WATCHED?

What Aquarius wants in sex is to feel close to her partner, to experience a wide range of sensations. Watching and being watched become important aspects as a relationship deepens. Initially, however, she is a little shy about him watching her.

"It's okay to be watched, but only by my boyfriend."

"If it makes him more excited, then yes . . ."

The Big "O"

HOW DO YOU REACH AN ORGASM AND HOW OFTEN?

A quickie may not always result in orgasm for Aquarius. But when her lover sets the stage with phone sex during the day and with sexual banter leading up to the act itself, Aquarius almost always climaxes. Most often this is through intercourse and oral sex.

WHAT'S YOUR FAVORITE POSITION?

For Aquarius to achieve orgasm via intercourse, she prefers oral sex first and then being on top and straddling her partner.

SOME PEOPLE ARE CONCERNED ABOUT BRINGING THEIR PARTNER TO CLIMAX BEFORE HAVING AN ORGASM THEMSELVES. OTHERS STRIVE TO REACH ORGASM TOGETHER. WHICH IS TRUE FOR YOU?

Cumming together is great, but Aquarius is usually the one to reach orgasm first.

"I need to cum first, and my partner feels the same way."

"I like to have one first."

"Multiple orgasms for a woman are best; string a man's out, I think."

"Both. Some days I just want him to get there and other times I want us both there at the same time."

"I want him to cum also, but I usually cum first."

 A Memory
"*Coming back from a bar, flashing people on a road, and getting so heated up. We drove so fast back to the apartment, ran upstairs, stripped as fast as we could for him to mount me doggie style and slam his cock deep inside me. Oh, how wonderful it was.*"

ARE YOU VOCAL DURING SEX?

The Aquarius woman loves to be vocal during sex. If she is in a private place, she allows herself free rein to express the fullness of her responses—both with words and moans of pleasure.

"It is my nature to be, but we live in an apartment building so I have to be less vocal than I would like."

"A little, we have small children in the house."

"It's up to my partner. I love to be vocal."

AFTER SEX WHAT DO YOU LIKE TO DO?

Following sex, Aquarius wants to stay home, cuddle a bit, perhaps spend a little quiet time together, and then go to sleep.

"Kiss passionately, hold hands, cuddle, listen to music, good conversation, sleep."

The Aquarius Man in His Own Words

A Memory
"I came home from work and found my mate, naked, waiting in our bed with her legs spread. I started to tongue her legs slowly, aiming for her pussy, and then I licked her pussy thoroughly until she had two or three orgasms. Then I fucked her hard and brought her to a final one before erupting deep inside her."

Attraction and Dating an Aquarius

WHAT ATTRACTS YOU TO SOMEONE?

For the Aquarius man, how a woman feels about herself and reflects that in her behavior is more of a turn-on than stereotypical good looks. On top of that, this is a man who has a need to contribute to his community so a woman who is involved in some form of civic endeavor, whether in her work or as a volunteer, is very attractive to him.

"I am drawn to a woman who gives off a dominant behavior, someone who believes in herself. As to looks, an average size body is about all that matters."

"Behavior, mostly their attitude about themselves, then looks. I do not like females who are grossly overweight."

"A person who is physically fit shows you that they take care of themselves. Natural beauty is essential. I enjoy active women who share some interests in common with mine. Sense of humor is important."

"Specific physical traits are not very significant with me. Weight is unimportant as long as it is not too extreme in either direction. What I like most is kindness, support for others, and intelligence."

WHAT MIGHT TURN YOU OFF?

Aquarius is the diplomat of the zodiac, known for being tactful and well mannered. Rude or generally poor behavior in public will turn off the Aquarius man more than almost any physical characteristic. About the only such turnoff for him is a woman who is considerably overweight.

"I do not like loud, vulgar, or obnoxious women. How they behave in public is a sample for me of what they would be like in a relationship."

"Women who are ignorant about the world and unconcerned about such matters do not interest me."

"I am turned off by bad attitudes and swearing, ignorant or obnoxious people, and poor hygiene."

"Traits that turn me off include talking too much about oneself, talking about other lovers, being a dull conversationalist, too clingy, or putting others down."

A Fantasy
"A hot night of passionate lovemaking after a long day of skiing at a mountaintop resort. I enjoy fantasizing about foreplay that involves slow movement, taking each other's clothes off, sipping on wine by a warm fireplace, sensual touching, alternating dominance."

WHAT DO YOU LIKE TO DO ON A DATE?

Aquarius is at his best in fairly large groups

where he can talk with a lot of people in a casual way. When he walks into the local breakfast place everyone calls out "Hi Joe!" He's that social. Still, he is not easy to get close to and may not have many intimate friends. As a result, Aquarius can be ill at ease in small groups, say getting together with his partner's family or closest friends, at least until the relationship is quite well established. He far prefers going out on active dates or spending evenings alone with his partner and sharing a meal at home.

"I like going to the theater, hiking, camping, fishing, and biking."

"Anything active, hiking, skiing, and also a quiet dinner and a movie [are] enjoyable."

"I enjoy sharing outdoor activities, walking around the city or having a home-cooked meal."

"Being outdoors in nature, hiking, going to the beach, or doing new things that I haven't tried before . . ."

ARE YOU FLIRTATIOUS?

Not really. Aquarius is a natural conversationalist, at ease talking with strangers in crowded clubs, at the office picnic, and in almost any new setting. Overall, he is sociable and can be charming rather than flirtatious.

"[I'm] not really that flirtatious. I do like to joke around to make women laugh."

"I can be tastefully, subtly, and playfully flirtatious; a good deal when instigated."

"I have been told that I am flirtatious, but I do not see it that way."

ARE YOU JEALOUS?

Aquarius is an even-tempered man. He's rational more than emotional, and capable of staying calm in a crisis. It would be very out of character for him to suffer from jealousy. Only to the extent that anyone is capable of feeling jealousy if provoked can Aquarius be jealous.

"If there is trust in the relationship I am not likely to get jealous."

"I tend not to be but have been with certain significant others in the past."

"I never thought I was jealous until recently. I have been finding myself getting jealous when the girl I am currently dating is talking to other guys."

HOW DO YOU FEEL ABOUT PUBLIC DISPLAYS OF AFFECTION?

For a man known to be quite proper in public, Aquarius is surprisingly at ease about public displays of affection. His attitude is that love is grand and happy; a good thing in this world. So why not show it off?

"I do not see anything wrong with it. When in the mood, the place means nothing."

"A little goes a long way. I am comfortable hugging, holding hands, a peck."

"I used to be very shy but with the woman I am seeing now, I am happy about showing my feelings in public."

 Memories

"My little pony girl bound helpless, legs wide apart, held by spreader bar, and me holding her harness and coming in from behind."

"A bit of struggle, a bit of restraining, and a lot of primal, carnal, sexual behavior."

Sexual Attitudes and Behaviors

HOW OFTEN DO YOU THINK ABOUT SEX AND HOW OFTEN PER WEEK DO YOU WANT TO HAVE SEX?

Aquarius seeks sensation, sexual and otherwise, and sex crosses his mind virtually every day. However, it takes some kind of trigger, usually verbal—a double entendre, an innuendo—to get the thought started. This Sign is content to have sex two or three times a week.

HOW LONG DO YOU LIKE TO SPEND HAVING SEX AND HOW MUCH OF THAT TIME IS FOREPLAY? DO YOU ENJOY QUICKIES?

Foreplay may well start hours before intimacy with sexy conversation, a little phone sex, and or a note in the briefcase describing activities planned for later in the day. His brain is an all-important organ when it comes to setting the romantic stage for Aquarius. When it comes to the act itself, he enjoys spending at least 30 minutes having sex, with 15 minutes devoted to foreplay. Quickies are fine, too, as well as an occasional marathon session.

"I enjoy quickies but I also like to spend hours having sex. I think you can never spend too much time on foreplay."

"I like to spend as long as it takes to get there. I enjoy quickies as well."

"When it comes to foreplay, I do not like spending much time: a little cuddling, touching, slow undressing, feeling bodies against each other."

WHAT TIME OF DAY DO YOU PREFER TO HAVE SEX?

Any time of day suits him fine. The only day part about which Aquarius is likely to have a strong opinion is morning. He either really likes sex first thing in the morning or he really dislikes it altogether.

"Time does not matter to me."

"In the daytime; I like light."

"Anytime except morning . . ."

HOW OFTEN PER WEEK DO YOU MASTURBATE?

Aquarius is a man of extremes. He may go through periods when he masturbates every day, and other times when he will do it less than once a week.

 Fantasies

"Being in front of strangers masturbating. Voyeurism is so hot. Being seduced or wanted, and having sex with a well-known celebrity."

"I imagine meeting a woman in a shopping mall or supermarket. There is instant attraction. Understanding we both want it we leave immediately, rush to her place, and make love fast and furious."

"All I need to think about is being on the water in a boat or in a small cabin in the woods, feeling close to nature."

HOW LONG DO YOU WANT TO KNOW SOMEONE BEFORE GETTING SEXUAL?

The short answer is, "not long." For Aquarius the stimulus to have sex comes from exciting conversation. If that kind of communication happens quickly, so will sex.

"I think one hour is sufficient. No, really, I don't think you have to know a woman long at all."

"The time frame matters very little. I know in short order if there is some sort of physical attraction."

"I don't have to know a woman at all. I will know if it is sexual upon meeting her."

"I believe in love at first sight. It could be on a first date if the feeling is right."

WHAT'S YOUR ATTITUDE TOWARD CASUAL SEX?

Aquarius does not enter into important or intimate relationships very easily. He craves physical sensation, so casual sex is simply fun for him. Certainly he realizes that anonymous sex may be unsafe, but he has few reservations about doing it.

"It is fine, if controlled and not indiscreet."

"Casual sex is fine, but not for people who are in exclusively committed relationships."

"It can be exciting, but unfortunately it can be unsafe and does not have much meaning."

"I know it is unsafe, but I love it."

DO YOU BELIEVE IN MONOGAMY?

An Aquarian man is charming, gentle, and easy to get along with. He is slow to reveal his feelings and in no rush to get married. He sees monogamy as an individual choice, but once in a committed relationship does value it. It may be difficult for him to sustain, however, particularly if his sex life is less than satisfactory.

"I think that if people are comfortable with monogamy they should practice it."

"Yes, it is important because I believe it holds together morals and ethics. Life would be empty without it."

"I believe in being monogamous, but that is just my personal preference. One relationship is difficult enough to manage at a time. I like the security of knowing that each individual in a relationship is being true to the other."

"I am and have always practiced monogamy, but I am curious about the idea of having something on the side. What stops me is that, from what I have heard, most open relationships have their downfalls."

DOES SEX HAVE A SPIRITUAL SIGNIFICANCE FOR YOU?

Aquarius makes connections more in the mind than in the physical realm. He has a tendency to keep his distance, and he avoids many emotional entanglements. Sex provides him with a way to get in touch with his feelings. As such, sex is very important to him, but not particularly spiritual.

"Perhaps sex with the right partner could, but I have not had that experience yet."

"Not that I know of so far . . ."

"It has at times in the past, but I do not consider sex spiritual on a regular basis."

 A Memory
"I was shopping and went into a Victoria's Secret. I saw a woman there, very hot, and I was enthralled. I was about 26 and she was maybe 35. We began caressing and had sex in the dressing room."

ARE YOU COMFORTABLE INITIATING SEXUAL ACTIVITIES?

Sort of. His sense of propriety shows here. The Aquarius man needs to be pretty at ease with a woman before he will broach the subject of becoming sexual. Too, he needs some signal from his partner that she is amenable.

"Yes, with someone I know."

"I prefer having certain conditions in place before initiating sex with a new partner. In other words, I want to be showered, have fresh breath, et cetera."

"Not necessarily. I feel like I am imposing or pressuring."

HOW DO YOU COMMUNICATE TO YOUR PARTNER YOUR SEXUAL WANTS AND NEEDS?

Here is a man who gets hot from sexy talk and for whom sexual excitement is maintained with sounds of pleasure. Aquarius may not want to participate in a verbal play-by-play during sex, but he is certainly comfortable expressing his likes, dislikes, and desires verbally.

"I tell her what to do most of the time."

"Verbally, only after I know her better."

"I tend to communicate mostly with words but would prefer gestures."

DO YOU THINK OF YOURSELF AS BEING IN THE MAINSTREAM SEXUALLY, MORE EXPERIMENTAL, OR OPEN TO ANYTHING?

Aquarius is a rather experimental lover who may enjoy some bondage, dominance and submission, ménage à trois, or using food along with sex. He also enjoys a certain amount of exhibitionism, is voyeuristic, and may like to have sex in public places. A beautiful foot with well-tended toenails will turn him on. He enjoys spanking a naughty partner. Sex toys are of little interest to him, limited only to vibrators and dildos. His fantasies are reflections of his sexual behaviors.

Fantasies

"It can be most anything, as long as she takes charge of me, controls every aspect and, keeps me locked up to prevent me from doing anything without her telling me so."

"In a lot of my fantasies I am the submissive one with two women dominating me."

"Dress her up in something girlie and spank her."

"Making it with my partner on our pool deck while the neighbors are watching."

HOW DO YOU DEMONSTRATE AFFECTION FOR YOUR PARTNER?

Aquarius is quietly attentive and shows his regard by helping his lover on her terms: by helping around the house and being willing to do a variety of errands. He is a wonderful listener and sounding board when she wants to work through a problem.

"Be there for her when she needs me without her asking . . ."

"Thoughtfulness such as helping with daily chores, surprising her with presents . . ."

"Random acts of kindness, doing the dishes, putting gas in the car. I try to be very aware and responsive, a good partner."

"Pamper her, do chores, get her cards, leave her notes . . ."

"Surprise gifts, doing chores around the house, cooking dinner frequently . . ."

The Five Senses

HOW IMPORTANT TO YOU IS THE SEXUAL ENVIRONMENT?

Bearing in mind that sex for Aquarius begins in the brain and his excitement is triggered verbally, the sexual environment is of little consequence to Aquarius. He does like the setting to be clean and dimly lit, but that's about it.

"Cleanliness is important; however, I have bypassed that on occasion in a fit of lust."

"Not important as long as it is clean."

"Not important at all."

"Except for when we do it outside, it should be very clean [and] with low light."

"As long as it is not dirty and we are alone, the particulars are not important."

A Memory

"A night after a good dinner with a couple of drinks and some very smooth music. It was traditional sex, a perfect evening with a warm breeze and the scent of salt air."

"Last winter in New Hampshire, in a warm room with a large hot tub and porn movies."

"In a hot tub, smell of chlorine and cold air, bodies collide, steam rising, feel of jets all over my body, wet bodies cling to every breath."

"A cold snowy night at her house, everything was so feminine, warm, candles lighting the room."

WHERE DO YOU LIKE TO HAVE SEX?

Sexy talk gets Aquarius so turned on that he won't want to wait to get home. Any dark corner can be fun. After all, Aquarius is a Sign that often seeks sensation. For many, therefore, having sex where there's a slight chance of being seen is a turn-on.

"I do not have a preference. Outdoors is nice; a public place would not be bad either."

"Anywhere . . . I like places where we might get caught, dangerous sex."

"Whenever and wherever I am turned on . . ."

WHAT PUTS YOU IN THE MOOD FOR SEX?

Aquarius is a verbal Sign. For him, ideas, thoughts, and discussions about sexual experiences and fantasies put him in the mood. He loves phone sex. Foreplay for him goes on throughout the workday with sexy calls back and forth to his lover. Later in the day, watching erotic videos or reading sexy scenes adds to his passion. Overall, words and the images they suggest turn this man on most.

"Talking about sex, passionate kissing, a massage, romantic settings, watching my lover undress, [the] sound of rain, poetry . . ."

"Environment, talking about sex, physical groping, passionate kisses . . ."

"A nice meal and conversation . . ."

"Nice music, mental activity, and anything in the porn line; as well as passionate kissing, my lover's nude body, and [the] sound of rain . . ."

WHAT'S YOUR ATTITUDE TOWARD PORNOGRAPHY?

Aquarius enjoys pornography up to a point, especially if it is of a more sophisticated type. Straightforward sex acts, one after another and without regard for setting or some sense of intrigue, interest him very little. Eroticism is more to his liking; X-rated movies—more than XXX-rated videos—and sexy talk are far more likely to get him turned on than scenes of bumping and grinding.

"I have mild interest in it. Sometimes I really enjoy looking at it, but not too often."

"I do not find hard core porn appealing . . . lyrical yes . . ."

"Most of it is of no interest to me and I really do not like it when it is degrading to women."

A Memory

"She lit candles in the bedroom, [and] then escorted me in by the hand. She slowly undressed me and gave me head. I reciprocated, undressing her and performing oral sex. We made love in the middle of the bed—not even turning down the covers—intensely fast, like two teenagers."

HOW MUCH CUDDLING DO YOU ENJOY, ASIDE FROM SEX?

His reputation is at odds with his own self-perception. Most often Aquarius is considered a somewhat distant personality, but he says that he enjoys cuddling very much. It would seem that he takes his cue mostly from his partner's behav-

ior. However, he must not feel smothered in a relationship and he does need his time alone.

"I like hugs a lot."

"I enjoy a lot of touching. I'm a very physical person."

"Very little; my wife does not enjoy it."

"I like a lot of cuddling. It is very important in my relationship."

HOW TACTILE AND HOW ORAL ARE YOU?

Bearing in mind that the word precedes the act, and that sexy talk is the true turn-on, when the actual sex begins Aquarius loves the tactile aspect of sex—to run his hands all over his lover.

"I love exploring a woman's body."

Kissing and oral sex acts rank at the top of his list of pleasures.

"I love everything from light to deep kisses, and all aspects of oral sex."

"Deep kissing, kissing all over [her] body, kissing breasts . . ."

WHAT SEX ACTS DO YOU LIKE MOST AND LEAST?

For day-to-day sex, his range of acts is within the traditional: from hugs and kisses to intercourse. When time permits and the setting is right, this Sign will go into the list of experimental behaviors that he enjoys. There is little Aquarius does not like sexually, but anal sex is probably least satisfactory to him.

"Massages, kissing, foreplay, oral sex, and intercourse . . ."

"Oral sex—both giving and receiving—and intercourse, along with breast fondling and mutual masturbation . . ."

"If it involves sex, I like it."

"I would have to pick anal sex as my least favorite because I have found that most women do not like it."

Fantasies

"I guess it is the most common one for guys: having sex with two women."

"I imagine a ménage à trois with a stranger. I usually envision anonymous sex, a raw physical act without any follow-up commitment. I imagine women with long, luxurious hair."

"Coming upon two beautiful women who are making love. I watch them for a while and then join them and enjoy servicing both of them while they do the same for me."

AS A LOVER, WHAT'S YOUR BEST SKILL?

The Aquarius man considers himself a very competent lover, especially in the way he moves his body. He is also gifted at oral sex and has no problem with the taste of a woman's secretions.

"I know how to please a woman. I can read what she wants."

"I am good at them all, especially the way I move."

"It is mostly how I use my body."

WHAT SMELLS AND TASTES ON YOUR PARTNER DO YOU ENJOY?

Stick to what is natural to please Aquarius most. Colognes and perfumes are seldom on his list of favorite aromas, and he doesn't care for flavored oils that disguise his lover's taste.

"My lover's skin, her sweat, and other body smells all please me."

"I enjoy the aroma of her hair, under her breasts, her pussy, all of her skin."

"Her skin, natural odors, and pheromones."

"I love to taste her pussy."

"I enjoy everything: her skin and her pussy, all of her juices."

"I love the taste of kisses, her salty nipples, her pussy, her ass, and her sweat."

FOR SOME PEOPLE THE TASTE OF THEIR PARTNER'S CUM OR SECRETIONS IS UNPLEASANT. IF THAT'S TRUE FOR YOU, WHAT DO YOU DO ABOUT THE TASTE?

Aquarius is a Sign that seeks sensation, seeks feeling experience in many areas of life and most certainly in sex. As a result, he has absolutely no problem in this area.

"I do not mind the taste; in fact, I enjoy it."

"The taste is not an issue for me."

"Her secretions are not unpleasant, but I do not kiss her mouth after she has performed oral sex [on me]."

A Memory

"I threw her over the desk in my office, pretending she was a student in trouble for poor behavior. I told her she would be kicked off the team if she didn't do exactly what I told her. I shoved it in her ass, and pummeled her anus bloody. I then came in her waiting mouth."

DO YOU ENJOY WATCHING YOUR PARTNER DURING SEX AND ORGASM? DO YOU ENJOY BEING WATCHED?

Aquarius may not have even thought about his lover looking at him during orgasm. His mind is more on words than images. But when he makes eye contact with his partner, he finds the experience far more erotic.

"I never thought about her watching me before. I think I would be okay with that."

"Being watched? I guess it's somewhat enjoyable. Maybe; I am not sure."

"I do not mind too much if I am watched, but I would rather not be the focus of attention."

The Big "O"

HOW DO YOU REACH AN ORGASM AND HOW OFTEN?

Keep his mind on the event at hand and Aquarius cums. Let his mind wander and Aquarius loses his erection. Dirty talk as orgasm nears sends him over the edge regardless of the position or the act.

"My mind can do it easier than my hand. I cum whenever I try."

"I climax through intercourse or masturbation all the time."

"The method varies: intercourse and oral sex, I cum all the time."

WHAT'S YOUR FAVORITE POSITION?

Variety, variety, variety. The Aquarius man is both a good lover and a satisfied one—as long as the event does not become routine.

"Face to face on our sides, woman on top, mutual oral sex . . ."

"Doggie style or man or woman on top so I can see her face . . ."

"Mutual oral sex and doggie style . . ."

SOME PEOPLE ARE CONCERNED ABOUT BRINGING THEIR PARTNER TO CLIMAX BEFORE HAVING AN ORGASM THEMSELVES. OTHERS STRIVE TO REACH ORGASM TOGETHER. WHICH IS TRUE FOR YOU?

Aquarius considers himself quite good at climaxing with his partner, but that is not a goal. As he has no trouble achieving climax, and knows that he will be satisfied ultimately, his aim is to please his lover.

"My first concern is to bring my lover to climax."

"I enjoy reaching orgasm simultaneously, but it doesn't always happen."

"I try to time it right but always make sure she has the first and the last orgasm."

ARE YOU VOCAL DURING SEX?

Leading up to the act, Aquarius is very talkative about sex. However, during sex itself, he is only moderately vocal. He does appreciate a woman who voices her satisfaction.

AFTER SEX WHAT DO YOU LIKE TO DO?

This man doesn't want to roll over and go to sleep. Aquarius wants to spend some time being close to his partner talking, watching a movie at home, or sharing food.

"Be massaged, shower together, stay in bed, listen to music, sleep, have some good conversation."

"I like to snuggle for a while, perhaps go out for a walk."

PISCES

February 19–March 20

THE FISH

Water Sign Pisces is a very sexual Sign, psychic and imaginative. Pisceans make wonderful writers, storytellers, and actors. They also have innate healing abilities, which make them well suited to the fields of medicine and counseling. Ruler of the feet, which are usually very well formed with this Sign, a foot massage will turn their thoughts to sex.

She says: "When we kiss we can melt an iceberg."

He says: "One memorable sex encounter was making love on the beach, in the waves. The fresh air and the sudden rush of cold water made it incredible."

"This is the miracle that happens every time to those who really love:
the more they give, the more they possess."
—Rainer Maria Rilke

The Pisces Woman in Her Own Words

A Memory

"On our honeymoon my husband and I made love on the bluffs of Block Island, Rhode Island. It was thrilling to be outside, with the waves crashing below us, and yet to be secluded. It felt like our own private island. We lay on pine needles with our naked bodies exposed to the chilly air. We were intense and loud, but very tender."

Attraction and Dating a Pisces

WHAT ATTRACTS YOU TO SOMEONE?

Pisces doesn't make answering questions about what attracts her easy. The last sign of the zodiac, Pisces is known to have some attributes of all the other Signs. When it comes to her sense of attraction, she incorporates the ideals of other signs.

"Lips, hair, eyes, confidence is very sexy, and his touch has to be soft yet firm and masculine, take control in the bedroom."

"He should take care of himself, be in shape, clean, good looking, nice eyes, large penis, well dressed."

"Clean shaven, penis more than six inches is nice, but most important, thick . . . Quick wit and dark hair . . . A man that walks tall and is sure of himself."

WHAT MIGHT TURN YOU OFF?

She is turned off most of all by men with negative attitudes and inflated self-images. In addition, as Pisces is a spiritual Sign, a man who is overly materialistic and places too much value on money and power will not satisfy her.

"When a man treats me with disrespect or makes me feel bad about myself. Arrogance is a huge turnoff."

"Smoking, loud and obnoxious behavior, disrespectful attitudes toward women . . ."

"Negative behavior; if a guy is really high on himself [it's] a big turnoff."

WHAT DO YOU ENJOY DOING ON A DATE?

Include water in one manner or another for the most satisfying date with Pisces. Activities she enjoys include swimming, water skiing, going for a ferry ride, having a picnic by a lake, or even visiting an aquarium.

"A drive to the beach, dinner . . . sex for dessert."

"Talking at a nice restaurant, holding hands, going for a stroll in the moonlight by the lake . . ."

"I am a movie buff, so movies would work for me. Discussing said movie over dinner gives you something in common to talk about when eating."

A Memory

"I was working on a cruise ship and had just begun dating a gorgeous young Australian man. On an overnight in Barcelona, Spain, I went to a gay club with a friend from the ship. I think I was the only straight chick there. Began flirting with gay men and they with my lover and me, which was a huge turn-on. My partner and I were then dancing in a tight crowd, getting very hot and very sweaty. We went into the bathroom. There

were TV screens all over playing gay porn, gay men giving each other head in the bathroom. It was sweltering, and smelly and finally nasty and very hot. We locked ourselves in a stall and had sex standing up using the toilets and walls as strategic props.

ARE YOU FLIRTATIOUS?

Pisces is a charming, masterful flirt. With grace, with easy conversation, with her ability to empathize and to read a man's mind, she reaches him and he is hooked. It doesn't hurt that she has captivating, luminous eyes.

"I don't like to lead people on. But if I want you, you will know it."

"I feel I am just being friendly, but I am told I flirt outrageously."

"I am a huge flirt. I have been told I flirt with every person in the room. I just think it is my charm."

ARE YOU JEALOUS?

Pisces is sensitive, empathetic, and psychic. She is quick to pick up on it if her lover is dividing his attention between her and another woman. Maybe she is not jealous per se, but she won't put up with that behavior.

"Very jealous. What is mine is mine. End of story."

"Guys are a dime a dozen, why be clingy?"

"I have grown more self-confident so I am less jealous. If the man I am with would rather be somewhere else, I give him my blessing. I would rather be alone and happy than with someone and miserable."

HOW DO YOU FEEL ABOUT PUBLIC DISPLAYS OF AFFECTION?

In the right place and at the right time Pisces loves public displays of affection. They should be in a romantic setting, such as in the park at sunset, cuddling in a late-night movie, and any other place apart from the eyes of children or others who might be offended.

"I am 100 percent behind public displays of affection."

"Simple displays are invigorating to see."

"Wonderful."

"Fine if spontaneous and short, great actually. Anything too close to coitus is really annoying to look at."

 A Memory

"One of the more exciting sexual encounters I've had involved nothing other than feeling up and down one another's bodies. The night started with conversation, getting to know each other, past experiences, et cetera. It developed into this extraordinary magnetic attraction. When our hands first touched, it was electric. Our fingertips were incredibly sensitive. Every part of my body tingled. We spent the rest of the evening with our clothes on, just feeling each other, mostly exploring each other's hands. It was almost indescribable, in some ways more sexual than intercourse."

Sexual Attitudes and Behaviors

HOW OFTEN DO YOU THINK ABOUT SEX AND HOW OFTEN PER WEEK DO YOU WANT TO HAVE SEX?

The Pisces woman thinks about sex daily, and would be happy to have sex that often as well. She will, however, content herself with having intercourse four times a week.

"If I am very attracted to the person, all the time . . ."

"At least every other day; I would like it daily."

HOW LONG DO YOU LIKE TO SPEND HAVING SEX AND HOW MUCH OF THAT TIME IS FOREPLAY? DO YOU ENJOY QUICKIES?

Pisces wants to spend at least an hour, preferable two, for sex. Erotic imagery, from videos to reading aloud passages from books, adds to her experience. She enjoys a fairly lengthy period of foreplay, lingering at it if her partner is skilled. She will settle for quickies only on occasion.

"I usually like to spend about an hour on foreplay and then about 15 minutes actually having sex."

"Foreplay, as much as it takes to get me hot, then bring it on (15 minutes to a half-hour)."

"I enjoy quickies but prefer a more romantic setting with lots of time to spend on my lover."

WHAT TIME OF DAY DO YOU LIKE TO HAVE SEX?

Pisces is comfortable having sex at any time, with some preference for late evening or nighttime.

"Evening is best, preferably around nine-ish, any later and I am too tired."

"In the morning when I first wake up . . . It is the time of day that I am least stressed."

 Fantasies

"Having my first sex encounter with a gorgeous woman while being watched by a man. Sex with two men at once, a group of men pleasuring me all at once, sweaty athletic sex, with Sting or Jude Law (yummy), spontaneous sex with a beautiful stranger in a doorway in a foreign city without ever exchanging a word."

"I fantasize about a sexual encounter with a woman and about watching two men together."

"A young girl teases me with her wet cunt, masturbating, while I am being held down and masturbated."

HOW OFTEN PER WEEK DO YOU MASTURBATE?

How often depends upon whether she has a partner. When involved, the Pisces woman almost never masturbates as she enjoys having sex so frequently.

"I don't masturbate. Honestly, why do it yourself if you can get someone else to do it?"

"When I'm not in a relationship, maybe three or four times a week; when in a relationship it's more like three or four times a month."

HOW LONG DO YOU WANT TO KNOW SOMEONE BEFORE GETTING SEXUAL?

For Pisces, it could be within a week or take as much as three months before she will get physical. It depends on the strength of the sexual attraction.

"The longer the better, but I am often impulsive."

"Foreplay can't come quick enough; that is, at least kissing. I love kissing. Actual sex, longer: maybe a few weeks."

"I have to be sure that person isn't going anywhere the day after our first sexual encounter."

WHAT'S YOUR ATTITUDE TOWARD CASUAL SEX?

Some Pisceans enjoy recreational sex, for the sheer physical release, but many Pisces women can't allow themselves to participate in it because their feelings get in the way.

"It's great so long as one can keep self-respect."

"I have a hard time with it emotionally."

"I really like sex, so casual sex is fine, but I would rather be in a relationship."

"I haven't been successful with it; emotions get involved."

DO YOU BELIEVE IN MONOGAMY?

Pisces does believe in monogamy, though she admits that practicing it isn't easy. She has a lot of sexual energy that needs satisfying. Sex partners outside a committed relationship may be fine as long as the relationship is open.

"I am not willing to share my man with anyone."

"Religiously yes, practically no. I am too spoiled not to be indulgent."

"I think it is biologically unnatural, but an interesting social, emotional development and can be a good goal for those who choose it. I am not sure it is right for me."

DOES SEX HAVE A SPIRITUAL SIGNIFICANCE FOR YOU?

Sometimes it does, but not always. Recreational sex to Pirsces is just that: pleasurable and entertaining but not necessarily spiritual. When there is commitment, sex may rise above the purely physical.

"It is the ultimate sharing experience."

"Two people share the most intimate moment, the most pleasurable of all sensations."

"It is like a really good session with a therapist or getting a badly needed makeover."

 A Memory

"I had met a wonderful man at a Renaissance fair. I went to his mobile home thinking we would have dinner, but instead he practically ravished me. He promptly removed my clothes and kicked into high gear. My body was on fire and I lost track of where his lips were. My nerves felt like they were on the outside of my body and I was electrified. After at least an hour of very intense foreplay, he made love to me like the wild Norwegian warrior he resembled. His long blonde hair was flying around him like he was a stallion and it was the best lovemaking session I had ever had. Afterward, we talked for hours, then slept, and in the morning we had another wild lovemaking session. Sadly, it did not work out and he is gone, but I still have the memories."

ARE YOU COMFORTABLE INITIATING SEXUAL ACTIVITIES?

Pisces has a curious combination of femininity, suggesting that she needs a protector and the self-confidence of a healing angel of mercy. Her gentleness is a turn-on for any man. Her inner strength makes her totally at ease initiating sex.

"Yes, very comfortable; in fact, I like it better that way."

"Yes, but most of the guys I have been with have been uncomfortable with me being the initiator."

HOW DO YOU COMMUNICATE TO YOUR PARTNER YOUR SEXUAL WANTS AND NEEDS?

Pisces communicates primarily through body motions. When she is in a comfortable relationship and over time, she will use words as well.

"Mostly gestures; my words don't come out the right way. Sometimes, they are not kind."

"I try to communicate verbally, [but] usually I am not good at that part."

"Whispered words, moans, noises, and guiding with my hands."

DO YOU THINK OF YOURSELF AS BEING IN THE MAINSTREAM SEXUALLY, MORE EXPERIMENTAL, OR OPEN TO ANYTHING?

A fairly experimental lover, Pisces enjoys having her feet massaged and loves incorporating food into sexual activities. She is also likely to try dominance and submission, spanking, wearing costumes, and using vibrators.

Even the most mainstream of Pisceans are likely to use vibrators, dildos, and occasionally butt plugs. They are willing to have sex in public places (preferably without being seen) and to try bondage, hot wax, and wearing leather and latex if these activities are introduced by a sensitive lover.

"By action I tend to be mainstream, but I am willing to try almost anything."

"I like to experiment with toys and positions."

Pisces is a romantic and sees sex as something of a drama or a performance in which she is the heroine. This often appears in her fantasy life, which may also include multiple partners, both male and female.

Fantasies

"Having my own female sex slave to play with as my husband watches."

"Being paraded about while wearing fetish garb and being rewarded after."

"Having two men licking and sucking every inch of my body."

"I fantasize about a sexual encounter with a woman, about watching two men together, about lesbian orgies."

"Candlelit dinner on the beach, skinny dipping, cuddling on the sand until the sun comes up."

HOW DO YOU DEMONSTRATE AFFECTION FOR YOUR PARTNER?

She is a nurturing lover and shows it in ways both romantic and practical, like sending him cards and small gifts. But in addition to that, Pisces has a healing nature. Her mere presence is reassuring and when she knows her lover is feeling stressed, without asking any questions, she goes out of her way to comfort him.

"I take care of him when he is sick, offer him massages, caress him. I cook for him, listen to him when he needs to let everything out. I call him sweet names."

"Make special foods he likes, massage, small gifts, special messages left on his cell phone."

"Cook his favorite meal, buy him something I know he would love."

The Five Senses

HOW IMPORTANT TO YOU IS THE SEXUAL ENVIRONMENT?

In the heat of the moment, lack of ambience won't turn her off but the Pisces woman is thrilled by a man who goes to the bother of creating a seductive setting with fresh sheets, a well-placed mirror, a hint of incense, candlelight, and soft music.

"Cleanliness is a must, [also] low lighting and music."

"Environment is very important as it sets a scene. If there is dirty laundry, loud rock music, and beer bottles around the room, suffice it to say I wouldn't be there."

Memories

"My boyfriend had a huge bathtub and filled it with oils and rose petals. We made love for hours in the water, while eating strawberries and drinking champagne."

"One night, my boyfriend and I spent over five hours together in the shower. We just went nuts and the water stayed hot. Our voices echoed. The shower was stimulating and we tried every position one could use in a standup shower stall. No extra candles, no puffy stuff: just pure, carnal lust."

"Once my partner and I went to a marina and sneaked onto a boat and had very wild sex on the floor of this boat with people nearby. It was very exciting to be so naughty and to be on a complete stranger's boat, not knowing if we would get caught. The sound of the water and the smell of the ocean [were] wonderful."

"It was having sex at the water's edge, on the beach, at night in Aruba. It was hot, humid, the water was warm. Waves slowly lapped the beach."

WHERE DO YOU LIKE TO HAVE SEX?

Water Sign Pisces frequently mentions water as a fun locale for sex. She enjoys settings such as on a boat, in a pool, at the beach, near a lake, and even out camping with the sound of a brook or stream nearby. Any of these will add to the pleasure of her experience.

"I am up for anything, but in the water is my favorite place to do it."

"Anywhere: I like creative, spontaneous places."

"Bedroom, over the sofa, in the shower, dining room table . . ."

WHAT PUTS YOU IN THE MOOD FOR SEX?

Pisces is naturally a wonderful actress and loves mythology. Going to the theater or watching a very dramatic film will tap into her emotions. Once stirred, her thoughts become romantic and then sexual. In addition, as a Water Sign, anything connected to water, from being near the ocean to the sound of rain, is sexy to her.

"The theater really turns me on, being outdoors when the weather is dramatic: thunder, snowstorm, windy. Anywhere with water . . ."

"Comfortable environment, low lights, yummy food and drink, good music. For some reason, sometimes, museums and the theater really turn me on."

WHAT'S YOUR ATTITUDE TOWARD PORNOGRAPHY?

The kind of pornography Pisces prefers has an aura of romance or drama. The heroine might be a captive on a pirate ship or a tragic, impoverished damsel in distress. Images could include orgies, incorporate lavish displays of food, or multiple sex acts occurring simultaneously.

"I like porn that is creative and artsy. The blatant dumb, fake, titty cum shot porn does nothing for me."

"I absolutely love porn. If I had the courage I'd be a porn star myself."

"I get turned on by porn movies and I like to read stories, but I don't need to have porn to be turned on."

 A Fantasy

"I'm a big fan of historical romance novels. I fantasize that I am an aristocratic English woman sailing on my family's ship to contact a relative in the Middle East about our trading company. Once in this foreign country, the ship is boarded and I am captured, sold as a slave, and wind up in the sultan's harem. Through my brains and beauty, I capture the sultan's heart and he falls desperately in love with me. He teaches me his language, history,

and religion and I become a faithful, loving wife and mother to his children."

HOW MUCH CUDDLING DO YOU ENJOY, ASIDE FROM SEX?

Pisces thinks cuddling is great before and after sex. She likes to cuddle on the sofa while watching TV, having her partner's hand on her leg when driving, and hugging on a park bench. She loves to cuddle just about anywhere, anytime.

"I adore cuddling, sitting on a couch, watching a great movie with my lover eating popcorn with legs all tangled like spaghetti, then reaching over to lick his fingers . . . oops, sorry, got carried away."

HOW TACTILE AND HOW ORAL ARE YOU?

Touch is great but all things oral are far more of a stimulus for Pisces' passion. She wants to feel ardor in her partner's kiss. She shows him how much he turns her on by the way she kisses and performs fellatio.

"When we kiss we can melt an iceberg."

"Kissing is my favorite activity. I enjoy giving oral pleasure to my lover, but only as an 'appetizer,' not as the entire meal."

"I enjoy sucking and licking over his body. I love giving my boyfriend oral: that really turns me on and I know that he loves it."

 A Memory

"My 20-something-year-old daughter had some friends visiting. I went upstairs to bed. Sometime later I was awakened by one of her friends, who was 21, touching me and gently kissing me as I lay in my bed. I could hear the TV, my daughter and her other friends down in the living room. He wanted me and was going to have me. His kisses were wonderful, shoving his tongue in my mouth and nipping and biting my lips and neck, running his hands in my hair, pushing my nightie up and fondling my breasts, licking and biting me. He was all over me. He moved around a lot. Missionary, to me riding him and giving head, to

doggie style with him licking my ass and squeezing my cheeks. We were at it for at least two hours before I came to my senses and asked him to leave. I hope we repeat the experience."

WHAT SEX ACTS DO YOU LIKE MOST AND LEAST?

Pisces, being a fairly experimental lover, enjoys sex with very few limits. Toys, trying out fetishes, and role-playing all add to her pleasure. If there's anything that doesn't thrill her, it's apt to be anal sex.

"My favorite sex acts include definitely kissing and intercourse, but I also very much enjoy teasing with my tongue, mouth, and hands, and even with words."

"I hate it when I am on top and the guy tries to sneak his finger in my butt . . . like I wouldn't notice."

"No anal sex. I have tried it and didn't enjoy it at all so that is off limits."

AS A LOVER, WHAT'S YOUR BEST SKILL?

Pisces is the most psychic woman in the zodiac and she knows what her lover wants, almost before he knows it himself. That way of being tuned in to her lover is her best sexual skill.

"Intuition and physical empathy . . . I am good at everything I do, or so I am told."

A Fantasy

"My sexual Prince Charming is adventurous, has fun with me, is good at suggesting new places, different positions. He knows exactly how long to tease and tantalize me. He makes me feel like a sex goddess in bed."

WHAT SMELLS AND TASTES ON YOUR PARTNER DO YOU ENJOY?

She loves the smell of her partner's clean skin right out of the shower, his colognes, and also body odors that are fresh. She enjoys the taste of his skin, his sweet mouth, and fresh sweat.

The Pisces woman may also be willing to incorporate foods, especially fruits, into her lovemaking.

"I like the smell of his skin, neck in particular, maybe a subtle cologne, shampoo; and as to tastes, salt on a sweaty neck, taste of ear lobes, taste of tongue."

"Sometimes after he has been working out and sweating, the smell of his skin is a huge turn-on. If he has just eaten something yummy, I love tasting it on his lips."

FOR SOME PEOPLE THE TASTE OF THEIR PARTNER'S CUM OR SECRETIONS IS UNPLEASANT. IF THAT'S TRUE FOR YOU, WHAT DO YOU DO ABOUT THE TASTE?

She may not complain about it but the taste, or perhaps more so the texture, is unappealing to her. Pisces prefers that her lover cum somewhere other than in her mouth.

"I love to give a blow job, but he knows better than to cum in my mouth."

"I do not and will not tell someone that they taste bad. If that happens [i.e., they taste bad] I will just go brush my teeth or wash my mouth."

DO YOU ENJOY WATCHING YOUR PARTNER DURING SEX AND ORGASM? DO YOU ENJOY BEING WATCHED?

She enjoys having her lover watch her when she's dressing, putting on makeup, and while she's giving him pleasure during oral sex. Too, Pisces gets turned on watching her lover during sex and orgasm; however, she isn't quite so sure how comfortable she is having him watch her climax.

"I'm a little self-conscious about him watching me."

"Being watched is fine, but I can't always look him in the eyes because he stares at me so intently."

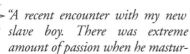

Memories

"A recent encounter with my new slave boy. There was extreme amount of passion when he masturbated for me. He was wiggling and squirming around, addressing me as 'Mistress.' I could smell his cologne. The touch of his freshly shaved balls was incredible. The sound of his whining and moaning was so erotic."

"We had gone out for a drink and a little music. When we got home, he was totally aggressive and we mostly had anal sex. It was violent. He ordered me around. It was the best."

The Big "O"

HOW DO YOU REACH AN ORGASM AND HOW OFTEN?

Pisces reaches orgasm quite easily, almost every time she has sex, by means of masturbation, oral sex, intercourse, or any combination of these.

"Through direct stimulation to my clitoris, hand, mouth; [his] penis; any way available . . ."

"With masturbation, all the time. With oral sex, it depends on how well it is done. With intercourse, often."

WHAT'S YOUR FAVORITE POSITION?

She enjoys a variety of sexual positions including doggie style, sixty-nine, man on top, and especially woman on top.

"I like a position that's sort of spooning. I throw my top leg over his and have intercourse and rub my clit on his thigh at the same time. Otherwise, being on top."

"I prefer my man on top, but orgasms happen more often and more intensely when I am on top."

SOME PEOPLE ARE CONCERNED ABOUT BRINGING THEIR PARTNER TO CLIMAX BEFORE HAVING AN ORGASM THEMSELVES. OTHERS STRIVE TO REACH ORGASM TOGETHER. WHICH IS TRUE FOR YOU?

Pisces is in no hurry during sex. She enjoys a fairly lengthy buildup and is not concerned about whether she and her lover reach orgasm together.

"It doesn't matter to my partner or me. I can have several orgasms in one session."

"I almost always have multiples, mine come way before my husband's, but if he cums first he makes sure I have mine, too."

ARE YOU VOCAL DURING SEX?

The Pisces woman is comfortable expressing herself during sex; how much so varies from being somewhat vocal to very much so.

"Extremely. I talk dirty and moan a lot."

"Depends on my mood and how playful I am."

A Fantasy

"Where my partner is so hot for me that he cannot control himself and he is rough. I love to be teased, to be made to beg for it, to . . . wait because I have no patience and it is exquisite torture."

AFTER SEX WHAT DO YOU LIKE TO DO?

After sex Pisces enjoys staying home. Most of the time she prefers to be alone with her partner, but a quiet get-together with a few friends is also pleasant.

"In general, I prefer staying in after sex. A warm shower, a snack, and some cuddling would be nice."

"Shower, cuddle up, watch television, rest, and talk."

The Pisces Man in His Own Words

A Memory

"We had a huge room in a romantic bed and breakfast. After dinner we relaxed, drank a lovely wine, [and] then shared a hot tub. We tried several different positions and collapsed into the huge bed afterward. Waking up and doing it again the next day."

Attraction and Dating a Pisces

WHAT ATTRACTS YOU TO SOMEONE?

Pisces is particular about the physical attributes that initially attract his attention. He is a leg man, into shoes. In addition, breast size is always important to him. After the initial attraction, qualities that hold his attention include a sense of humor, a positive attitude, and intelligence.

"I am attracted to women with joie de vivre, moderate sized breasts, and firm legs; women who take pride in themselves and who are physically fit and healthy."

"Well-formed breasts, lovely eyes, lips, easy on the makeup, nice legs; a feminine woman who enjoys being a woman."

"Enthusiasm, then looks, then physique. I like a firm ass, nice breasts, but will be happy with a very pretty face and a lot of excitement to be together."

WHAT MIGHT TURN YOU OFF?

The Pisces man is apt to be turned off by a woman who uses foul language, has bad teeth, or smokes. Most Pisces do not like tattoos or body piercings. In general, he is turned off by a woman who is extreme: too fat, overly self-absorbed, too clingy, or bitter about prior relationships.

"I don't like a woman who wears too much makeup, uses too much perfume, cuts her hair too short."

"I am turned off by rudeness, people who are very in your face, aggressive."

"Physical characteristics are rarely important as long as a woman is neat and clean. But, a woman who is rude or loud definitely turns me off."

WHAT DO YOU ENJOY DOING ON A DATE?

He is a romantic and enjoys walking by moonlight in quiet settings. As Pisces is a Water Sign, he loves to spend time near water— canoeing on a tranquil lake or walking along the shore listening to the sound of ocean waves. An ideal evening would be spent alone with his partner having dinner, perhaps seeing a movie, cuddling, and talking.

"I like to go to dinner and maybe to a club and dance a little, and then just go somewhere quiet to relax and get to know the person better by talking to her."

"Eating at a place where conversation can be heard easily."

"I enjoy good conversation, looking at a beautiful woman, and making her feel good about herself."

A Memory

"A long time ago. A memory that will last my lifetime. We were in a very cheap New York City hotel that we had to panhandle the money for. Bathroom down the hall, just a sink in the room; and the clerk unlocked the door and then left, taking the key. Stranded in the big city with no money but with the woman I loved. The room was hot, no air conditioner, small window facing a brick wall about 18 inches away. I propped a chair under the doorknob for some security. The sex was steamy. We set some records that night."

ARE YOU FLIRTATIOUS?

He is only mildly flirtatious. It is not Pisces' nature to be particularly forward. He likes to take his time getting to know a woman with quiet conversation before making any moves.

"I think that I seduce more than flirt, but I have been told that I do."

"I am flirtatious, but very little."

"Fairly flirtatious I am told. I try to guard myself a little, for fear of rejection."

A Fantasy

"I come home from work and my fiancée greets me wearing a revealing outfit that shows off her beautiful breasts. It is clear that she's horny and her hand goes immediately to my cock. She tells me she wants me to lick her pussy because she needs to cum."

ARE YOU JEALOUS?

He is somewhat jealous. When in a relationship, Pisces wants to know where his woman is and with whom. This is not about being controlling; rather, he is somewhat insecure and to him it just seems fair and natural that his partner would let him know what she is doing.

"When I'm with someone, I don't like seeing her flirt with another man."

"Sometimes, when I don't know where my girlfriend is I can be jealous."

"Yes, I can be very jealous, but only if I feel my relationship is being threatened."

Fantasies

"I imagine being with two women, light bondage, and domination."

"I fantasize about having a group of women just using their mouths and breasts to bring me to orgasm."

"I have fantasies of anal sex with large-breasted women."

HOW DO YOU FEEL ABOUT PUBLIC DISPLAYS OF AFFECTION?

The Pisces man enjoys public displays of affection, especially when the setting encourages them; for example, a beach at sunset or a moment in a romantic movie. He is a lover at heart and enjoys both participating in public displays and observing other people expressing their love for one another.

"I find them charming as long as there's no sexual content; then it's crass."

"When you love someone it's okay, but you don't have to stick your tongue down her throat for everyone to see."

"I'm fine with it as long as it's responsible."

"Small displays are okay—hand holding, the occasional quick kiss, nothing more."

"I love them."

Sexual Attitudes and Behaviors

HOW OFTEN DO YOU THINK ABOUT SEX AND HOW OFTEN PER WEEK DO YOU WANT TO HAVE SEX?

Pisces has a vivid imagination. Thoughts of sex occur frequently on a daily basis. These thoughts may be triggered by the sight of a woman wearing clothes of soft fabric in shades of pale blue and aqua. He is satisfied having sex four times a week.

"I'm not preoccupied with sex, but close enough. I'd like to have sex daily."

"I think about it daily; quite preoccupied with the thought of it and want it every day, but it's okay at least three times a week."

HOW LONG DO YOU LIKE TO SPEND HAVING SEX? DO YOU ENJOY QUICKIES?

Pisces is a man who doesn't like to be hurried. With him, quality counts more than quantity. Quality in a sex act requires times. He enjoys spending approximately two hours making love. He might like quickies on occasion, but that is truly not his preference.

"Sometimes long and drawn out, sometimes quick if the time is right. There's no set rule: sometimes a lot, sometimes none."

"Two to four hours each time, with lots of foreplay. I don't like quickies."

"I like sex to last an hour, maybe longer, and the seam between sex and foreplay should be unnoticeable. Quickies are fun, too."

"I like an hour and a half to two hours on sex. Sometimes all I do is foreplay. I can't say I enjoy quickies much."

WHAT TIME OF DAY DO YOU PREFER TO HAVE SEX?

There is something about the sun coming up, streaming through the bedroom windows for Pisces. It puts him in the mood. But when life intrudes, having sex at night is just fine.

"Day, afternoon, night, whatever, but it happens more on weekend mornings and weekday nights."

"It's great when we first wake up."

HOW OFTEN PER WEEK DO YOU MASTURBATE?

The Pisces male masturbates two to three times a week.

A Fantasy

"Two women begin by giving me a smoky blow job. One woman and I are going at it in the sixty-nine position while the second is sharing my cock. Then I eat the second one out as she performs oral sex on the first woman. After I bring off my woman, I mount her doggie style and she finishes off the other girl. We then kiss and caress for a long while as I alternate between the women's pussies. When I am all finished, the women clean me and each other up orally."

HOW LONG DO YOU WANT TO KNOW SOMEONE BEFORE GETTING SEXUAL?

The amount of time before getting sexual depends on the person and the situation, but regardless, Pisces needs to feel some amount of emotional connection. As a rule, for him waiting a few weeks before having sex is comfortable.

"I want to care very deeply for someone before having intercourse."

"A month or so . . ."

WHAT'S YOUR ATTITUDE TOWARD CASUAL SEX?

In general his answer is, "Yes, but . . ." Pisces is a sensitive Sign with a loving heart. He knows that casual sex is a poor substitute for making love.

"While I enjoy casual sex, I find that sex is most rewarding with someone to whom I have an emotional attachment."

"I think it's all right. But sometimes there are misunderstandings and it can become a problem."

"I enjoy it, but sex is best with someone I truly care about."

DO YOU BELIEVE IN MONOGAMY?

Pisces does not equivocate about this question. He is a faithful lover and believes in monogamy wholeheartedly.

"Yes I do. It is not right to mess with other people when you have your own love."

"Once you start to sleep with one person, you don't sleep with anyone else."

"Yes, once you commit to someone then have sex with only that person. You can masturbate to many people in your mind, but don't give your body to anyone else."

Memories

"I gave her a sexual massage, brought her to orgasm, held her, and had intercourse, and she cried that it was so good."

"I spent New Year's Eve with my partner. We were engaged in intercourse when the New Year arrived. All that shouting and fireworks . . . that was pretty outstanding."

"One night, after going out, my girlfriend and I barely made it through the door. We were just all over each other from the hall floor through the living room into the bedroom."

DOES SEX HAVE A SPIRITUAL SIGNIFICANCE FOR YOU?

Sex is many things to Pisces: physical gratification, spiritual connection, and a part of the whole performance of life. He likes to set the stage or perform on it, to get in touch with his romantic side, and last but not least, to show his prodigious ability to go on and on to satisfy his partner.

"Sex with someone you truly love enhances the experience that much more."

"It brings you closer to someone with whom you have already bonded."

"Yes, somewhat . . . I consider it making love."

"Yes. Sometimes our sex is as much spiritual as physical. It's the most intimate act."

ARE YOU COMFORTABLE INITIATING SEXUAL ACTIVITIES?

Pisces is highly intuitive, if not psychic. He picks up on a woman's cues that she is interested in him. And then, without being aggressive, he is comfortable initiating sexual activities.

"Yes, when I know it is welcomed or expected. Otherwise I never do."

"After I begin to sense that any advances would be welcome, I have no problem."

HOW DO YOU COMMUNICATE TO YOUR PARTNER YOUR SEXUAL WANTS AND NEEDS?

Never a particularly aggressive personality, Pisces depends upon his ability to communicate with his lover primarily through the movement of his body, the use of his hands, the look of pleasure on his face. This is not to suggest that he is shy on the subject, but rather that he uses his way of communicating non-verbally far more than by being direct and telling her how to please him.

"Gesture, encouragement, once in a while words . . ."

"I usually go with gestures and only sometimes words."

"Gestures more often, but I do verbalize a lot too."

"By touch in a sexual way or I just might say, 'I want to fuck you now.'"

Memories

"Making love in the waves. The fresh air and the sudden rush of cold water made it incredible."

"Having sex on a deserted ski lift . . . very cold, quiet and alone . . . very sexy."

"On a dune, under the sun, wind on my back, smell of the ocean."

"Belated honeymoon in Spain: having sex every day and taking a siesta afterward."

DO YOU THINK OF YOURSELF AS BEING IN THE MAINSTREAM SEXUALLY, MORE EXPERIMENTAL, OR OPEN TO ANYTHING?

A Pisces man is open to a range of sexuality from experimental all the way to very open. The most mainstream Pisces man will be turned on by his partner in sexy stockings and high heels or leather boots. On the experimental level, Pisces will try anal sex, dominance and submission, exhibitionism, sex in public places, spanking, and using food. And the most open Piscean will explore bondage, caressing or fondling his lover's feet, and fisting. This Pisces loves long fingernails, piercings, underwear, voyeurism, and water sports.

"I am open to anything and would like to try every experience. Unfortunately, people think you are weird if you bring it up. Even my wife thinks some of my ideas are weird."

The toys he may enjoy include vibrators and bondage accouterments.

"Vibrators are great (especially a cock ring/vibrator combo), as are spanking toys and light bondage stuff."

"I like to use vibrators and Ben-Wha balls, restraints, and soft toys such as fur when I go down on her."

"I enjoy using a butt plug while having sex."

Pisces' fantasy life is quite varied in terms of sexual practices, but is limited to one or at most two partners.

Fantasies
"We are lying in bed kissing each other from the neck down and that is where it would all start. We would have sex like crazy and add in a can of whipped cream and cherries."

"We are both wearing heavy latex or she is clad in fashionable leather and high heels. That image alone is all I need."

HOW DO YOU DEMONSTRATE AFFECTION FOR YOUR PARTNER?

Pisces is a sensitive and caring lover who demonstrates his affection with both attentions and small gifts. In so many ways he shows that he has observed her and knows what pleases her, by perhaps playing the music she enjoys and buying her daisies rather than the stereotypical long-stemmed roses.

"I am always there for her, buy her dinner, open car doors, spend a lot of time with her."

"Cuddling, trying to be as accommodating as possible, putting her needs above my own, doing special favors when asked."

"Massage, buying gifts for no reason, and because I am a musician, singing or writing songs for my lady love . . ."

The Five Senses

HOW IMPORTANT TO YOU IS THE SEXUAL ENVIRONMENT?

While the environment for sex may not be of great importance to Pisces, he does want privacy and he prefers that the place be clean. As to lighting, there are times when he likes to make love nude with the lights on to watch his partner's responses. There are other times when he prefers a dimly lit interior.

"The setting is not too important, privacy is the only requirement."

"Not terribly important, but it is always nice when the environment is pleasant."

"Cleanliness is first, enough light to see is important, not much else matters."

WHERE DO YOU LIKE TO HAVE SEX?

Considering his preference for privacy, Pisces' favorite place to have sex is the bedroom. Beyond that, he can be quite adventuresome on occasion and make out in public places; especially, being a Water Sign, at the beach or by a lake.

"Any room in the house, outside, public places if she would, anywhere as long as there is room to have sex without it being awkward or cumbersome . . ."

"Outdoors is my favorite, on the dunes at the beach."

"Against the car in warm summer rain, on a lovely warm beach, bed, couch . . ."

WHAT PUTS YOU IN THE MOOD FOR SEX?

Pisces is a highly sexual Sign. He is romantic and very connected emotionally to his partner. He has a gentle way about him that makes his lover want him. That alone puts him in the mood. In addition, if his lover has had a hard day or if the two of them have had a disagreement, he will want to comfort her with his skills in bed.

"Being with her does it for me almost anytime."

"Just being with my girl and smelling her perfume and hair . . ."

"Sitting near her and talking, feeling her play with my hair, just feeling her touch me . . . simply being close to her."

A Memory

"I had a wonderful encounter with three girls, a set of twins and a stripper. It was aggressive, each girl vying for my attention. The sight of the twins pulling me face to face for kisses or pushing each other off for their own pleasure was wild. The stripper only wanted to watch and masturbate, which was really cool. Whenever I looked at her she would smile and rub harder."

WHAT'S YOUR ATTITUDE TOWARD PORNOGRAPHY?

Being an empathetic and sensitive man, Pisces is also a bit of a performer at heart. And when he watches pornography he identifies with the actors. As a result, bad porn—where the actors show little emotional response for each other—will turn him off.

"I think it can be useful in some circumstances."

"There's nothing wrong with most porn."

"I own some pornography, but I can take it or leave it."

"I think it is fine and a good outlet for sexual feelings."

HOW MUCH CUDDLING DO YOU ENJOY, ASIDE FROM SEX?

Pisces is an emotional Water Sign who loves the opportunity to show his feelings by gently squeezing his partner's hand, by holding her arm, or by sitting close by her. He enjoys quite a lot of cuddling as a prelude to sex and apart from it.

"I am the type of guy who loves to cuddle. I would much rather stay inside and cuddle than be around a lot of people."

"Very much. Embracing, kissing, caressing are important to the closest sort of relationship."

"A lot, but never too much for any partner I have had."

HOW TACTILE AND HOW ORAL ARE YOU?

Here is a man who loves to linger over sex, to take each step slowly and savor it: the touch, the taste, the feel of her lips and nipples against his fingertips and then against his lips. It all runs together, the tactile and the oral.

"I am very tactile. I love the feeling of my fiancée's breasts in my hands and the feeling of her moist pussy on my mouth."

"It turns me on to go down on my fiancée, to suck on her breasts and neck, as well as deep kissing. We haven't done rimming yet, but the idea turns me on."

"I love to put my mouth everywhere. I could give oral sex every day."

"Cunnilingus, kissing the body, and rimming are all pleasurable for me and they thrill my partner."

Memories

"Sex while traveling. When we get away, stay in a hotel, she is hungry for sex."

"Just being with my girl makes for great sex. She is very nice, has a great body and she smells and tastes great."

"Recently I played with myself to orgasm while my fiancée hung her breasts in my face and watched."

WHAT SEX ACTS DO YOU LIKE MOST AND LEAST?

Pisces' favorite sex acts include the full range of cuddling, kissing, massage, oral sex, and intercourse. There is little about sex that he doesn't enjoy, but if he has to name a sex act that is his least favorite, it would be receiving anal sex.

"I enjoy kissing, oral sex, mutual masturbation, and intercourse. I don't like anal sex or bondage."

"I like it all . . . kissing, oral, intercourse, fondling, light anal play on her, mutual masturbation as well as watching masturbation."

"I enjoy most sex acts: intercourse, anal sex, fondling all over, kissing, oral sex, all of it. About the only thing I don't really enjoy is mutual masturbation. I want to touch the other person instead of watching her do it."

AS A LOVER, WHAT'S YOUR BEST SKILL?

Pisces, a psychic Sign, may not be able to predict the future, but he certainly knows how to read his partner. On top of that he has great stamina. Nobody lasts longer than Pisces. Overall, his best skill is his sensitivity to his lover.

"I am in good athletic shape. I can usually maintain an erection as long as I need to bring my partner off. Sometimes it takes a while. I try to mix up various movements to stimulate her fully."

"Knowing how to please the woman I am with, paying attention to what works for her and making sure that she is fulfilled each time."

Fantasies

"My lover met me in the park wearing a skirt, no underwear. I have her hike up the skirt, just a little, and ride me facing away from me."

"We take a walk in town. She is wearing a button-down shirt, no bra, and a skirt [but] no panties. We flash people from time to time, then find a spot in a department store and give each other oral sex."

WHAT SMELLS AND TASTES ON YOUR PARTNER DO YOU ENJOY?

He loves the aroma of his lover's clean skin, her breath, soap, her perfume, and the smell of fresh sheets. Pisces is also turned on by the taste of his partner's mouth and her genitals.

"I like the smell of her panties, pussy, her favorite cologne, her hair, and the taste of her lips, her juices, the salt of her sweat."

"Her perfume is very sexy and I love the smell of her hair. I enjoy all her juices."

"I am turned on by colognes and clean, fresh showered smells. I love the taste of her cum."

FOR SOME PEOPLE THE TASTE OF THEIR PARTNER'S CUM OR SECRETIONS IS UNPLEASANT. IF THAT'S TRUE FOR YOU, WHAT DO YOU DO ABOUT THE TASTE?

Pisces loves the taste of his partner and has no need to cover up the flavor.

"I love the taste of a woman's secretions. I have never found the experience bad."

"She tastes good to me. Only occasionally is it unpleasant; then I ignore it."

"I love the feel and the taste."

DO YOU ENJOY WATCHING YOUR PARTNER DURING SEX AND ORGASM? DO YOU ENJOY BEING WATCHED?

It turns the Pisces man on to watch his partner's pleasure, but he may be uncomfortable when she watches him—especially during orgasm.

The Big "O"

HOW DO YOU REACH AN ORGASM AND HOW OFTEN?

Known for endurance, the only time Pisces fails to achieve orgasm is when he is exhausted. The method is unimportant. Given enough foreplay, anything will get him off.

"Any type of sex will do it. The method doesn't really matter: intercourse, oral sex, or masturbation . . . I cum mostly through vaginal intercourse."

WHAT'S YOUR FAVORITE POSITION?

All positions are fine but what works most for him in terms of emotional gratification is maximum skin contact. As a result, Pisces' favorite positions for climaxing are being on top of his partner or having her on top of him.

"They all work; however, I like a position where I can look into her eyes."

"Missionary is best because my pubic bone rubs her clit."

A Fantasy

"*She comes to me by candlelight with incense burning. We share food and wine. I dress her in restrictive latex and high-heeled boots. She is suspended in a sling, and I play with her to exciting music. I let her down and we have passionate sex, followed by comforting cuddling and soft music. I undress her and bathe her. Afterward we share a romantic meal.*"

SOME PEOPLE ARE CONCERNED ABOUT BRINGING THEIR PARTNER TO CLIMAX BEFORE HAVING AN ORGASM THEMSELVES. OTHERS STRIVE TO REACH ORGASM TOGETHER. WHICH IS TRUE FOR YOU?

He prefers to achieve climax simultaneously with his partner and strives to make that happen. If it can't, Pisces wants his partner to cum first.

"It's important to me that she climaxes and is thrilled all the way."

"Ideally, I would like it to be simultaneous. If not, I'd want her to climax first."

"I want my partner to climax before I do. Then I allow myself to climax at almost the same time."

ARE YOU VOCAL DURING SEX?

Pisces is a vocal lover in terms of expressing his excitement, not with words, but with sounds of pleasure.

AFTER SEX WHAT DO YOU LIKE TO DO?

After sex, most of the time he wants to stay in, cuddle, talk, and perhaps listen to some music. On occasion, he would like to go out for a quiet dinner or perhaps a drive in the moonlight.

Sexual Compatibility through the Zodiac

Aries with Aries

TWO RAMS TOGETHER: *Can They Avoid Butting Heads?*

Any time two of the same Sign form a couple, there's conflict. There's no balance. Two Aries together is way too much fire. It becomes an ego contest. Whoever wins is the one with the most blessings from above. In bed there's no intrigue. It's slam-bam thank you ma'am and neither Aries knows how to broaden the perspective. Though both say they like spending quite a while having sex, these two wind up moving too quickly to feel gratified. For better sex, one needs to be more evasive and make the other work harder.

There are problems in the day-to-day relationship as well. When one Aries is having trouble, in all likelihood the other Aries is as well because both will be under similar astrological elements. He comes home from work saying, "I had the worst day. The guy in the next cubicle is driving me nuts." Partner Aries replies, "Wait 'til I tell you about my day." This is hardly comforting for either. In addition, Aries is apt to be abrupt verbally. No harm intended, but the Aries on the receiving end is easily wounded.

In an Aries/Aries pairing, the greatest likelihood for success occurs if one Aries is seven years or so older. An older partner may be more conciliatory and less likely to feel threatened by the other Aries' youthful exuberance and need to make all the rules. The older Aries may not mind pampering the younger one. Conversely, the younger Aries enjoys being indulged, even mothered to some extent.

Summary
In bed the Aries female needs to be directed by her lover so that the sex will not be so hurried and almost over before it begins. The Aries woman wants to prove her skills. She's especially proud of her abilities at oral sex. Her Aries male partner, passion ignited, will be thrilled to meet up with a woman of equal passion for a little while. But the Aries male needs to be inspired and the Aries female is too much his mirror image to bring anything new to his sexual repertoire. Result: unlikely long-term sexual satisfaction.

Aries with Taurus
THE RAM AND THE BULL: *The Dust Will Fly*

In the first days, Aries enchants Taurus and life is beautiful. Taurans grow up feeling that they were not loved enough, no matter how much they were loved. Along comes Aries, whose behavior consumes Taurus with passionate love. Meanwhile, Aries, longing to be doted on, is gratified by Taurus' total focus.

So what's the problem? Aries is bossy and Taurus will not be told what to do. Ask a Taurus for help, and you get it. Tell a Taurus to help, and you get an argument. Aries wants to be in control and while Taurus is very willing to be second in command and very willing to be supportive, Taurus will not follow orders. When Aries is aggressive, Taurus becomes unyielding. When speedy Aries says "Let's do it now," slow-moving Taurus asks, "Why, what's the hurry?"

In bed and out, this conflict of style undermines the long-term potential for a successful relationship. Taurus wants to luxuriate in sex, savoring it rather like a seven-course meal. For Aries, sex is more like the appetizer or the dessert. Over time, in the bedroom Aries would be bored to death with Taurus.

Out of the bedroom, Aries' readiness to do things at the drop of a hat runs headlong into Taurus' need to consider an action for a stretch of time before participating. What makes this combination so difficult is the conflict between the fundamental qualities of Aries—assertiveness and risk-taking—versus Taurus stability, receptivity, and need for security.

ARIES WOMAN AND TAURUS MAN
With a huge dose of optimism, it's possible to say that the Aries woman/Taurus man combination might work. It won't be easy, though. As dynamic, exciting, and delightful as an Aries woman can be, she's also demanding and independent. Taurus, on the other hand, is practical to a fault and won't be hurried. Her demands could strain their pocketbook, triggering his deepest fears relating to financial stability and security. She is apt to feel that he's just being obstinate. In the bedroom, where his favorite activity is passionate kissing all over his partner's body, she's impatient to get right to the core of the matter.

ARIES MAN AND TAURUS WOMAN
The Taurus woman makes a wonderful mate. She's loyal and devoted to her partner and family. She's usually an excellent cook and wants a man who's independent and self-assured. In most regards Aries fills the bill, if he doesn't order her about or expect her to mother him. The Taurus woman has something of a Cinderella fantasy, truly longing for the White Knight who will protect and love her. Even if she's highly accomplished herself, she wants a man who's capable of taking care of her financially. In return, she'll provide nourishment and comfort to please all of his senses.

Aries with Gemini
THE RAM AND THE TWINS: *Endless Possibilities*

Aries is the Sign of exploration; Gemini is the Sign of experimentation. These two traits are compatible and these Signs are a natural combination. While Gemini might be content to read and think about something, Aries will say, "Come on, let's go out and do it!" This enthusiasm is captivating to Gemini.

With Aries, what you see is what you get. Gemini, on the other hand, is a more complex and dual sign. Aries tends to focus on one thing at a time, while Gemini is apt to be involved in a dozen things simultaneously. It's part of Gemini's life path to try out many things. Gemini grows bored when life is too settled. Aries keeps Gemini guessing. With a less dynamic partner, Gemini pays inadequate attention, begins to withdraw, and soon everything falls apart. Aries' dynamism and intensity serve to keep Gemini steadfast.

When it comes to sex, Aries and Gemini are very well matched. Gemini intuitively knows to make Aries put a little more effort into lovemaking. Gemini is a verbal sign and keeps some banter going with Aries, asking questions, slowing the pace. As Aries likes being given sexual directions, it works that Gemini is the natural leader between these two. There is a minor problem but one that can grow over time if Gemini doesn't attend to it. Gemini is better with the hands than with the mouth or lips, but Aries is turned on by passionate kissing. For Aries the force in a lover's kiss is proof of love.

ARIES WOMAN AND GEMINI MAN

Sex is fun and frequent for the Aries woman and the Gemini man, and the duration is satisfying to both. The only area of possible difficulty in the sexual realm is that Aries is apt to find her Gemini lover too superficial. Unless he shows her his love passionately, unless he is forceful enough to convince her of the depth of his sexual energy, she will grow dissatisfied. Gemini certainly has powerful sexual energy. He just needs to demonstrate it in the ardor of his kiss. Meanwhile, if she is willing to introduce new elements to their lovemaking—the latest sex toy or a new porno video—Gemini's sexual fire will burn anew.

ARIES MAN AND GEMINI WOMAN

Aries, who wants to lead in most situations, is passionate sexually and loves the experimental willingness of Gemini. Though he may be too quick for some, as long as he sets the stage verbally with Gemini she'll be satisfied. He loves oral sex and performs it well. His passion ignites hers. To keep sex healthy over the years, Aries must remember to pay attention to Gemini, to what she's doing with her life, and to praise her for her achievements. She doesn't need a lot. But without some attention to her as an individual, she'll turn off in and out of bed.

Aries *with* Cancer
THE RAM AND THE CRAB: *Steam Up or Sputter Out?*

Aries is a Fire Sign. Cancer is a Water Sign. Together they produce steam, at least for a while. But water drowns fire, and Cancer's emotionalism may extinguish Aries' passion. Sustaining a relationship will require consistent effort. Yet relationships between these two are sometimes successful and can be gratifying when each accepts the other's differences.

Aries is a perpetual child and Cancer is the nurturing adult. Emotions make Aries decidedly uncomfortable, while Cancer is intensely emotional. Aries covers most feelings with anger. An upset Cancer needs to work through the feelings, to talk about them to release them. Nonetheless, when Aries wants comforting, Cancer is there, strong and loving, and that wonderful Aries courage provides reassurance when Cancer is upset.

In the bedroom, Aries is ready from the onset; however, Cancer needs time to work up steam. Sometimes Aries isn't sensitive enough to Cancer's moods and may believe that Cancer doesn't have a strong sex drive. Not true. Cancer is highly sexual.

The preferences of these Signs do differ. Aries is more conventional sexually whereas Cancer is more experimental. If dissatisfied by the sex in a relationship, Cancer will go looking outside. In public, Aries likes to show off his affection somewhat, while Cancer is more reserved. However, neither likes to be observed when having sex. Cancer may love making out in the woods, but certainly doesn't want to risk being watched. Sex in a secluded park or at least in a nearby B&B will revitalize this couple sexually every time.

ARIES WOMAN AND CANCER MAN

What the Cancer man wants most is oral sex and that's the Aries woman's forte. Her aim is to please her man. In the bedroom she's content to have him play the dominant male, and that kind of division of power is vital for a successful sexual relationship with Aries. Apart from sex Aries resents Cancer's domineering personality. She may be childlike in some ways, but she's also fiercely independent. A Cancer/Aries relationship will be short lived if he is overly controlling. In addition, Aries' abruptness, wounds Cancer, and he doesn't easily forgive her words. Over the long haul, this twosome may be headed for trouble.

ARIES MAN AND CANCER WOMAN

The Cancer woman likes the intensity of the Aries man's approach, but not his finale. He starts with great passion but moves on too fast and doesn't savor the effect he's having. She wants him to dally a while, to enjoy her breasts rather than rush to the heart of the matter. Sex improves if she reminds him about these rules and imposes them consistently with a firm, motherly hand. That's the message to Ms. Cancer. Sex will be best if Aries is given directions and he receives a spanking when he does not measure up. No kidding, most Aries enjoy getting spanked—gently.

Aries with Leo

THE RAM AND THE LION: *Fire Burning Bright*

Putting these two signs together is a challenge, but at least in bed it's great. Sexually, Aries and Leo are well matched. Both signs tend to be conventional in their range of behaviors. They love passionate kissing, feverish embraces, and quick sex as well as longer sessions. They both pride themselves on the strength of their sex drive.

There are some Aries and Leos who are involved in more extreme sex. Here, too, they match up quite perfectly in their choice of sexual experimentation, including bondage, dominance and submission, and using food in sex play. Among the toys they enjoy, also in the more traditional range, include dildos, vibrators, and cock rings.

A relationship can work, though it won't be easy. Common ground: both are quick thinking and spontaneous, and they like the same sorts of activities. But problems often arise because each may see the other as self-centered. Both Signs thrive on praise, but for different reasons. Aries is an insecure Sign and seeks ego gratification in all things. They need to be told how wonderful they are before they believe it themselves. Leos, on the other hand, have strong egos. They don't really need praise, though they do bask in it. Unfortunately, neither of these Signs gives out compliments frequently enough.

Another problem area is that both Aries and Leo are uncomfortable apologizing. Aries virtually chokes on the words "I'm sorry." Leo almost never admits to being wrong. In fact, on those rare occasions when Leo really is wrong, he'll gladly accept the other party's apology regardless.

ARIES WOMAN AND LEO MAN

In the bedroom, it doesn't matter whether Aries is the man and Leo the woman or the other way around. The sex is always good. The relationship works out better, however, when Leo is the man. The Aries female does not give much praise, and cocky Leo is self-assured enough not to be bothered by her less than effusive responses. On the other hand, he's wise enough to know that she desires and dotes on his attentions. She is the lady in red. Her temperament is fiery and she's proud to be a great lover. He's her match in passion and expression.

ARIES MAN AND LEO WOMAN

The Leo woman is a handful, a dominant personality. The Aries man cannot rule her, but she's a willing partner. He wants to be noticed. She loves an audience and her presence always inspires one. Imagine Mr. Aries entering a party expecting to be admired and finding Ms. Leo is the center of attention. Is he jealous? Turned on? Both. But, Aries loves Leo's energy, and in bed her passion matches his. The obstacle to long-term success lies in that area of praise. Ask any Lioness what turns her on and she'll say, with a big knowing grin, that she needs to be adored.

Aries *with* Virgo

THE RAM AND THE VIRGIN: *Passion or Punishment?*

Getting this relationship started is apt to be awkward. Virgo is attracted to Aries, but reticent to reveal feelings and waits for Aries to make the first move. Aries isn't shy, but wants encouragement. Virgo can be so poker-faced that Aries isn't sure Virgo is interested at all, leading to a stalemate. Once this is overcome, Virgo finds Aries' enthusiasm, spontaneity, and openness refreshing. Aries is balanced by Virgo's down-to-earth, practical approach to life. Aries is quicker to make a commitment than is Virgo, but once they enter into a monogamous relationship, both Signs are faithful.

Still, the differences between these Signs are vast, as these two do almost everything differently. For example, when getting ready for a vacation, Aries says, "Let the road take us where it may." Virgo, on the other hand, has at least two sets of maps and wants the route fully plotted before leaving home. Aries overlooks the details and trusts luck while Virgo is very detail oriented.

Aries can't stand criticism, and love on the part of Virgo is picking lint off the collar of his/her lover. During sex, Virgo will give instructions: a little to the left, a little to the right, do more of this, do more of that. That's fine in the bedroom, because Aries want to satisfy their lovers. Outside the bedroom, though, Rams want the freedom to do as they please and being nagged by Virgo is a turnoff. For this relationship to succeed, Virgo needs to be less critical and Aries must avoid becoming defensive.

ARIES WOMAN AND VIRGO MAN

The Aries woman's a handful and the Virgo man's turned on. He's a very sexual animal, though his sexuality isn't apparent in public. Publicly, he's the guy for whom casual dress means he's not wearing a tie and the keeping top button of his shirt undone. Their initial sex life will be lustful and exciting, though over time problems may ensue. Aries needs a very passionate, intense partner. Virgo is slower at the buildup and likes to take a lot longer in the act than Aries prefers. He's also rather repetitive in his performance, which can make sex feel routine. Virgo likes talking dirty, while Aries is more interested in action.

ARIES MAN AND VIRGO WOMAN

They'll drive each other crazy. The Virgo woman tries too hard to direct her Aries man, nagging him when he doesn't make that business call or get that promotion. He'll feel that nothing he does is good enough, and this is extremely hurtful because all he wants to do is please his partner. Virgo cares about her position in society. She's willing to work hard to get what she wants. Mr. Aries isn't as motivated. He wants to do well, but not at the expense of having fun. He won't delay gratification to the extent that Virgo will. Frustration will build and the passion will fizzle.

Aries with Libra
THE RAM AND THE SCALES: *Opposites Attract and Repel*

This relationship starts out well. Fire Sign Aries brings passion to an affair with Libra. Air Sign Libra cools things down some, making the sex last a little longer. In bed, passionate kissing comes first. Aries also loves having his/her head caressed and intense oral sex. Libra wants to satisfy Aries, but isn't interested in the same sexual acts. Libra prefers the missionary position and straightforward sex, while Aries loves doggie style and enjoys more variety. While anal sex may not be the favorite act for either Sign, it is a fairly common part of Libra's repertoire and extremely rare among Aries.

Libra enjoys the titillation of sex, talking about it; eroticism as opposed to pornography. Aries, on the other hand, is quite comfortable getting down and dirty. On top of this, Libra is quite romantic and while Aries will enjoy that, in the early days of a relationship, over time, he/she is apt to grow impatient. Aries' attitude is "Let's just get to it." Libra's pace in almost all things is too slow, too deliberate, for most Rams.

When there's a decision to be made, Libra wants to explore all avenues. Aries makes choices sooner than Libra can possibly even consider the options. When Aries tells Libra "this is what I want to do," Libra has a thousand questions. Aries gets annoyed at constantly having to explain his/her rationale. These signs hurt or confuse each other with their different styles of communication. Libra is subtle. Aries is blunt. Overall, this is not a promising long-term partnership.

ARIES WOMAN AND LIBRA MAN

The Aries woman is impulsive, headstrong, and decisive. She wants her Libra man to be equally sure of himself, but he isn't. If she initiates sex, "Honey, do you want to make love tonight?" his answer will be, "Sure, honey, if you do." This is infuriating to her. For Libra to satisfy Aries in and out of bed, he'll need to praise her, pump up her ego, and make some decisions—even when the issue at hand doesn't matter to him. In the bedroom, he'll want to please her and she'll want to impress him with her considerable skills and playfulness. Short term—okay. Long term, disappointing.

ARIES MAN AND LIBRA WOMAN

Sex is the best part of the Aries man/Libra woman partnership. Sustaining the relationship will be difficult. These two Signs are likely to quarrel furiously. Libra is a refined and mature woman while Aries is an irrepressible little boy. She wants an independent man who never tries to control her. She enjoys luxuries, being flattered, and she cares about the décor of her living space. Aries isn't much given to gift giving, nor generous with praise, and he can be oblivious to the environment—even his own. And if Mr. Aries allows himself to get out of shape, Libra will prove gifted in her ability to invent excuses to avoid sex.

Aries with Scorpio

THE RAM AND THE SCORPION: *Fatal Attraction*

Aries is by nature uncomplicated, falling in love at first sight and wanting to go straight home to bed. Scorpio is a sign of great depth and mystery. Initially Scorpio finds the directness, the "what you see is what you get" quality of Aries appealing, but also puzzling and he/she goes looking for underlying layers. The fact is that Aries isn't hiding anything. On the other hand, Aries doesn't understand Scorpio's depths. Scorpio always seems to be holding something back, even when he/she isn't.

Aries has an odd combination of vanity and insecurity and needs praise. Scorpio does little to ease this basic vulnerability. Aries is competitive. This is the Sign to which you say, "You're the best sex I've ever had." Scorpio, on the other hand, being jealous, never wants to hear those words. Scorpio knows full well that Aries has had other lovers. Scorpio just doesn't want to be confronted with that fact.

Both Scorpio and Aries are controlling signs, but Scorpio tends to be more powerful and Scorpio is assuredly more inflexible. One party has to concede. Generally the female of the species is a bit more conciliatory; therefore, in such a combination, putting an Aries female with a Scorpio man will be somewhat more satisfactory.

Sexually, Scorpions want to prove their sexual prowess. They want to thrill their partners. Aries is equally passionate, and both of these signs love oral sex. For sex, this is a great combination. For long-term relationships, it's not. Lust, yes. Love, no.

ARIES WOMAN AND SCORPIO MAN

This is a hot and heavy combination. The Scorpio man doesn't care whether lovemaking lasts five minutes or five hours, as long as it's good. Ms. Aries wants to lead, and she exhilarates Scorpio. And though he may feel rushed, Scorpio's certainly enraptured by Aries. If only the totality of a relationship were as uncomplicated as sex, these two could go through eternity consumed with passion. Sadly, in a life together, they burn each other out and when the love dies, it's too often replaced with equally powerful animosity. This can be the "fatal attraction" relationship. They never get over each other.

ARIES MAN AND SCORPIO WOMAN

The Aries man looks at his Scorpio lady adoringly. His hands touch every inch of her with amazing speed. She's afire. It's fabulous . . . for a while. His passion, his total involvement in sex is so exciting to her that he doesn't have to do much at all to please her, at first. Aries needs praise, and Scorpio knows to give it. But does he know that she worries about her body? Is she pretty enough? Naïve Aries, he doesn't know that Scorpio needs to be told she's beautiful. Beyond that, his sexual repertoire is limited to a little foreplay and then the main event. The Scorpio woman wants more.

Aries with Sagittarius

THE RAM AND THE ARCHER: *The Arrow Finds Its Mark*

An enviable couple. These two Fire Signs make a fine relationship in and out of bed. They share common interests, from hiking and camping to gambling. They're both social beings who like traveling, entertaining, and going out often. Aries enjoys playing the field, flirting, and being with several lovers before settling down. Once committed, Aries is a steadfast partner and loyal friend. Likewise, Sagittarius avoids grown-up responsibilities as long as possible, but when accepted, Sagittarius is a reliable, hard worker and a constant friend and lover.

The differences between these two Signs are matters of degree more than substance. They're both outgoing, though Aries is more flamboyant than Sagittarius. Sagittarius is more self-assured than Aries, even though Aries may give off the impression of confidence. Aries is a bit of a hothead. Most of the time Sagittarius is quite mellow and laid back, but you don't want to make the Archer angry. That temper may be rarely seen, but it's a force to deal with and when released, it comes out in a torrent of very cutting remarks. Aries is easily wounded.

In the initial stages of a relationship, Sagittarius will let Aries run the show. Over time, in a fairly subtle way, Sagittarius will take over. If Aries resists, Sagittarius will become more force-ful. In the long run, Sagittarius will get his/her way. While some Sun Signs might take offense at this behavior, the Aries female doesn't mind. The Aries male, on the other hand, might object, though not too rigorously.

ARIES WOMAN AND SAGITTARIUS MAN

This relationship begins like fireworks on the Fourth of July. The attraction is electric. The Aries woman and the Sagittarius man find a place to paw each other with more speed than they'd even want to tell their best friends. But the Sagittarius male is usually very well endowed and may be too much for the lady Ram to handle. Sex may be more painful than pleasurable, so though the relationship could be wonderful, if they don't find a way to handle the sex, she'll withdraw and he'll cheat on her. This would be a pity, as on most every level these two Signs complement and satisfy each other.

ARIES MAN AND SAGITTARIUS WOMAN

The Sagittarius woman likes a well-endowed man. If Aries isn't so fortunate, he should never joke about it, but rather prove his prowess with a combination of oral and manual skills. For the genuine stud Aries, Sagittarius will cherish a photo of that special treasure. Aries may be quicker to reach climax than the Archer, in which case he'd be wise to masturbate beforehand. Of course, when sufficiently aroused, Sagittarius might be glad to perform oral sex first, allow-ing for a slower follow-up session of intercourse. In other matters—daily living together, raising a family—they are at ease and comfortable together.

Aries with Capricorn
The Ram and the Goat: *Conflicting Species*

This is something of a business deal in that with mutual effort, each gets a substantial reward. Aries brings excitement to this relationship, while Capricorn brings stability. But this is not an easy pairing.

Both Signs have some tendency to be flirtatious as well as at least a little jealous. The Ram, ruled by the planet Mars, will let that Martian anger out. The Goat may withdraw in stony silence. In addition, Capricorn is so intent upon achieving and accomplishing in life that he/she may not put enough attention into the relationship. The Ram, left too much to his/her own devices, is apt to roam a field.

Aries recognizes the need for a partner who balances his/her impulsive nature. Capricorn does that. Capricorn is intrigued by the vitality of Aries and by the wonderful ability Aries has to be open to new things without prejudging. Capricorn has an opinion about almost everything. With a prodigious memory, when confronting something new, the Goat puts those opinions into categories with previous experiences. Aries approaches new things simply and openly.

In bed Aries is fairly mainstream, sticking to the basics of kissing, oral sex, and intercourse. Many Capricorns want to experiment with a wide range of sexual behaviors that may range from light bondage to sadomasochism. The Goat must go slowly to initiate Aries, and Aries must be open-minded if sex is to remain vital. Can this relationship last? Yes. Will it? That depends wholly on how much effort each brings to it.

ARIES WOMAN AND CAPRICORN MAN

While he's courting her, Capricorn buys Aries lovely gifts and treats her attentively. Once they're a couple, he turns his attention back to the fundamental Capricorn interests—business affairs. As a result, Aries feels betrayed, sex dies down, and the relationship ends up in jeopardy. This doesn't happen overnight. Initially, Aries hardly realizes that Capricorn's being inattentive. She's free to do what she wants without him checking up on her. Over time, she realizes that he simply isn't paying attention. No Aries woman will put up with that. She'll try to win him back with her prowess in the bedroom. It doesn't work that way with Capricorn.

ARIES MAN AND CAPRICORN WOMAN

Aries man/Capricorn woman is an awkward combination, but it's workable with mutual acceptance of significant differences. The Capricorn woman must acknowledge that Aries is a perpetual boy. If she finds his almost childlike enthusiasm charming, that's a plus. Aries must accept that Capricorn's far more down-to-earth and less excitable than he. She wants him to assume more responsibilities and he'll try to get her to take over running their lives. It won't be beneficial if she does. Ultimately, he'll blame her if he becomes dependent upon her. In matters of sex, Capricorn wants much more foreplay than Aries needs and his premature ejaculation will turn her off.

Aries *with* Aquarius
THE RAM AND THE WATER BEARER: *A Challenge*

Aquarius is enthusiastic about ideas. Aries is enthusiastic about life. As friends, business partners, or co-workers, they really hit it off. Sex is the only problem area. If it can be handled, these two will have a very successful, long-lasting relationship. Aquarius is a good intellectual lover, though sometimes not a good physical lover. Aquarius knows what to do and can talk a partner to the edge of ecstasy, but there's often little real passion behind the performance.

Aries is like a first-grade school child: impulsive, impatient, and assertive. Aries lets a partner know what is desired and expects a mate to come through. Even in sexual matters, Aries will be impatient if those needs aren't being met. The Ram tries very hard to satisfy a partner, sometimes performing acts he/she doesn't enjoy all that much. Aries expects that kind of consideration in return.

Aquarius is like an eleventh grader: grown up and well mannered. Aquarius knows you don't always get what you want immediately, that you have to be patient. Aries isn't patient. Aquarius is thoughtful and gifted at using words and conveying hopes and wishes. But the Water Bearer may also seem somewhat aloof and detached, while the Ram is entirely within the moment.

Words excite Aquarius. Kissing and actions turn on Aries. Phone sex was probably invented by an Aquarian. After all, sex begins in the brain. Aries wants the real thing or nothing at all. It's actions, not words, that get the Ram turned on.

ARIES WOMAN AND AQUARIUS MAN

Aries woman and Aquarius men make great friends. They enjoy similar activities and have similar attitudes. Unfortunately, sex may not be very satisfying. For great sex, he'll have to rev up his libido, and she'll need to temper hers. Initially, Aquarius is very appreciative of Aries' beauty. He cooks her dinner. He's genuinely thrilled when she comes home. He may love her completely, but his signs of affection don't produce the verbal warmth and enthusiasm needed to create adequate passion on the pillow. Somehow he's more into seeking sensation than true emotion. She's all about intensity. An occasional sexy lingerie, video, or sex toy will help.

ARIES MAN AND AQUARIUS WOMAN

Out in public the Aquarius woman is a charmer. Regardless of the nature of the event, she's at ease talking to all manner of people. Aquarius is vivacious and charming. Not that she seeks to hog the spotlight; rather, she has an easy way about her that others find appealing. She's a great conversationalist, a patient listener, and extremely attentive. But at home and in bed, she's far less attentive and just not very interested. The Aquarius female asks her Aries partner, "Are you done yet?" Then indeed he is. He wonders, "Where is she? Doesn't she know I'm striving to please her?"

Aries *with* Pisces
The Ram and the Fish: *An Odd Couple*

Pisces, the twelfth Sign of the zodiac, The Dustbin, collects some qualities of all previous signs, providing the Fishes with a wonderful ability to understand others and to be chameleon-like. Pisceans are great actors and writers, as a result. For the same reason, they are also fine healers. They have a sense when someone is sick or in need of nurturing. They are complex people. Aries is the first Sign of the zodiac, straightforward as a child. One can tell at a glance when Aries is happy or unhappy, annoyed or at peace with the world. While Pisces is subtle and diplomatic, Aries calls it like it is.

Pisceans seem able to get others to do their bidding so unobtrusively that their artful manipulation goes unnoticed. Without aggression or effort Pisces prevails. Is it hypnosis? Who knows! One thing's for sure, it's a far cry from Aries' no-holds-barred, direct approach. Pisces is among the most sensitive Signs in the zodiac. Aries can be pretty blunt.

Initially, this couple is great in bed. Pisces sees Aries as wonderfully strong, a decided turn-on, and Aries is intrigued by Pieces' experimentation with a variety of acts and accoutrements. But here too, in short order, they disappoint each other. Pisces loves sex to be like a screenplay. Aries doesn't want to go through all the romance—the lighting of candles and incense—things that Pisces loves. Aries wants to get right to the main event. Pisces wants time to enjoy seduction and the setting of the stage.

ARIES WOMAN AND PISCES MAN

The Pisces man brings his Aries flowers and entices her with poetry, wine, and song. She wants forceful sex, though. You better have a hard cock or you're history with Aries. Pisces wants to look deep into Aries' eyes, to read her very soul. Ms. Aries looks back simply. Nothing's hidden, but she's waiting for him to jump her bones while he's musing about ageless love. He's patient and will work to attain his ambitions. She's impatient and expects luck to work in her favor as she marches headlong toward her goal with an incomplete course of action outlined. In and out of bed, this is an unlikely duet.

ARIES MAN AND PISCES WOMAN

Aries wants to jump into bed at the beginning of the date . . . slam bam thank you ma'am. Pisces loves long, slow sex and is renowned for her staying power. Ms. Pisces wants romance. Mr. Aries wants risk. Aries loves an edge about sex, doing it in an unusual place such as the back row of the movie theater or on the kitchen floor with olive oil. Pisces wants sex in bed, complete with incense, soft music, and candlelight. Pisces is the woman who will strew rose petals around the bed in preparation for a night of sex. Unfortunately, Aries may not even notice.

Taurus with Taurus
TWO BULLS TOGETHER: *Let's Get Physical*

Frequently, when two like Signs get together there is competition, a sense of "who's in charge here." That's not the case with two Taurans. They love the same things: good food, a warm environment, and lengthy passionate sex. They're patient, kind, slow to anger, and loyal. They're romantic, and neither seeks to dominate the other. Even when it comes to their negative traits, each knows how to back off from the other rather than make a bad scene worse.

Taurus needs to be told "I love you," and Taurus accommodates. When one Bull is in a foul mood, the second knows not to press the issue. One needs a hug and the other complies. Above all else, Taurus needs stability and security and gets it with a Taurus partner.

Sex is long, romantic, sensual, and satisfying. For them, it feels as though the whole world has stopped. They really enjoy each other, but they can go broke putting too much time into the physical side of life. In bed it's great, but someone has to get up, go out, and earn the family paycheck.

The sex life is fundamentally conservative, sticking to lots of kissing, touching and massaging, and intercourse. As a result, sex may become routine in spite of each partner's regard for the other. In fantasy life, the sex is far more adventuresome. Exploring some of those fantasies—perhaps with an occasional can of whipped cream, introducing a sex toy, or wearing an unexpected costume—will add a certain spark.

Summary
She treats him like a king, is unfailingly loyal, and is attentive to his needs. She wants him to respect her and provide her with security and stability. As long as he pays the bills, or holds up his end of the bargain, the rewards will be substantial and the sex wonderful. Ms. Taurus rarely gets a headache, and if she really has one, she knows that sex will cure it. He's affectionate, helpful around the house, and enjoys buying her special gifts. As long as these two avoid being bullheaded in a disagreement, their relationship will be very agreeable indeed.

Taurus with Gemini
THE BULL AND THE TWINS: *Friends and Lovers*

On the friendship side of the relationship, Taurus and Gemini get along famously. Each has attributes that the other needs. Gemini, as the Sign of experimentation, brings liveliness and versatility and introduces Taurus to a broad range of experiences. Taurus, as the Sign of stability and security, provides Gemini with grounding and practicality. While Gemini's attention might wander, Taurus is ever steadfast and loyal. These factors account for the success and longevity of so many Gemini/Taurus couples.

In the bedroom, there are substantial differences in style and pleasure. Gemini wants spontaneity, while Taurus doesn't mind setting a date for sex. Gemini is content with about an hour for lovemaking; Taurus prefers it long and slow. Gemini wants to try many sexual behaviors, though variety doesn't necessarily entice Taurus. Taurus, the most physical sign in the zodiac, just loves sex and wants to be touched and kissed and licked and sucked, and can be thoroughly satisfied with repetitive foreplay. This would prove monotonous for Gemini.

The most difficult area for these two is the manner in which they approach problem solving. Gemini does multiple tasks at once, as he/she has a remarkable ability to focus on that one thing on which he or she is currently involved and to remain undistracted by all the other piles of unfinished business. Taurus does one thing and becomes unnerved by Gemini's seeming chaos. When worried, Gemini withdraws from the stress-producing situation and simply redirects focus to one of those myriad other endeavors. When Taurus is worried, there can be no other involvement. Taurus is relentless.

TAURUS WOMAN AND GEMINI MAN
Gemini's versatility in the bedroom excites his Taurus partner, and her rapture convinces him that he's a far better lover than he ever realized. In a long-term relationship, however, he may disappoint her, as she requires more time sexually than he may want to give. A mix of quickies and long sessions will help. The Taurus woman is steadfast and committed, but she can also be possessive and demanding. No one can be possessive with Gemini and have a lasting relationship. He may be inattentive to the relationship and she won't tolerate being ignored. There is good potential here, but also many pitfalls.

TAURUS MAN AND GEMINI WOMAN
When the relationship is new, Mr. Taurus loves the fact that Ms. Gemini has multiple orgasms before he climaxes. He feels like a great lover and continues his slow pace to orgasm. Over time, she's apt to grow impatient with these marathon sessions. Far less than halfway through, her quicksilver mind is planning the menu for tomorrow's dinner party. In addition, Gemini is an inveterate flirt, which drives jealous Taurus wild. He's a bit of a couch potato and she's highly social. With all that, these two frequently share a lasting and loving relationship based upon full acceptance of their many differences.

Taurus with Cancer
THE BULL AND THE CRAB: *Contented Combo*

Picture two kids playing in the mud, having a wonderful time, and you've got an image of

Taurus with Cancer. This is one of the most successful relationships, both socially and sexually.

These Signs have many qualities in common. Both love their homes and strive to create a welcoming environment. They enjoy working in their yards and preparing food for their friends and families. Planning and cooking a meal together is a sexual experience. They are both affectionate and openly loving, nurturing to each other and their circle of loved ones. They both have patient and tenacious natures. In their lesser traits, each provides balance for the other. Cancer is a worrier. Taurus is reassuring. Taurus frets about money. Cancer is confident about helping to provide it.

When Cancer is upset he/she wants to talk and Taurus is a great listener. When Taurus is upset and ready to talk, Cancer not only makes a wonderful listener, but also has a real knack for drawing Taurus out. Cancer is a sucker for a sob story, wanting to kiss it and make it better, and Taurus, strong and independent in some regards, appreciates a loving shoulder to lean on. Taurus respects the strength of Cancer, and Cancer appreciates the loyalty of Taurus.

In the sexual arena what makes this combination so successful is that both enjoy slow, primarily traditional sex including fairly lengthy foreplay, touching, and deep kissing. Taurus loves to explore every part of the body. Cancer luxuriates in this attention and returns the favor.

TAURUS WOMAN AND CANCER MAN

The Taurus woman and Cancer man never tire of listening to one another. She wants to be cared for but also needs her independence. The Cancer man intuitively understands that his Taurus female possesses great strength, as is proved by her incredible endurance in bed, as well as her remarkable steadiness in dealing with any emotional crisis involving the family. The only area where Taurus is truly fragile is regarding financial stability. Now Cancer, careful with money, is reassuring to Taurus. Cancer may tend to smother some woman, but he is so comfortable with Taurus that his possessive streak is not likely to be triggered.

TAURUS MAN AND CANCER WOMAN

The Cancer woman treats the home as a castle, decorating it and cultivating a garden. That and raising children are her fulfillment. Not only is she a loving homemaker, but also smooth as silk in bed. They both have strong sex drives and if time permits that would enjoy having sex daily. She's built well and even if she puts on weigh in later years, she still has a lovely shape. To whatever extent Taurus believes he was not adequately loved as a child, Cancer will more than make up for it. She will be a loving wife and nurturing mother all in one.

Taurus with Leo
THE BULL AND THE LION: *Incompatible Species*

Taurus and Leo, both Fixed Signs, respect one another. Taurus represents practicality and tenacity. Leo represents creativity, the willingness to take chances. In business and friendship, these qualities serve successfully as checks and balances for each other. In a love relationship, however, there are two key problems.

First, Fire Sign Leo is prone to snap judgments, while Earth Sign Taurus takes a long time to make decisions. Leo may misperceive this slowness of pace as indecisiveness. Wrong call. If Leo then tries to push Taurus toward a decision, Taurus will prove how well this Sign deserves to be called bullheaded. The second problem is sexual. Both signs are highly passionate but in very different ways. Leo wants variety, spontaneity, exploration, and a sense of urgency to feed passion. Leo wants play in the sexual act. For Taurus, passion is more about length, duration of the sex act, while Taurus doesn't do much exploring.

With Leo, sex has nothing to do with time. Sometimes it's quick, sometimes it's slow. For Taurus, a satisfying sexual encounter includes a tremendous amount of cuddling, touching, and deep kissing. Taurus is content with the conventional range of sex: hand holding, deep kissing, fondling, mutual masturbation, oral sex, and intercourse. Leo wants something more unconventional and a greater sense of ecstasy. Without that, Leo will get bored.

Taurus needs stability and security. Leo is extravagant; Taurus is straightforward and conservative. Leo is flamboyant, even outrageous. While this partnership is initially exciting, in the long term, they are truly at odds with each other.

TAURUS WOMAN AND LEO MAN

When upset, the Taurus woman is apt to toss cutting remarks at her Leo partner. Leo is not the most forgiving of Signs, and he has a long memory. Taurus' tendency to be abrupt will have significant impact and the effect will first be felt in the bedroom. She's curt. He's not interested. In addition, to please Leo, Taurus needs to spice up her act in bed. He's intense and forceful, while she wants longer, slower embraces and deeper kisses. He'll need to take more time building to the finale. This relationship is helped if Leo is successful in business, which is so important to Taurus' stability and security needs.

TAURUS MAN AND LEO WOMAN

Taurus treats Leo like a goddess, exactly what she wants. The strengths of the Taurus man—stability, steadfastness, and loyalty—are surprisingly comforting to the exuberant, dynamic Leo female. All is well if he doesn't bore her with his tendency to do the same things repeatedly (eat the same foods, maintain an unchanging pattern) and if she is not excessively demanding. Taurus must recognize that his Leo lover sometimes longs for shorter, more dynamic sex. Ms. Leo must understand that her Taurus lover takes longer to make choices than she does, and that this is no reflection on his manliness or his intelligence.

Taurus with Virgo

THE BULL AND THE VIRGIN: *Potent Potential*

These two Earth Signs are practical, straightforward, and caring. They make for a great combination in friendship, business, and love. While Taurus has great need for security and stability, Virgo's methodical, detail-oriented qualities are reassuring. Virgo, who makes a great friend—ready to help out, not looking for a pat on the back—is deeply appreciative of the loyalty and steadfastness of Taurus.

Taurus and Virgo inherently trust each other and generally appreciate similar activities centered on their home, food, and the pleasure of a close circle of intimate friends. They derive great pleasure out of togetherness, whether tending their garden or preparing dinners. They aren't likely to argue often and get over it fairly quickly when they do.

Problems in this relationship are few. They may arise when Taurus is self-indulgent or lazy, and when Virgo is nit-picking or faultfinding. Since Virgo works so hard at all aspects of life, he/she feels taken advantage of when a partner does not make an equal effort. Taurus is easily wounded by criticism.

Sexually, highly physical Taurus, who loves to lick, suck, and kiss, is gratified by Virgo's responsive hands caressing and fondling. If there ever are any problems in the bedroom, they come from the fact that Taurus is content with traditional sexual expression while Virgo may want to experience a far greater range of behaviors. If Virgo goes slowly, Taurus will gradually comply and respond enthusiastically. If rushed, Taurus will prove itself worthy of its symbol, the Bull.

TAURUS WOMAN AND VIRGO MAN

The Taurus woman is totally content with her Virgo man. He is the dominant one: not in an aggressive way, but in a protective way. He satisfies Taurus' need for security. These two possess a wonderful quality of togetherness. To the outsider, he may seem a little difficult, uptight, and self-righteous. She may seem a tad abrupt or demanding. But these two are unaware of, or at least unperturbed by, any such qualities. In matters sexual, their lovemaking is highly satisfying. They match each other in energy and in the nature of their sexual pleasures, or they reach to expand their repertoire for the other's pleasure.

TAURUS MAN AND VIRGO WOMAN

From their first encounter, the sexual heat with this couple is incendiary. He loves the way her hands lovingly and passionately enjoy his body, all of it. Taurus takes Virgo's breath away. He kisses her with a depth of passion that fulfills her fantasies. While the sex remains great, outside the bedroom problems arise. Virgo is more ambitious than Taurus, which triggers his insecurity. She may seem too much of a wheeler-dealer, forever trying to advance his career, often past the level of his feeling of competence. A long-term successful relationship depends on Virgo supporting, not nagging, the Taurus bull and on Taurus resisting a couch potato mentality.

Taurus with Libra
THE BULL AND THE SCALES: *Almost on the Balance Point*

More often than not, Earth and Air Signs are not very compatible. The Taurus/Libra twosome may be the exception to that rule. Even though they have many differences in temperament and style, some of these differences provide balance between the two Signs. Others just create stress. Passionate and romantic, both Signs are ruled by Venus, the planet of love and luxury.

Earth Sign Taurus is highly physical, loves to touch, and uses body language to express sexual needs and wants. Air Sign Libra is turned on verbally and communicates sexual wants more with words than with body language.

Both Signs enjoy taking their time, preferably an hour or more, for each sexual encounter, and they find quickies either not enjoyable or fun only on occasion. Food is a turn-on. For Taurus, sharing food is enough to turn thoughts to sex. For Libra, it can be fun to incorporate food with sex. In the sex act itself, Taurus loves the physicality, all the touching, while Libra loves the romance, wine, music, and candlelight.

Libra is an independent Sign. While Taurus has a strong personality, this Sign also has a dependent streak. The result is that Taurus may seem clingy or controlling to Libra, whereas Libra's self-contained behavior triggers Taurus' insecurities. Libra is ever romantic and sentimental, and enjoys the small tokens of love. Taurus is far more practical and when it comes to receiving gifts would prefer that a lover save up and buy something of consequence rather than wasting money on trivial trinkets.

TAURUS WOMAN AND LIBRA MAN

Taurus has a deep-seated need to rely on her man as her protector. When she listens to Libra struggling to make a decision, exploring and re-exploring his options, her fundamental insecurities can be triggered. However, his romantic gestures, words of love, and kindness are usually enough to keep her happy—as long as they share adequate financial stability. Her loyalty and devotion to him and their family and her attentiveness in the bedroom will satisfy him. The difficulty for these two, long term, will come only if Libra fails to understand how physical Taurus is, how important sex is to her.

TAURUS MAN AND LIBRA WOMAN

Taurus is the silent type, but it is words that turn Libra on. Though they share many interests and can live together harmoniously, to keep their sex life lively, Taurus must extend himself verbally. Conversely, he responds to the intensely physical and Libra must extend herself to turn him on with the use of her hands and body language before and during sex. Libra loves luxury and Taurus is concerned about financial stability. So if he is responsible for making the money, she must be watchful in her spending. By keeping all of this in mind, this twosome can enjoy an enduring relationship.

Taurus with Scorpio
THE SCORPION AND THE BULL: *Opposites Attract and Repel*

Scorpio and Taurus are opposite signs and while opposites do attract, the attraction may only work for the short term. Taurus is quite direct, often blunt. Scorpio is guarded in speech. When Taurus is upset and ready to talk, he/she will talk a blue streak. Secretive Scorpio, always afraid of saying too much and afraid of revealing too much, may find that behavior disarmingly attractive, for a while. Later, Scorpio is apt to become bored with Taurus' long tirades. Another problem is that Taurus' energy level is so different from Scorpio's. Scorpio is driven. Taurus has a lazy streak.

On the positive side, Taurus finds Scorpio receptive and understanding. Taurus wants protecting and Scorpio gladly complies. Regarding sex, Taurus is the most physical sign in the zodiac, loves to touch and be touched. Taurus is extremely sensual in all regards, luxuriating in warmth whether in front of the fireplace or at the beach in sunny climes. Taurus loves music, is very oral, and finds food a turn-on. Scorpio, with its highly sexy nature, matches Taurus' passion.

Taurus makes a great life partner: he's extremely loyal and never tolerates anyone speaking ill of his/her lover. Where Scorpio wants a profound relationship, yearns for a soul mate, Taurus can provide gratification. The problems come in when Taurus gets possessive. Scorpio's need for freedom causes Taurus insecurity. Taurus hates change, and Scorpio is forever changing things. Can this relationship work? Yes. Will it? That depends upon how these two choose to behave.

TAURUS WOMAN AND SCORPIO MAN

Ms. Taurus wants to feel secure. Mr. Scorpio exudes an aura of power and strength. She's drawn to that and captivated by his raw sexual magnetism. In bed, this is dynamite. Scorpio has staying power that satisfies Taurus and their sexual intensity is a match. Aside from sex, they have to accommodate marked differences. Taurus hates to be pushed into decisions in a manner she deems hasty. Scorpio can be insistent. He's quite emotional and can get into black moods that she's unable to draw him out of. When angry, Taurus too can withdraw into stony silence. These silences are disastrous to the relationship.

TAURUS MAN AND SCORPIO WOMAN

Mr. Taurus loves sex. Luckily, Ms. Scorpio frequently initiates lovemaking and knows exactly how to please him. She, being very sensual, loves the way his hands explore her body and show his awareness that she has more than one erogenous zone. He revels in her body, whether she's thin, a little overweight, or pregnant. Problems arise because Taurus isn't overly ambitious whereas Scorpio is driven. He wants to relax and enjoy himself; he's very much the couch potato. She's a workaholic. Scorpio respects Taurus' down-to-earth practicality but is sometimes bored by his commitment to routine. She wants much more variety in their life.

Taurus with Sagittarius
THE BULL AND THE ARCHER: *Curious Balance*

This is a surprisingly fantastic relationship because Taurus and Sagittarius have many fundamental differences. Taurus craves stability and security, while Sagittarius is a risk taker. Taurus is a bit of a coach potato. Sagittarius says, "Don't fence me in." Taurus is sensitive and easily wounded, and Sagittarius tends to shoot from the hip. Taurus prefers a life that centers on home entertaining and cookouts in the backyard. Sagittarius is an active Sign who enjoys travel, sports, and gambling. Taurus is a planner and Sagittarius is spontaneous.

What Taurus and Sagittarius have in common, which helps to overcome these disparities, is that they both love food and enjoy doing a variety of things together—as long as it is not too often for Taurus or too repetitive for Sagittarius. Taurus is ruled by Venus, the planet that represents sensual pleasures, while Sagittarius is ruled by Jupiter, the planet that rules extravagance and expansion. In a curious way, the stable earthbound Taurus energy can prove comforting to Sagittarius' wanderlust nature. The expansiveness and desire for broad horizons in Sagittarius helps shake Taurus loose.

The sex between these two is wonderful. Taurus likes it long and slow and Sagittarius has great endurance, like the Eveready battery, going and going and going. Sagittarius enjoys several experimental behaviors including anal sex, dominance and submission, spanking, and bondage. Taurus is rather mainstream in sexual expression, but is willing to explore. Both Signs like to incorporate food with sex. However, while Sagittarius may be into sex toys, Taurus is not interested.

TAURUS WOMAN AND SAGITTARIUS MAN

Here the sex is so good that it will help hold these two together when times are tough. And they are apt to get tough when it comes to setting priorities and dealing with money. Sagittarius spends more freely than Taurus would like because she worries about stability and family security. She wants the new SUV but the mortgage must be paid first. Sagittarius wants to spend a long weekend in Las Vegas, while Taurus wants a new washer/dryer. Sagittarius appreciates her loyalty and depth of love but will resent it if her practicality stifles his need to feel free of boundaries.

TAURUS MAN AND SAGITTARIUS WOMAN

Taurus is a man of solid quiet strength with confidence in his ability to resolve problems. He's ready to prove that though other men have been brutal, he represents all that is good in the male sex and will rescue his wounded dove. But Ms. Sagittarius is independent and strong, a far cry from Cinderella longing to be rescued. The sex can be great, though the relationship is difficult. She is a powerhouse and wants a strong, decisive man. Taurus, though no pushover, isn't the most assertive of men. If she nags and prods, he will withdraw into an immobile and stony silence.

Taurus with Capricorn
THE BULL AND THE GOAT: *Mutual Admiration*

This is a fine relationship, a mutual admiration society. Taurus and Capricorn work through their infrequent disagreements with little stress. Both are Earth Signs with equally strong libidos and can expect to have a lasting and enjoyable sex life. It isn't necessarily fireworks, but it is a slow and steady burn.

Taurans and most Capricorns are mainstream sexually, very into touch and kissing. They love to take their time in each sexual encounter, lingering over foreplay. Both want about 30 minutes to an hour for sex, half that for foreplay. They strive to achieve orgasm at the same time.

Some Capricorns are into the BDSM lifestyle. They want to explore the range of sexual practices of bondage, dominance and submission, and sadomasochism. The Goat may be able to coax the Bull into role-playing and bondage but not likely into accepting pain as part of sexual pleasure. If Taurus adopts the dominant role and Capricorn the submissive role, this relationship may work out better.

Neither Taurus nor Capricorn will be hurried. With Taurus, if one tries to get Taurus to make a decision quickly, the Bull will almost always say no. They do not want to be trapped into an unhappy situation by too hastily saying yes. Capricorn is a patient Sign, not likely to hurry Taurus. Taurus is not disturbed when Capricorn, who prefers to think things through without discussion, shares a decision only after having made it alone. In any kind of partnership—sexual, marital, or business—these two have most everything going for them.

TAURUS WOMAN AND CAPRICORN MAN

The Taurus woman wants to feel secure and protected and the hardworking Goat is very capable in this regard. Good sex on a steady basis is a given, especially if Capricorn remembers to compliment this loyal, loving woman. The only problem that may occur is if Taurus tries to maneuver Capricorn when she doesn't like a position he has taken. For one thing, Capricorn is a master of manipulation; this is part of his skill in business, and he knows what Taurus wants when she drops hints. It's better for her to say what's on her mind and ask him to consider her viewpoint. Typically, he will comply.

TAURUS MAN AND CAPRICORN WOMAN

Mr. Taurus wants to please his Capricorn woman in bed. He loves exploring her body with his hands and mouth. He lavishes compliments upon her. She may not want sex as often as he, but she certainly matches him in intensity. If Capricorn wants to try more experimental practices, Taurus is usually willing to go along. Overall, their sex life is rich and satisfying. They share similar values in lifestyle, respect material goods, and tend carefully to their home. She works hard creating a comfortable environment and is willing to bear some responsibility for the family's financial support. In return, the Taurus male is steadfast, loyal, and direct.

Taurus with Aquarius
THE BULL AND THE WATER BEARER: *No Common Ground*

Just think of these two symbols: the cool, calm Water Bearer versus the mighty and dangerous

Bull. There's no common ground. That's what it amounts to when you put these two Signs together into a love relationship.

Initially Taurus, who can be a bit reticent, is attracted by the Aquarian's ability to "work the crowd." Aquarius is everybody's buddy, having an extraordinary ability to fit in. The Water Bearer does the talking and finds a great listener in the Bull. As a friendship this pairing is just fine. In personal relationships, the problems are many.

Their pace and timing in life are at odds with each other. Together Aquarius and Taurus create an imbalance. Taurus moves slowly and hates to be rushed. Aquarius is a quick thinker and is off and running long before Taurus has digested the situation.

The diplomat of the zodiac, Aquarius is an Air Sign. In a crisis this is the person who knows how to stay focused on a rational, thinking plane. Conversely, Earth Sign Taurus gets right to the physical, what needs to be done, fixed, replaced, or repaired. Aquarius is thinking far ahead and expanding the perspective. They annoy each other. Aquarius says, "It's important to look at the big picture." Taurus says, "There's too much to do right here."

With sex, these two have a similar problem. Aquarius wants to talk about sex, while Taurus wants to just do it. They aren't in sync and, thus, satisfying the other becomes more pain than pleasure. Over time, Taurus is dissatisfied and Aquarius is bored.

TAURUS WOMAN AND AQUARIUS MAN

The natural diplomat of the zodiac, Aquarius is well liked, charming, and at ease with people. His wonderful ability to talk about a broad range of topics, places he's been, and all the people he knows, impresses Taurus. For his part, he's pleased to have such an attentive listener and he finds her warm, caring personality appealing. Unfortunately, the sex is seldom satisfying with this couple for more than a short while. The amount of time Taurus requires, and her conventional approach, won't light Aquarius' fire. His lack of ardor leaves her wanting. In a friendship they're fine. For romance, this union is not a good idea.

TAURUS MAN AND AQUARIUS WOMAN

Aquarius loves to talk about sex. She wants to idealize it. She can be an ardent lover occasionally, but it's verbal foreplay that really gets her going. Taurus is a quiet man, and great sex for him is all about touch and the use of his mouth for kissing, not talking. He moves slowly both in sex and in life. She's impatient and moves quickly. He seems rock solid but has an inner core that needs to feel assured that he is loved. He perceives her cool, calm behavior as detached and remote. He tries to hold on, she feels stifled.

Taurus with Pisces
THE BULL AND THE FISH: *Soul Mates in Paradise*

From the bedroom to the boardroom, Taurus and Pisces relate well. Both are sensitive, caring, and loyal Signs. Taurus provides practicality and Pisces provides intuition.

Highly emotional Pisces opens Taurus' emotional side. Taurus provides quiet strength to Pisces, who needs time to retreat and meditate. While some Sun Signs might be uncomfortable with these silent periods, Taurus is completely at ease with them. Taurus is concerned about stability, security, and family financial welfare. Pisces has a calming and assuring quality, and expresses confidence in their ability as a couple to resolve any problems.

What are the problems? In a disagreement Pisces is likely to give in, seemingly going along with Taurus. All too often, however, Pisces has just conceded in order to avoid conflict, but then goes on doing whatever he/she chooses. Taurus finds this behavior infuriating. On Taurus' part, the Bull has a tendency to be abrupt, which can trigger Pisces' defensiveness.

Taurus is ruled by Venus, the planet of physical love. Pisces is ruled by Neptune, the planet of spiritual love. These two Signs share a love affair that plays on both levels, making the relationship a true soul mate connection. Sex is instinctively right. Taurus is a mainstream lover, though quite vocal, and Pisces is a romantic who is very invested in bringing pleasure to a partner and is gratified to hear sounds of ecstasy. Pisces has great endurance and Taurus loves long, slow sex. Nobody needs to coach this happy couple. Their relationship can be fulfilling life long.

TAURUS WOMAN AND PISCES MAN

The Pisces man is great at romance. He remembers anniversaries, brings flowers, and lights candles. Sex is easy and satisfying. The Taurus woman wants to explore every inch of Pisces' body. He revels in her sensuality and responds in kind. Her skills with her hands are legendary. If he hadn't found sex to be a spiritual experience in the past, being with Taurus will change his mind. She's loyal and dependable, and makes him feel all the more a man—strong and protective. Taurus will never tolerate anyone speaking ill of her Pisces. He'll treat her like his queen and she will reward him with devotion.

TAURUS MAN AND PISCES WOMAN

Pisces has a vulnerable streak and wants a strong man. Taurus comforts her with his solid macho presentation. In bed, he tells her exactly what to do, and she likes it that way. The lovemaking, from kissing to oral sex and intercourse, is passionate. He's an attentive and sensitive lover. Pisces may want more experimentation, but Taurus will try new activities if she presents them as a fun choice. Romance and food put her in the mood, and her mere presence is all it takes for him. They have similar values and enjoy the same activities. This is a thoroughly well-matched couple.

Gemini with Gemini
TWO TWINS TOGETHER: *Complement or Chaos?*

Just imagine one hundred piles of unfinished business belonging to Gemini #1 and one hundred piles of unfinished business belonging to Gemini #2. And there you have it, life for two Geminis together: mutual chaos . . . and neither cares. Of course, somebody's got to go to the market, take out the trash, and pay the bills. One thing's for sure: these two better maintain separate checking accounts.

Geminis can talk with each other for hours and never run out of things to say. They love exploring a wide spectrum of life together. In the beginning, it's exciting, as Gemini feels unique among people and here he/she encounters a mirror image. But in fact, too much similarity is a problem. They get into power struggles and both are apt to deal with parallel difficulties simultaneously.

Bedroom activities are at first stimulating as each tries to impress the other with style and variety. But something is missing—the spark of a Fire Sign or the endurance of an Earth Sign. Over time, there just isn't enough variety and both Geminis become bored.

The tendency to be inconstant or shallow may also be exaggerated when two Geminis team up. In addition, Gemini is flirtatious and can be jealous. Two Geminis together trigger insecurities in each other. In time, each Gemini feels a longing for a partner who provides a stimulus or presents a feeling of stability, of being balanced or grounded. All these behaviors outside the bedroom undermine the relationship and everything backfires on them. This relationship is not likely to work.

Summary

She hugs and kisses every man in the room, just to be friendly, and he does the same to every woman. Heaven forbid anyone takes this seriously. Jealousy rears its ugly head, heated words ensue, and spicy sex follows. But too many such episodes will douse these flames. There's no balance here, no anchor, nothing to calm tense times or stimulate quiet ones. While each longs for emotional closeness, this isn't a natural Gemini trait. There remains a feeling of emptiness at the core. Only a very busy life outside the relationship will save this couple long term.

Gemini with Cancer

THE TWINS AND THE CRAB: *Sex—Sure Fire! Relationship—Doubtful*

Here we have two Sun Signs about as alike as night and day, and yet between the sheets it's a great sexual combination. Both Sun Signs range from experimental to very open in their sexual behaviors. Gemini lights Cancer's emotional fires, perhaps too much so. Cancer believes that Gemini shares common feelings, but Gemini doesn't.

Cancer comes from a feeling core, while Gemini comes from a more intellectual place. In other words, Cancer buys into the game and the sexual role-playing wholeheartedly with emotion and passion. Sex and love become wrapped up and synonymous. Gemini, on the other hand, manages to occupy the roles of experimenter and observer simultaneously, enjoying sex, loving sex, but seeing it as apart from or other than love. While Cancer gives himself/herself over with full abandon, Gemini retains a certain emotional distance. For Cancer, this complexity can create a kind of emotional maelstrom that may be too much to sustain.

Aside from the sex, personality trait by personality trait, these two have little in common. Gemini is restless and won't allow anyone to pin him/her down while Cancer is possessive. Cancer clings. Gemini tries to gain distance. Cancer grows insecure and tries to hold on tighter. Cancer feels deeply whereas Gemini shies away from emotion. Gemini is a nervous sign and Cancer worries. Each one sets off the other. They may love each other and all the while drive each other to distraction. On a scale of 1 to 10, this couple scores a 10 for sex but a mere 4 in a relationship.

GEMINI WOMAN AND CANCER MAN

Initially, she lights his fires. Gemini is full of sexual play and Cancer is thrilled. He is a deeply emotional man who tries to keep his feelings under wraps. She strips them away. And yet over time, Cancer strives to gain control as he begins to feel overwhelmed by his own emotions. If he strives too hard to control her, she will be turned off and will retaliate with wanton flirtatiousness and unkind words. Cancer wants to cling to Gemini and is resentful of the attention she pays to others. She is a generous and restless spirit who needs room to experience new horizons.

GEMINI MAN AND CANCER WOMAN

Surprise her. Cancer seems so much the lady, so much the good homebody, but she has a secret desire to be ravished in the woods. Gemini should take her there and listen to her say, less than convincingly, "Oh no! Not here," until she says, "Oh, that feels so good." For that foray into the woods a jug of wine and a loaf of bread will complete the afternoon. She's a sympathetic listener and he's a wonderful talker. This partnership starts off great. Later Gemini will have difficulty handling Cancer's moodiness and she may come to find him manipulative.

Gemini with Leo

THE TWINS AND THE LION: *Potential Paradise*

They love to talk, dance, and travel. They truly complement each other. Gemini loves to experiment and Leo loves to explore. Between the sheets this is a great combination. The one real obstacle to long-term bliss for this couple is that Gemini's flirtatiousness makes Leo intensely jealous. Leo, so full of himself/herself, won't put up with that. Gemini must curb the "friendly" act or Leo will take off and a potential life-long relationship will dissolve.

What Fire Sign Leo brings to Gemini is a spark of vitality, while Air Sign Gemini keeps the experience going. Leo might be a bit single-minded in approaching sex—passionate but set in specific ways—or might rush too quickly to climax. Gemini provides a balance. Gemini wants to talk things through: "Why are you doing that? What's that all about?" For Leo, sex is always hot and heavy. Gemini tempers things, which proves very satisfactory to Leo.

Leo likes being praised, adored, in fact. Gemini, attention elsewhere, may forget to lavish compliments. Leo, being outrageously self-confident, will overlook this Gemini lapse most of the time. But for these two to be truly happy, Gemini needs to remember that the Lion loves to have his mane stroked. He responds with lavish generosity when it is.

For Gemini, the biggest problem with Leo is that Leo is always right. In a disagreement, therefore, Gemini must be wrong. Clearly, Leo needs to give Gemini more credit for his/her wonderful intellect and ability to solve problems.

GEMINI WOMAN AND LEO MAN

This is a pretty ideal pairing. He's the passion; she's the variety. Leo explores every inch of her body, and Gemini is inspired by his attentions. What Gemini lacks in innate passion, she compensates for with curiosity. As long as variety is part of their sex life, they'll have great fun between the sheets, and it doesn't matter whether sex is short or lengthy. The relationship is equally successful as he takes charge and consistently reassures her that she has nothing to be nervous about. As long as her flirtatiousness doesn't threaten him, he'll be supportive of all her varied interests.

GEMINI MAN AND LEO WOMAN

Leo, a lioness in bed, loves intense and passionate sex. Gemini is more into versatility and play. The sexual part of this relationship will succeed, however, if Leo lets Gemini lead and Gemini remembers to tease Leo, bringing her closer and closer to climax, only to back away. This game will hold her interest through the years. In addition, the way he has of observing the changes in her body as she becomes excited fulfills her need for an audience. One warning: if Leo tries to take charge, Gemini will let her, but in time that will destroy the relationship.

Gemini with Virgo

THE TWINS AND THE VIRGIN: *Let the Madness Begin!*

Somewhere in the vast expanse of Mother Earth there are some happy Gemini/Virgo couples—but they are rare. These two have very little in common. Earth Sign Virgo generally deadens the Air for Gemini, who gets bored with Virgo's systematic approach to all of life, including sex. Gemini, wanting to try something new, somewhere else, somehow differently, makes Virgo fundamentally uncomfortable.

In a curious way, Gemini and Virgo have something important in common: a sense of order. Virgo knows exactly where everything is. The Virgo environment is tightly organized. Even when Virgo has many possessions and lives in a small place, there is seldom any clutter. Gemini loves clutter but in the midst of chaos can find anything. This form of order is beyond Virgo's comprehension. They drive each other berserk.

There are two types in the Virgo Sun Sign: Those who are mainstream in their sexuality and those who are willing to experiment. In bed, mainstream Virgo is wonderful with his or her hands and has a set pattern of behavior. For Gemini that predictability undermines passion. Virgo longs for eroticism, while Gemini wants raw sex. Virgo gets immersed in the act, while Gemini remains something of an observer.

Sex for Gemini and the more experimental Virgo is more satisfying, at least briefly, because Gemini enjoys trying out variations of sexual behaviors and sex toys galore. But even here, Virgo is likely to slip into routine, boring Gemini. Too, Gemini's desire for constant change is likely to unnerve Virgo.

GEMINI WOMAN AND VIRGO MAN

He knows just the right way to do it, whatever it is. Gemini knows one hundred ways to do the same thing. At first she is drawn to him because his practical, straightforward approach is reassuring and calming. Over time, this same endearing quality becomes annoying. Even in bed, Virgo believes you start at point A, progress through B and C to eventually end up at "O." Gemini knows full well that "O" can be moved to any number of places in the alphabet of sex. "O" may be great for a while, but it will become elusive before long.

GEMINI MAN AND VIRGO WOMAN

For Virgo, the smell and feel of clean sheets are a decided turn-on. Gemini has no clue when he last changed the bed. Interestingly, though she's called the Virgin, in bed Virgo can be dynamite in motion, sound effects, and all. She loves oral sex and in the early days of this relationship, it's great. But he'll want to check out pornography and an assortment of sex toys, and these rarely interest her at all. In other aspects of life, Virgo finds Gemini to be scattered and he sees her as critical. The relationship then spirals downward and sex is all but forgotten.

Gemini with Libra
THE TWINS AND THE SCALES: *Sexual Seduction*

The foundation of the Gemini/Libra relationship is their ability to communicate. They spend ten minutes having sex, then two hours discussing it. They could write the greatest romance novels together. She tells him how much she adores the feel of his hands on her skin. He replies that no one else has ever excited him so much. They look at each other lovingly, adoringly, blissfully. It is truly a mutual admiration society. They are content with each other in the outside world and at home in bed.

Libra debates extensively between two possibilities, whereas Gemini tends to explore dozens of them. In a relationship, each is comfortable with the other's need to discuss multiple options.

The only problem between these two is from a verbal standpoint. When Gemini gets upset, he/she is apt to say something that is quite cruel and cutting. Refined Libra rarely retaliates but always remembers.

Both Signs are affectionate by nature and rather easy-going. They will have a very active sex life that is both varied and fun, though it won't be overly passionate. Libra loves romance, while Gemini tends to get too quickly to the heart of the matter. If Libra brings variety into the bedroom, Gemini's curiosity will result in improved sex.

The one issue that could undermine their sex life is money problems. Libra loves luxury. Gemini may be disorganized. If neither attends to the checkbook and financial problems ensue, Gemini grows nervous and Libra becomes irritable. Needless to say, these are not the best energies to take into the bedroom.

GEMINI WOMAN AND LIBRA MAN

The Gemini woman and Libra man love to be out and about. Gemini circulates at any affair, charming all with the sway of her hips, a ready smile, and easy small talk. Mr. Libra sees her body as his trophy and observing others admiring his lover really turns him on. Libra, too, loves to be admired. He's proud of his physique and enjoys showing it off—especially on the beach. These two can make a relationship last a lifetime with their shared interests and relaxed easy interactions, as long as money is properly managed so that the coffers remain full and allow the music to play on.

GEMINI MAN AND LIBRA WOMAN

Libra wants to be treated to dinners and little gifts. She cares about her looks and wants to be admired. Gemini must remember to be attentive. In the bedroom, it's up to Libra to make the environment sensual so she'll feel most satisfied with the sexual encounter. If Gemini uses his wonderful gift for gab and skill with his hands, their lovemaking will be rich and rewarding. The relationship part is highly dependent upon Gemini's success in the business world. Libra wants a luxurious environment and a comfortable lifestyle. It costs a fair amount to live the way Libra enjoys.

Gemini with Scorpio

THE TWINS AND THE SCORPION: *Rarely the Twain Shall Meet*

Variety including the use of external stimulation, X-rated videos, and sex toys triggers Gemini's sexuality as well as Scorpio's. But primarily, Gemini is turned on by words while Scorpio is excited by emotion and feeling close. For a while, what they have in common in other interests, from travel to the arts, ideas about education and politics, helps these two out. Ultimately, the differences put a strain on the relationship. Jealous Scorpio plus flirtatious Gemini equals potential disaster.

They do virtually everything differently. Scorpio always takes the same street to get to a given, familiar destination. Gemini will find three alternate routes. When they get into the car, Scorpio expects Gemini to turn right but Gemini turns left. This sounds like a minor thing, but cumulatively it's annoying, and in bed it turns Scorpio off. Scorpio wants a certain kind of foreplay. Gemini does something else. The result is less than a rip-roaring "O."

While Gemini does myriad things at once, Scorpio moves inexorably toward one objective. Scorpio grows impatient as Gemini seems to leave everything dangling. Gemini just doesn't understand why Scorpio can't be more flexible. In addition, these two do not communicate well. When

Scorpio speaks, Gemini's attention may be elsewhere and he/she doesn't hear Scorpio. When triggered emotionally, Gemini uses words hurtfully. Scorpio never forgets and the words leave scars.

A long-distance relationship can work well for these two. They'd have time apart to devote to their separate interests. When together, Gemini would devote the attention, sexually and otherwise, that Scorpio requires.

GEMINI WOMAN AND SCORPIO MAN

This match is a potential death wish. Ms. Gemini flirts with all men, making Scorpio mad with jealousy. Sometimes his fury can turn to passion, and then when they're alone together, his pent-up emotion is released in torrid sex. Gemini knows scores of ways to excite Scorpio. She might meet him at the airport and slip a pair of her thong undies into his hand. Over time, their interests vary widely. They go separate ways and her sex drive wanes. His doesn't. The relationship is undermined. A substantial age difference between them would help, but under no circumstances is this an easy match.

GEMINI MAN AND SCORPIO WOMAN

He looks at his Scorpio woman, aware of her sexual magnetism, and believes that all other men want her. She's aware of his regard, loves it, and this, along with his intellectual curiosity and competence in so many areas, helps compensate for the disparity in their sexual drives. Scorpio's into passionate kissing and sexual abandon. His lovemaking is somewhat intellectual. He observes how she responds, whereas she wants to meld into his feelings. This couple is more likely to succeed if they come together in their late thirties or beyond or if there's an age difference of seven years or more.

Gemini with Sagittarius

THE TWINS AND THE ARCHER: *Opposites Attract and Repel*

Gemini and Sagittarius are opposite signs, which is both stimulating and difficult. The relationship is a struggle, rather like climbing a mountain, but that's a turn-on for Gemini. Unfortunately, their differences in temperament—Gemini has something of a detached quality, while Sagittarius displays more fiery passion—result in terrible sexual timing. When Gemini wants to take time, Sagittarius wants a quickie. And yet, they have many similarities in likes and dislikes. Both are sexually experimental, open to role-playing, bondage, and incorporating food with sex.

Neither Sign is possessive. Sagittarius is the laissez-faire sign of the zodiac. "I won't tell you what to do, don't tell me what to do." Gemini, too, has a restless need to be unfettered. But, in too many ways, these signs bring out the worst in each other. Sagittarius loves a good debate, even something of a verbal fight. Gemini finds this nerve-wracking. Sagittarius can cut loose with stinging barbs and is an inveterate tease. Gemini hates being teased and may retaliate with cruel words. They both have long memories and these exchanges build up resentment over time.

Gemini needs a variety of life experiences before settling down into one direction or with one life partner. Sagittarius struggles to find a balance between freedom and responsibility. Gemini is not ready for a committed relationship until the age of at least 29. Neither is Sagittarius, who is also known as the bachelor Sign of the zodiac. If these two take their time forming a committed relationship, there's more hope in the long term.

GEMINI WOMAN AND SAGITTARIUS MAN

Gemini woman and Sagittarius man share many interests—traveling, poetry, and types of music and film. Both want an active sex life, but Sagittarius must make an effort to get Gemini's full attention, voicing appreciation of her efforts to please him. Gemini must compliment Sagittarius on his endowment. If Sagittarius fails to attend to Gemini, she'll try making him jealous, but he might not even notice. She's a capable cook and loves her garden, but she's the nervous type who is constantly on the move. Conversely, he wants to relax in his home. Sagittarius needs quiet time and Gemini must allow him this meditation. This is not an easy partnering, but a relationship is possible.

GEMINI MAN AND SAGITTARIUS WOMAN

What works for these two is Sagittarius' independence. Gemini is into everything and needs time and space to pursue his own endeavors. Sagittarius doesn't crowd him and isn't demanding, but he best not mistake this for permission to ignore her. She'll shoot him dead with one of her proverbial arrows. She makes her expectations clear, and if they aren't met she'll become remote and sarcastic. Far from spurring him to greater success, this simply drives him away. In bed she wants more passionate kissing, more forceful sex than is the Gemini approach. This twosome requires ongoing effort to last in the long run.

Gemini with Capricorn

THE TWINS AND THE GOAT: *Success behind Closed Doors*

This combination is surprisingly successful. Air Signs like Gemini and Earth Signs like Capricorn usually stifle each other, but these two create balance. Why does it work? Because Gemini needs to be grounded and Capricorn is very pragmatic. Geminis are quite scattered in many aspects of life and have a tendency to move from one thing to another without going far enough toward the heart of any matter. Capricorns start on a path and are relentless in achieving their ambitions. Conversely, Capricorns can be too rooted to one spot. Gemini's multifaceted nature opens Capricorn to variety and to experiencing more of life. Gemini's youthful attitude helps lighten up Capricorn.

Gemini may not be materialistic, but he/she does like the opportunities that money allows. Hardworking Capricorn is generally quite successful. Perhaps he/she will contribute more to this couple's budget. In return, Gemini's ongoing interest in learning new things and willingness to try new things will keep Capricorn satisfied in and out of the bedroom.

A good many Capricorns are experimental sexually, keeping sex interesting for Gemini. With Gemini's tendency to be at once observer and participant, the added stimulus of behaviors such as bondage, dominance and submission, and using sex toys keeps this Sign focused. With the more mainstream Capricorn, Gemini is the one who brings experimentation into their sex life.

This couple faces two problems. First, Gemini is flirtatious and Capricorn has enormous pride. If Gemini is too friendly in the wrong circumstances, Capricorn will be mortified. Second, conservative Capricorn's need for order can be inhibiting to Gemini.

GEMINI WOMAN AND CAPRICORN MAN

Capricorn appreciates Gemini's vitality. He provides well for her, which is a decided turn-on for Gemini and leads to great sexual encounters. At virtually any gathering, this couple attracts attention: he is dignified and she exudes friendly flirtatiousness. She has wonderful social graces.

In bed, her playfulness, desire for variety, and interest in sex toys and pornography match the nature of the experimental Capricorn, and expand the horizons of the more mainstream Goat. If there is any problem it may come from the tendency of Capricorn to be too controlling. Ms. Gemini needs to feel free to pursue her own range of activities.

GEMINI MAN AND CAPRICORN WOMAN

He loves her stately appearance and appreciates her efforts to help him get ahead. Gemini's success is important to Capricorn because she has great pride, cares about appearances, and expects to live in a nice neighborhood and in a well-cared-for home surrounded by neatly trimmed hedges. Even if between them their income is substantial, she would prefer that her partner bring home the bigger slabs of bacon. Simply, harmony in their bedroom depends on Gemini's success in the boardroom. In that bedroom, a stock of sex toys, erotica, and pornography results in out-of-the-ordinary, memorable sex encounters.

Gemini with Aquarius
THE TWINS AND THE WATER BEARER: *If Not Lovers, Always Friends*

Gemini charm meets Aquarian friendliness. These two Air Signs have a wonderful ability to communicate endlessly. Most people talk primarily about themselves. These two are curious about the world at large, certainly about their community, and perhaps especially about their neighbors. They make great friends as well as successful business partners. All that's needed is somebody to be practical enough to take care of the nitty-gritty details. Easier said than done.

Aquarius is wonderful at brainstorming and bringing up streams of exciting ideas, but not at turning these into realities. Gemini may be overwhelmed by the vastness of the Aquarian's concepts, and is apt to rule out ways of implementing them as fast as Aquarius contrives them.

Aquarius is most at ease in a crowd and knows everyone casually. Gemini may feel slighted because the Water Bearer is so busy with all these other people. "You don't pay enough attention to me. You are too busy with your friends" may be the complaint.

There is a fundamental coolness in the nature of both Aquarius and Gemini. In love relationships, each longs for intimacy and yet is uncomfortable with it. Their sex life can be rich and varied as they compensate for this inherent lack of passion with wide ranging searches for sensation. Sound is always a stimulus. For Gemini, this may be music. For both Signs, it includes dirty talk, watching erotic movies, and occasionally exploring pornography. This can be a lifelong, comfortable and successful, if not overly passionate, relationship.

GEMINI WOMAN AND AQUARIUS MAN

He is always charming, even-tempered, and easy to talk to. Aquarius doesn't flirt or make Gemini feel insecure. He doesn't cross that boundary with her friends. He provides for her well and is successful in business because he's stable, loyal, and well respected. In the bedroom, he loves to look at her and admire her beauty. He loves to watch the way she becomes excited. They both enjoy making love with the lights on: "the better to see you with." Experimental lovers, they may enjoy bondage, dominance and submission, playing with a wide range of sex toys, and incorporating food.

GEMINI MAN AND AQUARIUS WOMAN

It's your brain, Mr. Gemini, not your physique that turns on Aquarius. It's the last book you read, the plans you've hatched, the ideas you express that get her juicy. Once in bed with her, she wants sex to be intense and not too lengthy. In other words, foreplay begins over dinner and continues with conversation on the ride home. A stream of words continues, leading all the way into the bedroom and throughout the shedding of clothes, Once ready to begin, you're going to get right to the heart of the matter. This relationship is comfortable and affectionate.

Gemini with Pisces

THE TWINS AND THE FISH: *For the Drama, an Audience*

The differences between these Signs are significant. Pisces is turned on by the sense of touch, passionate kissing, intense hugging, and fondling. Gemini's approach is as much intellectual as sensory. Gemini is observing as well as feeling, whereas Pisces is carried away by emotion. Pisces has extraordinary endurance in the bedroom. Gemini enjoys lingering over sex only some of the time.

And yet, there are strong connections. Pisces is a dual-natured Sign like Gemini, sometimes vibrant and dynamic, and other times moody and self-pitying. Oddly enough, this makes them quite compatible. One problem is that Gemini can become negative. Should that coincide with a self-pitying period for Pisces, the air will be heavy with thunderclouds; however, all in all this relationship is a fun thing.

The flexibility of both Signs helps this partnership flourish. From eating Indian food to Mexican cuisine, vegetarian to a pig roast, both Signs are willing to dip in. In the bedroom, Gemini wants to fool around with various toys. Pisces says, "The more the merrier." Pisces wants to approach sex as if it were a drama with Pisces as the leading victim. Gemini says, "Sure, why not. I'll play."

If they enjoy making a game of sex, with one responsible for setting the stage on Monday, the other responsible for Thursday, all goes well. If Gemini falls into sexual routine, resisting romance, Pisces will turn off. Conversely, now and then, Pisces must allow Gemini a quickie without any particular buildup so that Gemini can release some nervous tension.

GEMINI WOMAN AND PISCES MAN

Gemini's duality and Pisces multifaceted nature keep each other involved. He defines what he wants sexually, from kisses to costumes to positions to toys. Her willingness to accept a role in his fantasy plays out well in the bedroom. Outside the bedroom, for Pisces to satisfy Gemini he needs to become more decisive than the Pisces male often is. She does not want the burden of total responsibility for the relationship. Pisces has a curious, indirect way of getting what he wants. Gemini expects a more forthright, assertive behavior. If she perceives his subtlety as weakness, she will be turned off.

GEMINI MAN AND PISCES WOMAN

Gemini's curiosity and interest in learning new things intrigues Pisces. Her femininity reinforces his masculinity and she makes quite an effort to turn him on. With lacey negligees and silky teddies, satin sheets, candlelight, and a whiff of perfume, Pisces sets the stage for an ideal night of sex. He has a romantic streak and enjoys a sensual setting, and all these romantic trappings enhance the sexual experience for him. Sometimes he might prefer pornography to lace and frills. This fits for her as she has a fantasy about being kidnapped by a dashing pirate. Bondage and some dominance and submission will suit her fine.

Cancer with Cancer

TWO CRABS: *Two Close for Comfort*

Cancers are highly emotional people. When the lights are out the sex is terrific, but the relationship is far from paradise. Two of the same Signs together represent a doubling up of all that Sign's inherent qualities, the bad along with the good. On the positive side, both are highly sexual and enjoy the same amount, duration, and types of sexual behaviors. They have similar timing and strive to satisfy each other.

Beyond the bedroom, they share common interests, caring most about family, home, and food. They love to shop for antiques, are great bargain hunters, and are generally frugal and quite good with money. Money is important to Cancers, and the Crab is usually quite successful. Being an intuitive Water Sign and having a warm personality sets them up to be well liked on the job and to maintain close relationships with their bosses and co-workers. So the sex can be great and money shouldn't be an issue, but still this is not likely to be a happy couple.

Problems surface over matters of control and dominance. Cancer is a controlling Sign, and will resent a partner who tries to run the show. Cancer also needs to feel loved and the power struggle with another Cancer is likely to undermine any loving feelings. In addition, Cancer has a suspicious streak, which only plays into the tendency to dominate. As both have the same instincts, the result is lack of trust and at the very least, a difficult relationship to maintain.

Summary

Two Cancerians in lust have a fine time of it. Two Cancerians in love have to beware the tendency to be controlling and must plan on always working at this relationship to keep it healthy. As friends it's a cinch. They share a love for gardening and cooking as well as entertaining friends in their homes. If a love relationship is to survive, she must remember that he needs to be told he's loved as much as she needs to hear it. He must not badger her about where she's been, with whom, and how much she spent. He must trust her.

Cancer with Leo

THE CRAB AND THE LION: *Pleasant Potential*

This combination has plenty of potential, though it also has pitfalls. On the positive side, the sex is great. Leo strives to please Cancer with gifted hands and mouth. The vitality of Fire Sign Leo excites Cancer. Cancer relies on sensitivity and intuition to know what a lover wants and needs. In addition, the loving Water Sign nature of Cancer provides a balance for the Lion's occasionally hyper energy.

Problems crop up when one Sign tries to dominate the other. Leo gives off an aura of competence and willingness to handle considerable responsibility. People always ask Leo to run the show. Since Cancer has a decidedly domineering streak, the Crab won't allow Leo to play king of the jungle, at least not all of the time. Cancer is strong and capable, and doesn't want or need to be ruled. A steady, loving partner is more to the Crab's liking. Also, Leo can be arrogant, which upsets Cancer, and Cancer can be moody, which Leo finds annoying.

Cancer wants attention, in the relationship and out among friends and family, but seldom has the personal magnetism Leo is known for. Just think of their symbols:, the noble Lion versus the side-stepping Crab. Cancer is very nice and charming in a quiet way, but Leo shines in public. Cancer may resent the attention heaped on Leo. The Lion needs to compensate by showering affection on the Crab at home and being mindful of the amount of oxygen he/she takes up when out in a group.

CANCER WOMAN AND LEO MAN

Cancer wants to take over but Leo is the king. No problem. Leo is in control outside the white picket fence surrounding her dream house. Inside, he must acknowledge that the home is her domain. Sex can be great fun if they use their power struggle to their advantage. One night, Leo can be the master and Cancer his slave. After all, Leo is a sucker for a damsel in distress. He loves a woman to be soft and sensual, but also strong and purposeful in life. Ms. Cancer is every bit of that and she'll prove it when it's her turn to play mistress.

CANCER MAN AND LEO WOMAN

If Cancer holds true to his Sign, he'll be successful in business and able to provide for Leo in the luxurious lifestyle that she wishes to enjoy. Leo's competence, vitality, and loyalty provide Cancer the comfort and love he desires. Ms. Leo, wanting to be adored, is thrilled with Cancer's attention to her body. Her responsiveness makes him feel all the more like a wonderful lover. Out in public, like a peacock, Leo displays herself and commands attention when entering a room. Cancer needs to beware of letting jealousy take over or she'll respond with all the power of an outraged Lioness.

Cancer with Virgo

THE VIRGIN AND THE CRAB: *Don't Worry, Be Happy*

A fine combination. Water Sign Cancer operates from the intuitive, emotional center while Earth Sign Virgo is more pragmatic and logical. Virgo is attentive to detail, a perfectionist, and since Cancer is something of a worrier, this behavior is actually comforting. Both are very social, but Cancer has a remarkable capacity to draw people close. In a brief conversation Cancer can learn all about another's childhood, current lover, and career. Virgo can spend weeks conversing with people without finding out half of this information.

Virgo can be fussy and hypercritical, and tends to go on and on about a situation. Cancer enjoys listening. When Virgo is hard on himself/herself Cancer is nurturing and accepting. Cancers can be moody and over-emotional, but Virgo takes this in stride. When they have disagreements, they avoid confrontation. Though not overly significant, there are a few areas of conflict. Virgo has a sarcastic streak and Cancer is easily wounded. Cancer can be too dependent or clingy. Virgo is a strong partner but doesn't want to shoulder all responsibilities.

Both enjoy having sex at least three to four times weekly, and they like sex to be fairly lengthy. Variety isn't necessary, but an experimental range of activities suits both well. They enjoy erotica, some pornography, and using sex toys such as vibrators and dildos, either store-bought or hand-carved or from the produce department at the supermarket. Virgo is all about sensual touch, and Cancer represents emotional expressiveness. Their mix of personality traits and behaviors makes for great sex and a solid, loving relationship.

CANCER WOMAN AND VIRGO MAN

This partnership is as good as it gets. Cancer loves to nurture, cook, tend to the home and family, and is more than happy to assume responsibility for the whole traditional feminine sphere. Her Virgo mate dominates in the business world. In the bedroom, this is equally successful. While Virgo might be matter-of-fact in his sexuality, Cancer encourages him to be more expressive. Virgo has the most wonderful capacity with his hands. Cancer loves deep kissing and is both sensitive and emotive. For the Virgo open to exploring a wider range of sexuality, Cancer is a willing partner.

CANCER MAN AND VIRGO WOMAN

Cancer loves his home, family, and good food. Virgo keeps that house impeccably neat and cooks a luscious meal. She's pleasant and well mannered, if not overly warm. In the relationship Cancer tends to be rather domineering, but Virgo is quite comfortable in the supportive role. There are few problems in the bedroom as both of them enjoy frequent sex, but routine may dominate over passion. Cancer, likely to be the more experimental partner, can spice things up by suggesting variety. The more open Virgo will be very receptive. The mainstream Virgin will at least give some new behaviors a try.

Cancer with Libra

THE CRAB AND THE SCALES: *Out of Balance*

One might think that Cancer, Sign of home and family, would be comfortably matched with Libra, Sign of marriage and partnership. But, Air Sign Libra, wanting to avoid conflict and sometimes striving for peace at any price, may come across to sensitive Cancer as emotionally detached. Conversely, Libra may find Water Sign Cancer overly emotional and moody. Yet, when they first meet, Cancer notices Libra's easy elegance and Libra is drawn to Cancer's warmth and accessibility.

Libra gets turned on by praise and Cancer is expressive: "I love your body. I love to touch your skin." Cancer wants action, to be kissed and caressed, and Libra is an attentive lover. So far so good; however, Libra cannot be pushed and spends a long time making decisions. Cancer can be domineering and is given to worry, a quality often triggered by Libra's seeming indecisiveness.

In the bedroom, Libra enjoys a sensual environment with satin sheets, a hint of incense, and a well-placed mirror. Cancer, much earthier in nature and less concerned with the setting, enjoys having sex in the woods, near water, and when at home, all that really matters is a modicum of cleanliness. Sex for Libra begins with verbal stimulation, viewing erotica, or phone sex. That's always hot. Libra often likes anal sex, which is not appealing to Cancer. Cancer is generally content with oral sex and intercourse, and enjoys experimentation to add intensity. Overall, it isn't likely for the Scales to find balance or the Crab a happy home in this twosome.

CANCER WOMAN AND LIBRA MAN

On the positive side, Libra's gentleness and calm demeanor is soothing to emotional Cancer, while Cancer's nurturing, supportive personality makes Libra feels loved and protected. On the negative side, she gets anxious. He is laid back and says, "Don't worry." She feels patronized. Sexually, Libra gets turned on by words, mood music, and soft lighting. With Cancer it's food, a touch, and a sense of emotional closeness. He wants romantic sex. She wants fervor. She may assume too much responsibility for their sex life and, in time, resent him for not reaching out to her. The sex may be good but this relationship is tough.

CANCER MAN AND LIBRA WOMAN

The Libra woman likes sex slow, passionate, and romantic. The Cancer man prefers it urgent and a bit rough. She wants the comfort of her boudoir. He loves the variety of sex in nature or on the kitchen table. She wants to be treated as an object of luxury. In fact, each wants to be indulged by the other and if they both extend themselves, this match has a chance, though they have a hard road ahead of them. A kind word, an occasional flower, or an evening out will go far to keep gentle, loving Libra content. In return, Cancer is happy with a home-cooked meal and an aura of love.

Cancer with Scorpio

THE CRAB AND THE SCORPION: *Love Bites*

Two intuitive Water Signs make one great pair. They talk easily about everything, operate from of their emotions, and are sensitive, caring partners. When Cancer is distressed, maybe Scorpio doesn't prod as much as Cancer would like, but Cancer knows that Scorpio is reliable.

Cancer is a perplexing Sign, remarkably strong in terms of its nurturing, loving qualities, but also prone to worry. Scorpio's strength is comforting. Scorpio may feel deeply distressed about a problem, but doesn't worry. Instead, Scorpio focuses on finding solutions. Scorpio has quiet periods and believes that he/she can work problems out alone. In fact, Scorpio resolves matters far better by bouncing them off someone else. Cancer knows this and patiently strives to draw out Scorpio. Scorpio relishes Cancer's doting nature. When Scorpio gets a cold, Cancer makes chicken soup.

Their lovemaking is passionate and so charged with feeling that they experience a sense of oneness. The act becomes truly spiritual. Certain sex toys are appealing to secretive Scorpio, namely blindfolds, and Cancer likes to experiment with food. Differences in pace will need accommodating, as Cancer wants sex to last longer than Scorpio. There are also Scorpios for whom rough sex and crude talk are part of the sexual experience. This may be a turnoff for Cancer.

The only potential relationship problem in this match is that Cancer has a domineering personality, and nobody is going to be in charge of Scorpio . . . at least not for long. Otherwise, this couple has the compatibility to be tremendously successful in the long term.

CANCER WOMAN AND SCORPIO MAN

The Scorpio man assumes the responsibilities of supporting the family in a relationship. Conversely, the Cancer woman makes their house a home and is happily the doting wife and mother. In sex, she wants tenderness and lots of foreplay. He wants to please his lover, and delays his own gratification until she's thoroughly satisfied. They tend to like the same range of sex acts and both are willing to experiment with different behaviors. Bondage will be fun, as will a light spanking. There may be times when Cancer's moodiness pushes Scorpio into deeper silences, which only provokes Cancer's insecurities and a tendency toward jealousy. Aside from that, the relationship is easy.

CANCER MAN AND SCORPIO WOMAN

He's sensitive and in touch with his feelings. She's charmed by his romantic, caring ways. Her intensity reinforces his. The kissing is passionate, their timing is almost always in sync, and they frequently achieve orgasm simultaneously. But lust doesn't conquer all. For the Cancer man, the center of life is home and family. While that's also central to the Scorpio woman, she also needs fulfillment in her own right. When Cancer treats Scorpio with trust, and supports her need for independence, she remains a loving and committed partner. As long as Scorpio gives Cancer the attention he wants, he'll be comfortable while she's off doing her own thing.

Cancer with Sagittarius

THE CRAB AND THE ARCHER: *Tough Going, but Possible*

Cancer's motto is "Home sweet home." Sagittarius says, "Don't fence me in." Cancer's symbol, the Crab, is a creature that moves sideways, a creature that is cautious and stays inside its own home. Sagittarius is the Archer, whose arrow flies straight to its mark. In other words, Cancer has a sensitive, self-protective nature while Sagittarius is at times reckless and always direct—to the point of bluntness. Without intending to hurt, Sagittarius' words leave their mark and Cancer, with a remarkable memory, will bear the scars forever.

The beginning of this relationship is fun. Cancer is excited by Sagittarius' broad and expansive ideas. Sagittarius is turned on by Cancer's warmth and attentiveness. They have a great time together in public. Where Cancer is a bit reticent, Sagittarius is self-assured. Both are passionate and intense lovers and highly oral and both will strive to impress the other.

They can be great friends, and in business these two could balance each other very well. Cancer would hold down the home base, and Sagittarius would be out in the field dealing with the public. A personal relationship is more difficult to sustain, however.

Sagittarius has an aura of cool detachment or aloofness, which can trigger Cancer's insecurity and resentment. Cancer will try, in all ways possible, to entice the Archer to stay within their home territory. In this union, neither will be long satisfied. Even though the sex may be terrific, these signs are opposites in goals and temperaments, and their fundamental differences make sustaining a long-term relationship very tough.

CANCER WOMAN AND SAGITTARIUS MAN

Mr. Sagittarius is the bachelor of the zodiac. Ms. Cancer, the mother figure, wants commitment. She pushes. He resists, yet she charms him and really turns him on. His skill in bed satisfies the highly sexual Crab. He wants to be the aggressor though often Cancer tries to take over. He needs freedom and can be distant. She wants security and may be cloying. He wants to daydream. She wants to talk. All of this is difficult, but Sagittarius enjoys how Cancer is loving, loyal, attentive, and a pleasure to be with in public. They enjoy doing many things together and the sex is good.

CANCER MAN AND SAGITTARIUS WOMAN

The Cancer man wants the all-American ideal: house with white picket fence, two kids, a dog and a cat, and a wife who stays within that fence tending to the home and family. While the Sagittarius woman may fulfill this dream, she will not be stifled. He must do well. She needs to feel proud of her partner. He must stay in good shape physically and maintain his sense of humor. If he disagrees with her, he'd better be prepared for a long, well-thought-out argument. She knows her mind and is no pushover. Sex is the easy part. He likes a lot of it and her libido matches his.

Cancer with Capricorn

THE CRAB AND THE GOAT: *Opposites Attract and Repel*

As a business combination, the balance of Cancerian intuition and Capricorn practicality is fine. A long-term romantic relationship is more difficult. Cancerian mottoes include, "Home is where the heart is, "A man's home is his castle," and "The way to a man's heart is through his stomach." Capricorn thinks, "Don't hang your dirty linen in public," "Keep your cards close to your chest," and "What will the neighbors think?"

If this couple had only enough money to paint either the interior or the exterior of their house, Cancer would paint the inside and Capricorn would paint the outside. For Capricorn the well-kept house projects an image of success. For Cancer, an inviting atmosphere, the smells of cinnamon and coffee, and the welcome mat at the front door are far more important.

Cancer is sensitive, intuitive, and perhaps the most emotional of all the Signs. Capricorn is pragmatic, matter-of-fact, takes a logical approach, and tends to be reserved. Both can be controlling, and neither takes that well from another. Cancer would respond with moodiness and Capricorn with manipulation.

Sex for these two starts out great. Working to keep the physical relationship healthy will go far to help this couple stay together. Their sex life begins with lots of intensity, both like it to last 30 to 60 minutes, and they enjoy the same range of behaviors. Over time, however, even in their sex life, Cancer will find Capricorn distant and Capricorn will find Cancer too emotional.

CANCER WOMAN AND CAPRICORN MAN

The Cancer woman/Capricorn man union is characterized first by a strong sexual attraction and, for a while, steamy sex. In time, however, Capricorn's rather staid presentation proves disappointing to Cancer. In addition, their approach to everyday life is uncomfortably different. The dishwasher leaks all over the floor, the kids have turned the kitchen into a makeshift waterslide, and Cancer is distraught. Capricorn doesn't understand all of her emotion. His response to such crises is, "We'll fix it." Cancer finds this response cold. She needs comforting, and a hug would go far with her. In addition, Capricorn is a workaholic and may have less time for family than Cancer desires.

CANCER MAN AND CAPRICORN WOMAN

The Capricorn woman is a loyal mate who'll help her Cancer man succeed in the business world. She will always look appropriate, never seek center stage, and quietly prepare a comfortable environment. His success is very important to her. She may not be seeking diamonds and yachts, but a decent house in a good neighborhood is essential. In the bedroom, Capricorn doesn't like to hurry. She'll thrill Cancer, slow and easy in a teasing manner, until his heart's pounding. And she's every bit as oral as he is. The success of this relationship ultimately depends on Cancer doing well in the business world.

Cancer with Aquarius
THE CRAB AND THE WATER BEARER: *If Not Passion, Then Contentment*

Most often when a Water Sign like Cancer connects with an Air Sign like Aquarius, you get steam . . . a whole lot of instant reaction that dissipates rapidly into nothingness. Surprise! This Water and Air couple has the potential to be a far better combination than expected, though it won't be easy.

The best part for Aquarius is that Cancer provides warmth, open affection, and commitment, qualities that comfort Aquarius, who is well mannered, diplomatic, and friendly— though emotionally detached. For Cancer, it's the brilliance of the Aquarian mind, the social aspect with people around all the time, and the amount of variety Aquarius always has that are so appealing. While Cancer might normally be content within the confines of that single-family house surrounded by the white picket fence, Aquarius broadens the perspective.

Sex is an area of potential difficulty for this couple. Cancer may be willing to experiment with some sex toys, a few costumes, and some food in the sex play, but not much more than that. Cancer's approach to sex is all about getting deep into the feelings of intimacy and passion. Aquarius, seeking sensation, wants to probe deeper into fetishes. This is not necessarily a comfortable foray for Cancer. Aquarius is more about observing, experimenting, and exploring new territory. "Try that toy and see how it feels." Cancer may be dissatisfied, and Aquarius does not comprehend what's missing. All in all, if Cancer and Aquarius strive to overcome the problems in the bedroom, they can sustain a contented and respectful, albeit not overly passionate, relationship.

CANCER WOMAN AND AQUARIUS MAN

The Aquarius man swaggers into a room with his hands in his pockets: relaxed, charming, and at ease in the crowd. But his hands are in his pockets for a reason. He's just not a touchy-feely kind of guy. His Cancer woman is arm candy, charming, so attentive to him. She wants to hold on; he wants freedom to roam the crowd. As intrigued as she is with him, if he doesn't pay more attention to her, she'll soon be out looking for a new lover. In the bedroom, Aquarius loves to look at naked Cancer and to talk about sex, but his performance falls short. She had better climax before he does or she won't at all.

CANCER MAN AND AQUARIUS WOMAN

The Cancer man provides for Aquarius well and will continually be turned on by her beauty and social skills. In public, he finds her fascinating, though her flirtatiousness may trigger his possessiveness. At home, he finds her detached. The center of Cancer's life is his own private acre, but Aquarius cares about the world as a whole. She won't understand his complaints because she sees herself as an appropriate wife: loyal, ready for sex most anytime, friendly, and even-tempered. She needs her freedom. She appreciates the love Cancer shows her, but she won't be happy in a gilded cage. For this couple, quality time together works better than quantity time.

Cancer *with* Pisces

THE CRAB AND THE FISH: *True Love That Lasts Forever*

Frequently, when two Water Signs get together all you get is drenched. Where's the substance of Earth, the vitality of Fire, the stimulus of Air? With Cancer and Pisces, though, no such problem exists. Instead, they make for a playground romance. Their affection and shared emotions create the typical, "falling in love, living in the little house in the woods happily ever after" fairytale relationship.

Cancer wants the all-American dream lifestyle: a house with white picket fence, two kids, a cat, and a dog. Pisces shares that dream, and extends it out from their private half acre into the community. They make a loving couple, have a very gratifying sex life, and most of the time are very in sync with each other.

Okay, there can be problems. Sometimes Cancer may be crabby and moody, and Pisces has occasional bouts of self-pity. If there should be an argument, Pisces will seem to yield and Cancer believes they've come to an agreement. All too often, however, Pisces has just stopped arguing and may go right on doing whatever he/she wants. Simply put, Pisces can't be pushed—cajoled perhaps, but not pushed. Cancer should know that fighting with Pisces is like punching a rubber wall. Walk away and the wall just resumes its previous condition.

These two are so well suited, however, that they work through tough and demanding periods. This is truly the couple that can look forward to celebrating their golden anniversary, still as much in love as they were in their teens.

CANCER WOMAN AND PISCES MAN

The sex is good, passionate, frequent, and mutually gratifying for this couple. They have such similar likes and dislikes, and neither needs much instruction on how to please the other. The Pisces man may be more interested in variety and role-playing than the Cancer woman, who is usually amenable to experiment—just not too much or too often. The only real problem for these two is that she's more ambitious than he. Cancer wants nice things and, given her desire for him to succeed, is very apt to nag. Pisces may become annoyed at this and say, Pisces style, "Yes, dear," and then blithely go on his way.

CANCER MAN AND PISCES WOMAN

This is a fine match in the bedroom, in the living room, and even in the woods. The Cancer man and Pisces woman share the same values regarding home and family. Both are loving, not particularly aggressive, and unlikely to become involved in long-lasting arguments. Cancer is the more assertive of the two Signs, good for business. He's complimentary, which bolsters Ms. Pisces' ego, and he's sympathetic when she's having a bad day. They are equally sensitive and remarkably tuned in to the other's sexual needs. Pisces will create a sensual environment and Cancer thinks to bring flowers now and then for no special reason.

Leo with Leo

TWO LIONS TOGETHER: *Fire, Fire Burning Bright*

Fire Sign Leo is open, direct, personable, and easy to get along with—if one remembers that Leo is always right. Really, Leo is right most of the time. But when Leo is wrong, the Lion still prefers the other person to apologize. Put two Leos together and there will be occasions when both are right, but have different opinions. In the big picture, this is a tough relationship to sustain, but the benefits are worth the effort.

Leo is a performer, needs an audience, and, when given attention and praise, reciprocates with generosity. In public, each enjoys holding court, which might lead to competition, but more often than not, generosity of spirit prevails. This Sign is also extravagant, but fortunate, so money need not be a problem.

Leo is such a competent Sign that others frequently ask them to assume responsibilities at work and in the community. Leo has a hard time saying no, and with so many activities outside the home, may have less than adequate energy to attend to a partner, which won't suit Leo #2 at all well.

Leo/Leo sex is great, and ranges from mainstream to experimental that includes bondage, dominance and submission, and having sex in public places. They like it often and approach the act with intensity. It's a mark of pride to please the partner. They share similar interests and are active people who enjoy being out with friends, traveling, and attending concerts and movies. Overall, their life together can be passionate, rewarding, and fun.

Summary

Sometimes the Lioness is a bit too demanding of her audience and can be tedious. Sometimes the Lion is a tad egotistical. Both are somewhat sloppy, as if their "den" wasn't important. They enjoy sex more, however, if the bedroom is made inviting with gentle aromas, candles, and dim lights. Sex is hot and heavy. They take their time, want sex almost every day, and often prefer a couple of rounds. It's usually the female Leo who takes over in bed, consuming her mate and proving that at least in this realm, this king isn't her master—he's a puppet.

Leo with Virgo

THE LION AND THE VIRGIN: *An Odd Couple*

Leo is sort of sloppy and Virgo can be too neat. Long term they aggravate one another. Virgo is always picking on Leo for things that Leo finds inconsequential. Leo says, "So what?" Put these two between the sheets, however, and it's quite fine. Leo, the actor, enjoys Virgo, the director, saying "a little to the left, a little to the right."

Their differences are many. Leo has an optimistic attitude in life: "I'm an open book; you can know everything about me because I'm wonderful." The Lion is dynamic, extravagant, and a risk taker. Virgo is cautious and does not volunteer much personal information until feeling quite secure in a relationship. Virgo is a discriminating, hard working, and dependable friend.

Sexually, Leo is intense and passionate. The Lion begins the sexual experience like a burst of flame, may want to have an orgasm and then start all over more slowly the second time around. Virgo likes longer, slower, more protracted foreplay, and many enjoy far greater experimentation than is true of Leo.

Leo needs to be adored. A sexual turn-on for Leo is being praised during foreplay and sex. Virgo is short on compliments. Leo wants to be trusted, not questioned, by his/or partner and Virgo questions everything. Virgo wants appreciation for the hard work and effort that he/she puts into the relationship, but Leo doesn't see why a relationship should be so much work. Over the years, the contrast between these two personalities makes this combo difficult to sustain in any meaningful and fulfilling way.

LEO WOMAN AND VIRGO MAN

His posture is so erect that he looks totally sure of himself, but Mr. Virgo doesn't put himself forward unless he is confident of his surroundings and circumstances. Ms. Leo makes an entrance wherever she goes, as if there were a spotlight shining on her. Virgo is turned on by her exuberant self-confidence. In bed, he wants to explore every curve of her catlike body. The fiery Leo woman wants to get right to the heart of the matter. Over the years, Leo's sex drive proves to be far greater than Virgo's. In addition, if Virgo doesn't compliment her enough, someone else will.

LEO MAN AND VIRGO WOMAN

Virgo's busy hands match Leo's passion. Where Leo might rush to orgasm, Virgo slows him down. Her hands linger lovingly over parts of his body; he never knew they could produce such exquisite sensations. Leo is happy taking directions in bed because the result is Virgo's thorough satisfaction, proving Leo's prowess. Outside the bedroom, Leo is the natural leader, king of the jungle and, in most regards, this suits Virgo well. Problems arise, however, when Leo's extravagance triggers Virgo's insecurity. Then she's apt to become critical and nagging, which Leo finds annoying. In a long-term relationship, this pairing is not ideal.

Leo with Libra

THE LION AND THE SCALES: *Cozy Balance*

Fire Signs like Leo and Air Signs like Libra are generally a harmonious match. Libra loves Leo's exuberance and Leo is turned on by Libra's style and gentle disposition. Libra wants a steadfast, independent partner. Cuddling is great. Cloying is not. Libra wants to be free to roam around, to be admired, and to flirt. Leo is okay with this, as long as it is obviously just playful; the Lion has a jealous streak. But Libra knows this and is attentive to her Lion.

Leo wants a loyal, devoted audience and he has that in Libra, who is delighted by Leo's sense of humor. They take pleasure in their well-tended house and yard, though they'd prefer to have someone else do the tending. They are both spontaneous and either might suggest, "Let's pack our bags and take off for the weekend." Neither is overly critical or demanding.

Sex is comfortable, whether it lasts an hour or five minutes, and sometimes passionate. It's always satisfying. Both like sex acts that range into the experimental: some role-playing, a bit of dominance and submission, and a little food play. The setting is more important to Libra, but Leo is willing to accommodate.

Money may be a problem in this relationhip. Leo is extravagant and Libra is the Sign of luxury. They want to live well. So, Leo's exuberance in buying the latest technology gizmo or plasma TV best be matched by his/her income, and Libra's acquisitive streak must also be balanced with matching funds or serious disagreements will arise.

LEO WOMAN AND LIBRA MAN

In bed, the Lioness loves to be teased. She'll try getting him inside her quickly. If Libra holds off and tantalizes her, she'll be ever more passionate. Leo loves oral sex and swallows Libra whole. Libra must honor his commitments. If she catches him in a lie, he's history. She's turned on by confidence. Libra needn't be the macho man—though that won't hurt—but Leo must know that she can rely on him. A pair of cowboy boots will go over well. She'll appreciate his kindness and return it with devotion. No one will ever dare criticize her Libra man to a Lioness.

LEO MAN AND LIBRA WOMAN

Leo is the knight in shining armor who loves to rescue the damsel in distress. He's passionate about all aspects of life, work, play, and sex. He expects devotion and to be treated like a king, and he'll reward his partner generously for her efforts. The Libra woman is tuned in to the Lion's needs, and most of the time she's willing to fill them. She will lose him in a short period of time if she gets tired of that role. It's easy for her to turn him on. She's like a plush poodle, and he's thrilled by her luxurious aura.

Leo with Scorpio
THE LION AND THE SCORPION: *An Uphill Battle*

The Leo/Scorpio pairing is difficult because both Signs are strong-headed and obstinate. Still, this relationship has a chance. Scorpio and Leo are Fixed Signs: they have profound respect for each other. Scorpio brings devotion to the relationship and Leo brings enthusiasm. Leo admires Scorpio's resourcefulness, while Scorpio finds Leo's natural leadership ability and charm highly appealing. Sexually, they're both very passionate and open to a fair range of sexual exploration, though Scorpio may be more experimental than Leo. Scorpio strives to satisfy Leo by staying attuned to him/her. Leo gets very carried away. Scorpio enjoys the excursion and is content to let Leo lead, at least in the bedroom.

Their differences, however, are vast. Leo is outgoing, direct, flamboyant, and self-assured to the point of being arrogant. Scorpio is guarded and reserved, and can't begin to match Leo's bottomless self-confidence. In fact, Scorpio envies it and strives to learn from it. Leo wants

Scorpio to take more chances and Scorpio wants Leo to calm down some. A strong sense of humor is an invaluable asset.

The biggest problem in the relationship from Leo's point of view is Scorpio's stubbornness. As Scorpio sees it, Leo is temperamental and demanding. Leo likes to be right. In fact, Leo is convinced that he/she is always right. Scorpio may adore Leo and be willing to concede most of the time, but not always. If, over time, Scorpio becomes more confrontational and less willing to say "Yes, Dear," Leo is liable to turn off and the sex life could die out.

LEO WOMAN AND SCORPIO MAN

Sex may be the best part of this twosome. Scorpio matches Leo's passion and sex is explosive initially. She loves the traditional macho male. Scorpio may give off an aura of great self-confidence but he has his areas of doubt. Leo is a powerhouse, a natural leader; and only content when she is adored. Scorpio doesn't want a leader for a partner, and while he admires his exuberant Leo, he isn't big on adoration. He can also be possessive and that never sits well with the Lioness. When angry, he broods and she rants. Scorpio's silences and Leo's extravagances work against these two.

LEO MAN AND SCORPIO WOMAN

Sexually, while the Scorpio woman has a large appetite and a willingness to experiment, she keeps this reality to herself. Leo is content with hot and heavy, fairly mainstream lovemaking. He's not overly attuned to her subtleties. This relationship would improve if Scorpio told Leo directly what turns her on. It's surprising that she is reticent about her sexual needs when she so often nags him in other areas, a trait that disturbs him no end. Leo's public exuberance makes Scorpio uncomfortable, as she is so concerned about doing the wrong thing and committing a social faux pas. Clearly, Leo and Scorpio are better friends than lovers.

Leo *with* Sagittarius
THE LION AND THE ARCHER: *Play Time*

The Leo/Sagittarius combination is playful and highly sexual. Two Fire Signs together can be explosive, as this element is known for wanting to dominate all relationships. Leo and Sagittarius are successful because Sagittarius is the least aggressive of the Fire Signs and is, in fact, pretty mellow.

In all aspects of life—sex included—Leo is energetic, vital, and enthusiastic. Even the most sophisticated, mature, and seemingly controlled Leo has a playful quality. Sagittarius is dazzled, charmed, and smitten by his/her partner. Sagittarius is the philosopher of the zodiac and has a remarkable ability to take a long view of life. Conversely, Leo is acquisitive, the quintessential consumer, and completely involved in the moment. Each finds the other's outlook intriguing. In the bedroom, Sagittarius wants to impress Leo with force and duration. Leo responds with fervor and intensity. Whether mainstream or more experimental in range of sexuality, each will find a willing partner in the other.

There are a couple of problems with this pairing. Sagittarius speaks his/her mind without thinking through the effect of those words. Leo is easily wounded. Also, Sagittarius resents Leo's "I'm always right" attitude. A problem area for Leo: Sagittarius is the gambler of the zodiac and not above cutting corners to achieve his/her ends. Though Leo may tell an occasional lie, to the extent that anybody will, this Sign is by nature honest and adamant about principles. In spite of these problems, the Lion and the Archer are fundamentally well suited and likely to share a happy, long-lasting relationship.

LEO WOMAN AND SAGITTARIUS MAN

The Leo woman is passionate and seeks to dominate in the bedroom—but secretly wants her partner to be the aggressor. Sagittarius is laid back and easygoing. He thoroughly enjoys the way Leo devours him. Big mistake. Sagittarius considers himself the all-American stud and has a reputation for being well endowed. To keep her happy, he has to assert himself. Both prefer mainstream sex, though they think of themselves as being experimental. A lot of kissing, plenty of buildup, and the occasional sex toy keep their love life lusty. Outside the bedroom, these Signs share similar interests. Both are highly social; enjoy movies, theater, and traveling; and get along very easily.

LEO MAN AND SAGITTARIUS WOMAN

Sexually, this is a great match. Mr. Leo and Ms. Sagittarius are equally passionate and enjoy the same range of sexual activities. Leo has great self-confidence but doesn't like being criticized. By the very force of his personality, he's used to people treating him royally. Initially, Sagittarius, smitten by Leo's dynamism and boyish smile, pays appropriate homage. Within about a year, she'll begin letting him know where he isn't coming through for her. His ego may be so wounded by this that he loses desire for her. If she will listen to her thoughts before speaking, and if he retains his sense of humor, this relationship can flourish through time.

Leo *with* Capricorn

THE LION AND THE GOAT: *Unnatural Pairing*

Imagine going to a large party. Somewhere in the middle of the room one person stands surrounded by a group. That's Leo, the center of attention, holding forth with charming stories, an actor's delivery, and a captivating personality. In another part of the room is a striking figure: stately, composed, calm, quiet, and compelling. This is Capricorn. The Goat notices Leo and finds the Lion's energy sexually exciting.

After Leo tires of entertaining the crowd, he/she notices Capricorn and is equally drawn. As soon as Leo recognizes what's going on, Leo is ready for the main event. No way, not with Capricorn. Capricorn wants the wining and dining, the romance of a courtship. If Leo hangs out for a while and impresses Capricorn sufficiently, they will retire to someplace more private. Sadly, it's not likely that sparks will fly.

Though Capricorn has the reputation for being staid and conservative and Leo for being a dynamo, when it comes to sex Capricorn is far more open and experimental. Initially the sex can be great. Over time, though, Capricorn wants to take it slow and Leo moves fast, eventually undermining the sexual expression.

Where Capricorn is reserved, frugal, and pragmatic Leo is expressive, extravagant, and optimistic/trusting. Capricorn represents the work ethic, Leo trusts to luck. While clearly they respect each other and may have a loving friendship, their fundamental differences are vast. Over the long haul, this pairing is a tough combination.

LEO WOMAN AND CAPRICORN MAN

Leo is luscious, entrancing, vital, and fun. She loves Broadway Theater and Bourbon Street jazz, and champagne as well as beer. Capricorn knows he must woo his Lioness, but he takes too few trips to Cordon Bleu and too many to McDonald's. In the bedroom, he's a thorough and skillful lover, and he enjoys lingering over sex. Leo is more intensely passionate and prefers a shorter sexual encounter. In business, what these two offer each other is dynamite. Her charm and his attention to detail make an unbeatable combination. In a long-term personal affair, however, Leo irritates Capricorn and Capricorn suffocates Leo.

LEO MAN AND CAPRICORN WOMAN

Capricorn looks so hot. Leo's turned on and ready. She maintains her distance and Leo sees that he's not going to feel satin sheets anytime soon, not until he gives Capricorn what she wants. In fact, until Leo comes through, Capricorn will have quite an epidemic of headaches. Leo must court Capricorn to get into her pants. She knows that she brings important aspects to a relationship: willingness to work hard, diplomacy, and caution. She is not wasteful, and her demands are both fair and reasonable. Unfortunately, Leo will see these efforts merely as demands that inhibit his joie de vivre.

Leo with Aquarius

THE LION AND THE WATER BEARER: *Opposites Attract and Repel*

Leo is charmed by Aquarius' dignity and adept conversational skills. The Water Bearer, preferring to observe, stays somewhat on the sidelines, enjoying flirting and talking quietly. Aquarius is drawn to the open vibrancy of Leo, for whom all the world's a stage, with the Lion very much in its center.

The Aquarius/Leo relationship is cordial. In business and friendship this union can be satisfying. On the personal level, these Signs do not bring out the best in each other. Aquarius feels unappreciated as Leo is so focused on his/her own activities. Leo finds Aquarius emotionally detached. Sex for Aquarius begins with verbal seduction early in the day. Anticipation is heightened by sexy phone chats. All this talk about sex becomes tedious for Leo, who just wants to do something. By the time Aquarius is finished talking about sex, Leo is too tired to actually have sex.

Leos are concerned about being forthright. Aquarians temper their words to the situation. Think of Aquarius as the ambassador, sent to the hot spots of the world to mediate. It's a good thing that Aquarius keeps cool and chooses words with care. Leo comes to distrust this seemingly cagey quality.

Leo is a Sign of summer and is ruled by the Sun, all hot and fiery. Aquarius is a Winter Sign: cool, crisp, and emotionally reserved. These Signs are as different as fire and ice, and their personalities—especially in intimate relationships—do not mesh. As Sun Sign pairs go, these two make among the worst of combinations.

LEO WOMAN AND AQUARIUS MAN

The Leo woman has the ability to draw attention to herself effortlessly even in the largest crowd. She gets close to people easily and enjoys exuberant personal relationships. Aquarius stays somewhat remote. He's a great conversationalist but reveals little about himself. Ms. Leo does not see that at first. She notes that everyone seems to know him and like him, and this is very true. The thing is, they just don't know him well. The Lioness has strong likes and dislikes, while Aquarius is quite even-tempered. In bed, while Leo doesn't care whether the sex is long or short, she does require passion and praise. He's too analytical for her and she feels unappreciated.

LEO MAN AND AQUARIUS WOMAN

The Aquarius woman's elegance captures Leo's attention. She finds him fascinating and listens intently. In no time they're at his place or hers, clothes flying in all directions. She's all words, praising his body, the texture of his hair, the power of his arms. He's all action. He lifts her onto the bed, pins her down, and bites her ear. She can't move. Sex is great for a few weeks, but then he finds her approach too dependent on verbal stimulation and she wants to try variations that don't interest him. Add that to their personality differences, and this twosome soon splits.

Leo *with* Pisces

THE LION AND THE FISH: *Incompatible Species*

Initially, this is a fun pairing. Pisces is such a romantic and so good at giving praise that Leo is delighted. The sex is passionate. Pisces, with a strong constitution, keeps things going a lot longer than Leo is used to. Pisces brings new elements to lovemaking: incense, candles, and different settings. Both Signs are experimental in the sexual range, Pisces more so than Leo. They enjoy sex in public places; using costumes, leather, or latex; and are turned on by sexy underwear. Leo finds tattoos and shaved genitals exciting. Pisces likes to use hot wax and ice cubes in sex play and may well have a foot fetish. If sex is the beginning and the end between these two, all's well. As a relationship, troubles lie ahead for the two.

Leo is a powerful sign, willing to confront problems head on. Pisces is also strong—the Sign of medicine and healing—but the Fish is not confrontational. Pisces depends upon negotiation, quiet maneuvering, and doing what is needed as a matter of expediency to get what is desired. Leo sees this as a lack of scruples and is turned off.

Pisces has a need for retreat, for time to meditate. Leo may feel shut out by this. The Fish also has short periods of self-pity, for which Leo has no patience. The Lion is all about action, often precipitously. Pisces is all about intuition and makes decisions based on belief and instinct. Neither is overly pragmatic. Life's mundane details undermine their stability as a couple.

LEO WOMAN AND PISCES MAN

Leo has grand ideas. She wants to own a big spread, or travel the globe, or gamble in Las Vegas, or mix with the societal elite. She has a need to be known and appreciated beyond the confines of her home. Pisces wants to live in a solid neighborhood, serve on the board of the church, raise his kids quietly, and pay his bills on time. She is extravagant and feels suffocated by a tight budget. She wants him to do more, to be more, to bring home more. Pisces is content with who and what he is. Beyond the ecstasy of early sex, these two have precious little in common.

LEO MAN AND PISCES WOMAN

Pisces is rather quiet and somewhat shy. Leo is inordinately outgoing, maybe a bit loud. He will not tolerate being criticized about his behavior in public. She cringes. Whatever brings them together in the first place? Well, she has large, luminous eyes that speak of mysteries. He finds her endlessly alluring. At first his excessive self-confidence is captivating. She expects him to be somewhat different at home, and of course he's not. Leo is what he is at all times. Pisces is a chameleon. Beyond a few wonderful passionate tumbles beneath the sheets, these Signs are not well suited to each other at all.

Virgo with Virgo

TWO VIRGINS TOGETHER: *Let's Try That Again*

Put two Virgos together and you've got a kind of tape recorder specialist on sexual relations. They get it all down and replay it over and over, testing and analyzing who's outperforming whom, and in their minds, they're having fun. After all, Virgo is a perfectionist who wants to do everything right. So when Virgo gives directions in the bedroom to "do more of this; no, no, more to the right; yes, that feels wonderful" all goes fairly well. But there can be a problem because between these two, there is no spark, no unexpected energy.

Doubling up the good qualities of Virgo, practicality, directness, and the willingness to work hard and be supportive, is fine. Doubling up on the negative qualities, nitpicking and needing to examine and reexamine all things, becomes tedious. And while Virgo is a highly critical Sign, Virgo also doesn't take criticism well. The good news is that these problems are surmountable. Virgo/Virgo can make for a very successful couple. Each simply needs to guard against being overly fault finding—both need to let some matters go without extensive rehashing.

Back to the sex scene. Virgo is a Sign that comes in two extremes: very conservative with a modest sex drive and very experimental with a strong libido. This couple will have a contented and friendly relationship even if their sex drive is mismatched, though one will certainly miss the passion. Bring on the sex toys or plug in a porno DVD. Try a little bondage. Stretching beyond vanilla sex is one way to provide the needed spark in this relationship.

Summary
Virgo females are very matter-of-fact, but they are decidedly feminine and appreciate romantic gestures. A flower now and then, cooking dinner for her, and dimming the lights will bring loving rewards. If his sex drive is lower than hers, he must remember to initiate sex on occasion. She's willing to start things off most of the time but she's apt to get a tad cranky if he doesn't reach out to her now and then. Living well (not being rich) matters to her. She's willing to help support the family, but a clear division of responsibilities is necessary because she won't shoulder more than her fair share.

Virgo with Libra

THE VIRGIN AND THE SCALES: *An Uneasy Balance*

Virgo and Libra are fine as friends and business partners, but as lovers, they're mismatched in bed and out. Though good-hearted, Virgo is given to complaining and nitpicking, which is hurtful to Libra. Libra enjoys chattering about almost anything while Virgo is not big on small talk. On the positive side, both Signs strive to avoid confrontation. It violates Libra's gentle, polite nature and innate struggle for balance and is at odds with the Virgin's cool, objective, analytical approach to problem solving.

Regarding sex, Virgo generally programs everything, including the time and place for coitus, and follows a set process from foreplay to climax. Earth Sign Virgo is turned on by touch and spends lots of time during foreplay exploring a partner's body with inquisitive and exciting fingers. Sometimes Virgo likes to get down and dirty with raunchy sex talk and the use of pornography.

Libra, an Air Sign, needs verbal setup to get in the mood. The more sexy talk—tantalizing, not crude—the readier he/she is. Libra dislikes anything harsh, is far less structured, prefers spontaneity, and likes kissing more than extensive touching.

Sex may work out better if these two explore some fetishes and experiment with a variety of sex toys. Libra's interest in sex may be greater in the area of fetishistic role-playing accoutrements than Virgo's, but Virgo is curious enough and usually willing to try new things. Virgo needs to remember that Libra wants romance. A compromise between these two may be difficult but could also be a lot of fun.

VIRGO WOMAN AND LIBRA MAN

Virgo's quiet self-assurance and straightforward demeanor attract Libra. She is appropriate in public: neat and well groomed. He comes across as such a nice person, very at ease and charming. Virgo is almost surprised by his attentions. Things get sexual quite quickly and, initially, it's hot and heavy. With the passing of time, Libra comes to find Virgo too cool and analytical. His indifference to small matters makes her feel like she's responsible for everything—where they go and what they do—in bed and in daily life. She wants decisiveness but he wants to relax. Initially this pairing is exciting, but over time it will prove unfulfilling.

VIRGO MAN AND LIBRA WOMAN

The general impression of the Libra female is charming, relaxed, and at ease with herself. Virgo is attracted to her beauty, dignity, and decorum. At the same time, Virgo's erect posture, careful behavior, and quiet presence turn Libra's head. Their first encounters in bed are wonderful. She's romantic and her kisses are passionate. He explores every part of her body with his mouth as well as with his hands. Virgo's pace is thorough and slow. In time, however, this pace bores Libra. Her lack of intensity cools his passion. Eventually, their personality and sexual differences undermine the staying power of this relationship.

Virgo with Scorpio
THE VIRGIN AND THE SCORPION: *The Sting Becomes a Love Tap*

Virgo/Scorpio is a great combination. A natural chemistry draws these two together in a bond that grows over time into mutual respect. Virgo and Scorpio share a quiet, almost subterranean, connection that provides comfort for both. They can talk about anything and rarely upset each other. Virgo is down-to-earth, straightforward, and direct. With Virgo, what you see is what you get. This is a quality that Scorpio admires. For Virgo, who has a tendency to worry, Scorpio is steadying and reassuring.

Scorpio appreciates Virgo's work ethic on the job, at home, and in his/her social life. Where Virgo may suffer from feelings of self-doubt, Scorpio's profound strength is comforting. Virgo is wonderful about assisting a partner in achieving his/her goals. Scorpio is good at encouraging Virgo to stretch for new objectives. Virgo is not put off by Scorpio's silences and Scorpio does not object to Virgo's fussiness. In fact, trait for trait, both Signs are accepting of and comfortable with the other's little quirks.

The sex will be comfortable, even quite passionate, as Scorpio knows how to energize Virgo, to get Virgo to let go of the structured or predictable, and to become more spontaneous. Conversely, Virgo knows how to prolong the experience and tease Scorpio to greater heights. Virgo wants sex frequently; it's good for one's health, and Scorpio is glad to oblige. The only area of difference is that Scorpio likes varying the length of time for sex, enjoying quickies as well as longer sessions. Virgo is more into marathon sex.

VIRGO WOMAN AND SCORPIO MAN

Virgo is unselfish and devoted to Scorpio, who matches her devotion with loyalty. She sincerely believes that life is fair, that hard work and consistent effort will be met with success. He is a fatalist and knows life doesn't necessarily work out the way he wants. He is there to comfort Virgo when life proves itself to be less than fair. In matters of sex, Scorpio should take the lead to add passion. Virgo should open up to new possibilities. If Scorpio is sensitive and gentle enough to help her open up, their sex life can be rich and rewarding.

VIRGO MAN AND SCORPIO WOMAN

This relationship is based upon friendship, similar interests, and an almost brother/sister kind of familiarity. Talking and working together is easy, sex is a bit of a struggle. It's great initially but what makes Scorpio happy today won't work tomorrow, and it takes her a while to explain what she wants. Virgo's hands do turn her on but his repetitive process bores her and turns her off. Variety is the answer. Sex is crucial to the long-terms success of this relationship and a good sex life depends upon her willingness to tell him what she wants, and his about introducing variations.

Virgo with Sagittarius

THE VIRGIN AND THE ARCHER: *A Mixed Metaphor*

This relationship represents a conflict both physically and emotionally. Sagittarius takes a rather breezy approach to love and sex. Virgo is very serious—a perfectionist—even about lovemaking. Both Signs like to spend about one hour having sex, but they spend this time very differently. Sagittarius wants to romanticize sex, to drag it out, make it interesting, and discuss it whereas Virgo wants to focus squarely on the sex. Virgo wants time to run his/her hands over every inch of Sagittarius' body, but Sagittarius' passion is turned off by this almost analytical exploration.

Virgo is the worker of the zodiac. Sagittarius is the philosopher. Virgo attends to all details, while Sagittarius takes the long view. Work for Virgo is getting things done. Work for Sagittarius may be more thinking things through. Virgo is mature at an early age, ready to accept considerable responsibility even while still a teenager. Sagittarius struggles to find balance between freedom and responsibility. In the younger years Sagittarius avoids responsibility for fear that it will limit freedom. Later Sagittarius becomes very responsible, but this Sign never gives up the quest for fun and pleasure.

Virgo will have to make a terrific effort to remember hearts and flowers, violins, and the gentle scent of vanilla to keep Sagittarius happy in the bedroom. Sagittarius will have to be more focused and help Virgo with the nitty-gritty aspects of life to make this relationship last more than a short while. Fundamentally, Virgo feels threatened and insecure with Sagittarius, and Sagittarius feels stifled by Virgo.

VIRGO WOMAN AND SAGITTARIUS MAN

Sagittarius is so charming and Virgo is attracted at once by his warmth and grace. He finds her quiet, serious gaze enchanting. Although he isn't aggressive, he is apt to want the relationship to become sexual well before she's ready. The first rolls in the hay are exciting. Virgo is a force in bed, sound effects and all. Unfortunately, this heat won't keep this couple cozy. He's a flirt and she resents it, even if she is also flirtatious. In public, Sagittarius works his charm on all comers. Ms. Virgo is embarrassed. If his behavior triggers her jealousy, she'll back all the way out.

VIRGO MAN AND SAGITTARIUS WOMAN

Her walk, her swaying hips immediately turn Virgo on. In bed, he explores her abdomen as if he's never seen one. At first it's all fire. But outside the bedroom his anal-retentive approach to most of life drives Sagittarius mad. He wants to plan; she wants to be spontaneous. She's a bit light-hearted about love. He's very serious. She wants candles and incense; he's content with clean sheets. He has a schedule for everything while she wants to read the paper or take a walk. He attends to work. She wants to climb mountains. This is a mismatched pair.

Virgo with Capricorn
THE VIRGIN AND THE GOAT: *Add a Little Spice*

Virgo and Capricorn will not have a passionate love affair, but rather a stable relationship that can last through time. These Signs have a great deal in common. They enjoy traveling, talking, and working together. They're down-to-earth, practical, and have respect for order. Virgo is a remarkably loyal partner as is Capricorn. They both expect a lot of themselves and, therefore, from their partners.

In the bedroom, what starts out great can get dull. Initially they enjoy exploring each other's bodies. They both have fabulous hands with which they make the whole body an erogenous zone. Over time, this sex play, lacking in spontaneity, can become predictable and unexciting. Going outside the mainstream will spice up their sex life.

Remember that though Virgo is known as the Virgin Sign, many Virgos are into exploring physical stimulus and sensations far beyond traditional intercourse and oral sex. Could it be that their puritanical outer behavior hides a lustful interior that almost embarrasses them? Without doubt, Virgos are quiet about their secret, wild bedroom excursions. In Capricorn, this Virgo finds a willing partner.

Capricorn likes experimental sex. Still, introducing such things as bondage, discipline, and sadomasochism must be done with care. This is the couple who may enjoy exploring sexual role-playing and the entire BDSM lifestyle. Virgos are perfectionists. Perhaps they expect spankings when their performance is less than perfect. Capricorn—the master, the military general—is all too ready to administer the punishment.

VIRGO WOMAN AND CAPRICORN MAN

This is an ideal couple, though romance may be lacking. Mr. Capricorn provides very well for Ms. Virgo, who cares for him diligently. Even in lovemaking Virgo strives to perform perfectly. She strives to become a master at oral sex, working at the technique until her practice proves perfect. Her hands are extraordinary at exciting him to the brink of climax. But the bedroom behaviors become almost scripted and predictable. The unforeseen needs to be added. A simple sex toy like a tickler, a vibrator, or a blindfold will go far to stimulate the only weak link in this otherwise solid chain.

VIRGO MAN AND CAPRICORN WOMAN

Ms. Capricorn doesn't ask for much . . . not directly anyway. Yet somehow she manages to communicate that she enjoys skiing in Aspen or vacations in Paris or perhaps cruises in the Caribbean. She'll settle for a B&B by the ocean. The point is that Capricorn works very hard to keep her loved one happy. Her home is impeccable. The garden is productive and dinners are tasty and nutritious. She's a dutiful and generous sexual partner. For all of this, she expects a reward. Without one, life in the bedroom will prove downright chilly. Nobody gets headaches more frequently than a dissatisfied Capricorn.

Virgo with Aquarius
THE VIRGIN AND THE WATER BEARER: *But How Do You Feel?*

The Virgo/Aquarius combination is most successful as a friendship. Both Signs are slow to reveal much about their private lives. Virgo wants to be sure that a developing relationship could become more than a casual acquaintanceship before actually opening up. Aquarius isn't merely being guarded; Aquarius just doesn't reveal personal information.

Major problems for these two come from their emotional cores. Virgo may feel things intensely but isn't expressive. Aquarius operates from intellect and inspiration rather than from feelings. Therefore, when there are relationship problems, Virgo chooses to analyze them in depth. Aquarius wants to discuss things at length but neither is comfortable getting at the emotional underpinnings. In time what's left is a polite, well-mannered life without much warmth.

Sexually, these two are decidedly mismatched. Words are the trigger to get Aquarius juicy. Touch turns on Virgo. Sexy talk over dinner is enough to put Aquarius on the edge of orgasm. Virgo, conversely, needs a fair amount of foreplay to reach that plateau. Sex can work for this couple if Virgo is open to experimenting with behaviors beyond the mainstream range. Aquarius is often willing to try fetishes, role-playing, and the use of toys and equipment. Though the motive for this is sensation, as opposed to being carried away with passion, the result can be exciting lovemaking for both Aquarius and Virgo. Overall, Aquarius' sex drive is lesser than Virgo's. If Aquarius hopes to keep Virgo from looking for a "side order," Aquarius must rev up the internal sex drive.

VIRGO WOMAN AND AQUARIUS MAN

Aquarius is ardent and attentive in the beginning of a relationship, less so later on. Once Virgo lets her guard down, she's totally committed. His coolness, then, triggers her insecurity. Sex is frequent and if both are into toys, role-playing, costumes, and bondage, it will be fulfilling. But emotionally, neither Sign does much to warm up the other. Virgo is the more sexual of the two, and Aquarius is responsive when she initiates sex. But she wants him to be the aggressor. Her need to examine and reexamine all matters is tedious to him. This relationship can and often does work, but it isn't based on common ground and it's never easy.

VIRGO MAN AND AQUARIUS WOMAN

When love is new, Ms. Aquarius might turn up at his apartment in a fur coat and spiked heels . . . and nothing else. Over dinner the erotic and graphic sex talk has Virgo at the verge of climax. Unfortunately, the event itself doesn't match the hype. For Aquarius, sex starts and builds in the brain. For Virgo, words get him ready but touch, taste, and smells make the actual act so rewarding. Her foreplay is conversation; his is physical sensation. Virgo and Aquarius may be wonderful friends, even loving companions, but the sexual mismatch makes this a tough combination to sustain for long.

Virgo with Pisces

THE VIRGIN AND THE FISH: *Worth Getting Your Feet Wet*

Virgo and Pisces is a hot and heavy combination: hard to live with, hard to live without. They are opposite Signs, but remember that opposites repel as well as attract. Virgo provides stability and down to earth practicality. Pisces provides emotional warmth and sexual intensity. Pisces is highly spiritual. Virgo is matter-of-fact. This attraction is difficult to sustain because while Virgo is certainly fascinated by the emotional world Pisces inhabits, he/she also finds it overwhelming—possibly enough to leave.

Virgo is not usually a pushy or aggressive sign, but rather one comfortable having someone else in the director's position. However, with Pisces, which is such a flexible Sign, Virgo may become highly domineering. When there's a disagreement, Virgo may enjoy a good debate, but Pisces tends to retreat. Virgo then believes that a resolution has been reached when, in fact, Pisces has merely stopped arguing without necessarily conceding.

Those Virgos who are experimental in their lovemaking are better mates for passionate Pisces. In this twosome, Virgo will have free rein to explore all the kinkiness that he/she desires, as Pisces likes to act out sex fantasies. Generally, Pisces wants half as much time for lovemaking as most Virgos prefer. It is not that Pisces lacks endurance, far from it. Pisces can keep on going right through the night, exhausting most Virgos. The difference is in the buildup. Virgo needs a lot of stimulus to become truly turned on. With far less foreplay, when the stage is well set, Pisces is ready.

VIRGO WOMAN AND PISCES MAN

Both Virgo and Pisces have a desire to live well, and the Pisces man is generally successful in the business world. He'll find his Virgo woman to be budget conscious and generally frugal. She's the practical one. He's the romantic. Pisces sends flowers when Virgo really wants a dishwasher. Of course, if these two can afford both, she won't object to the flowers. The sex should be phenomenal because Pisces enjoys Virgo's efforts with her hands and mouth. He is expressive in his appreciation of her mastery of oral sex. He will enjoy her desire to be spanked, and he will want her to return the favor.

VIRGO MAN AND PISCES WOMAN

The Pisces woman must be more direct in telling her Virgo partner what she wants and needs in all aspects of their relationship. He won't try to read her mind. She's a supportive life partner, a caring lover, and considers sex the bonding of two souls. He's practical and devoted, but sees sex as a release of stress, good for one's health. Ruffles, frills, and more than two pillows on the bed are a waste in Virgo's eyes. This relationship can be great if Virgo remembers to bring Pisces an occasional flower and to light some candles every once in a while. That, along with his masterful hands, will satisfy Pisces both physically and emotionally.

Libra with Libra

THE SCALES WITH THE SCALES: *Yes . . . No . . . Well, Maybe*

Venus—planet of love and beauty, of harmony and elegance—rules Libra. Libra hates people who are demanding, loud, and crude in public. Two such kind, truly nice individuals should make a wonderful twosome, right? Not necessarily.

Libra strives to avoid confrontations by backing away from touchy issues and even denying that certain problems exist. Unfortunately, denial doesn't make things better. Time passes, frustrations build, and eventually outpours a lengthy list of remembered grievances. Imagine the distress produced when items that were supposedly of no concern appear on the list. For this relationship to succeed, both Libras must face problems when they arise.

Libra is reputedly indecisive. Well, that's not accurate. Libra sees many possibilities and must weigh them before making a choice because once having chosen Libra will stick to that position. It does, therefore, take Libra a long time to make a decision. Two Libras have a doubly difficult time settling on a course of action whether the decision is minor ("Your place or mine?") or major ("Should we buy a house? Which one? Should we have children?"). Over time this behavior proves tedious and creates a state of confusion, of emotional instability. Sex, therefore, doesn't produce much satisfaction.

In fact, after the initial heat of an affair passes, it isn't easy to keep the sexual spark going. Perhaps the best way for this couple to maintain excitement in their sex life is to have other partners on the side or to enter a ménage à trois arrangement.

Summary

Her beautiful body is his trophy. He is more than happy to show her off. He too enjoys compliments, and much of the time she provides them. She wants at least some luxury in her life. While she's willing to participate in earning the household income, he must contribute his fair share to provide those little extras or her dissatisfaction will be apparent in the bedroom. Sex may not be that important to her but she wants to make him happy. If he tells her what he wants, she will accommodate. Expanding their range of sexual expression will help Libra/Libra keep sex from becoming routine.

Libra with Scorpio

THE SCALES AND THE SCORPION: *A Mixed Metaphor*

Initially ardent, it is soon obvious that Libra and Scorpio have distinctly different styles in the bedroom. This leads ultimately to lukewarm sex and an unsatisfying relationship. Signs that come side by side, as Libra and Scorpio do, seldom complement each other.

Libra, genuinely nice, gentle, and good-natured, seeks to avoid strife. This Sign is refined and also self-indulgent. Scorpio, intense, driven, and relentless, will not back away from a confrontation. Scorpios would never describe themselves as "nice." Scorpions might think of themselves as good, committed, and caring—but never nice. Scorpios have fierce tempers. They want intensity, emotion, and passion in their lives. Libra is even-tempered and strives for a life of contentment. Libra wants to go out with friends to movies, sports events, and flower shows. Scorpio is often content to stay at home and work on some project or other.

When it comes to sex, most Librans are true to their Sign. They want sex to be something lofty, elegant, and not too sweaty or messy. Scorpio is capable of getting down and dirty. Sex is easiest between those Librans who are more relaxed, even a bit crude, and the more highly refined Scorpios. However, the differences in personality and approach to almost every aspect of daily life still make true connection between these Signs quite difficult.

If Libra will confront problems more directly and if Scorpio will avoid prodding or nagging, if Libra lets down all guards and allows Scorpio to devour him or her, this couple has a better chance for success in the long term.

LIBRA WOMAN AND SCORPIO MAN

Sex may be the best part of the Libra woman/Scorpio man relationship. His hands and tongue lovingly explore her body, and she revels in the way he responds to her. His passion feeds into her fantasies. She is the favorite in a harem and he is her sheik. In the relationship, however, Scorpio's brooding moods distress Libra. Conversely, Libra's tendency to deny that problems exist is unsettling to Scorpio. He sees that she's upset and asks, "What's wrong?" She says, "Nothing." The communication fails and undermines the sexual relationship. The remedy is for him to open up to her verbally, and for her to acknowledge problems when they surface.

LIBRA MAN AND SCORPIO WOMAN

The sex for these two is good for a while, as Libra is swept up in Scorpio's passion and Scorpio enjoys pushing Libra's boundaries of sexual expression. She is extremely forceful. The energy she exudes intimidates many men. Ms Scorpio is dynamic and driven. Mr. Libra has a lazy streak. While a masculine sign, Libras are quite gentle. The time it takes him to reach a decision is unnerving to Scorpio. She is likely to react by nagging and pushing for a conclusion. These two are apt to bring out the worst in each other, which bodes ill for a long-term relationship.

Libra with Sagittarius
THE SCALES AND THE ARCHER: *Perfect Balance*

This is a fun combination. Libra and Sagittarius share similar likes and dislikes, from traveling and camping, to gambling and spiritual retreats. They have a good time with sex and like to try it anywhere: on the beach, on the rooftops, and certainly in the woods. They may also enjoy making videos of their lovemaking, as Sagittarius is a natural performer and Libra is a bit of an exhibitionist.

Libra, the Sign of marriage, understands that the best relationships are between people who stand beside each other as mutually independent partners. Libra is not looking for a mate to lean upon and will not tolerate someone who is clingy or cloying. In self-reliant Sagittarius, whose motto is "Don't fence me in," Libra finds perfect balance.

The Archer is a dependable lover once ready to settle down, but nobody can rush a Sagittarian. Libra isn't pushy. Sagittarius is social and outgoing, frank, outspoken, charming, and witty. The Archer does have a temper and can be secretive, but Libra has a knack for helping stressed-out Sagittarius regain his/her normal affable demeanor.

Until Libra is ready for commitment, he/she can be very shallow in romance. After all, Libra is ruled by Venus, the planet of beauty and physical love. Libra loves sex. Sagittarius, more passionate sexually, adds heat to Libra's calmer approach. With or without sex toys, within the range of mainstream sex or exploring outside its boundaries, these two match each other well and have all it takes for a successful relationship.

LIBRA WOMAN AND SAGITTARIUS MAN

Libra is pretty, charming, and refined. She's like the flower in the field. Sagittarius is the centaur: half man, half beast. His attraction to her is totally natural. They are as well suited to each other as any couple can be and all aspects of the relationship, including sex, are satisfactory. Until he's ready to settle down, he's the undisputed bachelor of the zodiac. Notoriously well endowed, Sagittarius enjoys many affairs. Libra loves love and can be quite fickle until she too decides on a mate. If these two come together when both are ready for commitment, the relationship can last forever.

LIBRA MAN AND SAGITTARIUS WOMAN

The Sagittarius woman is sincere and the Libra man is diplomatic. Both are friendly, outgoing, and independent. She may be overly frank and he overly cautious, but these traits hardly cause problems. The attraction between these two is immediate. She knows her mind far better than he knows his. She's decisive, to the point, and has an exceptional ability to cut to the core. This trait is invaluable in helping Libra work through all the variables when struggling with a decision. Sex is fun and easy. They bring out the best in each other, expanding their sexual vocabulary into the experimental range, which keeps passion alive in the bedroom long term.

Libra with Capricorn
THE SCALES AND THE GOAT: *An Odd Balance*

Air Sign Libra and Earth Sign Capricorn might be expected to kick up more dust than to build anything solid as they have trait after trait at odds with each other, and yet the attraction is powerful. What brings them together?

The positives: Reserved Capricorn is charmed by the warmth and effortless people skills of Libra. Libra is drawn to Capricorn's quiet, courteous demeanor. Luxury-loving Libra appreciates Capricorn's hard-driving, goal-orientated focus. Each is supportive of the other's ambitions. Both seek to avoid confrontation. Capricorn gets quiet and withdraws when there's discord. Libra backs away from arguments and tries to find a compromise.

As to the differences, Libra is sociable while Capricorn is reserved. Libra is relaxed, impressionable, and a bit lazy. Capricorn is on guard, somewhat suspicious, and the hardest worker in the zodiac.

In bed, Capricorn likes to take it slow and easy, build to considerable intensity, and enjoys getting sweaty in the process. Libra appreciates a slow, verbal buildup, a shorter session between the sheets, and rarely breaks a sweat even though the sex is always satisfying. Librans are generally rather conservative in their sexual behavior, while some Capricorns travel on the outer edges of mainstream sex. Put these two together and the affair is likely to be brief. A sexually moderate Capricorn and a somewhat experimental Libra will enjoy each other far more. Long term, this relationship may work but will require ongoing effort.

LIBRA WOMAN AND CAPRICORN MAN

For the Libra woman, sex is a tool to get what she wants. The Capricorn man is a great provider. As long as Capricorn provides well, Libra performs well. Libra will happily sit on the plush pillows that Capricorn proudly provided. When Libra is treated well, she brags about her Capricorn's marvelous qualities. This praise, and the attention it brings to Capricorn, helps him to succeed in life. This is an unlikely combination but one that can be successful. This success depends on Capricorn being more of a romantic (give her the occasional flower) and Libra understanding that Capricorn's lack of sentimentality doesn't mean he's not in love with her.

LIBRA MAN AND CAPRICORN WOMAN

In a traditional couple, where the man provides the primary income, this twosome is apt to have difficulty. Though the Libra man loves luxury, he isn't as hardworking or driven as the Capricorn woman. If in the courtship days, he leads her to believe that he will provide well, he better come through. Ms. Capricorn isn't very agreeable when she feels that she's been misled. When he provides well, he'll find Capricorn to be loyal, supportive, and willing to treat him royally in bed. She's more adventurous than Libra, and if he encourages her to unleash her imagination, she'll fulfill his deepest fantasies.

Libra with Aquarius
THE SCALES AND THE WATER BEARER: *A Delightful Duo*

The Libra/Aquarius couple loves to talk about everything, including sex. Sometimes their sexy conversations are more exciting than the act itself. In fact, sex may last five minutes though the conversation could carry them across a walking tour of Europe. Aquarians wants sex very often; they're on a quest for deep emotional response. What they find with Libra is more friendship than passion, but the quality of the communication and sense of companionship make for a rewarding, life-long connection.

For both Signs, triggering other senses will create the mood for sex. Reading erotic literature aloud is a major turn-on. Sexy videos are great. Nothing crude, but rather those that are more erotic than pornographic will do just fine. Dinner beside the river, with a view of a mountain range, by a fireplace, or in the woods is a sensual stimulus. The environment turns this pair on. Indoors, lighting is important: not too bright. The scent of vanilla is appealing.

What's needed to make sex more rewarding for this couple is a spark of surprise, bringing in the unexpected. Otherwise sex will be a bit dull. Libra and Aquarius can compensate by using their wonderful minds to explore new toys, games, and approaches. They go out to dinner. She's not wearing underwear. She sits beside him and during dinner slips his hand under her skirt. He brings home a new vibrator or tickler, blindfolds her, and begins to use it. All in all these two can have a satisfying sex life and a very successful lifelong relationship.

LIBRA WOMAN AND AQUARIUS MAN
Mr. Aquarius has a gentle heart, but he's seldom overly romantic. To turn on Ms. Libra he'll need to extend himself. Is it too much to ask that he occasionally light some candles? She wants to be treated well, like an object of value, to be wined and dined on occasion—even after they've been together for many years. He appreciates the way she takes time making decisions and that she includes him in the process. Their sex life will be satisfactory, though mostly mainstream. Introducing a costume or a sex toy, perhaps something involving electricity, could spice thing up.

LIBRA MAN AND AQUARIUS WOMAN
Aquarius is a gorgeous woman who turns the head of every man in the room. Underneath her pleasing exterior, though, she's decidedly cool. It's a man's mind that turns her on. If Libra becomes intellectually lazy, she's gone. When Libra wants to try something new in his life, Aquarius will encourage him and be both his cheerleader and his coach. She's strong and assertive as well as good tempered and loyal. In return, Libra gives her the respect, praise, and appreciation she desires and adds romance to her nature. When there's something on her mind, he's an excellent listener and knows that she wants his attention, not his advice. This pairing scores a 5 for sex and a perfect 10 for relationship potential.

Libra with Pisces
THE SCALES AND THE FISH: *A Mixed Metaphor*

Air Sign Libra mixed with Water Sign Pisces just goes flat. It starts out well enough. Pisces is idealistic, giving, gentle, refined, and devoted. Libra shares many of these traits and at first they regard each other as being extremely similar. They aren't. In fact, their personality differences give rise to a general imbalance in the relationship. Pisces is a complex sign, not dominant but not about to be led either. Libra is a subtle Sign, and though independent, Libra doesn't like to take charge.

Libra's overall energy is very pleasant and genuinely nice. In a long-term relationship and for exciting sex, Libra needs someone with raw energy. It's the Fire Signs who ignite their passion. A Water Sign like Pisces is fundamentally emotional and doesn't provide the spark of passion that Libra needs. Conversely, Pisces longs for a person who is decidedly earthy, very physical. Perhaps these two can be great friends, but they ultimately will not satisfy one another in a sexual relationship.

Sex in the early days will be wonderful. Pisces' romanticism is exciting to Libra, who enjoys seduction: candles and incense to create the mood. For a while they have fun setting the stage and luxuriating in sensual pleasure; however, these Signs are turned on by very different things. Talking about sex off and on throughout the day is part of Libra's foreplay. With Pisces, foreplay begins in the bedroom. In the course of the relationship, while Pisces continues to desire romance, Libra is more satisfied simply fulfilling a sexual urge.

LIBRA WOMAN AND PISCES MAN
The Libra woman loves beautiful things. Things that others consider luxuries are necessities for this woman. Her bedroom is incomplete without a proper vanity, bed skirt, matching curtains, and an upholstered chair. She's a generous lover when her needs are met; less so when she feels they aren't. The Pisces man isn't overly ambitious and Libra's desires may be too much for him to fulfill. Libra can be lazy but will pick on Pisces for not being more aggressive. She'll nag him to be more and do more. He'll be turned off. She won't argue, but she will grow chilly. These Signs bring out the worst in each other.

LIBRA MAN AND PISCES WOMAN
Ms. Pisces wants a screenplay setting for sex. She longs for Libra to whisper in her ear that she brings out the pirate in him, that he envisions himself sailing the seven seas with her as his sex slave. The Libra man may not be flamboyant about it, but he yearns for admiration from his partner. She may be threatened by his behavior in public, which she sees as flirtatious. When accused, he'll deny it vehemently. She's far more sensitive than he is and he wounds her unintentionally. Pisces will become depressed or self-pitying when Libra gets on his case. Different needs. Different styles. A tough combo.

Scorpio with Scorpio
TWO SCORPIONS TOGETHER: *Passion or Poison?*

Two Scorpios: both powerhouses, both passionate, both suspicious, and both jealous. They are inherently competitive, and the sex is incredibly exciting. From the minute a sexual encounter begins, each Scorpio is out to impress the other with both duration and intensity.

They have the same likes and dislikes. Kissing gets things started; being taken by force or having the other do the initiating is a turn-on. They like taking time before going to the most erogenous zone, building up fairly quickly but with control and coming to a simultaneous earth-moving orgasm.

Scorpios react to each other the way magnets do: they either pull together or push apart. The attraction is instantaneous and breathtaking, or both parties warily keep a careful distance. Even their body language makes this apparent. They either face each other openly or lower their heads and keep their arms wrapped across their chests.

There is no balance when two like Signs get together. Rather, there is a doubling up of all the characteristics, good and bad, that each Sign possesses. Scorpio is both secretive and on a deep level, somewhat insecure. Seemingly without provocation, one Scorpio may turn on the other, issuing accusations that come from unresolved or even unfounded suspicions. Should these two get into an angry debate or suffer an ugly breakup, the grudge is likely to continue eternally. If there is ever to be any peace on the planet for two Scorpios, it is crucial that each be totally open with the other.

Summary

The Scorpio pair is sensitive to one another, has great timing, and experiences incendiary sex. Each is able to fill the other's desire, knowing instinctively what the other is feeling. If they are off to a great start, Scorpio's flirtatious nature can bring out Scorpio's jealous nature. When a Scorpio woman is out with her lover, she expects his undivided attention. If he lets his flirtatious eyes wander around the room, her behavior later will prove to be the living example of the expression "Hell has no fury like a woman scorned." In bed this may be dynamite. Outside it is just plain war.

Scorpio with Sagittarius
THE SCORPION AND THE ARCHER: *Don't Worry, Be Happy*

Scorpio/Sagittarius is a difficult pairing, but one with potential. Sagittarius, the zodiac's philosopher, says, "The goal of life is happiness." Scorpio doesn't understand this idea. When life is going well, Scorpio waits guardedly for something to go wrong. When life is tough, Scorpio is calm, confident, and ready to take action. Sagittarius is certainly up to life's challenges but feels quite content when life is good. Sagittarius' optimism brightens Scorpio. Scorpio's quiet depth comforts Sagittarius.

When Scorpio wants to achieve something, the approach is like a laser beam, moving straight ahead, unswerving, to accomplish that goal. Sagittarius prefers to take in a broad overview before choosing a course of action. The Archer wants to see the entire forest. Scorpio can be put off by what he/she views as a cursory overview. Sagittarius believes Scorpio has too narrow a perspective.

Sagittarius is famous for letting fly words that cut like arrows. Though powerful, Scorpio is also a highly emotional, easily hurt Water Sign with a remarkable memory. Those words leave indelible scars. In bed, add Scorpio's passion to Sagittarius' endurance for a steamy result. The sex may not be overly varied, but it is passionate and satisfying. Sagittarius may be open to anal sex. Scorpio generally isn't. Otherwise their pleasures are parallel, including the occasional use of sex toys and having sex in out-of-the-ordinary locations.

For this relationship to succeed, maturity is needed. Scorpio must back off from competition and enjoy the ardent nature of Sagittarius. Sagittarius needs to beware of shooting from the hip.

SCORPIO WOMAN AND SAGITTARIUS MAN

The Sagittarius man finds his Scorpio lady sexually exciting and intellectually stimulating. He is not bothered when Scorpio is in a silent mood. In bed, she knows exactly what to touch, what to kiss, and what to squeeze. He proves himself a fine lover with the use of his hands and tongue. The difficulty in this relationship is that he's used to speaking directly without censoring himself. He may unwittingly hurt Scorpio deeply. The foundation of their relationship is friendship. If each remembers to regard the other as a friend and to remain sensitive to the effect they have on one another, this relationship can succeed very well.

SCORPIO MAN AND SAGITTARIUS WOMAN

Sagittarius has the remarkable ability to size up people and situations, often out loud, with little regard for the effect of her words. This distresses Scorpio, whether or not he's at the receiving end. For upbeat Sagittarius, handling Scorpio's silences is difficult. For both, the effort to make this relationship work is well worth it. Scorpio finds Sagittarius an exciting life partner and a wonderful lover who is somewhat open to sexual experimentation. They enjoy setting the stage for romantic sex. For both, it doesn't matter whether the sex is long or short, as long as it's good.

Scorpio with Capricorn
THE SCORPION AND THE GOAT: *The Perfect Pair*

Ideal balance here. Scorpio represents the power of desire and has a great need for accomplishment. Capricorn is motivated to achieve, ambitious, and among the hardest workers in the zodiac. When Capricorn needs to make a decision, the Goat keeps the subject closely guarded, telling nobody what ideas or plans are on tap until quite certain of a course or direction. This behavior might be disconcerting to some but not to Scorpio, who is secretive by nature. Scorpio is far more emotional than Capricorn, and this serves to soften what appears to be the overly pragmatic approach to life that Capricorn projects. There are few differences between these two Signs, but one is important. Capricorn cares enormously what other people think and Scorpio simply doesn't. The physical relationship is satisfying, as these two are similar in almost all aspects of sexuality. They like the same sex acts, frequency, and forcefulness. The amount of time spent in a sexual encounter is of little importance to either Sign. Both are experimental and Capricorn will match Scorpio fetish for fetish, from bondage to ménage à trois all the way to orgies and, in some cases, sadomasochism.

While Scorpio's possessiveness turns off several other Signs, Capricorn finds this quality reassuring. Some might find Capricorn impersonal, but Scorpio is comfortable knowing there is ample compensation in the richness of their sex life.

SCORPIO WOMAN AND CAPRICORN MAN

The Scorpio woman and Capricorn man are compatible in virtually all aspects of life, from their value systems to their long-term goals. Where there are differences of opinion, they respect the other's right to have them. Capricorn's hard work ethic matches the energy Scorpio puts in at work and at home. Capricorn is a steady partner and a caring lover. He is quite often interested in experimenting with fetishistic behaviors and various sex toys. Scorpio won't want that to be a steady diet—sometimes she likes romance—but is very ready to try activities like bondage. A blindfold will almost always turn her on.

SCORPIO MAN AND CAPRICORN WOMAN

Capricorn is drawn to her Scorpio man's mysterious aura. He loves the way she behaves in public. He is jealous and she is seldom flirtatious. The sex is lusty as his relentless assault thrills her and her willingness to explore beyond the bounds of vanilla sex stirs his passion. He can be crass and talk dirty in the bedroom. That's fine, but if he behaves that way in public or among friends, Capricorn will be sorely embarrassed. She is a very private person. Regardless of what goes on at home, in public she is decorum itself and expects the same of her mate.

Scorpio with Aquarius

THE SCORPION AND THE WATER BEARER: *Conflicting Species*

"You like potato and I like potahto. You like tomato and I like tomahto. Potato, potahto, Tomato, tomahto . . ." sums it up. These two just don't speak the same language. Exceptions may exist, but generally Scorpio and Aquarius make an incredibly difficult relationship. In love affairs, after a while, they simply annoy each other.

Neither Sign is even likely to find the other sexually attractive. When they do, the first few encounters will be intense, but the passion is unlikely to last. Aquarius seeks sensation through sex, trying a variety of approaches but from an intellectual core. Scorpio is all about getting down, dirty, and sweaty.

When Scorpio is after something, the objective is the only focus. Scorpio aims straight ahead, stripping away all that is superfluous to attain that end. To Aquarius this is very limiting. Aquarius, after that same objective, sees ten new elements to enrich the goal and must, therefore, take a very different and circuitous path. Scorpio finds this maddening. When Scorpio wants comforting Aquarius offers levelheaded advice. When in an emotional state the last thing Scorpio wants is calm advice. And when Aquarius is distressed, getting an emotional response from Scorpio only makes matters worse.

For Aquarius, seduction is word play. For Scorpio, it's "Let's get to the point." For Aquarius, the sexiest part of the body is the brain. For Scorpio, it is smack dab between the legs. A long-distance relationship may be the most satisfying option for this unlikely twosome.

SCORPIO WOMAN AND AQUARIUS MAN

She says, "I've had the worst day." He says, "Let's sit down and talk." Scorpio wants comfort, not conversation, and she finds Aquarius remote. He's turned off by her over-emotionalism. Yet he wants to "feel," he wants emotional sensation. He loves to make love, but the experience is more one of trying things out rather than hot lusty, sweaty passion. As Aquarius sifts most of life's circumstances through the intellect, Scorpio uses her feelings. These differences—she perceives him as cold, he sees her as moody—drive a wedge between them. The relationship is undermined and the sex dies off.

SCORPIO MAN AND AQUARIUS WOMAN

There is a phenomenal initial attraction with this pairing, but these two really don't understand each other. Scorpio focuses on what is immediately in front of him. Aquarius expands on everything. He's overwhelmed by what he sees as lack of focus, and she's annoyed at his seemingly narrow view. They both want romance, but they define it differently. He's in touch with his feelings, she isn't. He wants sex. She wants seduction. Her responses are cerebral while his are earthy. He's always ready sexually. She needs to be talked into arousal and he's unwilling to work that hard. As a result, sex diminishes, and without an active, gratifying sex life, Scorpio will cheat.

Scorpio *with* Pisces
THE SCORPION AND THE FISH: *Happy Surf and Turf*

This is a great combination in friendship, business, and sexual relationships. Scorpio and Pisces share similar values and pleasures. They cherish their families and enjoy the comfort and quiet of staying at home. They love to cuddle, aside from sex, but also need privacy and periods of retreat. Pisces can be self-pitying; Scorpio provides strength and comfort. Sometimes Scorpio has a difficult time opening up, but Pisces has an uncanny ability to understand what's going on inside the secretive Scorpion. Their communications have an ESP quality, somehow going beyond words. This empathy extends to the bedroom.

These two can spend a week making love without surfacing for anything beyond room service. Scorpios believe that nobody is their equal at lovemaking. In Pisces they have met their match. Pisceans have super endurance and never get burned out. Sexually, these two passionate signs enjoy almost anything, anywhere, anytime. Their timing is in sync and they frequently achieve orgasm simultaneously.

One difference between them is that Scorpio exudes a kind of energy force field, seen by all as extremely strong, whereas Pisces, not an aggressive Sign, may seem to be weak. Surprise! Surprise! Pisces has a remarkable ability, perhaps hypnotic, to convince people to accept his/her opinion.

Scorpio and Pisces are sensitive, emotional, and empathetic Water Signs. Being near the water, from the ocean to a lake or a stream, helps them stay in touch with themselves and each other. This is a relationship that can prove gratifying forever in life and in love.

SCORPIO WOMAN AND PISCES MAN
Scorpio is so powerful that she overwhelms many men . . . but not Pisces. He's sensitive to her needs and self-confident enough not to be threatened by her strength. In bed, Pisces has remarkable staying power and is exhilarated by Scorpio's passion. He keeps the action going. She makes sure they both arrive. She'll set the stage for their lovemaking with low lights and incense. He'll provide the lust, satisfying her desire to be ravished. In the relationship they respect each other's differences. She accepts and trusts his decision-making abilities. He's at ease when she makes significant changes in her life. Steamy sex. Lifelong commitment.

SCORPIO MAN AND PISCES WOMAN
Pisces has an active fantasy life in which her role is the leading victim. The hero, a powerful tycoon or swashbuckling pirate, takes her by force in a fashion more romantic than frightening. This is part of the all-encompassing experience of sex for her. Scorpio embodies if not dark brooding qualities, at least a sense of intrigue and mystery. This couple rarely has a disagreement, but when they do the same endurance that powers their sex life feeds their battle. Happily, after the battle comes making up, a whole night's worth, with her having multiple orgasms. The Scorpio man and Pisces woman can enjoy a lifelong love affair.

Sagittarius with Sagittarius
TWO ARCHERS TOGETHER: *Cupid's Arrow or a Poison Dart?*

Sagittarius is both the Sign of the risk-taking gambler and the philosopher who knows that the goal of life is happiness. Sagittarius has a laid-back, mellow personality, is willing to take chances, and can be hard to pin down. The Archer won't be dictated to by others and does not tell others how to live their lives. Since Jupiter, the planet of abundance, rules Sagittarius, most of the time they're lucky.

Sagittarius is impulsive and prone to making spontaneous decisions, from little ones like getting away for the weekend, to big ones like moving cross-country. They are in no hurry to grow up, but when they accept responsibility they usually handle it well. Staying happy, however, requites keeping a bit of play in their lives.

In all their relationships, they love debating topics from politics to films to economics to the environment. Sometimes emotions get out of hand and the friendly debate becomes an argument. This is the greatest pitfall for this couple because the Archer may let fly a stinging arrow: words that cut. Then the fun debate gives rise to criticism and defensiveness.

For sex, neither is overly concerned about the setting. Sagittarians enjoy sex in varied locations such as the woods or the beach. Still, the sex is best when one bothers to set the stage by dimming the lights, lighting incense, and playing soft music. The fulfillment of the sex may not be wonderful unless one strives to vary the actions, but the enjoyment that each finds with the total personality of another Sagittarius will be great.

Summary

She admits to being jealous; he says he is not. She believes in monogamy; he will strive for it but would enjoy an open relationship were it possible. He sees himself as the all-American stud: well hung and proud of it. She loves oral sex and appreciates her mate's endowment. Doing it outside where someone else might catch them is a thrill. And yet sex won't be the best part of this relationship; friendship will be. Sagittarians tend to see the big picture, the forest, and overlook the details of the trees. In this relationship someone has to pay attention to mundane, daily reality.

Sagittarius with Capricorn
THE ARCHER AND THE GOAT: *A Worthwhile Challenge*

Sagittarius/Capricorn is a great combination. Both are sincere and dependable, and they balance each other. Capricorn is inspired by Sagittarius' imagination. Since Capricorns can be overly pragmatic, they're apt to lose touch with their own creativity. Dreamer Sagittarius looks at the sky and in the clouds sees castles and dragons. Capricorn says, "It looks like rain."

Capricorn is cautious. Sagittarius is spontaneous, apt to wake up on a Saturday morning and say, "I feel like getting out of town. Pack your bags. Let's go." Capricorn asks, "Where are we going? How long will it take to get there? Where are we staying? How much will it cost?"

In the bedroom, Sagittarius strives to excite Capricorn with busy hands, oral sex, and inspired body moves. Capricorn's responsiveness stimulates Sagittarius to be more inventive, and this is something that the Archer finds rewarding. Sexually, Capricorn runs the gamut from mainstream to very experimental. Sagittarius is an experimental lover, so sex with mainstream Capricorn won't be quite as satisfactory. But those Capricorns who enjoy a wider range of sexual practices, perhaps including bondage and S&M, may find a very willing partner in the Archer.

There are a few areas of potential trouble. Sagittarius, the gambler of the zodiac and less than cautious with money, may cause frugal Capricorn stress. Ambitious Capricorn is apt to be disconcerted by Sagittarius's laid-back attitude. Where Sagittarius may be blunt, Capricorn will be diplomatic. But both are good-hearted and strive to meet the needs of the other.

SAGITTARIUS WOMAN AND CAPRICORN MAN

Sagittarius' friendly, outgoing personality attracts Capricorn. She is seductive and he picks up on her body heat. In bed, Capricorn's endurance matches her passion. Sex in the pine forest or on a lonely hillside thrills her, and the fear of being caught turns him on. Sometimes, his frugality may annoy her. For him dinner and a movie may mean McDonald's and a rented video. That's fine most of the time, but if he doesn't spring for a four-star restaurant and tickets to the latest hit movie occasionally, Sagittarius will become impatient. When she gets angry, this woman holds nothing back. He'll know exactly where he stands with her.

SAGITTARIUS MAN AND CAPRICORN WOMAN

Initially the attraction is mutual. The Capricorn woman is very conscious of her public appearance. Her style and grace attract Sagittarius' attention. In return, his friendly, outgoing demeanor is very appealing and helps her to relax. He knows not to rush her, as she is not the one-night-stand type. When they do make it to the bedroom the sex is intense, varied, and mutually gratifying. The only problem area for this relationship is if Sagittarius does not perform well in the workplace and can't provide adequately for Capricorn. If this happens, she will develop headache upon headache.

Sagittarius with Aquarius
THE ARCHER AND THE WATER BEARER: *As Good As It Gets*

This is the perfect, happy couple. Where they go is always exciting, whether it's a Cape Cod B&B or a ski lodge in Aspen. Sagittarius and Aquarius always have the best sex when they get away from it all. It is then that Sagittarius turns full attention to sex and won't be distracted. Aquarius, too, is able to focus on the business at hand, which is pleasure, when away from work-related business.

Sagittarius is a Fire Sign. Aquarius is an Air Sign. These two elements are always compatible, whether as friends, colleagues, or lovers. Neither Sign triggers insecurity in the other. Sagittarius needs freedom and Aquarius is not possessive. Both enjoy a wide range of activities that might include traveling, sports, the arts, and charitable functions.

The Archer and the Water Bearer are truly made for each other. While Aquarius has a less than lustrous reputation sexually, Sagittarius has the ability to heat things up. For Aquarius, not only initial excitement, but also all through the sexual experience, words are the primary stimulus. Sagittarius can tell a wonderful story; in fact, Sagittarius will turn Aquarius on as much by talking about sex as with kisses or sensual touching.

Sagittarius is somewhat experimental in the approach to sex, enjoying outdoor sessions and some bondage or role-playing. The Archer isn't overly interested in sex toys or sexual behaviors such as S&M. Sagittarius may enjoy long sex sessions on occasion, but most of the time prefers to get to the heart of the matter fairly quickly. This suits Aquarius perfectly.

SAGITTARIUS WOMAN AND AQUARIUS MAN

Aquarius loves looking at his Sagittarius woman, preferably nude. His verbal appreciation turns her on. She tries ever harder to find creative ways to stimulate their sex life with sexy lingerie and by seducing him at unexpected times. She may start the day with promises of things to come later. An occasional phone call for some dirty talk adds to his anticipation. They both love traveling, fine food, and the arts. She may like sports and gambling more than he, but this is a minor difference. Her laid-back nature matches his easygoing demeanor, and they have what it takes for a lifelong loving relationship.

SAGITTARIUS MAN AND AQUARIUS WOMAN

The Aquarius woman is stunning and her aura is electric. She's an attentive listener and is well informed on a wide range of subjects. Should the conversation turn to sex, she reveals an extensive knowledge of erotica. The Sagittarius man is enthralled and apt to take her home to bed that very night. When the relationship is new, the sex will be intense and over fast. These two are more likely to have repeated sex in one session than lengthy or protracted foreplay. As life partners, they balance each other well. Her social graces help him in business and his relaxed presence in public does the same for her.

Sagittarius with Pisces
THE ARCHER AND THE FISH: *An Uphill Battle*

The war, the conflict, is non-stop in this pairing. For Sagittarius, who loves a good debate, the comparison of philosophies is stimulating, and Sagittarius is curious about Pisces' ideas. Nonetheless, sometimes Sagittarius finds Pisces petty. This is a tough combination for a long-term relationship. Both in bed and out, this combination is more of an experiment than anything else.

There are some areas of compatibility, however. Both Signs are thoughtful and spiritual, though Sagittarius is more religious in a traditional sense and Pisces is more open to New Age ideas. Sagittarius is the philosopher who seeks balance between freedom and responsibility, who seeks happiness. Pisces is the Sign of sacrifice and service, seeking spiritual fulfillment.

The differences are vast. Pisces is sensitive and refined; Sagittarius is blunt, rash, and at least in speech, capable of crudeness. Pisces can be hard to pin down. As the twelfth Sign of the zodiac, Pisces possesses some of the characteristics of all Signs. It is also a dual Sign, two fishes swimming in opposite directions. This indicates Pisces' complexities. Sagittarius is sincere, honest to a fault, independent, and upbeat. Sagittarius has a remarkable ability for shrugging things off. Pisces wallows in problems for a bit and is given to self-pity.

Both are passionate lovers so the sex will be extraordinary initially. It is all the other aspects of this relationship—the practical realities and philosophical differences—that prove destructive. After a while, even in bed, fiery Sagittarius and watery Pisces produce more fizzle than sizzle. Pisces wants far more romance and drama, while Sagittarius wants more energetic expressions of passion.

SAGITTARIUS WOMAN AND PISCES MAN

She's more assertive than he is and relies on Pisces to be successful in the world of affairs. If he isn't, Sagittarius expresses her displeasure in blunt terms, more critical than constructive. Her bluntness inhibits his sexual performance. He wants a supportive, trusting partner who brings out the best in his gentle soul. She wants a sense of adventure, not a quiet cocoon. Ms. Sagittarius is by nature a full partner, not the doting little woman. Sex will be passionate as both are experimental lovers who enjoy stimulating each other to ever-greater satisfaction. Outside the bedroom, however, this is a mismatched duo.

SAGITTARIUS MAN AND PISCES WOMAN

He wants to go camping; she wants to shop for lacy curtains and frilly dust ruffles. He wants to go to the track but she prefers the ballet. He wants spontaneity. She wants to plan ahead. She wants him to admire her femininity and to be powerful and protective. He wants her to be independent outside the bedroom and self-assured in it. Sex may be the best part of their relationship, as both enjoy taking their time and having sex outside—especially in or beside water. But the relationship itself is not an easy one to maintain.

Capricorn with Capricorn

TWO GOATS: *No Head Butting, Just Contentment*

Contented in public and private, the Capricorn couple goes out looking terrific and turns heads. In bed this relationship is dynamic because each wants to impress the other. The sex is long, easy, and enjoyable.

Capricorn finds one classic style of dress and sticks with it, one hairstyle worn for decades, one favorite path to walk through the park. Stability and constancy are the earmarks of this Sign. Sound boring? It's not. Capricorn knows how to simplify trivialities to allow time for the more important aspects of life.

These wise Goats are willing to delay and deny pleasure until significant goals have been accomplished. Their pride requires that they be seen as upstanding members of the community. In fact, they care enormously about what the neighbors will say. With similar values and commitment to take the proper steps to achieve them, two Capricorns have solid mutual respect and great potential.

Capricorn, the hardest worker in the zodiac, is indefatigable and exceptionally persistent. These qualities applied in the bedroom make Capricorn an excellent lover. The Goat does not take sex lightly. Behind closed doors, Capricorn's reticence dissolves and passion is released. Sex is usually slow and drawn out, showing this Sun Sign's qualities of endurance and persistence. Capricorn is a lover with a mission: to please a partner. While most Capricorns enjoy primarily conventional sex, there is a good-sized group within this Sun Sign that loves more varied sex play. They are turned on by bondage, dominance and submission, and possibly sadomasochism.

Summary

She is supportive of her mate in public. She presents herself well and strives to help him advance his career. At home, neither is extravagant; they live modestly and rarely rack up debt. Whether their home is grandiose or small, they maintain it impeccably. In lovemaking, he prefers lengthy sex and enjoys quickies only occasionally. She is open to both. They are equally adept at using their hands and mouths for sexual exploration as each puts so much effort into pleasing the other. He will strive to satisfy her first. Sex may not be varied, except among the fetishists in this Sign, but it will always be thoroughly satisfying.

Capricorn with Aquarius

THE GOAT AND THE WATER BEARER: *Interest or Irritation?*

Though the attraction between Capricorn and Aquarius may be powerful, this is a difficult connection in the bedroom and in all aspects of the relationship. Capricorn is practical and cautious, whereas Aquarius seems so open and full of inspiration. It looks easy for Aquarius to enter a crowd and talk with people. Capricorn is more guarded.

Initially Aquarius finds comfort in that wonderful Capricorn sense of grounding and stability. Later, this same quality seems stifling. For Capricorn, there is frustration trying to feel closer, more connected. Aquarius remains somehow distant.

When these two get into conversation, though, they may have very different opinions and the interaction is stimulating. One stimulus leads to another, and what is truly a developing friendship appears to be a fledgling romance.

Once they tumble onto a bed, a couch, or any other suitable site, their differences become glaringly apparent. Capricorn, like all Earth Signs, enjoys physicality in all forms. Sex is a release from the confines of proper behavior. Aquarius is more turned on by words and erotica than by the messy, sweaty sex that is more to Capricorn's liking. For sex to be satisfactory, Capricorn must set the stage verbally to excite Aquarius. Aquarius has to talk less and do more to satisfy Capricorn.

Capricorn wants to plan ahead and make a date for sex, and likes to repeat the same performance. If it worked once why change it? It ain't broke, why fix it? Aquarius gets bored. In the short term, this pair will enjoy interest and excitement; in the long term, they're in for irritation.

CAPRICORN WOMAN AND AQUARIUS MAN

He's refined, charming in public, and popular at work. Mr. Aquarius tends to be successful and can provide Ms. Capricorn with a comfortable lifestyle. She needs that. Capricorn puts effort into her job, home, friendships, and family. If her mate doesn't measure up, she loses respect for him and her sex drive shrivels. He gets hot watching her strut around the bedroom and undress slowly. His turn-on is cerebral. The act is almost secondary to that mental foreplay. For success in the bedroom, in addition to the effort he makes to bring her to climax, Aquarius must also strive to make the buildup more passionate.

CAPRICORN MAN AND AQUARIUS WOMAN

Aquarius' stately and elegant looks—not provocative but decidedly alluring—catch Capricorn's eye. He watches Aquarius charm people with her eager interest and easy flow of conversation. This conservative man, his three-piece suit buttoned over a passionate heart is, turned on. With all their differences, if they hope for any kind of successful long-term relationship Ms. Aquarius has to do less talking and more touching. Mr. Capricorn, on the other hand, has to start verbal foreplay hours before the grand finale. Capricorn has the ability to delay his own orgasm in order to satisfy his partner. Prolonging sex is no way to prove his love to Aquarius.

Capricorn with Pisces
THE GOAT AND THE FISH: *Contented Species*

As highly compatible Signs, Capricorn and Pisces relate to each other comfortably in all types of relationships, from friendship to business to romance. They are inherently in sync with one another and are comfortable discussing most topics without friction. They have the potential to be an enviably happy couple.

Capricorn's pragmatism is perfectly balanced by Pisces' idealism. Capricorn is cautious and Pisces is expansive. Capricorn bases choices upon the careful study of the circumstances. Impressionable Pisces may indeed examine information, but when it comes to making a decision, the Fishes depend far more upon intuition. Pisces is also a more social Sign than Capricorn, and this helps ease Capricorns' reservations when dealing with groups of people. Capricorn is the stabilizing energy when Pisces' fancies grow a bit wild.

In matters sexual, both Signs are noted for their endurance. They like to take their time and linger over a fairly lengthy buildup of touching, kissing, and oral sex. They understand each other in bed and require little guidance from one to the other to obtain maximum pleasure. The difference in their sexual expression has to do with the importance of romance and a sense of stage set that is so vital for Pisces. Typically, Capricorn doesn't care about the environment, as long as it is clean. Pisces, on the other hand, wants a setting that gives rise to fantasies. A well-placed mirror, silky draperies, or satin sheets as well as messages of love make Pisces wet with anticipation.

CAPRICORN WOMAN AND PISCES MAN

Status matters to the Capricorn woman. She needs her mate to be hardworking and to share her goal of achieving and accomplishing. He needn't be a doctor or a lawyer, but if he's a factory worker he should at least be a superintendent or the best producer in his unit. Overall, his work ethic is a turn-on to Capricorn. Ultimately, Pisces is the romantic in this relationship. In his sexual fantasies, he's the man behind the scenes whose strength saves the day. He wants to satisfy his partner in all ways, and he enjoys having sex repeatedly. She matches his passion, though she may not share his fantasies.

CAPRICORN MAN AND PISCES WOMAN

The Capricorn man provides the hardworking stability that the Pisces woman craves. In return, Pisces provides a hospitable, refined, and loving home. When she is occasionally self-pitying or negative, Capricorn maintains a reserved and steady demeanor. While he might be overly reserved or conservative, she encourages him to open up and relax. They have compatible likes and dislikes in most areas. In the bedroom, Pisces takes charge of supplying the romance: the wine and roses. Capricorn fantasizes about dominating her and she will be his damsel in distress. The only warning: he might be thinking whips and chains while she may welcome only light bondage and vibrators.

Aquarius with Aquarius
TWO WATER BEARERS TOGETHER: *Stimulate the Mind and the Sex Will Follow*

This is the buddy relationship: "You do your thing and I'll do mine." Both are independent people and while apt to find one job, one house, and one model car and stay with each forever, Aquarius will not tolerate feeling possessed in a relationship.

They love to discuss their activities. When Aquarians talk about the things they feel passionately, from politics to the arts, from careers to cars, their passion spills over into sexual energy. For Air Sign Aquarius, conversation stimulates the mind. The Water Bearer says the most important sex organ is the brain.

More than chemistry and physical beauty, ideas are what turn on and dominate sexual excitement for Aquarius. Erotic literature and talking dirty are sure turn-ons. While pornographic videos may be stimulating to him, for her they might be a total turnoff. In either case, since porn is dependent upon images more than words, it isn't the turn-on of choice for Aquarians.

There are times when words are not the best way for Aquarians to communicate—emotional times when a touch or a hug goes much further than words. This is when Aquarians need to put aside the cool, calm, collected behavior, get in touch with feelings, and demonstrate affection directly.

As these two make very good friends and share all basic likes and dislikes, they may very well be able to make a lifelong relationship work. Sex will not be the most important part of their union, but it will be satisfying.

Summary

He looks stately. She looks hot. Their conversation is lively, even passionate. They quickly escape to a private spot and rip off each other's clothes. Sex is urgent, lasting about 30 minutes perhaps followed by some conversation or a walk. Then they do it all over again. They diverge from each other in terms of preferred range of sexuality. She likes the tried and true: kissing and intercourse; he wants to experiment. For both, the sex drive is stimulated by erotic ideas and images, such as reading a sexy novel aloud to movies such as *9 1/2 Weeks*.

Aquarius *with* Pisces
THE WATER BEARER AND THE FISH: *More Friction Than Fun and Games*

Aquarius/Pisces is a rare and uncomfortable combination. Aquarius is rational where Pisces is intuitive. Aquarius confronts situations. Pisces recedes from them. Aquarius is cool and diplomatic, detached and impersonal. Aquarius enjoys being in public but is uncomfortable with intimacy. Pisces is emotional; creates very intense friendships; is romantic and sentimental; and enjoys nostalgia. In fact, Pisces has a strong need to stay connected to the past, whereas Aquarius is excited about the future. A Pisces is apt to belong to the local historical society or the preservation commission. An Aquarius is likely to serve on the community planning board.

When it comes to sex, talking dirty and reading excerpts from erotic literature turns Aquarius on. This is new and different to Pisces, who will respond . . . for a while. Pisces wants romance and a stage set for sex. The environment is of little matter to Aquarius. Yes, Pisces' passion turns Aquarius on in the beginning of the relationship; over time, Aquarius gets bored with the long sex sessions Pisces so loves. In addition, Aquarius' aloofness triggers feelings of uncertainty in Pisces, who is then likely to get clingy. This will be unacceptable to the independent Aquarius.

For more than a passing fling, Aquarius has to talk less and romance more with mood-setting items like wine, music, and roses. Pisces needs to stimulate that wonderful Aquarius brain with conversation. Best advice for the would-be Aquarius/Pisces couples: have a long enough courtship, at least two years, before holding the wedding ceremony.

AQUARIUS WOMAN AND PISCES MAN

The Pisces man brings his Aquarius lover flowers, which is nice, but she'd prefer a subscription to the latest new-trends magazine. He has mementos from past relationships. She has something of a jealous streak and doesn't understand why he keeps them. He is methodical and takes time to arrive at a decision. She thinks quickly and lands on new plans in a heartbeat. He changes his mind frequently. She adheres to her positions. In an argument, he'll concede and then do whatever he pleases. She loves his gentleness but then becomes impatient and accuses him of seeming weak. They argue, he becomes silent, and the process repeats. This is a truly mismatched twosome.

AQUARIUS MAN AND PISCES WOMAN

His ideas appeal to her and his interest in others inspires her. She thinks, "How similar we are." They aren't. Pisces' interest in others comes from her compassion; Aquarius' comes from his intellect. He stays cool in the face of tragedy, and she mistakes this for lack of feelings. Aquarius is far from being unemotional, but he doesn't operate from a feeling center. For him, the world of ideas is most important. He wants to figure out how to handle problems. He'll step in too often for Pisces, not understanding that she's strong, though highly emotional. Sex will be too quick for her, too vanilla for him.

Pisces *with* Pisces

TWO FISH TOGETHER: *Happily Swimming Round and Round*

Pisces is an idealistic, sensitive, and refined Sign. It rules medicine and healing; many Pisces work with sick and needy people. These fields require strength, the strength of compassion and not aggression.

Pisceans manage to achieve their objectives by a sort of maneuvering more akin to hypnosis than to overt assertive behavior. Pisces is not known for being particularly direct in confronting difficulties. This is a problem in all of their relationships and particularly between two Pisces.

Because Pisceans so wish to avoid confrontation, they may concede in a discussion only to go off and do whatever they want to do. This is not a successful way to conduct a partnership. Simply put, Pisces needs to learn how to say, "I understand your position, but I don't agree with you."

In a new relationship, two Pisces are like happy flower children out there making love, not war; following the music wherever it may take them; and enjoying a great sex life. They want to have sex virtually every day and enjoy a range of experimental sexual activities at a leisurely, romantic pace.

What is necessary to ensure that Pisces will make a relationship last long term is a division of labor. Someone has to get out of bed and be practical. Someone has to deal with the everyday mundane realities. Neither wants to, and each tries to maneuver the other into doing it. Solve this problem and these two Fishes can swim successfully side by side.

Summary

Each thinks, "Never have I known anyone who understood me this well, who could sympathize when I am worried and share my feelings. Never have I known anyone who responded to me this well in bed." Each picks up the other's most subtle clues. The physical compatibility is phenomenal. They share spiritual values as well, and will feel like soul mates. Overall, if one Pisces is independently wealthy so that the other Pisces can buy satin sheets, rose petals, and loads of throw pillows, the relationship may stand the test of time. Otherwise, both must learn to stick to a schedule and a budget, and to resist the urge to go shopping when feeling depressed.

The Astrology of Great Sex Questionnaire

Part I: Background Information

Date of birth: _____ Time of birth: _____

City and State of birth: _____

Male/Female: _____ Gay/Straight/Bisexual: _____

Marital status: _____

How often do you think about sex? (Daily, weekly, preoccupied with it, seldom)

_____

How much time do you like to spend having sex? (One hour, half-hour, more, less) How much of that is foreplay?

_____

_____

Do you enjoy quickies? _____

Are you sexually in the mainstream, more experimental, or open to anything?

_____

_____

How often per week do you masturbate?

_____

What's your attitude toward casual sex? (Love it, it's fine, it's immoral, it's unsafe, other)

_____

_____

Do you believe in monogamy? Why?

_____

_____

Does sex have a spiritual significance for you? How so?

_____

_____

_____

_____

What's your attitude toward pornography? (Love it, hate it, no interest)

_____

_____

Part 2: Attraction

What attracts you to someone? What turns you on? (Please specify physical characteristics, specific behaviors, attitudes, etc.)

_____

_____

_____

_____

What might turn you off?

_____

_____

_____

Are you flirtatious and, if so, how much?

_____

_____

Are you jealous?

_____

Part 3: Developing the Relationship

What do you enjoy doing on a date?

_____

_____

_____

_____

How much cuddling do you enjoy, aside from sex?

_____

_____

How do you demonstrate affection for your partner? (Specific acts of kindness)

_____

_____

How do you feel about public displays of affection?

_____

_____

How long do you want to know someone before getting sexual?

_____

_____

Part 4: Foreplay

Are you comfortable initiating sexual activities?

_____

_____

What puts you in the mood for sex? (Favorite music, nature of the environment, kind of food, aromas, activities such as eating, showering, watching porn videos, other)

_____

_____

_____

_____

Part 5: Having Sex

Where do you like to have sex?

_____

_____

How important is the sexual environment to you? (Cleanliness, orderliness, lighting, décor, etc.)

_____

_____

What time of day do you prefer to have sex?

_____

How tactile are you? Do you like to run your hands over your lover's body? (A lot, a little)

_____

_____

How oral are you? (How much do you enjoy deep kissing on the mouth, kissing your lover's body, cunnilingus and fellatio, rimming, other)

_____

_____

How do you communicate to your partner your wants and needs, by words or gestures or both?

_____

_____

What sex acts do you like most? (Kissing, oral sex, intercourse, anal sex, mutual masturbation, fondling breasts, other)

_____

_____

What sex acts do you like least?

_____

_____

Are you vocal during sex? A lot or a little?

_____

How do you reach an orgasm? (Through intercourse, oral sex, masturbation, combination, anal sex)

_____

How often do you reach orgasm? (All the time, often, seldom)

_____

Some people are very concerned about bringing their partner to climax before having an orgasm themselves. Others strive to reach orgasm together. Which is true for you?

_____

What's the best position for you to achieve orgasm? (Man/woman on top, doggie style, spooning [stomach to back], facing side by side, sixty-nine)

_____

_____

For some people the taste of their partner's cum or secretions is unpleasant. If that's true for you, what do you do about the taste?

_____

_____

_____

How do you handle his cum? (Swallow, rub it on yourself, other)

_____

_____

How often per week do you want to have sex?

_____

After sex what do you like to do? (Go out together, shower, sleep, take a walk, etc.)

_____

_____

Part 6: Intimacy

Do you enjoy watching your partner during sex and orgasm?

_____

Do you enjoy being watched?

_____

What smells on your partner do you enjoy? (Skin, particular body parts, her panties, colognes, other)

_____

What tastes on your partner do you enjoy?

_____

_____

Part 7: Fantasies and Fetishes

All people experience sex fantasies; we use them to arouse ourselves for self-pleasure and with a partner. Describe your sex fantasies.

_____

_____

_____

_____

_____

_____

As a lover, what's your best skill? (How you use your hands, tongue, body, other)

_____

_____

Describe a wonderful sexual encounter—romantic or aggressive—complete with sights, smells, sounds, and location that made it extraordinary for you.

_____

_____

_____

_____

_____

_____

Check off the fetishes/toys/behaviors you've tried:

___ Using sex toys (dildos, vibrators, body clips, etc. Please specify)

___ Anal (giving)	___ Anal (receiving)	___ Bondage
___ Chains	___ Cross-dressing	___ Dominance & Submission
___ Electricity	___ Enemas	___ Exhibitionism
___ Feet	___ Fisting (giving)	___ Fisting (receiving)
___ Hairy (men/women)	___ Hot wax/ice cubes	___ Interracial
___ Leather and Latex	___ Long fingernails	___ Ménage à trois
___ Orgies	___ Piercings	___ Sadomasochism
___ Sex in public places	___ Shaved (men/women)	___ Shoes and boots
___ Spanking	___ Tattoos	___ Underwear
___ Uniforms (men/women)	___ Using food	___ Voyeurism
___ Water sports	___ Wearing costumes	
___ Other (specify)		

THANK YOU FOR ANSWERING THIS QUESTIONNAIRE

© 2000 Astrology Research Institute Venus

About the Author

Myrna Lamb has been a professional astrologer for more than 30 years, overlapping a 20-year career in radio. On the air, Myrna has hosted a variety of call-in programs, first on astrology, and then a general advice show syndicated on NBC/Talknet and broadcast on three hundred radio stations nationwide. Her next talk shows aired midmorning on media giant WGY in Albany, New York, and then on WPRO, Providence, Rhode Island. Currently, in addition to seeing clients and writing a series of sex and astrology books, Lamb has an astrology talk show that airs on WPRO. She also writes a weekly astrology column.

Lamb's background is eclectic. After completing her liberal arts education, she went on to earn a Bachelor of Fine Arts degree in painting from Rhode Island School of Design. She spent her senior year in Italy on the European Honors Program and speaks fluent Italian. While in college Lamb completed one year of equity apprenticeship at Trinity Repertory Theater in Rhode Island. She holds Master of Arts degrees in teaching and psychology and has taught art on every level from preschool through college, in private classes, public middle school, and at Rhode Island School of Design.

Myrna has been married to Robert Lamb for 38 years. They have two beloved daughters and three grandchildren. They live in Lincoln, Rhode Island, in an early American home that they have faithfully restored.

About the Artist

Robert Lamb has been a sculptor, calligrapher, and painter for 50 years. He graduated from the United States Merchant Marine Academy at King's Point and served as a merchant marine throughout World War II. He earned a Bachelor of Fine Arts degree in 1952 from Rhode Island School of Design and a Master of Fine Arts degree from Cornell University in 1954. He has taught at both of these colleges as well as in private classes.

Lamb has exhibited at the National Sculpture Society in New York City, the RISD Museum of Art, and Cornell University. Currently his work is in numerous galleries across the country. He is represented in many private collections, including the Hirschhorn Collection in Washington, DC.

Paintings and Sculptures in This Book, by Robert Lamb

COVER	Acrylic paint	9" x 12"
ARIES	Mixed Media	10" x 11"
TAURUS	Gouache	8" x 12"
GEMINI	Gouache	10" x 13"
CANCER	Slate Relief	11" x 15"
LEO	Bronze Relief	12" x 14"
VIRGO	Marble Torsos	20" x 15"
LIBRA	Polychrome Bronze	12"
SCORPIO	Bronze Relief	3" x 6"
SAGITTARIUS	Epoxy Resin	3 1/2" x 5 1/2"
CAPRICORN	Slate Relief	8" x 9 1/2"
AQUARIUS	Acrylic paint	9" x 13"
PISCES	Mono Print	10" x 12"